FROM CLICK TO BOOM

PRINCETON STUDIES IN
CONTEMPORARY CHINA

Mary Gallagher and Yu Xie, Series Editors

From Click to Boom

THE POLITICAL ECONOMY OF E-COMMERCE IN CHINA

LIZHI LIU

PRINCETON UNIVERSITY PRESS

PRINCETON & OXFORD

Published by Princeton University Press
41 William Street, Princeton, New Jersey 08540
99 Banbury Road, Oxford OX2 6JX

press.princeton.edu

All Rights Reserved

Library of Congress Cataloging-in-Publication Data

Names: Liu, Lizhi (Political economist), author.
Title: From click to boom : the political economy of e-commerce in China /
    Lizhi Liu.
Description: Princeton : Princeton University Press, [2024] | Series: Princeton
    studies in contemporary China | Includes bibliographical references and index.
Identifiers: LCCN 2024007458 (print) | LCCN 2024007459 (ebook) |
    ISBN 9780691254104 (paperback) | ISBN 9780691254098 (hardback) |
    ISBN 9780691254111 (ebook)
Subjects: LCSH: Electronic commerce—Political aspects—China. |
    Economic development—China.
Classification: LCC HF5548.325.C6 L577 2024 (print) | LCC HF5548.325.C6 (ebook)
LC record available at https://lccn.loc.gov/2024007458
LC ebook record available at https://lccn.loc.gov/2024007459

British Library Cataloging-in-Publication Data is available

Editorial: Bridget Flannery-McCoy and Alena Chekanov
Production Editorial: Ali Parrington
Jacket/Cover Design: Hunter Finch
Production: Lauren Reese
Publicity: William Pagdatoon
Copyeditor: Leah Caldwell

This book has been composed in Arno

10 9 8 7 6 5 4 3 2 1

CONTENTS

PREFACE

WHILE MANY consider writing a book a long and arduous journey, for me, it has been an adventure—an endeavor I wasn't sure I could complete but chose to pursue nonetheless.

This research project began during my doctoral studies at Stanford, sparked not by a gap in the literature but a casual conversation. A friend's enthusiasm for how e-commerce transformed struggling villages in China captivated me. The idea that technology could democratize market access and uplift remote communities resonated deeply. After a brief trip to China and witnessing first-hand the transformative impact of e-commerce, I became so intrigued that I chose it as the topic of my PhD dissertation.

Yet I soon grasped the risky nature of the research project. E-commerce, still nascent at the time, presented a complex landscape to unravel. It also stood as an unconventional topic within my home discipline of political science, with minimal prior research and an unclear theoretical path. Unlike delving into a well-established field, I found myself needing to lay the foundation from scratch.

My biggest hurdle emerged from the data frontier. Crafting a successful dissertation in my field—and improving job prospects in academia thereafter—often requires not just qualitative evidence but fine-grained data for statistical analysis. However, acquiring e-commerce data proved challenging due to its scarcity and proprietary nature. Along this journey, frustration became a constant companion. After more than a year of fieldwork in China, with crucial data still elusive, I contemplated abandoning the topic for something more manageable, pondering whether switching tracks would bring me closer to the finish line.

On the brink of giving up, I revisited my fieldwork notes, which evoked memories of encounters from different corners of China: with private entrepreneurs, government officials, platform employees, and industry experts. Among these, the most memorable moments arose from interactions with online merchants who had incredibly humble beginnings.

I once conducted an interview on a brisk winter day, right on the street, with a village elder selling fish. Little did passersby know that he was also an online merchant. Before being introduced to e-commerce by his son, he had never even touched a computer. To provide online customer service, he taught himself to type, albeit with just one finger. His friends playfully dubbed him a kung fu master practicing "one-finger zen" every day.

I also met a young man in a humble warehouse whose parents were initially worried about his online gaming addiction. However, his exposure to the digital world unexpectedly became the catalyst for launching his own online business. Eventually, his parents quit their jobs to support their son's venture, and the store achieved annual sales of 100 million RMB. At the time, as an unemployed PhD student, I was astonished to learn that this successful businessman before me was only fifteen years old.

These reminiscences reminded me of one thing: the e-commerce boom is not just about large sales figures; it embodies grassroots transformations unfolding throughout China and the world, impacting the lives of countless ordinary people. While not everyone I interviewed benefited from e-commerce—reflecting the market's disruptive nature and inherent imperfections—no one could deny the significance of this burgeoning phenomenon.

I ultimately chose to stick with this project and continue studying what I deemed important, thinking it was okay if I couldn't reach the finish line, as long as I gained valuable insights along the way. As the concept of "finish line" ceased to loom as a grand prize above me, I began to genuinely enjoy this adventure. And before I realized it, I found myself sitting on my rocking chair, typing out this final paragraph of the preface.

ACKNOWLEDGMENTS

THIS BOOK would never have come to fruition without the support of my family, teachers, colleagues, and friends.

Since this book began as a doctoral dissertation at Stanford University, I would like to first extend my deepest gratitude to my advisers at Stanford University: Jean Oi, Barry Weingast, Lisa Blaydes, and Michael Tomz. Without their care and support, I would not have traveled half as far. Jean, as my dissertation committee chair, provided unwavering support and encouragement to this project, urging me to persevere and never take "no" for an answer. Her dedication to problem-driven research and her pursuit of excellence have profoundly influenced my scholarly approach. Barry is my adviser and coauthor. I have learned tremendously from his polymathic style of research, which encouraged me to think outside the box and beyond disciplinary boundaries. I will always remember fondly his witty remarks, his deep commitment to research (despite writing extensively on commitment problems of various forms), and his Caltech rules. Lisa is a fantastic adviser with great research insight. I was constantly amazed by her intellectual acumen and her ability to get my point even before I finished my sentence. Mike is one of the sharpest and most eloquent scholars I have ever met. I knew that if I could answer his "three-part question"—essentially three bullets that could tear a research project apart—I would probably survive a tough audience anywhere.

My sincere appreciation also goes to Andrew Walder, Xueguang Zhou, and Phillip Lipscy. While they are not my advisers, they have committed precious time to guiding me throughout the research for this book.

In the process of revising this manuscript, I benefited from the insightful comments provided by the participants of my book conference: Henry Farrell, Mary Gallagher, Edmund Malesky, and Kellee Tsai. Earlier drafts or individual chapters of this manuscript have also received feedback at invited talks at MIT, Stanford, Harvard, Penn, UChicago, UCSD, USC, NYU, University of Washington, INSEAD, and King's College London. I am grateful to Iza Ding, Hanming Fang, Douglas Fuller, Yue Hou, Haifeng Huang, Yasheng Huang, Nan Jia, Daniel Mattingly, Zikai Li, Tao Lin, Barry Naughton, Jean Oi, Margaret Pearson, Molly Roberts, Susan Shirk, Thomas Streinz, Xin Sun, Susan Whiting,

Yuhua Wang, and Siqi Zheng for providing extensive comments that improved the manuscript.

I also hold deep appreciation for my colleagues at Georgetown University. Paul Almeida, Heather Berry, Marc Busch, Jasmina Chauvin, David Dunahay, Scott Ganz, Jenny Guardado, Rahul Gupta, Brad Jensen, Yunan Ji, Jeffrey Macher, Andreas Kern, Diana Kim, Suh Yeon Kim, Marko Klasnja, Ning Leng, Kristen Looney, John Mayo, Kathleen McNamara, Nathan Miller, Ferdinando Monte, Abraham Newman, Irfan Nooruddin, Ken Opalo, Charly Porcher, Dennis Quinn, Pietra Rivoli, Nita Rudra, Joel Simmons, Katalin Springel, Yuhki Tajima, Jennifer Tobin, Laia Balcells Ventura, Erik Voeten, Stephen Weymouth, and many others have fostered a collegial intellectual environment that helped me grow, both professionally and personally.

I am also thankful for my teachers, friends, and colleagues at other institutions who helped me at various stages. They include, but are not limited to, Yuen Yuen Ang, Liang Chen, Ling Chen, Jidong Chen, Jonathan Chu, Victor Couture, Bruce Dickson, Iza Ding, Greg Distelhorst, Benjamin Faber, Hongbing Gao, Francisco Garfias, Yizhen Gu, Li Guo, Zhaowen Guo, Jennifer Haskell, Yue Hou, Haifeng Huang, Xian Huang, Nan Jia, Zhengwei Jiang, Azusa Katagiri, Xiaojun Li, Xiaoming Li, Adam Liu, Hanzhang Liu, Fengming Lu, Peter Lorentzen, Reed Lei, Xiaobo Lv, Xiao Ma, Daniel Mattingly, Eric Min (and his legos), Lynette Ong, Sungmin Rho, Meg Rithmire, Kenneth Scheve, Zhenzhong Sheng, Weiyi Shi, Ken Shotts, Brian Silverman, Lijun Sun, Haixiao Wang, Wei Wang, Yuhua Wang, Rachel Wellhausen, Brian Wu, Rachel Wu, Jian Xu, Xu Xu, Yiqing Xu, Fang Ye, Ming Zeng, Dong Zhang, Ruxi Zhang, Tongtong Zhang, Wentao Zhang, Wei Zheng, and Qiang Zhou.

I would like to express my sincere appreciation for the financial assistance provided by the following institutions: the Bill and Melinda Gates Foundation, the Lynde and Harry Bradley Foundation, Weiss Family Program Fund, the Chiang Ching-Kuo Foundation, the John and Jackie Lewis Fund, Stanford Center of International Development (SCID), the Stanford Institute for Innovation in Developing Economies (SEED), the Graduate Research Opportunities at Stanford (GRO), the Clausen Center of UC-Berkeley, and the Stanford Center at Peking University. Additionally, I am grateful to AliResearch for facilitating field interviews and providing data support during various stages of my research. Portions of chapters 3 and 5 were originally published, respectively, as Lizhi Liu and Barry R. Weingast, 2017, "Taobao, Federalism, and the Emergence of Law, Chinese Style," *Minnesota Law Review* 102: 1563, and Victor Couture, Benjamin Faber, Yizhen Gu, and Lizhi Liu, 2021, "Connecting the Countryside via E-Commerce: Evidence from China," *American Economic Review: Insights* 3, no. 1: 35–50, and they are reproduced with permission of the corresponding journals.

I want to thank the editors at Princeton University Press—Bridget Flannery-McCoy, Alena Chekanov, and Ali Parrington—for their tireless work in support of this book, and Mary Gallagher and Yu Xie for including this book in the Princeton Studies in Contemporary China series, and Leah Caldwell for her careful copyediting of the manuscript, as well as the two anonymous reviewers who supported the publication of this work.

Finally, I wish to express my heartfelt gratitude to my family. My parents and in-laws—Jishun Liu, Lingling Deng, Richard Koo, and Yvette Koo—have showered me with their love, care, and support. Wesley, my partner, has been a constant source of joy and excitement in my life since our first encounter in a PhD class at Stanford. His optimism and sense of humor provided uplift during moments when my research seemed to hit a dead end. The birth of our son, Dao-er (道迩), coincided with the manuscript being under review. We named him after the teachings of Xun Zi, a Chinese Confucian philosopher from the Warring States era, who wrote, "Even if it's a short path, one can't complete it without taking the necessary steps (道虽迩, 不行不至)." Like many endeavors, including the marathon of writing this book, there are no shortcuts. I am glad I made it.

This book is dedicated to my family.

FROM CLICK TO BOOM

1

Introduction

From Click to Boom

WANTOU VILLAGE, nestled in China's Shandong Province, sits in a region long marked by economic deprivation. For centuries, the Yellow River frequently flooded the region and acidified the soil, making it unsuitable for farming. Local households traditionally relied on crafting straw wickerwork for livelihoods, but the local market was limited. In the late 2000s, a returning migrant ventured into selling these handicrafts on Taobao.com, China's largest online trading platform, and quickly amassed a fortune. His success lured other villagers to follow suit. Since then, e-commerce has transformed the entire village—even its walls. The wall slogans that once exhorted the Communist Party's one-child policy have been replaced by e-commerce advertisements like "running around for a living away from home doesn't beat selling on Taobao at home" (在外东奔西跑, 不如在家淘宝).[1]

Gyatsoling Rinpoche, who is recognized as a Tibetan living Buddha (the reincarnation of a past spiritual leader), started shopping online in 2014 to purchase religious items like yak butter lamps and candles. To his delight, he discovered that these items were cheaper online and that delivery only took four to five days to his temple in Chamdo, a city perched on the "Roof of the World," where brick-and-mortar options were limited due to high altitude, inclement weather, and a scattered population.[2]

The two anecdotes above are by no means unique. As of late 2022, around 850 million Chinese individuals engaged in online shopping, with 69 million directly or indirectly employed in sectors related to e-commerce.[3] The avid online shoppers refer to themselves as members of the "Hand-Chopping Party" (剁手党), humorously vowing to sever their hands to resist the temptation to splurge again. The spending spree peaks every year on the unofficial holiday of Singles' Day (November 11)—the world's biggest shopping bonanza, which generated four billion parcels in 2020.[4] If these parcels were arranged side by side, they would encircle the Earth at the equator approximately thirty times.[5]

China's e-commerce market is remarkable not only in absolute size but also in relative terms. Since 2013, China has consistently held the position of the world's largest e-commerce market. Nearly 50 percent of global online retail sales took place in China,[6] while the country accounted for only about 13 percent of global consumption in 2023, reflecting the country's disproportionate development in e-commerce compared to other nations. Jack Ma, a prominent figure in China's e-commerce landscape, encapsulated this disparity by stating: "In the US, e-commerce is the dessert, but in China, it is the main course."[7]

More importantly, e-commerce has been a catalyst for widespread socioeconomic transformations in China beyond the confines of the online market. For example, the burgeoning popularity of e-commerce has facilitated the rapid adoption of digital payment and mobile wallets, propelling China toward a cashless society. Even beggars have adapted, now collecting alms through QR codes. Not everyone was happy about this transformation, though. In Hangzhou, a leading cashless city, two individuals robbed three convenience stores in a single night—yielding a meager sum of 1,800 yuan ($260) in cash. Their unawareness of the city's cashless nature—as they were not local residents—inadvertently turned the criminal endeavors into a comical misadventure.[8]

There are many more headline issues in China linked to the e-commerce boom: the development of highly efficient logistics and express delivery industries, which now employ robots and drones in sorting and delivering packages; the rise of powerful platforms and the fall of brick-and-mortar stores; advancements in big data analytics and artificial intelligence capabilities; the emergence of novel industries like live streaming; concerns about data security and platforms' monopolistic behaviors—and the list goes on.

It is therefore not an exaggeration to assert, as *Businessweek* does, that "e-commerce has transformed China" (电商改变中国).[9]

The Paradoxical Market

This now-evident boom was, however, unanticipated. In the early 2000s, China's e-commerce sales were meager, lagging far behind other major economies.[10] Researchers of the period held a bleak view about the sector's growth prospects, citing various obstacles to e-commerce development: a lack of technological and public infrastructures; citizens' concerns about the safety (or lack thereof) of online transactions; the Chinese government's unclear policy stance toward this nascent industry; and an insufficient complementary service industry.[11]

Indeed, China's extraordinary online market seems to defy conventional wisdom in many aspects.

First, many political economists argue that strong formal institutions— including state-provided secure property rights, contract enforcement, and the rule of law—are crucial prerequisites for bolstering efficient markets.[12] For example, a strong legal system can prevent trading partners from engaging in fraud and breaching contracts, thereby nurturing trust and stimulating market activity.

A strong legal system should be particularly vital to the growth of e-commerce. After all, online transactions are not conducted face to face, and sellers and buyers are easily dissuaded by fraud, counterfeits, and information asymmetry. While many legal institutions are not specifically designed to regulate online activities, they play a pivotal role in preempting issues that could infiltrate the online market. For example, in countries with lax regulations on counterfeits, citizens naturally harbor skepticism toward online transactions, preferring face-to-face exchanges that enable product inspection before payment.

Nonetheless, China's e-commerce market took off *without* strong formal institutions to support it. A case study on China's e-commerce market in the 2000s highlighted this point: "China lacked norms and laws regulating online behaviors and preventing online fraud . . . In the US if you place a bid, it's a contract, and by law you need to fulfill that bid if you win the auction. That's very clear. People would be afraid of getting sued if they did not abide by that contract. In China people don't care. 'I place a bid, I don't want it anymore, tough luck.'"[13] Although China later made strides in legal developments that govern online transactions—including advancements in the general legal system (e.g., the Civil Code enacted in 2020) and the online sphere (e.g., the implementation of the E-Commerce Law in 2019 and the establishment of three specialized internet courts in 2017–18)—these legal frameworks emerged *after* the e-commerce boom. This aligns with the findings of Donald Clark, Peter Murrell, and Susan Whiting (2007), who show that improvements in China's legal system are generally a *consequence* rather than a *cause* of market growth.

Second, conventional wisdom also suggests that, in countries lacking strong legal institutions, market transactions often rely on personal networks, social ties, or face-to-face exchanges to proceed. Citizens prefer trading with acquaintances or familiar vendors because repeated interactions can hold the trading parties mutually accountable, thereby fostering honesty and trust in trade. In contrast, impersonal exchanges with strangers are often hindered by trust issues in environments lacking legal protections.

Yet most e-commerce transactions in China are *impersonal exchanges between small, anonymous traders in distant localities*. Trading parties are often strangers to each other, and they do not repeatedly interact due to limited consumer loyalty. One may assume that consumers buy from these unfamiliar vendors due to their large size or offering of branded products. However, in reality, China's dominant e-commerce model revolves around marketplaces.[14] Major e-commerce platforms like Taobao/Tmall and Pinduoduo do not sell their own products but host tens of millions of third-party sellers.[15] These sellers are predominantly small-scale, or even microbusinesses, and the majority of sales in the market come from nonbranded products or lesser-known brands.[16] Given the setup, why do Chinese consumers ever trust and trade with online strangers when legal protections remain weak?

The third counterintuitive aspect of China's e-commerce market is its leapfrog development. Many would naturally anticipate larger e-commerce markets in developed economies compared to China. Despite China's rapid growth, it remains a developing country by many international standards, with GDP per capita only about one-sixth of the US level in 2023. Developed economies have wealthier citizens, a stronger spending culture, and more widespread internet coverage, all of which are conducive to e-commerce development. Additionally, developed economies have stronger legal institutions and higher credit card adoption rates, which should offer better protection for online purchases and foster e-commerce growth.

However, China leapfrogged developed economies in e-commerce within a short period of time. In 2006, China's online retail sales were merely 3 percent of those in the United States. Yet within a decade, its online sales overtook those of the United States and the United Kingdom combined.[17] In 2019, China's online retail sales accounted for 21 percent of the country's total retail sales, almost double that of the United States (11 percent).[18] This leapfrogging trend applies not only to overall market size (see Figure 1.1) but also on a per capita basis. Compared to online shoppers in the United States, their Chinese counterparts make online purchases more frequently and conduct more than half (59 percent) of total monthly purchases online.[19]

Lastly, even more perplexing is the Chinese government's attitude toward the online market, which contradicts two prevailing notions. First, the Chinese internet is often depicted as a giant cage marked by pervasive censorship and state control, suppressing innovation.[20] However, it is often overlooked that there is a duality in China's control over the internet. While social media and communication aspects of the internet have always been tightly regulated, China's control over the economic facet of the internet has been much more lenient.[21] This autonomy has paved the way for e-commerce to act as a catalyst for innovations like mobile payment, AI, and smart logistics.

Moreover, China is known for its state capitalist economy, characterized by a large sector of state-owned enterprises (SOE) and active government

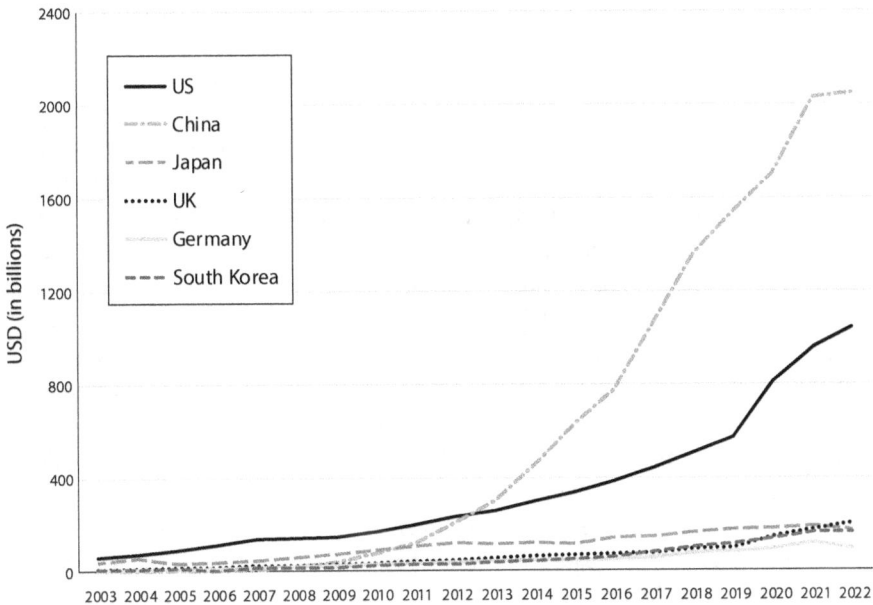

FIGURE 1.1. Online Retail Sales in China and Major Developed Economies (2003–22). *Notes*: In 2003, China's online retail sales amounted to only 0.47 billion USD, which was the lowest among the six countries depicted in the figure. This figure represented just 1/120th and 1/80th of the size of the online retail sales in the United States and Japan, respectively. *Source*: The data is derived from nominal online retail sales collected from various official sources and converted into USD using yearly average currency exchange rates provided by OECD. In the case of Japan, only business-to-consumer (B2C) e-commerce data is included, as consumer-to-consumer (C2C) e-commerce data is unavailable for many years.

intervention in economic affairs. Nevertheless, for as long as two decades preceding 2020, the Chinese government refrained from imposing stringent regulations on e-commerce, and SOEs had little presence in the market. While regulations were eventually tightened in 2020, it's noteworthy that this regulatory adjustment occurred *much later* than expected. Given the government's historically interventionist stance and formidable regulatory power, its prolonged leniency toward a highly disruptive industry dominated by private firms is surprising.

The Puzzles and Answers in Brief

These counterintuitive aspects of China's e-commerce market raise many questions.

If neither formal institutions nor informal networks apply, what constitutes the institutional foundations of this ostensibly well-functioning market? Why do customers trust trading with strangers despite the considerable risks involved? If legal institutions are so important for undergirding a market, why did the e-commerce boom happen in China, where the legal environment was weaker than in developed economies? Why did the Chinese authoritarian government, which has great capacity to directly regulate e-commerce, refrain from doing so for a surprisingly prolonged period? What are the political and economic effects of this paradoxical market boom?

These questions have not been thoroughly examined or even raised. Despite the rising prominence of e-commerce, boasting 2.6 billion users worldwide, many pundits, scholars, and journalists still treat e-commerce as merely a novel technology, a business model, and a market channel substituting for brick-and-mortar stores. Little heed has been paid to the *political-economic* aspects of e-commerce, particularly in non-Western contexts: its role as an institutional builder (creating institutions where the government fails to); a policy instrument (strategic government use of e-commerce to advance policy agendas); a catalyst for structural change (how e-commerce platforms reorganize state-business relations); and a battlefield for power (how governments interact with large platforms).[22]

This book represents a decade-long endeavor to analyze the political-economic dynamics of China's e-commerce market, the world's largest. Drawing on extensive field interviews, firsthand observations, and a wealth of original and proprietary data, this book aims to unravel China's seemingly paradoxical e-commerce boom and its consequences. Below, I offer a glimpse into some key findings of the book, addressing the questions raised earlier:

i. The institutional foundations of China's e-commerce market are neither formal institutional rules nor informal networks such as personal relationships. The market largely relies on the digital institutions provided by privately owned, mutually competing e-commerce platforms. Importantly, the state acquiesced, endorsed, and even partnered with this private provision of economic institutions despite its disruptive nature. This case is an example of China's novel route to institution building: *institutional outsourcing*,[23] in which the state implicitly or explicitly outsources institutional functions to key private actors such as digital platforms. This initially ad hoc process later became more explicit and formalized.

ii. China's e-commerce development has leapfrogged that of developed economies not *despite* its weaker rule of law, but partly *because* of it. China's e-commerce market is predominantly platform based. Compared to developed economies, China faced greater deficits in formal market institutions, and lower baseline trust among users in online transactions. Consequently, Chinese e-commerce platforms were compelled to establish more developed private market institutions (e.g., contract enforcement, fraud management, dispute resolution, and cheap access to loans) to instill trust among users—a necessity less pronounced for their Western counterparts operating in rule-of-law environments. These highly developed platform institutions have facilitated China's e-commerce growth. More importantly, equipped with such strong institutional capacity, platforms have evolved into "points of control" through which the Chinese state can strengthen its economic, legal, and political functions.[24]

iii. Institutional outsourcing explains why the Chinese state refrained from directly regulating the e-commerce market for a very long time, despite having the means to do so. E-commerce helps stimulate domestic consumption and entrepreneurship, which are crucial for China's growth. However, the market's nature, involving long-distance trade between strangers, requires strong market institutions in place to make people trust and trade. Yet, like in many developing countries, China's state-provided institutions are insufficient to support such a market, particularly in the early 2000s, when the e-commerce market first emerged. Reforming government institutions is a prolonged process fraught with political obstacles. Outsourcing economic and legal functions to private platforms, on the other hand, allows the state to build market institutions, strengthen policy enforcement, and foster institutional experiments—without undertaking these challenging tasks directly. It also allows the authoritarian government to distance itself from any public dissatisfaction that may arise from bad governance or failed institutional experiments.

iv. Institutional outsourcing to private platforms does not negate the need for government regulations; rather, regulations and outsourcing are closely interconnected. Without effective state oversight, large private platforms may exploit users and misuse their growing market influence, adversely affecting the quality of private institutions and, consequently, diminishing economic efficiency of institutional outsourcing. Conversely, if state regulations are excessively strict and arbitrary, they can impede the autonomy of private actors, stifling innovation and hindering institutional building, thereby also diminishing the efficiency of institutional outsourcing. Therefore, striking a balance between the power of platforms and the regulatory role of the state is crucial. The turbulent regulatory shifts in China regarding platforms—moving from a long-standing "hands-off" policy to a 2.5-year "regulatory storm," and more recently back to a supportive stance—illustrate the challenge of finding the right balance to avoid both regulatory vacuums and excessive control.

v. The institutional aspect of China's e-commerce development makes it more than a technological phenomenon. E-commerce has political-economic effects at both the individual and systematic levels. It generates individual-level effects on household welfare and digital inequality. At the systemic level, e-commerce fosters a national common market undergirded by a set of impersonal rules and digital enforcement, which, to some extent, erodes the authority of local governments. It also leads to a reorganization of the relations between the central government, local governments, and the economic agents.

While this book is contextualized in China's e-commerce market, its underlying theme is to investigate a central question in political economy: How can states foster growth in the absence of formal economic institutions, or if those institutions are frail? This question bothers many developing countries striving to prosper.

China's e-commerce boom suggests a potential growth strategy: encouraging the private development of economic institutions—particularly third-party enforcement—to foster *large-scale impersonal exchange*. This involves greatly expanding transactions among strangers in a society, enabling them to confidently trade with one another regardless of personal relationships or social identities. In the subsequent sections, I elucidate why large-scale impersonal exchange matters for growth, why most developing countries struggle to cultivate it, and China's approach to foster the e-commerce market—a nationwide market full of impersonal exchange.

Large-Scale Impersonal Exchange as a Source of Growth

From Personalized Exchange to Impersonal Exchange

To understand why large-scale impersonal exchange matters, we first need to go over the three types of exchange in human history, as summarized by Nobel laureate Douglass North: personalized, limited-scale, and large-scale impersonal exchanges.

Personalized exchange has existed throughout economic history, dating back to primitive societies. North characterizes this type of exchange as involving "small-scale production and local trade," facilitated by conditions such as "repeat dealing" or "cultural homogeneity (a shared set of values)" between trading partners. Notably, such exchange can occur without the need for third-party enforcement, such as legal enforcement of contracts.[25] Examples of personalized exchange include trading with a friend or consistently buying from the same vendor. In contemporary societies, especially in the developing world, where legal enforcement of contracts may be weak, personalized exchange prevails. For example, personal relationships, or *guanxi*, are considered critical in business dealings in China. People are inclined to trade with acquaintances because familiarity can reduce information asymmetry between trading partners, and repeated interactions can hold each other accountable. However, under personalized exchange, the available pool of potential trading partners is rather small, restricting the scope of the market and a country's growth potential.

To grow an economy, trade must expand beyond a small geographic entity or a culturally homogenous group: it must shift to *impersonal exchange*. This often refers to trading with unknowns—individuals who lack a personal acquaintanceship and anticipate no future engagements.[26] However, impersonal trade poses a significant challenge: establishing trust between strangers. The trust issue stems from substantial information asymmetry between unfamiliar trading partners. Without expectations for future interactions or the possibility of retaliation, there is a natural incentive for dishonest practices. Therefore, institutions play a vital role in facilitating impersonal exchange by assuring parties that contracts and property will be protected.

Impersonal exchange can be classified into two categories based on the governing institutions for trade. The first type is *limited-scale impersonal exchange*. This form of exchange relies on social and informal constraints to address the trust problem. In this scenario, trading parties are bound by "kinship ties, bonding, exchanging hostages, or adherence to merchant codes of conduct"; and "frequently the exchange is set within the context of elaborate rituals and religious precepts to constrain the participants."[27] For instance, even without personal familiarity, traders can securely trade with unknown members of other social groups if those groups have norms to effectively police their members' behavior. An example of this mode of exchange is long-distance and cross-cultural trade in medieval Europe. Because social constraints only work when both trading parties are embedded in social organizations, this type of impersonal exchange remains limited in scale.

The ideal form of exchange to foster an extensive market is "impersonal exchange with third-party enforcement."[28] I refer to it as *large-scale impersonal exchange* to distinguish it from the impersonal exchange that relies on social constraints for enforcement. In this scenario, the enforcement typically stems from a state-provided legal system that is both impartial and effective.[29] This impartial legal enforcement can alter the incentive structure for trading partners, discouraging dishonesty and opportunistic behavior. As a result, individuals can engage in trade confidently, regardless of their personal knowledge or social identity. This, in turn, stimulates market expansion, encouraging the division of labor, specialization, and ultimately contributing to economic prosperity. North regards impersonal exchange with third-party enforcement as "a critical underpinning of successful modern economies involved in the complex contracting necessary for modern economic growth."[30]

Institutional Hurdles in Developing Countries

According to North and Greif, the emergence of large-scale impersonal exchange is key to the rise of the West.[31] Yet very few developing states have successfully followed this path. The key to large-scale impersonal exchange—impartial legal enforcement—rarely exists outside of Western democracies. Why?

One factor is simply that developing countries lag behind in the market development stage. It took centuries for today's advanced economies to construct and refine market institutions. Similarly, latecomer countries need time to acquire the technical expertise and human capital essential for constructing such institutions and ensuring strong enforcement.

Meanwhile, political barriers frequently hinder the establishment of a strong rule of law in markets. Impartial legal enforcement requires treating everyone equally, regardless of whether they are a prince or a pauper, or whether a firm is politically connected or not. Achieving this often requires the establishment of strong formal institutions such as limited government and an independent court system to curb the arbitrary actions of rulers and resist political intervention in the ruling process. Yet political elites often resist being subjected to the law, fearing that an independent judiciary will undermine their authority. For instance, China has long stressed the importance of Communist Party leadership and supervision in the legal system. Zhou Qiang, the former head of China's Supreme People's Court, stated in 2017, "We should resolutely resist erroneous influence from the West: 'constitutional democracy,' 'separation of powers' and 'independence of the judiciary.' . . . We must make clear our stand and dare to show the sword."[32]

The lack of independent judiciaries makes it challenging for impartial legal enforcement to emerge. For instance, according to Jian Xu's (2020) empirical findings, even in economic domains where there is greater judicial independence than in the political realm, Chinese judges consider the political implications of their rulings. This results in a bias favoring politically connected companies, such as state-owned enterprises.

The lack of strong rule of law and impartial legal enforcement explains why it is rare to see large-scale impersonal exchange in developing countries. Instead, personalized exchange or limited-scale impersonal exchange prevail. For example, personal relationships are important for business dealings in China.[33]

Impersonal exchange exists on a limited scale, often based on social connections such as shared hometowns or kinship ties in places like Chaoshan. In some cases, large firms that have brand names and reputations can overcome the trust problem in impersonal exchange. Yet smaller businesses and individual sellers face more difficulties to assure their trading partners, relying more on personal or social networks to conduct business.[34]

This deficiency of large-scale impersonal exchange in China limits the scope of the domestic market, leaving much growth potential untapped. However, at the earlier phase of development, the Chinese government managed to generate substantial growth through an alternative strategy. This growth strategy does not rely on full-fledged market institutions (such as rule of law) as prerequisites for growth. It proved very successful—until recently.

China's Previous Route to Growth—and Its Limitations

A large body of scholarship has been dedicated to deciphering the so-called China miracle: why China has managed to achieve extraordinary growth with formal institutions that appear ill-suited for economic development by Western standards. For example, China does not have Western-style rule of law, credible checks on the executive power, secure property rights, or a clear separation of government and business.

While China does not have strong rule of law, it has established alternative institutional foundations for growth. This involves a combination of economic decentralization and political centralization.[35] On the economic front, the central government has delegated substantial authority to local governments, allowing them to improvise and enforce policies that drive the local economy.[36] Politically, the central government maintains a firm grip on local officials. Since the promotion of local officials is determined from above (in the nomenklatura system), they are strongly motivated to comply with central government directives, including those pertaining to economic guidelines.[37]

Within this institutional framework, China's past growth trajectory exhibits three key characteristics. (1) *State-led development*: the state is deeply involved in the economy. It maintains a sizable SOE sector and engages in state-led investment and industrial policy. (2) *Preferential treatment*: the state controls substantial business resources (e.g., bank loans, permits, and land), but these resources are limited. Absent strong formal institutions that ensure universal support to all businesses, the state grants preferential treatment to large firms (e.g., some foreign-invested firms or national/regional champions) and those with political connections (e.g., SOEs, connected private firms). (3) *Localized solutions* to development challenges and *interjurisdictional competition*: local governments are the primary drivers of the national economy. They formulate and implement policies tailored to local conditions, and competition among them encourages the adoption of market-friendly policies.[38]

These institutional arrangements fueled significant growth during China's early development stages, because they were well aligned with the country's dual growth drivers at that time—fixed-asset investments and exports. For example, state-led investments in critical infrastructure such as roads, bridges, electrical grids, and telecommunications effectively addressed China's infrastructural gaps, propelling overall economic development. Intense competition among local governments motivated them to offer policy incentives, enticing foreign businesses to relocate manufacturing lines to China, which significantly boosted the nation's exports. Through preferential treatment, the state prioritized allocating limited resources to large, relatively productive firms capable of managing exports, manufacturing, and infrastructure projects.

Nevertheless, by the mid-2000s, both of China's primary growth engines began losing momentum. For one thing, China's fixed-asset investments had reached the point of diminishing returns. There were ample issues related to infrastructure projects, such as overinvestment, investment misallocation, environmental problems, industrial overcapacity, and local debt problems. For another, China's excessive dependence on exports makes it vulnerable to protectionist backlash from countries such as the United States and to shocks in the global market.[39] The financial crisis of 2007–8 turned the risk into a reality. China's export slump brought lean times to the manufacturing industry and created risks of mass unemployment.[40]

Recognizing the urgency for new avenues of growth, the Chinese leadership started to advocate "economic rebalancing." This strategy first appeared as a guiding idea behind the country's economic policymaking around the mid-2000s, and it later became the central objective of China's Twelfth Five-Year Plan in 2011. Economic rebalancing aims to shift China's economic structure from an investment- and export-driven model to one led by domestic consumption and indigenous innovation. (In hindsight, China's efforts toward rebalancing have yielded limited overall results thus far, partly due to unforeseen circumstances compelling China to stick to traditional economic stimulus measures such as investments.[41] Nonetheless, the government's *intention* for rebalancing indeed prompted certain policy adjustments in favor of domestic consumption, including promoting e-commerce.)

The shift toward a consumption-driven model required expanding the domestic market. Despite China's already sizable domestic market, there existed considerable untapped potential for growth. With weak rule of law, market transactions often took place within personal networks or local markets. Therefore, a crucial step toward expanding domestic trading activities would be to establish a national common market characterized by large-scale impersonal exchanges, granting national market access not only to "whales" (large firms) but also to "minnows" (SMEs and individual traders). This would enable consumers to access a much greater variety of products, thereby stimulating household consumption.

Establishing large-scale impersonal exchange, however, seemed difficult in China. Conventional wisdom deems that this market usually comes with strong rule of law and impartial legal enforcement, which is not readily available in China. Some of China's institutional features also fall short in supporting such a market, potentially hurting it. For example, interjurisdictional competition incentivizes local governments to engage in protectionism and erect trade barriers on the borders of subnational jurisdictions, which may hurt the emergence of a national common market.[42] Furthermore, preferential treatment toward large and connected firms undermines the growth of small- and medium-sized enterprises despite their increasing significance in the Chinese economy.

Hence, it is intriguing to witness the rise of China's 800-million-user e-commerce market. This expansive and impersonal marketplace enables transactions among distant and unfamiliar traders, mainly comprised of SMEs and individual sellers. Such a market demands robust institutional frameworks to uphold contracts and deter fraud. But where do these institutions come from?

Institutional Outsourcing to Digital Platforms

Since the 2000s, China has effectively embraced a novel route to institutional building and enforcement: offloading it onto digital platforms.

I use the term "institutional outsourcing" to describe the scenario that, when state-provided formal institutions are absent, weak, or difficult to enforce, the government—either implicitly or explicitly—outsources a portion of its economic, political, or social functions to private actors of a certain type, which I call private regulatory intermediaries (PRIs), including digital platforms.

PRIs are not ordinary private actors. They possess the capability to provide private rules to either help the state establish new institutions or enforce existing institutions.[43] In cases where state-provided formal institutions are absent, PRIs develop private *substitutes*. Conversely, when formal institutions are already in place, PRIs can act as *supplements*, enhancing the enforcement of existing state institutions.

In chapter 2, I elaborate on which government institutional functions can or cannot be outsourced and why only a select few private actors qualify as PRIs. This discussion also explains why digital platforms are particularly suited to serve as PRIs compared to other private actors. Not all private actors can provide private governance, but as multi-sided markets, platforms' business models require them to establish private institutions for the various user groups they host. Platforms can also serve a large population, potentially the entire society, as their private institutions have remarkable scalability due to the zero marginal cost of digital products. Moreover, platforms can utilize extensive data and sophisticated algorithms to automatically detect rule violations and enforce regulations. Through techniques like A/B testing, platforms can also experiment with institutional modifications, promptly gather user feedback, and rapidly adapt to changing market conditions.

In the following, I use China's 800-million-user e-commerce market as the context to explain how institutional outsourcing works.

Private Institutional Building by E-Commerce Platforms

In China, the vast majority of e-commerce transactions occur on platforms rather than independent websites. These large e-commerce platforms are not merely connectors of sellers and buyers; they also play a pivotal role in institutional development.

Consider China's largest e-commerce platform, Taobao, owned by Alibaba. It contributes to the country's institutional development in three ways. First, Taobao has established strong private institutions to enforce contracts, prevent fraud, and settle disputes, effectively compensating for the lack of formal institutional support provided by the state. These private institutions include an escrow payment system, a sophisticated reputation mechanism, a credit scoring system, a fraud detection program, and even a unique jury-like system where millions of users voluntarily participate in adjudicating cases or shaping platform rules. These institutions have been widely adopted by other platforms, leading to a spillover effect (see chapter 3). Second, once platform institutions are established, the state can leverage them to enhance its legal enforcement. For instance, since 2015, the Supreme People's Court has collaborated with major platforms such as Taobao, JD, and WeChat to enforce debt repayment, reducing debtors' credit ratings and limiting their ability to purchase expensive items online.[44] Third, the state occasionally formalizes widely used private institutions, such as third-party payment services and platforms' online return policy, as shown in chapter 3.

It is crucial to acknowledge that, in Western countries, platforms such as Amazon or eBay also incorporate private institutions for contract enforcement or fraud prevention. However, these institutions are not as sophisticated as their Chinese counterparts due to lower demand. China's weaker underlying legal enforcement results in a higher prevalence of counterfeiting and fraud. Consequently, platforms in China face greater challenges in earning user trust and facilitating trade on their platforms. To overcome these obstacles, they must develop much stronger institutions and enforcement capabilities. The need for stronger institutions is illustrated in chapter 3 through the Taobao-eBay battle in the Chinese market in the early 2000s. eBay's transplanted institutions from Western countries proved insufficient to assure Chinese users of the safety of online transactions. In contrast, Taobao's focus on trust-building was the main reason it defeated eBay, despite eBay's first-mover advantage and much greater resources.

Interestingly, my discussions with platform rule makers in China revealed their acute awareness of the functional overlaps between state institutions and platform institutions. They didn't simply regard platform rules as internal company policies—they recognized their broader societal impact and their intricate relationship with the legal frameworks of the state. One platform employee shared: "We face similar market problems in the online market as government officials do in the offline market, albeit employing different methods to fix the problem."[45] Some platform rule makers even harbored ambitions to influence China's formal legal development, recognizing the possibility that the state might formalize platform rules that have proven effective.[46] This shows that the role platforms have played in institutional development is not entirely incidental but intentional to some degree.

The State's Outsourcing

Meanwhile, the state either acquiesces and gives implicit consent to platforms' private institutional building (*de facto outsourcing*), or explicitly delegates institutional functions to digital platforms through formal contracts or agreements (*de jure outsourcing*).

De jure outsourcing is clear-cut: it entails the state's observable action to outsource governance functions to platforms. For example, as discussed in chapter 3, China's Anti-Corruption and Bribery Bureau formally entered into a memorandum with Alibaba to delegate certain legal functions, aiming to combat commercial bribery. Moreover, as summarized in chapter 4, since the mid-2010s, nearly all provincial-level governments have signed strategic collaboration agreements with major platforms across diverse domains, including cloud computing, big data, rural e-commerce, and Smart City initiatives.

De facto outsourcing, however, requires additional clarification. This form of institutional outsourcing entails *deliberate inaction* by the state: despite having the capability to intervene or subvert private rules, it chooses not to. A prime example of de facto outsourcing can be seen in China's approach to the e-commerce market before 2020, when, despite the significant disruptions and controversies caused by e-commerce platforms, the Chinese government refrained from imposing stringent regulations for two decades. This hands-off approach granted platforms considerable autonomy to conduct institutional experiments and thrive, serving as a pivotal driver behind China's e-commerce boom.

The absence of stringent regulations did not stem from a lack of information about the issues caused by the e-commerce sector. Indeed, there were repeated calls from vested interests in China urging the government to impose strict regulations on the sector or even to ban it. For instance, in the early 2010s, state-owned banks repeatedly urged the government to ban Yu'E Bao, Alibaba's fintech money market fund, which rapidly redirected deposits away from banks. In 2015, e-commerce led to waves of closure of brick-and-mortar stores, prompting vehement criticism from many private entrepreneurs who denounced it as a "virtual" economy harmful to the "real" economy. In response, the government then resisted the pressure and avoided imposing stringent regulations on the e-commerce sector.

Some may also question whether the absence of stringent regulations reflects the government's inability to control platform power. This assertion may hold true in other countries, where governments are captured by powerful private businesses or where they are required to undergo lengthy legal processes to enact regulations. However, in China, the authoritarian government possesses many regulatory tools at its disposal. For instance, it retains ultimate control over the country's internet connectivity, evident from the internet cutoff in the entire Xinjiang region for ten months following an ethnic riot in 2009.[47] Moreover, from 2018 to 2019, the government decisively shut down the popular 200-million-user app Neihan Duanzi and mandated the closure of all peer-to-peer (P2P) lending platforms—numbering in the thousands—within a two-year period,[48] showcasing its capacity to intervene and shut down platforms when deemed necessary.

Instead, de facto outsourcing entails a situation where the government exercised *strategic nonregulation* over the e-commerce market before 2020. Unlike most government policies that entail active measures, strategic nonregulation involves a practice of *non-doing*—deliberately avoiding excessive regulations on emerging industries to foster their development. In contrast to industrial policies that provide businesses with land or capital, strategic nonregulation instead offers the much-needed autonomy in a country where government intervention can be frequent.

There is direct evidence of de facto outsourcing, indicating that the government strategically refrained from hasty regulations on the e-commerce sector. A research report conducted by a central government agency confirms that a key contributor to China's e-commerce growth is the "lax regulatory environment . . . with all levels of government encouraging experimentation and innovation without excessive intervention."[49] For example, in 2015, the State Administration of Taxation prohibited local tax authorities at all levels from conducting any tax inspections on e-commerce organizations.[50] In a similar vein, the State Administration for Industry and Commerce stressed in 2013 and again in 2016 that individual online stores were not required to register with local governments and obtain official business licenses.[51] These findings resonate with insights gained from interviews with local officials during the mid-2010s. For example, a provincial-level official from Shaanxi Province emphasized, while instructing other officials on e-commerce promotion, that the government's role is to "cultivate fertile ground" rather than dictate which crops should be planted.[52]

After 2020, China implemented stricter regulations on digital platforms. However, as shown in chapter 6, the goal of these regulations is not to shut down the private governance provided by platforms but to align it more closely with the state's interests. Consequently, institutional outsourcing has persisted. Despite heightened oversight, the state has maintained collaborations with platforms in rulemaking and governance provision. A notable post-2020 trend, however, is the increase in de jure outsourcing. Platforms are increasingly pursuing formal arrangements (such as memoranda of understanding or collaborative contracts) with the government to clearly define their responsibilities, request formal exemptions for accidental law breaches, and minimize compliance risks.[53]

The Regulatory Dilemma

Outsourcing institutional functions from the state to platforms does not always exempt platforms from government regulations. China's regulatory approach to e-commerce platforms has undergone significant fluctuations. Initially, until late 2020, the Chinese government maintained a hands-off approach with minimal regulations. Then, between late 2020 and mid-2023, there was a severe crackdown on big tech companies. Finally, in mid-2023, the government eased regulations and returned to a supportive stance. How can we interpret these regulatory swings, and why did the Chinese government turn to regulate platforms despite their outsourcing relationship?

In fact, regulation, or the latent capacity to regulate, is intricately linked to institutional outsourcing. First, if the authoritarian government lacks ex-ante confidence in its ultimate control over these platforms, it would not allow platforms to grow and wield such substantial influence. According to a Chinese legal scholar familiar with policymakers, the government's confidence in its own regulatory capacities—particularly its ability to exercise the "nuclear option" of shutting down the internet—led to an initial hands-off approach toward internet firms.[54] Second, government regulations act as a post facto mechanism to address issues in private governance. Without government regulations, large platforms may exploit their users, leading to a decline in institutional quality. Meanwhile, the state's outsourcing of institutional functions to platforms generates principal-agent problems. Through regulation, the government ensures that private platforms align with its political and economic visions, thereby facilitating a more seamless delegation of institutional functions.

The real problem is not whether digital platforms should be regulated, but how. The government faces a regulatory dilemma: inadequate regulation may lead to platform abuse of market power, while excessive regulation stifles private institutional innovation. In both scenarios, the quality of private institutions deteriorates, undermining the efficiency of institutional outsourcing. Achieving optimal economic outcomes requires striking a balance between platform and state powers: platforms must not be unchecked, and the state should avoid excessive intervention.

China's erratic regulatory shifts toward platforms underscore the difficulty in achieving the right balance. Chapter 6 elucidates how China's 2020–23 regulatory crackdown resulted from a situation where "platforms overstepped" and "the state overreacted."[55] It details how, due to the absence of robust state regulations before 2020, major private platforms overstepped their boundaries and exploited their market power, resulting in problems regarding data privacy, algorithmic manipulation, and anticompetitive behaviors, all of which harmed consumer welfare. While there were valid economic reasons for tightening regulations, the Chinese government overreacted to the challenges posed by platforms. It initiated a campaign-style crackdown on the tech sector with a high level of seriousness and intensity, often referred to as a "regulatory storm." This overreaction was likely driven by the influence of communist ideology, the absence of checks on executive power within the political system, and overconfidence in its regulatory capacity. The 2020–23 regulatory crackdown on platforms had dire consequences: the campaign-style enforcement significantly diminished tech firms' market value and profitability, injecting policy uncertainty into the broader economy. Ultimately, economic pressures prompted the government to halt the regulatory storm in 2023.

The Political and Economic Effects of E-Commerce

This book also examines the political-economic effects of China's flourishing e-commerce sector. Among e-commerce's multifaceted effects, I focus on two aspects that are central to China's economic and political governance.

The book presents the first causal evidence of e-commerce's effects on household welfare, as detailed in chapter 5. Despite prevalent anecdotes regarding the economic effects of e-commerce, there remains a dearth of rigorous empirical research to quantify the effects and identify the channels through which it influences household welfare. The study exploited a rare opportunity to conduct a field experiment in China, randomizing first-time e-commerce access across one hundred villages in three provinces. This experimental intervention is combined with transaction and shipping records from the e-commerce platform, price surveys of local retailers, and pre- and post-treatment household survey data. The findings suggest that e-commerce benefits the average rural household primarily through consumption effects (i.e., enhancing their purchasing power by reducing the cost of living) rather than production effects (such as increasing nominal income or stimulating entrepreneurship). Meanwhile, significant heterogeneity exists among the beneficiaries of e-commerce, with younger, wealthier households, as well as those residing in more remote villages, deriving greater benefits. The research has implications for inequality and rural development in the digital age.

In addition to exploring the economic impacts of e-commerce, the book investigates how e-commerce reshapes state-business relations, drawing evidence from interviews, an original national survey, and web-scraped store-level data. The central inquiry revolves around whether e-commerce will foster the rise of an independent business class in China. This question is crucial because, in other national contexts, the rise of a bourgeoisie independent of the state could precipitate political changes, such as demands for political rights or even democracy.

I find that, on the one hand, e-commerce indeed makes private merchants more autonomous from local governments. In China's economically decentralized system, local governments enjoy substantial power to support and regulate the local economy. Yet e-commerce has partially changed this status quo by offering national market access and private institutional support to private businesses. Local governments encounter difficulties in closing the regulatory gap, facing information gaps and coordination problems in regulating these online merchants. As a result, e-commerce participation seems to partially "liberate" private merchants from local government oversight.

However, this does not mean that e-commerce has created an autonomous business class; rather, private merchants remain regulated by the state, though indirectly, through large platforms. In chapter 4, I illustrate how the increased autonomy of private merchants results in a shifted dependency on platforms and how platforms establish extensive connections with central and local governments, serving as intermediaries of state authority to regulate merchants. Thus, the rise of e-commerce does not eradicate state-business interactions; rather, it centralizes them and moves the locus of interactions from the individual level to the platform level.

Methods of Inquiry

When this research was initially undertaken, given the rapid growth and relatively nascent nature of China's e-commerce market, there was a scarcity of prior research and publicly accessible micro-level data. Consequently, my research relied heavily on firsthand and proprietary data obtained through extensive fieldwork in different parts of China (see Figure 1.2). The research design comprised a mixed-methods approach, integrating both qualitative and quantitative research methodologies (see Table 1.1).

Qualitative Research

My qualitative research comprises three main parts. First, I conducted over two hundred semi-structured interviews. These interviews took place either in person during my fourteen months of fieldwork (intermittently between 2013 and 2016) across six provinces and two municipalities in China, or in the form of phone interviews (conducted between 2017 and 2023), when fieldwork was not possible. These interviews helped inform the book's theoretical framework, laying the foundation for the follow-up quantitative analysis. To attenuate research bias, I interviewed all major parties participating in or affected by the e-commerce industry, including online and offline merchants, online and offline buyers, village cadres, officials at the county/city/provincial levels of government, employees of various e-commerce platforms, and industries supporting e-commerce such as logistics and online marketing companies. My interviewees represented a diverse selection of geographic areas (i.e., urban/rural, coastal/inland, developed/underdeveloped) to reflect regional variations.

Second, I conducted online ethnographic research from 2013 to 2022 to counter problems common in field interviews, such as various forms of interviewer effects and snowball sample biases.[56] Unlike prior research that has used public forums and discussion boards for online ethnographic work,[57] I closely followed conversations in several invite-only, e-commerce-focused chat groups on WeChat, China's billion-user social media messaging app. Each e-commerce-focused chat group comprises up to five hundred members, including e-commerce sellers, government officials, platform employees, and researchers from various institutes. These groups conduct real-time, interactive discussions about the latest developments in e-commerce. Following the daily chats enabled me to: (1) garner truthful opinions in the absence of disturbing interview effects, (2) reach a large sample of subjects who were otherwise inaccessible, and, most importantly, (3) verify the long-term validity and stability of the theoretical framework derived from the field interviews.

Third, I performed content analysis of numerous e-commerce-related policies, news, platform regulations, and internal documents from local governments and platform companies.

Quantitative Research

On the quantitative side, this book exploits five datasets that are either original or to which exclusive access was granted. These datasets involve both observational and experimental studies. The first one draws on web-scraped infor-

TABLE 1.1. Summary of Research Methods and Data

Type	Methods	Description
Qualitative	Semi-structured interviews	Conducted more than 200 interviews over 14 months of fieldwork
	Online ethnography	Followed conversations in e-commerce-focused chat groups for 9 years
	Content analysis	Analyzed news, policies, and internal documents from local governments and platform companies
Quantitative	Web-scraped data	Analyzed web-scraped data from 1.76 million online stores
	National online survey	Surveyed 3,280 business owners (1,920 online merchants and 1,360 offline merchants)
	Randomized control trial	Randomized e-commerce access across 100 villages in combination with three sets of newly collected microdata:
		• Surveyed a random sample of 2,800/3,800 households within the 100 villages in two rounds
		• Surveyed local physical stores within the 100 villages for two rounds and collected 11,500 price quotes per round
		• Obtained 28 million transaction records from a large platform

mation from 1.76 million online stores that actively operated on China's largest e-commerce platform, Taobao.com, in December 2014. The raw dataset includes product-level data for each online store (e.g., store name, location, and each product's description, category, and price). By aggregating fine-grained information on individual stores at the level of the city/prefecture where each store was registered, the dataset helps uncover the regional distribution of China's e-commerce industry.

The second dataset is the China Entrepreneurs Survey, an original national survey of online and offline merchants. This survey provides rich information about the demographic, socioeconomic, and political variables of individual merchants. It enables statistical analysis of how the rise of e-commerce has altered merchants' political beliefs and relationships with local officials.

An additional three datasets were created in relation to a large-scale randomized controlled trial (RCT), also known as a field experiment, conducted in collaboration with a major e-commerce platform. The RCT involves randomizing first-time e-commerce connection across one hundred villages situated in eight counties of three provinces of China. This intervention is combined with three sets of newly collected microdata: (1) two rounds of

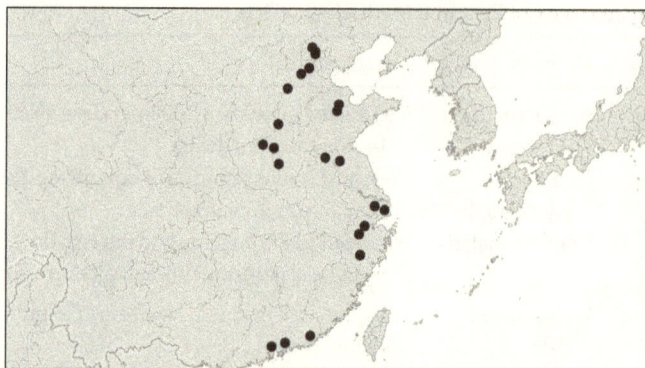

FIGURE 1.2. Map of Fieldwork Sites. *Notes*: The fieldwork sites include Beijing, Shanghai, Henan Province (Zhengzhou, Mengzhou), Shandong Province (Boxing, Feicheng, Zibo), Hebei Province (Shijiazhuang, Gaobeidian), Guangdong Province (Guangzhou, Jieyang), Zhejiang Province (Hangzhou, Tonglu, Lishui), and Jiangsu Province (Suzhou, Xuzhou).

longitudinal survey data collected from 2,800/3,800 households (roughly 8,600 individuals) per round, (2) two rounds of price surveys on local retailers, including 11,500 price quotes per round, and (3) 27.8 million transaction and shipping records obtained from the firm's internal database. As the first of its kind, this field experiment helps causally identify the impact of e-commerce on rural household welfare (e.g., cost of living, source of income).

Road Map

The remainder of the book proceeds as follows.

Part I examines the institutional foundations of China's e-commerce market.

Chapter 2 elaborates the theory of institutional outsourcing. It begins by describing a key puzzle in political economy: how developing states build strong market-supporting institutions under political constraints. I review existing theories on institutional building—the formal institutions approach, the competitive federalism approach, and the social connections approach—and discuss the limitations of each. I then introduce the theory of institutional outsourcing, defining the concept of outsourcing and specifying what government institutions can or cannot outsource. Importantly, the chapter explores why only a small group of private actors—which I term private regulatory intermediaries (PRIs)—possess the necessary capabilities to facilitate institution-building within this outsourcing framework, and why digital platforms qualify as PRIs. Lastly, I analyze the political logic of institutional outsourcing, as well as the durability and limitations of outsourcing to platforms as an approach to institutional development.

Chapter 3 applies the theory of institutional outsourcing to elucidate the institutional foundations of China's e-commerce market. In China, the overwhelming majority of e-commerce transactions occur on platforms rather than independent websites. These large private platforms serve as providers of robust market institutions when formal institutions remain inadequate. Through a case study on Taobao, I illustrate how large platforms establish strong private institutions to enforce contracts, prevent fraud, settle disputes, and allocate resources in a weak-rule-of-law environment. Furthermore, I illustrate how China's efforts to rebalance its economy prompted the government to not only tolerate but actively promote private institutional innovation by e-commerce platforms for an extended period, laying the groundwork for China's e-commerce boom. Furthermore, I provide concrete examples of institutional outsourcing from the state to platforms, indicating that such outsourcing has become more explicit and institutionalized over time.

Part II of the book examines the economic and political effects of China's e-commerce market.

Chapter 4 examines how e-commerce has affected the relationships between the central government, local governments, and economic agents, including the platforms and private merchants. Using data from field interviews, web-scraped store information, and an original national survey of private merchants, this chapter finds that the rise of e-commerce has restructured state-business relations. It centralizes these ties at the platform level, redirecting the locus of political engagement from individual merchants to these platforms. In particular, the chapter documents numerous strategic collaborations between platforms and the state, underscoring the growing significance of platform-state interactions.

Chapter 5 investigates and quantifies the various effects of e-commerce access. It first examines how e-commerce influences rural areas, focusing on the welfare of rural households. The investigation leverages the combination of a field experiment and the new collection of microdata. Furthermore, the chapter extends its analysis beyond the rural context, juxtaposing the experimental outcomes with other research findings to extrapolate the effects of e-commerce in urban settings. It also discusses aspects of e-commerce impact that are challenging to quantify but merit further research.

Chapter 6 delves into the reasons behind the Chinese government's evolving regulatory approach toward platforms: transitioning from a hands-off stance before 2020, to a period of regulatory crackdown from late 2020 to mid-2023, and finally returning to a supportive stance thereafter. Additionally, it examines the evolution of institutional outsourcing across these distinct periods.

Chapter 7 encapsulates the book's main findings and broad implications. I discuss how the study of e-commerce can offer valuable insights into significant shifts in China's political-economic landscape. These shifts encompass the evolving growth trajectory in China, the blurring of state-business boundaries, the increasingly collaborative provision of governance in China, and the dual-faceted politics of the internet, where commerce and control are intricately intertwined. Additionally, I examine supplementary cases from various global contexts, such as Grab, SafeBoda, the darknet market, US regulations on online child pornography and hate speech, and Facebook's "Supreme Court," to assess the circumstances under which the institutional outsourcing framework can or cannot be effectively applied. Finally, the chapter concludes by contemplating the future direction of China's e-commerce industry.

2

Institutional Outsourcing

A PUBLIC-PRIVATE COLLABORATION
ON INSTITUTIONAL BUILDING

Nightlights and Institutions

Orbiting over East Asia, an astronaut took a nighttime satellite image of the Korean Peninsula.[1] Seen from the International Space Station, North Korea looks like a dark abyss ringed by the radiant glow of lights from South Korea. As nighttime luminosity is often used as a measure of economic activity, this image vividly illustrates the startling economic disparity between the two Koreas.

More importantly, the image implies a key driver of economic development. South and North Korea used to be a unified country that shared rules, culture, ethnicity, and geography. They also had comparable levels of economic development. After World War II, Korea was arbitrarily divided into two. This triggered what social scientists call "a natural experiment" in institutional change: since then, the North and South have been governed by radically different institutions. Since other common factors that drive economic growth are held constant—including geography, culture, and prior governing rules—the economic divergence after the split can be plausibly attributed to these differences in institutions.[2] The satellite image endorses a powerful finding in political economy: institutions are a fundamental cause of long-term growth.[3]

Institutions are crucial, yet most states struggle to develop effective governance institutions. Out of approximately two hundred countries globally, only about two dozen have established strong rule of law systems to bolster their markets.[4] Most developing countries either lack state-provided market institutions or have ones that are weak or extractive in nature.

Numerous factors contribute to this deficit. Some states lack the technical know-how and human capital for institutional development, and the process itself takes time. However, in many cases, the primary obstacle is political. Rulers may hesitate to embrace strong formal institutions such as the rule of law that constrain their arbitrary actions.[5] Additionally, entrenched interests often resist institutional reforms since economic restructuring usually entails redistributing wealth, prompting those at risk of losing to collectively block such changes.

Therefore, a central puzzle in political economy is how developing states can build strong market-supporting institutions crucial for economic growth, particularly under political constraints.

Preview of the Chapter

In this chapter, I propose a theoretical framework of how developing countries can build institutions—what I call *institutional outsourcing*.[6] When faced with political barriers to adopting strong formal institutions, the state can—either implicitly or explicitly—outsource a substantial number of economic, political, and social functions to a certain type of private actor, which I call private regulatory intermediaries (PRIs). PRIs can offer (imperfect) private substitutes or complements for institutions the state is unwilling or unable to supply. Where formal institutions are absent, PRIs develop private *substitutes* for state institutions, but when formal institutions are already in place, PRIs can serve as *complements* to strengthen the enforcement of state institutions.

Importantly, not all private actors qualify as PRIs—only a select few that can provide private-order institutions and meet three criteria simultaneously: encompassing, impersonal, and limited. Large digital platforms are among these qualified actors.

I then use the framework of institutional outsourcing to explicate the institutional foundations of China's e-commerce market. I argue that in this market, major e-commerce platforms (hereafter: platforms) are not simply exchange platforms, but PRIs that perform legal and social functions including contract enforcement, fraud prevention, dispute resolution, and resource allocation. The state has largely acquiesced to platforms serving as private suppliers of market-supporting institutions, or even actively encouraged this behavior. Although the state's outsourcing of institutional functions to platforms initially took the form of implicit acquiescence (de facto outsourcing), this practice has become increasingly institutionalized and explicit (de jure outsourcing), as shown by various collaboration agreements signed between platform companies and different levels of government. Such collaborations have continued even after 2020, when the Chinese government tightened its control over digital platforms.

As a digital route to institutional development, institutional outsourcing to platforms offers several advantages over other approaches, such as the formal institutions approach, competitive federalism approach, and social connections approach. For instance, institutional outsourcing helps the government tackle the technical complexities of institutional development without directly handling them. Moreover, it is much less politically constraining than directly reforming formal institutions. Outsourcing to private actors allows the state to stand above the provision of services; if a privately operated institution fails, the state can abandon it without tarnishing its own reputation.

However, institutional outsourcing to digital platforms also presents its own set of challenges. Maintaining the high quality of private institutions demands a nuanced balance between public and private regulatory powers: the state needs to regulate platforms to prevent their abuse of power while granting them enough autonomy for innovation.

The absence of government regulations can lead to a deterioration in the quality of private institutions. For example, big platforms tend to grow larger due to network effects, and without constraints, they may engage in monopolistic behaviors and abuse their dominant positions. Moreover, digital platforms rely on algorithms and collect vast amounts of personal data to enforce institutional functions, raising concerns about algorithmic bias, privacy, and data manipulation. To remedy these problems, certain government regulations on digital platforms are necessary.

However, excessive state regulations can stifle institutional innovation by platforms and equally hamper the quality of private institutions. In such a scenario, institutional outsourcing can still continue, but platforms may bear an undue compliance burden. This could weaken their incentives to pursue meaningful and potentially risky innovation to avoid penalties.

Therefore, institutional outsourcing is most effective when a delicate balance exists between state and platform powers, ensuring that both sides are somewhat constrained and do not act arbitrarily.

Institutions and Market Development: Existing Theories and Limitations

Market-supporting institutions are "rules of the game"[7] that sustain the legal order, enforce contracts, protect property rights, and enable equal access to market resources, such as loans. These institutions foster growth by mitigating several fundamental problems in trade: information asymmetry between trading parties,[8] traders' inability to credibly commit to contractual obligations,[9] and the risk of expropriation by those who have coercive power.[10]

While market institutions are crucial to economic growth, not all states have them. The developed West is already equipped with institutions to support markets. These institutions—including strong rule of law, parliaments, and independent judiciaries—enforce contracts and secure property rights by constraining rulers from acting arbitrarily.[11] By contrast, formal institutions in developing countries are often weak, ineffectual, or subject to the whims of political elites. Even worse, many developing countries are stuck with the unfortunate combination of weak formal institutions and low growth. They are unable to escape what Ang calls the "poverty trap," a self-reinforcing equilibrium in which weak institutions fail to generate sufficient growth, and low growth in turn fails to provide the necessary resources to build strong institutions.[12]

Can developing countries grow under a weak rule of law and build market-supporting institutions along the way? The answer is yes. Past studies on China and other emerging economies have identified three approaches: the formal institutions approach, the competitive federalism approach, and the social connections approach. This section assesses the strengths and limitations of each approach.

Formal Institutions Approach

One solution to the lack of market support is to strengthen formal institutions. A common method, termed "institutional monocropping" by Peter Evans, involves transplanting idealized Anglo-Saxon governance institutions to the developing world.[13] International organizations have long promoted this practice, making governance reforms a condition for developing countries to receive aid.[14] The underlying assumption is that a best-practice model exists and can transcend cultural and national circumstances.

However, institutional transplants have rarely succeeded due to political barriers.[15] Developing countries tend to either staunchly resist Western institutions or only adopt them on paper. Various types of political obstacles have stood in the way of reform, such as the ruling elites' reluctance to cede arbitrary powers,[16] a lack of doorstep conditions to transition to an "open access order" society,[17] and the failure to restrain early winners from blocking the reform process.[18]

Fundamentally, as Yuen Yuen Ang's work insightfully indicates, one model cannot fit all states.[19] Ang argues that development is a co-evolutionary process in which the state and markets mutually adapt. That is, developing countries can harness weak institutions as raw materials for building markets and foster improvisation among ground-level agents to develop policies that are conducive to market development. This process in iteration produces both stronger institutions and higher growth.

Indeed, China has avoided wholesale adoption of Western institutions. Instead, it has gradually reformed its formal institutions. A key feature of this process is *compartmentalizing* institutional development by issue area: focusing on developing economic institutions while postponing major political reforms, such as introducing elections and constitutional government.[20] This approach has allowed China to develop market institutions without significantly constraining the ruler's power.[21]

However, this compartmentalization can lead to only partial development of formal market institutions. In a state-capitalist country like China, where the state plays a significant role in the economy, it is challenging to fully separate economic and political issues. As a result, building robust formal institutions, even for economic matters, will inevitably face political obstacles.

To illustrate this, Barry Weingast and I write about how China undersupplied legal institutions in markets due to the "authoritarian's legal dilemma."[22] We start with the premise that authoritarian states want to maximize economic growth but minimize political opposition. The state therefore seeks to fully support private law (e.g., laws that protect contracts and property rights) but constrain the development of public law (e.g., citizens' rights and constitutions). Unfortunately, these two goals are incompatible. Establishing an independent judiciary that *only supplies* private law is difficult. To fully establish private law, the state must establish a strong and independent judiciary in the commercial area. However, if a judiciary is truly strong and independent in private law, it cannot credibly commit to avoid constraining the autocrat by extending its power to public law. Given the state's especially strong presence in the Chinese economy—for example, a large sector of state-owned enterprises and the government's frequent use of industrial policies and market interventions—commercial issues are often political as well. Therefore, knowing that an independent judiciary could be politically constraining in the future, ruling elites would never grant judiciary independence, even in the commercial arena. This is why compartmentalization cannot generate fully developed market institutions and why it leaves untapped growth potential.

In summary, reforming formal institutions can help support markets, but reforms have a ceiling. Developing states face multiple political barriers that make it difficult to fully implement the formal institutions approach.

Competitive Federalism Approach

Competitive federalism combines two key elements: the decentralization of authority from national to subnational governments and the competition among these subnational governments to attract citizens and businesses. Unlike the formal institutions approach, competitive federalism highlights the primary role of subnational governments in spearheading the national economy. These subnational entities implement pro-market policies such as tax incentives and business subsidies. Many of these policies do not involve formal institutional reforms, and when they do, the resulting changes are typically regional.

An influential body of literature credits China's economic success to its unique version of competitive federalism.[23] While not technically a federal country, China is one of the world's most economically decentralized states, as indicated by high subnational shares of government revenue and expenditure.[24] The policymaking process is what Yuen Yuen Ang calls "directed improvisation": the central authority sets out broad policy directives and leaves the policy details and implementation to local governments, which are the main drivers of economic development.[25]

Local governments in China are driven to develop markets due to strong incentives to compete for economic success. Unlike many countries where interjurisdictional competition is driven by bottom-up electoral pressure, in China, the central government encourages competition among local governments through fiscal revenue and official promotions.

From the 1980s to the early 1990s, China adopted a revenue-sharing fiscal contracting system, where local governments transferred a portion of their tax revenues to the higher level and kept the rest. This incentivized local officials to boost the local economy since higher tax revenues led to larger local budgets.[26] In 1994, the tax-sharing reform disbanded the system and reclassified taxes in favor of the central government. However, local governments continued to have strong incentives to urbanize the economy because they retained exclusive rights to taxes on the service, construction, and real estate industries.[27] Another key incentive for local officials is their promotion prospects. While China is economically decentralized, the central government retains substantial control over local officials' careers. Since their career advancement largely depends on their economic performance rankings, local officials are strongly motivated to foster growth in their jurisdictions.[28]

A key drawback of the competitive federalism approach is that it does not ensure a national market. In China, the combination of decentralization and interjurisdictional competition gives local governments both the means and incentives to erect trade barriers against one another.[29] The central government lacks the necessary information to police such behavior effectively.[30] This leads to problems such as localized corruption and patronage networks, regional protectionism, beggar-thy-neighbor policies, and, in an extreme form, fragmented markets along the borders of subnational units.[31] For example, Panle Jia Barwick, Shengmao Cao, and Shanjun Li (2021) find home provincial bias in China's auto market that is caused by protectionist policies such as subsidies to local brands. Counterfactual analysis shows that such local protection leads to a total consumer welfare loss of 21.9 billion RMB. These problems jeopardize long-term economic development.

In short, when the central means of containing local protectionism are insufficient, which is often the case in China, competitive federalism encourages internal trade barriers on the borders of subnational jurisdictions. This outcome diminishes the prospects of a national common market and makes economies of scale more difficult to achieve.

Social Connections Approach

Unlike the formal institution and competitive federalism approaches, the social connections approach focuses on microlevel, informal institutions like kinship ties, friendships, and acquaintance networks to facilitate market transactions. While social connections aid business in all societies, they are particularly crucial in developing countries. Where formal market institutions remain weak, informal networks serve as substitutes to support market activities.[32]

Social connections are crucial because they help enforce contracts. Personal relationships and repeated interactions can bind trading parties and reduce transaction costs. In his study of crony capitalism, David Kang (2002) argues that personal relationships between entrepreneurs and politicians can "lead to better information, monitoring, and sanctioning," thereby strengthening property rights for private businesses. Similarly, Katherine Xin and Jone Pearce (1996) highlight the importance of guanxi (i.e., personal relationships) in Chinese business dealings.[33]

Moreover, personal connections with political elites help reduce expropriation risks for private entrepreneurs in developing countries. To grow a market, it is crucial to solve a commitment problem: asset holders will not invest if the government cannot credibly commit to protecting their property rights. While developed countries have checks and balances to constrain government expropriation, developing countries often lack such constraints. However, in developing countries, the government can still credibly commit to protecting a subset of asset holders who have political connections and share rents with government officials. These asset holders' property will be protected because "the intermingling of economic and political elites means that it is extremely difficult to break the implicit contract between government and the privileged asset holders."[34]

However, markets that rely heavily on personal connections as supporting institutions have at least three downsides. First, social connections often lead to the misallocation of economic resources. Corruption and other types of economic inefficiency are often involved in relationship-based market transactions.

Small- and medium-sized traders are particularly disadvantaged, because they often lack the necessary resources and political capital to advance their interests. The second downside is that social connections can be unstable. As Haber points out, "The fact that crony systems ultimately depend on the personal connections of particular asset holders and government actors means that the commitments of the government are credible only so long as that particular government is in power."[35] Finally yet importantly, because social relationships are difficult to scale up, this approach constrains the size of the market. Although social connections provide expedient support to markets in developing states, these connections often hamper a society's overall economic efficiency, especially over time.

Summary

These three approaches have contributed to China's economic growth despite the country lacking strong formal institutions by Western standards. However, each approach has inherent limitations. Reforming formal institutions is time-consuming and often faces strong opposition from political elites with vested interests. The other two approaches tend to limit the scope of economic activities due to difficulties in sustaining trade beyond local markets and personal networks. For example, competitive federalism promotes regional markets but can hinder the creation of a national common market, affecting economies of scale. Similarly, the social connections approach restricts market scalability and tends to foster corruption and favoritism.

During the earlier stages of the Chinese economy, the limitations of the existing approaches were less evident. When China relied heavily on fixed-asset investments and exports as the main growth drivers, establishing a national common market for internal trade and domestic consumption was less important. Personal networks were also sufficient for generating growth when China's overall scope of trade was limited.

However, as China struggles out of poverty and enters the "middle-income" phase, a new approach to institutional building is needed to complement the existing approaches. To sustain growth, China must promote broad-based exchange and development. This involves boosting domestic consumption and democratizing market access, ensuring that all sellers and buyers, regardless of size and location, can easily access the national market. Therefore, it is essential to build strong market institutions to facilitate long-distance, impersonal exchanges and develop a national common market. While the ideal route involves government reforms to the legal system, such reforms take time and often encounter political obstacles. With this in mind, what novel path should China pursue to build market institutions?

Clues from the Past

According to historian Fernand Braudel, "The present . . . [is] in large measure the prisoner of a past . . . and the past with its rules, its differences and its similarities, [is] the indispensable key to any serious understanding of the present."[36]

Indeed, historical precedents of private governance inform a path forward. Economic agents in various countries supplying private rules and adjudication mechanisms when a state apparatus was nonexistent or weak. For instance, during the California gold rush, the police department in San Francisco was initially nonexistent and then "considered as worse than the private criminals" after its establishment.[37] To combat crime, local merchants organized a private organization, the San Francisco Patrol Special Police, in 1847. Currently, this private police force still patrols neighborhoods at the request of private clients and has long operated alongside the government police under the city's charter. Other examples of private governance in different areas include medieval merchants, the diamond and cotton industries,[38] cattle ranchers,[39] pirates,[40] nineteenth-century American railroads,[41] and stock exchanges.[42]

While in some cases the state did not exist or was weak, in other cases, strong political authorities strategically outsourced governing functions to private actors, leading to blurred lines between public and private regulatory powers. The most prominent examples are the company states or corporate republics established during the first wave of globalization, including the British and Dutch East India companies over vast parts of India and Southeast Asia and the Hudson's Bay Company in North America. These companies were authorized by royal charters and enjoyed a monopoly on trade and, more importantly, extensive political powers including tax collection, diplomacy, and war-making on behalf of the Crown. This wide range of functions made the company states hybrid entities: they were a combination of profit-seeking companies and sovereign states.[43] As historians J. C. Sharman and Andrew Phillips forcefully argue, these company states are "the most important actors in the crucial formative stages of the modern international system."[44] In this process, private actors took on the major role of building institutions; the state remained in the background, providing implicit consent or explicit endorsement.

Since the mid-2000s, a parallel route of institutional development has emerged in China: institutional outsourcing to privately owned digital platforms. Under the authoritarian government's initial acquiescence and later overt support, powerful digital platforms have served as private institutional builders, filling in the governance gap left by the state.

While the idea of private regulatory power is not new, institutional outsourcing is not an exact replica of the historical examples. Digital platforms constitute a special type of private actor, and the institutions they develop differ from many historical examples of private-order institutions. The political context of contemporary China is also unique. The Chinese Communist Party (CCP) has long feared that an overly powerful private sector could threaten the regime. It is therefore puzzling to see the emergence of powerful private platforms in China, particularly given their critical role in building market institutions and providing governance. Why were SOEs not given this role? The next section explains what institutional outsourcing is and the political logic underlying this concept.

Institutional Outsourcing to Digital Platforms

Institutional outsourcing is a public-private collaborative effort to build institutions. When the state confronts political barriers to establishing strong formal institutions, it strategically outsources a portion of its institutional functions to a special type of private actor—what I call private regulatory intermediaries (PRIs). For example, large digital platforms in China serve as PRIs. With the state's acquiescence or active support, these platforms privately substitute—or complement—formal state institutions.

For example, in the e-commerce market, platforms are propelled to provide private institutions to enforce contracts, prevent fraud, and settle disputes because state-provided formal institutions are insufficient. By allowing these private institutions to develop and flourish, the state can foster market growth and delay the painful process of directly reforming formal institutions. It can also exploit these private institutions to strengthen legal enforcement, political control, and social governance. In some cases, digital platforms can even serve as sites of institutional experiments, in which the state formalizes private rules. In this way, institutional outsourcing to digital platforms provides a novel solution to market failure and the governance deficit in China. It also highlights an alternative route to institution building.

Institutional outsourcing differs from public-private partnerships (PPPs), although they overlap in some circumstances. In a typical PPP, the state and private actors work together under a cooperative agreement to produce a product or service (e.g., building roads or highways). Institutional outsourcing, however, is not about producing a specific product or service; it involves making rules or providing governance. Unlike PPPs, institutional outsourcing can also occur with the state's acquiescence, even without contractual agreements.

The concept of institutional outsourcing overlaps with, but is distinct from, the delegation seen in many earlier Chinese reforms. In the 1980s and 1990s, as demonstrated by Susan Shirk (1993), Gabriella Montinola, Yingyi Qian, and Barry Weingast (1995), the Chinese central government delegated powers to provincial governments, encouraging them to conduct policy experiments to stimulate the economy. During China's globalization process, China imported foreign institutions and effectively outsourced power to foreign entities, as noted by Douglas Fuller (2005, 2016), Edward Steinfeld (2010), and Steven Wilson (2009). Unlike these historical delegations, institutional outsourcing in this book involves transferring government authority to domestic private actors. Importantly, not all private actors can perform this role—the concept also defines the conditions under which private actors qualify as PRIs to provide private institutions for the state.

To clarify the concept of institutional outsourcing, I will elaborate on its building blocks: what constitutes outsourcing, institutional functions that can be outsourced, what defines PRIs, and why digital platforms qualify as PRIs.

Defining Outsourcing

I define outsourcing as the state either acquiescing to private actors building institutions and governance (*de facto outsourcing*) or explicitly delegating institutional functions to them through clear consent, contracts, or agreements (*de jure outsourcing*).

De jure outsourcing is straightforward. It involves the state's observable action to endorse or utilize private rules. For example, chapter 3 discusses how China's Anti-Corruption and Bribery Bureau affiliated to the Supreme People's Procuratorate signed a formal memorandum with Alibaba, outsourcing certain legal functions to platforms to curb commercial bribery.

De facto outsourcing, however, requires further clarification. This form of institutional outsourcing entails *deliberate inaction*: while the state has the means to intervene or subvert private rules, it chooses not to, implying implicit consent to the private actor's authority. However, not all instances of state inaction are de facto outsourcing. For example, a state's failure to address a mafia group may result from a lack of knowledge or limited capacity, not implicit consent, and should not be interpreted as de facto outsourcing.

In contrast, China's e-commerce market has exhibited de facto outsourcing. Until 2020, the state largely respected the private rules established by e-commerce platforms, despite being aware of these rules and having the ability to shut the platforms down (as it forced peer-to-peer lending platforms to close).[45] Given China's history of market intervention, the lack of action towards these large platforms for two decades suggests state consent or acquiescence. Even after 2020, when the Chinese government implemented stringent regulations on e-commerce platforms, de facto outsourcing persisted, albeit with a diminished degree of consent towards private ruling. After all, these regulations were not intended to shut down the platforms or dismantle their private governance structures. The state still allows private actors' assertion of authority in the e-commerce market.

Comparing the two forms of institutional outsourcing, de facto outsourcing is more common and often preferable for the state than de jure outsourcing. De facto outsourcing does not require explicit consent or contracts, making it flexible and costless for the state while granting the private actor more autonomy. The state may also fear that formal contracts with certain private actors but not others (de jure outsourcing) could generate moral hazards and undermine market fairness.

Lastly, outsourcing differs from two related concepts: delegation and forbearance. Outsourcing is broader than delegation: delegation involves a formal and written contract, while outsourcing also includes acquiescence. Additionally, outsourcing differs from forbearance, which Alisa Holland defines as the government choosing not to enforce laws to gain political support (e.g., not regulating street vending to attract votes from the poor).[46] While both forbearance and de facto outsourcing involve state tolerance, they differ in nature. Forbearance overlooks clearly illegal actions that the state could enforce, whereas institutional outsourcing allows activities that provide private governance. These activities are not necessarily illegal and often occur when laws are absent, unclear, or unenforceable. For example, digital platforms may step in to address regulatory gaps or enhance the state's enforcement power in China.

Choosing Institutions to Outsource

While this book focuses on the state's outsourcing of economic functions, in this section I discuss what institutional functions can be outsourced in general. To illustrate this point, I build on a typology used by Acemoglu and Johnson[47] to consider two distinct dimensions of institutions: (1) socioeconomic versus political institutions and (2) horizontal versus vertical institutions.[48] Because dimension (1) is self-explanatory, I explain dimension (2) below, and discuss how (2) interacts with dimension (1).

Horizontal institutions govern relations among private agents (e.g., ordinary citizens and businesses), many of which involve economic and social matters, such as contract enforcement, family matters, and disease control. Vertical institutions involve relations between the state or elites and citizens. Some of them concern economic issues, such as property rights institutions that prevent government expropriation. Most vertical institutions, however, deal with political problems. These vertical political institutions can be further categorized according to whether they impose *top-down* coercion (i.e., coercive institutions) or facilitate *bottom-up* participation (i.e., participatory institutions).

To predict which institutions can be outsourced, I assume that ruling elites seek to achieve two goals simultaneously: maximizing economic growth and minimizing political opposition.[49] For example, because the Chinese Communist Party derives an important part of its legitimacy from economic performance, it wants to maximize growth. At the same time, as an authoritarian regime, it wants to maintain political power by minimizing public opposition. I also assume that this joint utility function guides the state's major decisions, including which institutions to outsource. These assumptions lead to several predictions, which I explain using examples from China.

- In general, the state is more likely to outsource *economic and social* institutions than *political* institutions to private actors, which helps maximize economic benefits and minimize political challenges to the ruler. For example, the Chinese government has outsourced economic functions to digital platforms in the online market, as well as some pandemic control functions, including designing the coronavirus tracking app.
- The state is also more likely to outsource horizontal institutions than vertical institutions. This is because vertical institutions govern relations between the government and citizens, imposing greater constraints on the government. Therefore, within economic institutions, the government is more likely to outsource horizontal institutions (e.g., fraud prevention or contract enforcement) than vertical institutions (e.g., property rights against state expropriation), which is the case in the e-commerce market (see chapter 3). In a multilayer government system, the central government may still outsource some vertical institutions to constrain the power of local governments, such as using private institutions to reduce expropriation by local governments.
- Although less likely to occur, the state may outsource vertical and political institutions to private actors. To minimize political risk, it is more likely to outsource *top-down coercive* institutions rather than bottom-up participatory institutions. In China, the government has outsourced censorship and surveillance functions to major social media platforms.[50]

In summary, the government of a developing country is more likely to outsource horizontal institutions that govern economic and social functions than vertical institutions. If it does outsource the latter, it is more likely be top-down coercive functions (such as surveillance and censorship) than bottom-up participatory institutions. In this book, I focus on the state's outsourcing of economic functions.

Defining Private Regulatory Intermediaries (PRIs)

To qualify as a PRI, a private actor must be able to supply private rules. Most private actors do not meet this criterion because they only provide products, not rules. For example, myriad small businesses produce apps on the IOS App Store, but only Apple Inc. gets to set the rules.

However, merely having the capability to offer private governance is insufficient for a PRI. To qualify, they need to meet additional criteria. The rationale behind institutional outsourcing is that when the government fails to provide strong formal institutions, it outsources this responsibility to PRIs. Therefore, PRIs must be capable of establishing institutions that approximate key aspects of strong formal institutions: encompassing and impersonal.

- *Encompassing*: To approximate the functions of strong public institutions, PRIs must provide inclusive private institutions that serve all market participants. This requires PRIs to have a broad interest in the market's overall success, rather than representing specific industries or groups. Otherwise, they may prioritize narrow interests over general welfare, making them unsuitable substitutes for public entities.[51] For example, while a merchant guild also provides private governance among its members, it only represents the narrow interests of merchants. By contrast, a market owner has an encompassing interest in the market's overall success. Given that more merchants in the market attract more consumers and vice versa, a market owner must balance the interests of both merchants and consumers to maximize sales.
- *Impersonal*: Another key attribute of strong formal institutions such as the rule of law is impersonality, which involves "treating everyone the same without regard to their individual identity."[52] To reflect this attribute, PRIs must establish institutional rules with impersonal characteristics rather than basing decisions on social identities. A private ruling system based on personal or social ties will not be scalable, making it difficult to substitute for public institutions. For instance, the Maghribi Traders' "code of conduct" was a social norm that governed an ethnically homogeneous group in the Middle Ages.[53] In the modern era, rules based on social, ethnic, and religious networks often cannot be scaled up to the whole society. This scalability limitation makes it difficult for these private rules to substitute for good

public institutions. Hence, PRIs need to be able to supply institutional rules with impersonal traits.

For institutional outsourcing to occur, it is not enough for a private actor to be capable; the state must also be willing to outsource. This leads to the third condition for a PRI: being limited.

- *Limited*: A PRI should be limited in scope so the state does not perceive it to be a powerful threat that can capture or subvert its authority. If a PRI does not meet this condition, the ruling elites will not tolerate the private exercise of institutional functions, and outsourcing will not take place.

Why Digital Platforms Qualify as PRIs

Digital platforms are well positioned as PRIs due to their distinct business model.

To begin with, the business model of digital platforms requires them to supply private institutions. Traditional businesses typically follow a *pipeline* model with a *linear* value chain—acquiring inputs, designing and manufacturing products, and finally selling these products, thereby creating value in a sequential manner.[54] In stark contrast, platforms are by definition two-sided or multisided markets. They create value by fostering connections within and between different user groups. For example, e-commerce platforms operate as a marketplace in which sellers and buyers can interact; social media platforms bring together content providers and consumers, and ride-hailing apps link passengers and drivers. This value creation requires platforms to establish and enforce private rules for user interactions.

More importantly, the private institutions created by digital platforms are remarkably scalable. They can serve a large population, potentially encompassing all members of society. This scalability stems from two sources. First, digital platforms benefit from network effects. As a platform's value increases with each new user, it fosters a virtuous cycle of attracting even more users and enhancing overall appeal. Second, a critical feature of digital platforms is their near-zero marginal cost: serving each additional user becomes practically costless once the platform infrastructure is established, as replicating digital products involves minimal costs. This scalability also sets platforms apart from many other private actors that face significant incremental costs (such as physical investments) to expand their reach.

In addition to their ability to offer private governance, digital platforms also meet the additional criteria required for being PRIs.

First, digital platforms have encompassing interests in the overall success of the market. As defined above, platforms host multiple user groups and benefit from the value created by the interactions between these groups. Due to network effects, the key to success for a platform is encouraging all user groups to stay in the market. This requires them to enact rules that balance the competing interests of the user groups.[55] For example, if a platform only protects buyers, then sellers will exit; with fewer sellers in the market, buyers will also move to other platforms, leading to the platform's failure.

Second, although platform governance involves human decision-making and execution, a substantial portion of it relies on largely impersonal, algorithm-based enforcement to regulate exchanges between users. This characteristic renders platform rules and online institutions scalable because they do not rely on social relationships to operate.

Third, while digital platforms wield considerable influence, their power remains constrained. Unlike certain private groups with violent potential or physical capabilities, platforms primarily rely on reputational and digital enforcement within their own virtual domains. Meanwhile, the Chinese authoritarian government has various tools at its disposal to control these platforms, such as internet cutoffs, data regulations, and antitrust measures. These efforts prevent platforms from monopolizing the market and becoming substantial threats to the state.

The Political Logic of Institutional Outsourcing

Why would a government relinquish—or at least implicitly tolerate encroachment on—its authority? This practice is particularly counterintuitive in China, which does not resemble "captured" states where private corporate interests steer politics. The CCP is known for its tight grip on the corporate sector and deep distrust of private firms. So why does the Chinese government outsource institutional functions to private platforms?

General Logic of Outsourcing

Outsourcing generally serves the interests of the central government in three ways. First, it helps the government tackle the technical complexity associated with institutional development. When it comes to governing rapidly evolving fields like e-commerce, a high level of expertise is required. Such expertise is often not readily available within the government and can be excessively costly to cultivate in-house. In contrast, platforms have acquired the necessary expertise through continuous experimentation on the best governing institutions to outperform their competitors. Consequently, it is cost-effective for governments to outsource some of the rulemaking authority to private entities. This motivation for delegation, rooted in expertise, resonates with the findings of Walter Mattli and Tim Büthe (2005): in highly technical domains such as setting global accounting standards, governments frequently opt to delegate authority to private organizations with the relevant expertise.

Second, even where the government has expertise or formal institutions exist, the cost of using them can be high. While laws may exist on paper, their enforcement can be challenging. For instance, e-commerce users can, in theory, use the state-provided small-claims procedure for resolving disputes. However, the time and effort required can still be prohibitively high, especially for everyday transactions between parties in different areas. In contrast, online dispute resolution systems provided by digital platforms are more accessible and cheaper. Unlike formal institutions, which evolve slowly due to high reform costs, private institutions are more adaptable and responsive to market demands.

A third advantage for the central government is that outsourcing allows the authoritarian state to divert blame. By outsourcing rule-making to platforms, the government can disassociate itself from failures when institutional experiments go wrong. Private platforms bear the risk of failure and shock from reforms, buffering tensions that would otherwise be directed at the state. The state can then take a neutral role in mediating conflicts between platforms and users.

For example, Taobao faced several waves of seller protests after making major rule changes. The largest, "October Rising" (十月围城), took place in October 2011 after Taobao substantially increased the membership fees and cash deposits required for sellers on Taobao Mall (the predecessor of Tmall) in an effort to reduce the number of counterfeit and substandard products sold on the platform. The rule change was made without warning and disproportionately hurt small sellers. Nearly fifty thousand sellers formed an "anti-Taobao alliance" and initiated a storm of digital protests to disrupt the online market: they simultaneously ordered many products from big retailers, left nasty reviews, and requested refunds, leading to the closure of many stores. Thousands even protested at Alibaba's headquarters in Hangzhou. The dispute was eventually resolved after the government stepped in to mediate. Taobao conceded by revising the fee schedules and offering 1.8 billion RMB to help small businesses use its platform.[56]

The above logic of outsourcing has a historical parallel. Since the beginning of China's market reforms, the central government has delegated substantial economic authority to local governments to distance itself from the provision of services. The central directives usually consist of broad and vague guidelines and leave sufficient room for local governments to fill in the details. This arrangement has allowed local governments to engage in policy innovation and experimentation, which has moved reforms forward.[57] It has also allowed the center to benefit from and scale up successful local experiments without being held responsible for failures.[58] This partly explains why Chinese citizens exhibit "hierarchical trust": they tend to trust more in the center than in local authorities; they blame the latter for bad policies and implementation problems.[59]

Why Outsource to Platforms?

Apart from the general logic of outsourcing, why would the central government outsource institutional functions to *digital platforms* rather than to local governments, as is more common in China's previous reforms? I have already shown that digital platforms qualify as PRIs. Two additional features make them attractive candidates.

First, platforms' ability to collect and analyze a key economic asset—data—gives them unparalleled advantages over state agents in executing certain functions.[60] By employing techniques such as A/B testing, platforms can experiment with institutional modifications, promptly gather user feedback, and rapidly adapt to changing market conditions. Moreover, the combination of data and algorithms also help automatically detect rule violations and effectively enforce the institutions in place, which is not easily achievable through traditional execution methods employed by local governments.

The second advantageous feature is the geographical transcendence of digital platforms, which bolsters the central government's authority and facilitates the consistent execution of policies across regions. While local governments can also implement central policies, their significant autonomy within China's economic system can lead to issues such as withholding local information from the center, distorting policy implementation, and engaging in local protectionism. National platforms provide some means for the central government to check the power of local governments, potentially aiding in its recentralization of power.[61] For example, platforms can serve as centralized data collection tools, mitigating the center's information disadvantage vis-à-vis local governments and ensuring the consistent implementation of central policies across regions. Additionally, by breaking down internal trade barriers, platforms further weaken local governments' authority, revenues, and rent creation (see chapter 4 for empirical evidence for this).[62]

Why Outsource to Private Actors?

One may still wonder why private ownership of platforms matters.[63] Theoretically, a state-owned enterprise (SOE) can offer the same digital services. As a regime insider, SOEs pose less of a threat to the authoritarian government.

However, outsourcing to private firms carries important benefits. As demonstrated earlier, outsourcing enables the government to deflect blame when institutional experiments fail. Mattli and Büthe (2005) emphasize that outsourcing to private actors, rather than public entities, enhances the government's ability to avoid responsibility because private actors are frequently perceived as separate from the government.[64]

More importantly, private ownership is key to improving economic efficiency under institutional outsourcing. It can incentivize platforms to remain competitive and continuously improve the quality of their services. By contrast, SOEs receive preferential treatment from the state, which can lead to decreased motivation for competition and innovation.[65] For example, SOEs are generally less profitable than private companies because the state usually provides bailouts when they exceed their budget constraints, a phenomenon known as "soft-budget constraints."[66]

SOEs would therefore be unable to compete in the aggressive platform industries. For instance, Jike Search—the state-run search engine with the sports legend Deng Yaping as CEO—failed miserably in 2013, allegedly wasting 2 billion RMB (about $320 million).[67] Another state-run search engine ChinaSo.com—jointly managed by the state-run news outlets Xinhua News Agency and *People's Daily*—remains operational but is rarely used.[68] Similarly, in e-commerce, after observing the success of private platforms like Taobao, many local governments attempted to build their own e-commerce platforms to sell local products. Almost all of these government-sponsored initiatives failed. Perhaps the only exception is Yiwugo.com, a B2B platform jointly built by the Yiwu city government and the government-run Zhejiang China Commodities City Group Co Ltd. Its success is likely due to the city's hosting of the world's largest offline small commodity wholesale market, providing a strong foundation for the online market. An e-commerce expert explained: "Platform business has network effects. Customers will naturally choose to buy from the largest private platforms where most sellers are. Why would you buy from these new platforms built by local governments when you have better alternatives?"[69]

Given that SOEs cannot emerge organically from competition, there arises the question of whether the state will nationalize dominant private platforms. Indeed, some Chinese scholars have advocated for nationalization, claiming that large platforms function as public utilities and that data, being highly vital, should not be controlled by private entities.[70] This radical standpoint has so far garnered minimal support within China. While the government has been reported to acquire "golden shares" in certain local subsidiaries of Big Tech companies,[71] it has not pursued outright nationalization. In fact, from an economic perspective, it seems more advantageous to the state to keep platforms in private hands. A platform employee, whom I interviewed, expressed little concern about nationalization. He remarked: "The government certainly has the authority to nationalize the platform. But if a private platform were to become a SOE with the implicit backing of the state, its motivation to compete and innovate would be gone. Consequently, its economic efficiency and service quality would certainly decline, and users would seek alternatives."[72]

Durability of Institutional Outsourcing

Institutional outsourcing from the state to private platforms can generally endure when two conditions are satisfied. First, the platform needs to provide institutions and services that appeal to users without arbitrarily exploiting them. Failing to do so can expose the platform to government regulatory crackdown, user exodus, and, in extreme cases, internal collapse. Second, the state needs to maintain its basic support for platforms without arbitrarily banning them or imposing insurmountable compliance costs. Otherwise, platforms may lose incentives to innovate and could collapse, leading to widespread unemployment and social instability, which pose significant problems for the state.

Various mechanisms are in place to ensure the aforementioned conditions are met. Essentially, there are constraints on both the state and platforms that limit their ability to act arbitrarily and incentivize cooperation. These mechanisms provide durability to the outsourcing relationship, making it costly, if not impossible, to reverse.

Limits on Platforms' Arbitrary Power

To constrain platforms' arbitrary power to exploit users, several mechanisms are at play.

USER PROTEST AND CROSS-PLATFORM COMPETITION

One mechanism to constrain a platform's arbitrary acts is user protest. In an authoritarian state, it is politically risky to openly criticize or initiate collective action against the government. This risk is reduced if citizens demand rights from, or protest against, a rulemaking company rather than the state. The threat of a user revolt can sometimes prevent platforms from creating arbitrary rules.

For example, as previously mentioned, the abrupt rule changes at Taobao in 2011 ignited a substantial wave of seller protests, famously known as the October Rising. This protest movement saw the formation of an anti-Taobao alliance, with thousands of sellers staging physical demonstrations at Alibaba's headquarters. In response to these protests, Taobao implemented changes to prevent future unrest. Instead of immediately implementing new rules as they had done previously, they introduced a seven-day buffer period for public notice of new rules and started to hold rule hearings and discussions before rule changes.[73]

Another mechanism is cross-platform competition. Competition weakens platforms' incentives to exploit users, as users can opt to migrate to other platforms. The fierce cross-platform competition stems from the fact that most buyers and sellers use multiple platforms simultaneously; for sellers in particular, this constitutes a risk-pooling strategy—that is, "not putting all the eggs in one basket."[74] The minimal hurdles to switching between platforms foster intense rivalry, not just among firms offering similar services but also those providing entirely different ones. As Google's former executive chairman Eric Schmidt said, Google's biggest competitor in search is Amazon, rather than another search engine.[75] Likewise, WeChat—Tencent's flagship social media app—added the WeChat Store and Pay functions after 2011 and immediately became a challenger to Alibaba's e-commerce business. At least by the time of writing, vibrant competition continues to thrive in China's digital economy. In e-commerce, Alibaba, Pinduoduo (PDD), and JD vigorously compete, with none able to establish a monopoly. Notably, PDD emerged after Alibaba and JD had already consolidated the market, surprising many analysts who had previously thought there was limited room for new entrants.

Nevertheless, the enduring efficacy of this competitive mechanism remains uncertain. While platform competition is theoretically just "one click away," platforms use various strategies to impede users from switching, such as loyalty programs and personalized services based on extensive user data. Moreover, platform economies are inherently "winner-takes-all" businesses. As multisided markets, platforms exhibit network effects—either direct (more sellers attract more buyers and vice versa) or indirect (more users and data improve service). These network effects generate increasing returns to scale, potentially making large platforms even more dominant. This raises the question of whether large platforms might begin to exploit their users as the market consolidates.

GOVERNMENT REGULATION

Even if market competition subsides or user protests fail to hold platforms accountable, there is a more important mechanism to constrain large platforms—China's authoritarian government. In addition to its economic rationale, the Chinese state also has political motivations to regulate private platforms to prevent them from becoming monopolies. Private monopoly firms are too powerful to be politically safe for the CCP, which is deeply concerned about private capital capturing the state. The authoritarian state has many ways to regulate platforms.

At the most fundamental level, the government has ultimate control over the country's internet connection. The Cybersecurity Law passed in 2016 stipulates that the government can cut off or limit internet service during a crisis for national security.[76] Even before the law's passage, the government had demonstrated its ability and resolve to take such action. Internet access was blocked in the entire Xinjiang region for ten months following an ethnic riot in 2009.[77]

Apart from its ability to cut off the internet, the authoritarian state has a plethora of methods to constrain platform power. For example, the government engages in antitrust regulations when large platforms abuse their market power.[78] E-commerce platforms like Alibaba used to lock sellers into exclusive deals, forcing them to shut down their stores on other platforms. The State Administration for Market Regulation declared this "either-or restriction" to be anticompetitive and illegal. In 2021, Alibaba was fined a record amount of $2.8 billion (4 percent of its total 2019 sales in China) for engaging in such practices. Other tech giants, including Baidu and Tencent, were also fined for antitrust violations that year.[79]

The state also blocks entry when platform economies prove to be too disruptive to traditional businesses. For example, in 2014, the central bank suspended Alibaba and Tencent's plans to issue virtual credit cards, a move that directly challenged the credit card business of state-owned banks.[80] In some cases, the state doesn't need to implement actual regulatory measures. The stock market's sensitivity to even a hint of regulatory actions effectively pressures major tech companies. For example, Tencent's stock price dropped by 4 percent after an article in the *People's Daily Online*, the CCP's mouthpiece, criticized its online game "Honor of Kings" as addictive and harmful.[81]

The fact that platforms' power is constrained by the state, however, leads to another question. If the authoritarian government is so powerful, how does it assure the platforms that it will not confiscate them and subvert their private institutions?

Limits on the State's Arbitrary Power

Some people assume the Chinese government has unconstrained power over private firms because it lacks a Western-style system of checks and balances. Yet China's political system features fragmented authoritarianism: there are structural and procedural constraints in the policymaking process, which leaves room for bureaucratic bargaining and business lobbying.[82] News reports indicate a revolving door phenomenon: Chinese tech firms have hired high-level ex-regulators to deal with government relations and fend off regulatory crackdowns.[83] The interviews I conducted for this study also indicate that tech firms frequently engage in lobbying activities to win support from the government, including "lobbying for e-commerce to be written into the Government Work Report,"[84] a key document laying out each year's policy priorities.

More importantly, the Chinese state is constrained by its own goal of promoting economic growth to sustain its legitimacy, jobs, and social stability. While the authoritarian government faces few procedural constraints to prevent it from cracking down on the private sector, arbitrary policymaking can jeopardize economic growth and social stability. Consequently, the government may eventually refrain from acting arbitrarily. For example, in early 2022, after a year of regulatory actions against Big Tech that led to plunging stock prices and widespread layoffs, the government eased off the tech clampdown to support the economy.[85] Therefore, while the state regulates platforms, it has been careful to not subvert major platforms for three reasons.

The first reason is the sheer size of the major platforms.[86] For instance, more than 800 million sellers and buyers rely on Taobao for jobs and shopping. The government would generate public anger and risk social instability if it shut down such a large platform. Recent studies on regulatory entrepreneurship also suggest that tech companies have inherent advantages—such as being scalable and highly connected to users—that they can use to leverage popular support against resistant officials or overly protectionist rules.[87]

Second, many state and platform interests are aligned. The state benefits from well-functioning platforms that create jobs, boost innovation, and stimulate development. Technology platforms are also critical to government plans to shift the country's growth engines from investment and export to domestic consumption and services. For example, e-commerce stimulates consumption and creates jobs in related service industries (e.g., online retailing, customer service, and logistics). In 2012 alone, the e-commerce sector generated more than two million jobs directly and twelve million indirectly,[88] which has alleviated central government concerns about large-scale unemployment and subsequent social instability as the Chinese economy slows down.

Additionally, major tech platforms have forged political ties by accepting investments from funds that are government-backed or run by the scions of Chinese leaders. According to the New York Times, "Most of Alibaba's new investors in 2012, including the sovereign wealth funds CITIC Capital and CDB Capital, were . . . state-owned."[89] Around the same time, Alibaba also received investments from a subsidiary of Boyu Capital, of which former President Jiang Zemin's grandson is a partner. Boyu's investment of $400 million gained more than $1 billion after Alibaba's initial public offering (IPO).[90] More recently, China's National Social Security Fund has invested in Ant Financial, the company that runs Alipay.[91] Other e-commerce and tech firms such as JD Digits have also received investments from government-backed funds.[92] While these investments do not exempt tech firms from government regulations, they mean that the state has direct economic stakes in their success.

The above analysis by no means suggests that digital platforms are completely safe from state expropriation. Rather, it shows that the central government would pay a high price for shutting down large platforms. At least in the short to medium term, institutional outsourcing helps strengthen the authoritarian state rather than undermine it. This provides incentives for the state to not break the outsourcing relationship.

The Interconnectedness of Outsourcing and Regulation

A key implication of the analysis is that outsourcing and regulation are two sides of the same coin in institutional outsourcing. On the one hand, outsourcing to private platforms would not occur if the authoritarian government lacked ex-ante confidence in its ultimate control over these platforms. According to a Chinese legal scholar familiar with policymakers, the Chinese government's strong confidence in its own regulatory capacities—particularly its ability to exercise the "nuclear option" of shutting down the internet—has led to an initial hands-off approach toward internet firms.[93] On the other hand, regulation serves as an ex-post mechanism to fix the problems of private governance. Without proper state regulations, private platforms may exploit users and abuse their market power as they expand. Consequently, the quality of private institutions would deteriorate, hampering the efficiency of institutional outsourcing.

While some level of government regulation on platforms is necessary, arbitrary and overly stringent regulations would backfire. Excessive regulation risks stifling the autonomy and innovation of platforms. This could also result in a decline in the quality of private institutions and hurt the economic outcomes of institutional outsourcing.

In summary, while institutional outsourcing can generally endure, its economic efficiency can fluctuate significantly depending on the balance of private and public regulatory powers. For optimal outcomes, neither the state nor the platform should be overly dominant in the outsourcing relationship.

Limitations of Institutional Outsourcing

Institutional outsourcing has its limitations. Not all institutions can be outsourced, and platforms' institutions are not perfect substitutes for public institutions, even if they fill gaps left by the state.

The enforcement capabilities of digital platforms are inherently limited. When a user violates a platform rule, the typical consequences may include a decrease in their online rating, freezing of funds in their online wallet, or, in extreme cases, the suspension of their account. These penalties are not as severe as those imposed by law enforcement. For instance, the banned individual can open a new account or use others' accounts to access the platform. Detecting such behaviors is challenging because platforms lack offline enforcement authority unless they collaborate with law enforcement. This helps explain why counterfeits and fraudulent activities persist in the online marketplace despite the platforms' efforts to establish institutions.

Moreover, decisions driven by big data and algorithms do not inherently lead to optimal outcomes. In 2017, Jack Ma provocatively advocated for the revival of the planned economy, arguing that the integration of big data and AI could close the information gaps that historically caused such models to fail.[94] However, this claim has been criticized for several reasons. First, big data is not necessarily representative or high-quality. Using such data for algorithmic training can produce biased outcomes—a classic case of "garbage in, garbage out." Additionally, algorithmic bias and interpretability issues can further hinder the effectiveness of digital governance. Another major concern is economic agency. When data plays a crucial role in resource allocation, market actors have strong incentives to manipulate it, leading to distorted data and, consequently, misallocated resources. This issue is exemplified by the practice of "brushing," where sellers create fake orders to manipulate product rankings, thereby undermining the governance capabilities of platforms.

Other challenges arise from the abuse of market power by private platforms, especially if public regulations do not keep pace. As Lord Acton famously contended, "Power tends to corrupt and absolute power corrupts absolutely"; this applies not only to public entities but also to private actors that wield regulatory powers. Two major problems exist. The first problem is that platforms' commercial interests do not always align with public interests. Although a PRI by definition has an encompassing interest in its own market, it does not necessarily serve the interests of the whole society. To maximize its rents, a profit-driven PRI can engage in anticompetitive behaviors at the expense of its rivals, leading to antitrust concerns. Second, like government officials who wield power, private agents who enforce private rules may also abuse their power, leading to corruption. For example, the platform employee may collude with a seller to artificially boost their sales and reviews in exchange for bribes. I will discuss both problems further in chapter 6.

Finally, finding the right balance between private and public regulatory powers to achieve the best economic outcomes is challenging. When private platforms expand, they have the potential to overstep their bounds and exploit their market power. Conversely, there is the risk of an authoritarian government imposing excessively stringent regulations on platforms. As discussed in chapter 6, China has experienced tumultuous shifts in its regulatory approach to platforms, transitioning from a long-standing hands-off policy to a regulatory storm and then returning to a supportive stance on platforms. This pendulum swing in regulatory approaches underscores the challenge of striking the right balance, avoiding both regulatory vacuums and excessive control.

Concluding Remarks

In this chapter, I have conceptualized institutional outsourcing to digital platforms and explained how it enables institutional development. In the next chapter, I use the concept to explain the political foundations of China's e-commerce market of 800 million users, focusing on Taobao as an analytical case.

Two caveats must be noted. First, institutional outsourcing is not the only route to institutional development and is likely a short-term solution for addressing market problems like fraud and contract violations. In the long run, formal institutions may still need to catch up to fundamentally eradicate these problems. For example, despite platforms' efforts, counterfeit products remain a significant problem for e-commerce. A key reason is that China's legislation on counterfeits is lax and outdated. Between 1993 and 2017, China's per capita GDP increased nearly twentyfold, yet the penalty for individuals who falsify product quality inspection results or issue false certificates remained unchanged at up to 50,000 RMB (less than $8,000). This penalty is minimal compared to the potential profits from counterfeiting.[95] This indicates that, while platforms' private institutions have their own merits—they are flexible and can quickly adapt to changing market needs—their enforcement power rarely goes beyond the platform. In many cases, public regulation is still needed to fix the root problem.

I do not argue that institutional outsourcing is a Pareto efficient or the best approach to developing market institutions, nor do I claim that government-initiated legal reforms are unnecessary. However, institutional outsourcing is more politically feasible than the lengthy process of directly reforming formal institutions. According to Dani Rodrik, this makes it a *second-best* institution.[96] Such institutions often perform better than the most economically efficient institutions in developing countries due to political barriers that are hard to overcome in the short term.[97] This logic of *trading economic efficiency for political expediency* is also at the heart of many other reforms in China.

3

Making Institutions Work

THE POLITICAL FOUNDATIONS OF CHINA'S
E-COMMERCE MARKET

Winning against the Odds

Shark vs. Crocodile

In 2003, all the stars aligned for eBay to build an e-commerce empire in China. Through the acquisition of EachNet, the nation's leading online auction platform, eBay swiftly claimed a commanding 85 percent market share.[1] For Meg Whitman, eBay's CEO at the time, China was a "must-win" to achieve global dominance.[2] In the ensuing years, eBay forged exclusive partnerships with major web portals to thwart competitors' advertisements and committed substantial investments to signal "an unmistakable commitment and an unstoppable determination to be number one in China."[3]

Nevertheless, eBay's remarkable momentum was disrupted by an unexpected contender: Alibaba. Alibaba was founded in 1999 by former English teacher Jack Ma. The company initially only had online business-to-business (B2B) wholesale platforms, facilitating Chinese small- and medium-sized enterprises to sell worldwide. As eBay entered China, Alibaba swiftly sensed that eBay would encroach on Alibaba's user base, since Chinese buyers would struggle to distinguish small business sellers on Alibaba from individual vendors on eBay. Therefore, in 2003, Alibaba unveiled Taobao.com, a rival consumer-to-consumer (C2C) platform, as a defensive move against eBay.

All signs indicated a clear victory for eBay over Taobao. By 2003, eBay was globally recognized, with annual net revenues exceeding a billion dollars. Its first-mover advantage and strong network effects made it appear unbeatable. In contrast, Alibaba was relatively unknown and had only achieved positive cash flow the previous year.

However, the battle yielded a surprising outcome. In merely four years, eBay/EachNet's market share plummeted from 72.4 percent in late 2003 to a

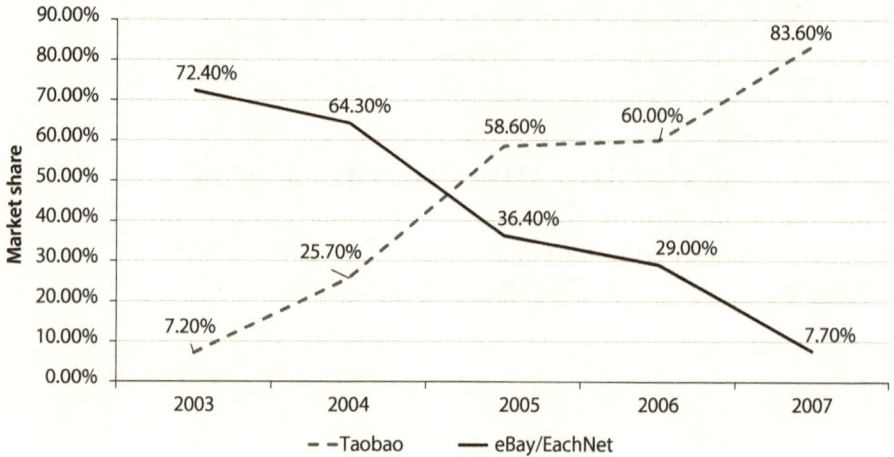

FIGURE 3.1. C2C Market Shares of Taobao and eBay China/EachNet (2003–7). *Notes*: Adapted from Barnett et al. (2010).

mere 7.7 percent in 2007, while Taobao's surged from 7.2 percent to over 80 percent (Figure 3.1). This dismal performance prompted eBay to withdraw from China.

How did David defeat Goliath? A remark by Jack Ma provides the answer: "eBay may be a shark in the ocean, but I am a crocodile in the Yangtze River. If we fight in the ocean, we lose—but if we fight in the river, we win."[4]

A key distinction between the "ocean" and the "river" is their institutional environments. Unlike developed markets, early 2000s China faced institutional voids—an absence or inadequacy of institutions like a strong legal system, efficient arbitration mechanisms, and credit card systems. These institutions are crucial for preventing issues in e-commerce. For example, a strong legal system would reduce counterfeit products, and credit cards protect consumers against online scams. However, prior research indicates that these institutions were lacking in China during the Taobao-eBay battle:

"China . . . lacked norms and laws to support online exchange, and had not yet developed the technological and financial infrastructures needed to facilitate online auctions . . . In the US if you place a bid, it's a contract, and by law you need to fulfill that bid if you win the auction. That's very clear. People would be afraid of getting sued if they did not abide by that contract. In China people don't care. 'I place a bid, I don't want it anymore, tough luck.' . . . In 2002, a survey conducted by China Internet Network Information Center found that 13.9 percent of online buyers had the experience of not receiving goods they had paid for."[5]

As a result, Chinese consumers exhibited notably lower trust in e-commerce compared to Americans. To encourage adoption, China-based platforms needed stronger online institutions to build trust. eBay overlooked this difference and merely transplanted their US model to China, failing to assure Chinese consumers of transaction safety. In contrast, as a local company, Taobao leveraged its deep understanding of the Chinese market and built institutions that fostered user trust.

The Game Changer: Alipay

A critical institution behind Taobao's triumph is the invention of Alipay. This seemingly small step in improving the online payment systems resulted in a great leap for Alibaba's e-commerce business.

In the early stages after Taobao's launch, employees noticed a peculiar trend: although users were enthusiastic about online trading, they rarely completed transactions on the platform. This was due to a simple dilemma: should the seller ship the products first, or should the buyer pay first? Neither party wanted to kickstart the process, fearing that the other might not fulfill their contractual obligations afterward.[6] Consequently, most early transactions on Taobao were only partially online. Users would identify trading partners online but meet in person to exchange products and cash, limiting e-commerce to local trades where in-person exchanges were feasible.[7] Fundamentally, this problem stemmed from the aforementioned institutional voids: without strong institutions to ensure the fulfillment of contractual obligations, trust levels were low, causing trade to stagnate.

After numerous attempts to solve the trust problem, Taobao introduced Alipay, a game changer. As acknowledged by the chief strategy officer of Ant Financial (Alibaba's financial subsidiary), "If there were no Alipay, there would be no today's Alibaba."[8] On the surface, Alipay might seem like just another online payment system, similar to PayPal. However, what distinguishes Alipay is its integration of a *mandatory escrow system* (担保支付) into the online payment process.

Alipay is vital in building user trust. Unlike PayPal or credit cards, where the buyer's payment is directly transferred to the seller upon order placement, Alipay's escrow service ensures that the payment is released to the seller only after the buyer receives the product and is satisfied with it (Figure 3.2).[9] If either party is unsatisfied with the transaction, Alipay freezes the payment, prompting dispute resolution. By withholding payment until both parties are satisfied, the escrow system ensures both sides fulfill their contractual obligations.

While Alipay involved little new technology, it was a major institutional innovation that triggered substantial growth in online transactions. In particular,

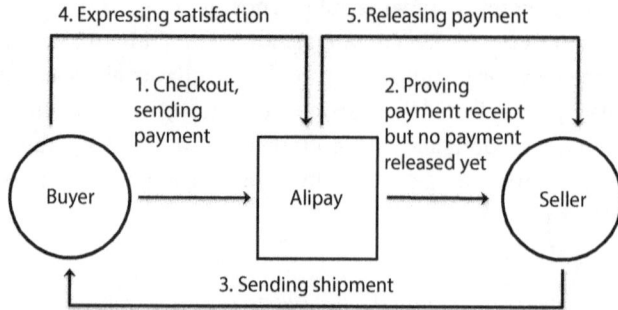

FIGURE 3.2. Alipay's Escrow Service (Steps 1–5). *Notes:* After an order is placed, the buyer sends the payment to Alipay's escrow account rather than paying the seller directly (step 1). Alipay then notifies the seller to send the product to the buyer (steps 2 and 3). If the buyer expresses satisfaction within fifteen days after receiving the product (step 4), Alipay will immediately release the payment to the seller (step 5). If the buyer does not take any action, the money will be automatically sent to the seller after fifteen days. If either the buyer or seller is unsatisfied with the transaction, neither party receives the payment. The money will be kept in escrow and frozen, forcing both parties to seek dispute resolution.

it unleashed the potential of long-distance trade, as individuals no longer needed to meet in person to establish trust. Alipay's first transaction took place in October 2003, which enabled the international sale of a secondhand camera between Xi'an, China, and Yokohama, Japan.[10] By early 2004, 70 percent of Taobao products included Alipay as one of the payment options.[11] Taobao later made Alipay compulsory for all transactions.

By contrast, eBay China failed to prioritize trust as a central element of its institutional design until it was too late. The Chinese company that eBay acquired, EachNet, recognized the importance of trust and even introduced a beta version of an escrow service prior to Alipay. Unfortunately, this crucial advancement was halted to make room for the introduction of PayPal in China.[12] A year after Alipay was created, eBay China finally launched its own payment escrow system, called "An Fu Tong" (安付通). However, this endeavor proved unsuccessful, as users often confused An Fu Tong with PayPal, exacerbating eBay's challenges.

The Political Backdrop

Apart from Alipay, one crucial factor behind Taobao's success is often overlooked: the Chinese government's tolerance to Alibaba's institutional innovations in legally ambiguous domains. At the time of Alipay's inception, China's financial industry was predominantly controlled by state-owned banks. Non-bank third-party payment systems, including Alipay, lacked the legal authorization to issue direct online payments. The legal risks associated with launching Alipay were so substantial that Jack Ma had to reassure his staff by saying, "If someone needs to go to jail for Alipay, let it be me."[13] The government was informed about Alipay from the outset, since Alibaba decided to provide monthly updates to alleviate suspicions.[14] However, for nearly eight years, the government maintained a regulatory-free environment in this specific domain rather than cracking down on it. Eventually, in 2010, the central bank legitimized third-party payment systems, and, a year later, the government issued the first electronic payment licenses to twenty-seven domestic enterprises, including Alipay and Tencent's Tenpay.

Not only did the government acquiesce, but in the mid-2010s, it actively encouraged the disruptive innovations introduced by Alipay and other private payment platforms, disregarding pleas from state-owned businesses to ban these platforms. A notable example is the launch of a money market fund called "Yu'E Bao" (余额宝, meaning "leftover treasure") by Alipay in 2013. This offering allowed consumers to earn much higher interest rates by keeping their funds within Alipay, resulting in a rapid diversion of deposits away from state-owned banks. Despite strong complaints from state-owned banks, China's central bank chief sided with the private sector, claiming that Yu'E Bao and similar products would definitely not be banned. On another occasion, then-Premier Li Keqiang even praised these fintech innovations as a means to reform the Chinese economy, incentivizing the mighty state-owned banks to change.[15]

Over the years, as Alipay became widely adopted and an integral part of the country's digital infrastructure, the Chinese government partnered with it to strengthen legal enforcement. In 2018, it took only forty minutes for two courts in Beijing and Hangzhou to coordinate and investigate a suspect's Alipay record.[16] In 2022, the Public Security Bureau of Chaoyang District in Beijing also collaborated with Alipay to jointly develop an Anti-Fraud Early Warning System, targeting scammers.[17]

It may seem paradoxical that an authoritarian government, possessing significant regulatory capabilities, would allow private firms to flout rules and even challenge the business interests of the state-owned sector. In fact, it points to a broader governmental strategy that I call *strategic nonregulation*. This nonregulation does not come from an inability to rule; rather, it is a deliberate choice by the government to refrain from stringent regulation, thereby creating space for the market development and innovation. Particularly when dealing with new industries (such as e-commerce, fintech, ride sharing, and other parts of the digital economy), the Chinese government often follows a principle of "development first, regulation later" (先发展, 再监管). It adopts a "wait and see" stance and regulates only when the time is ripe. In the case of e-commerce, the Chinese government waited nearly two decades before implementing stricter regulations in late 2020. This delay allowed ample time for private digital institutions like Alipay to emerge and fill the governance gap left by the state.

Preview of the Chapter

The anecdote about Alipay illustrates the logic of institutional outsourcing: why digital platforms create private institutions and why the state engages in outsourcing. Initially, the state did not shut down Alipay despite its disruptions to vested interests (i.e., de facto outsourcing). Later, the government legalized Alipay and collaborated with platforms to strengthen state institutions and legal enforcement (i.e., de jure outsourcing).

The rest of the chapter extends this logic to a full analysis of institutional outsourcing in the e-commerce market. I organize the discussion by examining two enabling conditions for institutional outsourcing and demonstrating how they are both present in China's e-commerce market.

First, a private regulatory intermediary (PRI) must exist to provide substitutes for formal market-supporting institutions. China's e-commerce market meets this condition. I first show that this market is platform based: most of China's e-commerce transactions take place on platforms rather than on independent websites. I then draw from a case study on Taobao, China's largest e-commerce platform, and demonstrate how platforms provide private substitutes for formal market institutions, including contract enforcement, fraud prevention, dispute resolution, and resource allocation. Taobao's system includes a complex reputation mechanism, a credit score, a fraud detection program, and even a jury-like system in which ordinary users can vote to adjudicate cases or change the platform's rules. Taobao has therefore begun to supply many aspects of institutional infrastructure to fill the governance gap left by the state.

Turning to the second enabling condition for institutional outsourcing: the state must willingly acquiesce to or actively encourage PRIs to serve as private suppliers of market institutions. Between the mid-2000s and late 2010s, China's broad political-economic ambition—economic rebalancing—made the government receptive to private institutional innovation in e-commerce and other aspects of the digital economy. This hands-off approach granted the e-commerce sector considerable autonomy, crucial for China's emergence as the world's largest e-commerce market. Over time, institutional outsourcing has evolved from tacit consent to become more overt and institutionalized, manifesting through a multitude of collaborative agreements between the state and various platforms. To demonstrate this trend, I offer concrete examples of how the state outsources institutions to platforms.

How E-Commerce Platforms Serve as PRIs in China's E-Commerce Market

Let's start the analysis with the first condition for institutional outsourcing: PRIs must *exist* to provide (at least partial) substitutes for formal market-supporting institutions. This section elaborates why e-commerce platforms serve as PRIs in China's e-commerce market and how they provide market institutions in a weak-rule-of-law environment.

China's Platform-Based E-Commerce Market

An important feature of China's e-commerce market is that it is platform-based. In 2011, 90 percent of China's online retail transactions occurred on platforms rather than independent websites, contrasting sharply with the United States, where only 24 percent of transactions were platform-based (see Table 3.1).[18] For example, when buying products like Nike shoes, Chinese consumers strongly prefer shopping on e-commerce platforms over the brand's independent website. Conversely, in the United States, consumers are more likely to make purchases from Nike.com rather than Amazon.

At first glance, China-based platforms might seem like mere replicas of their American counterparts, such as eBay or Amazon. They all match sellers and buyers, and they have all built online institutions to foster user trust. However, Chinese platforms are compelled to develop more sophisticated institutions to gain trust compared to their Western counterparts. This is because China's weaker legal environment has led to a higher prevalence of counterfeits and market fraud and a lower level of baseline trust within society. Platforms must therefore bridge the gap in formal institutions.

This also explains why platform-based e-commerce transactions are much more prevalent in China than in the United States. In the United States, shopping on independent websites is not as risky due to the stronger underlying legal system, lower instances of counterfeits, and widespread adoption of credit cards to prevent fraud. This is not the case in China. Therefore, Chinese consumers gravitate toward platforms, which have developed robust private institutions to enforce contracts and protect users.

In the following section, I use the case of China's largest e-commerce platform, Taobao, to illustrate how Chinese platforms develop private substitutes for market institutions that the state has yet to provide.

TABLE 3.1. Platforms vs. Independent Websites in Online Retail:
China vs. the United States (2011)

	Market Share of Platforms	Market Share of Independent Websites
United States	24%	76%
China	90%	10%

Source: McKinsey Global Institute (2013).

Taobao: The World's Largest Bazaar

In this book, I use "Taobao" to refer to two closely related sites: Taobao.com and its spin-off site Taobao Mall (Tmall.com).[19] Taobao, which means "searching for treasure," is the world's most popular online shopping platform by gross merchandise value (GMV). As a major revenue hub for Alibaba, Taobao paved the way for Alibaba's 2014 listing on the New York Stock Exchange, in what was then the world's largest initial public offering.

Taobao's business model mirrors eBay's in many ways. Like eBay, it operates as a virtual marketplace facilitating transactions between buyers and third-party sellers, rather than directly selling products. However, unlike eBay, Taobao predominantly hosts new products instead of second-hand items.

Taobao is a gigantic market. In fiscal year 2020, the platform hosted ten million online stores and 726 million active buyers, amassing a GMV of $945 billion[20]—more than Amazon and eBay combined and higher than the annual sales of Walmart Global, the world's largest brick-and-mortar retailer. If this GMV were nominal GDP, Taobao would have been the seventeenth largest economy in the world in 2019, between Indonesia and the Netherlands. In terms of product category, Taobao mainly sells physical products, but it also provides virtual products and services. For example, as of 2016, the largest product category (42.29 percent of online stores' major product category) was "Apparel, Shoes, Accessories, and Beauty Products," and over 7 percent of the Taobao stores provided a wide range of "Household Services," such as home cleaning, photo editing, data processing, and furniture repairs (Table 3.2).

Compared with its Western counterparts, Taobao features a significantly broader range of products, spanning from fresh crabs and pets to 18.5-meter dragon boats for racing, and even bad debt (Figure 3.4). For example, in 2023, a state-owned construction firm listed forty-three bad debts totaling 79 million RMB (approximately $11 million) for auction on the platform.[21] Some of the more peculiar items on Taobao have captured the attention of foreign media. These include products such as the "Dog Translator" (claimed to translate dog sounds into human language); "Recharge Your IQ" (a mysterious

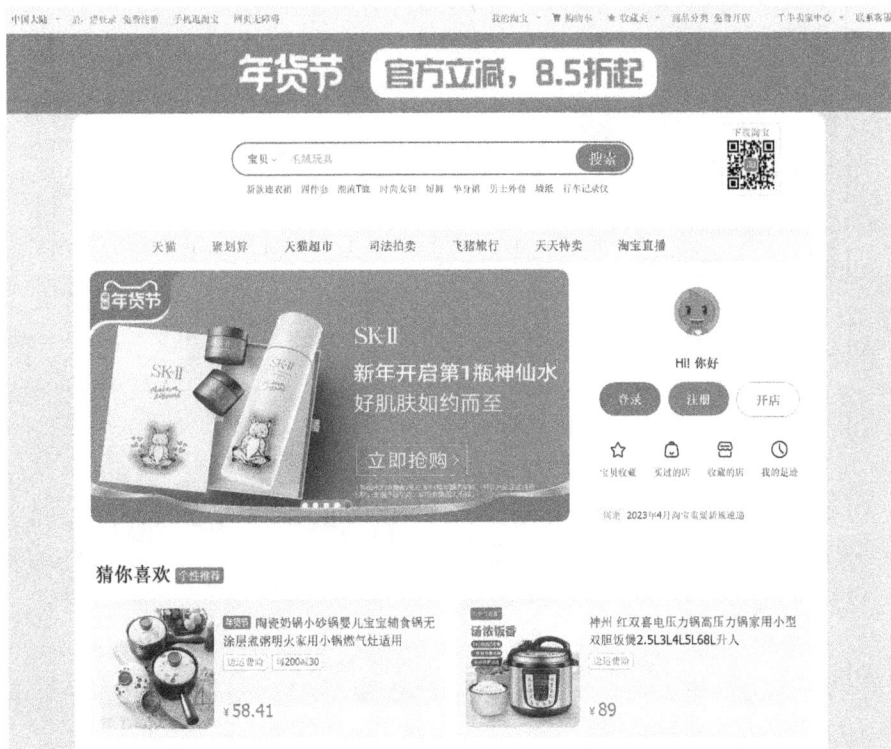

FIGURE 3.3. Taobao's Website Layout.

product with glowing reviews such as: "Before charging my IQ, I could hardly remember my girlfriend's name"); "Noisy-Neighbor Revenge Machine" (i.e., a vibration motor that can be attached to the ceiling and shake the floor of noisy upstairs neighbors); "Hire Somebody to Express Your Love" (for shy or unromantic people); and "Breakup Insurance" involving celebrity couples (i.e., purchasers could get double payback if the celebrity couple breaks up within a year).[22]

What further distinguishes Taobao is that its sellers are not limited to individuals and businesses. Courts, customs, state-owned banks, and asset management companies also use the site to auction government-seized or distressed assets. For example, as early as 2014, more than five hundred Chinese local courts had established storefronts to sell seized property, some of which was confiscated during the government's anticorruption campaign. The rationale for moving such auctions online is to increase transparency and reduce related-party transactions. Assets for sale included three Boeing 747 freighters (two

FIGURE 3.4. Examples of Eccentric Products on Taobao. (*top*) Dragon Boat, (*middle*) Court-seized Assets, (*bottom*) Bad debt sold for 4.45 million RMB (approximately $700,000).

TABLE 3.2. Share of Online Stores in Major Product Categories

Major Product Category	China Entrepreneurs Survey (CES)	Taobao Online Merchant Survey (TOMS)
Secondhand & Used Products	4.06%	2.62%
Apparel, Shoes, Accessories & Beauty Products	42.29%	36.35%
Personalized Products & Creative Design	5.99%	0.95%
Household Products	10.99%	9.98%
Mother & Baby Products	6.67%	7.11%
Auto Parts & Accessories	1.56%	1.95%
Household Services	7.19%	5.92%
Food & Health Care Products	9.17%	5.34%
Electronics & Appliances	5.68%	9.22%
Investment Goods & Collectibles	0.94%	2.2%
Leisure & Culture	1.88%	15.31%
Other	3.59%	3.04%
Survey Year	**2016**	**2012**
N	**1,920**	**58,793**

Notes: While there is no fine-grained data on the total number of product listings on Taobao, two surveys in 2012 and 2016 reveal the major product categories. The Taobao Online Merchant Survey (TOMS) is a nationally representative survey of Taobao's online merchant population conducted in 2012. The survey was conducted by Taobao, and data on major product categories were compiled from the company's account information. The China Entrepreneurs Survey (CES) is an original survey I conducted in 2016. The online merchant sample from CES is close to the TOMS sample. The information on major product categories in CES is based on self-reported data. See chapter 4 for a description of both surveys.

successfully sold for 48 million in total) and a 156-meter-high unfinished skyscraper.[23]

This is why Chinese netizens call Taobao an "omnipotent market" (万能的淘宝), a place where "there's nothing you can't find, only what you haven't imagined yet."[24]

Taobao's Ecosystem of Institutions

How did Taobao achieve its current market status?

The introductory anecdote of Alipay indicates that platform institutions serve as key catalysts for Taobao's market growth. Indeed, Taobao has created an ecosystem of private institutions that address various types of transaction problems and fraud (Figure 3.5). Backed by big data and artificial intelligence analytics, these institutions are intimately connected and jointly contribute to

m

a   Rating system   d

House of Representatives

Transactions on Taobao   b   Alipay   e   Big data   g   Sesame Credit

l

c   Dispute resolution system   f   h   Fraud risk management

j

k

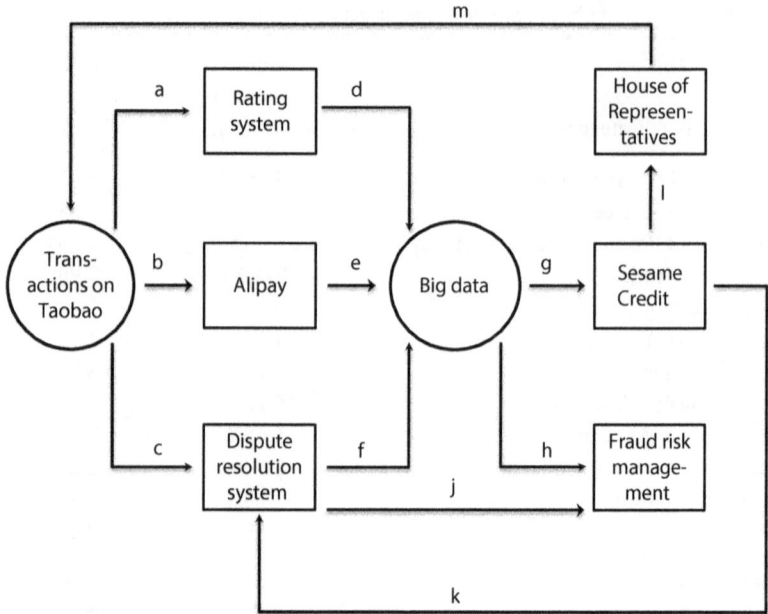

FIGURE 3.5. Taobao's Ecosystem of Institutions. *Notes:* The flowchart illustrates how different parts of Taobao's institutions are intimately connected and mutually supportive of one another, when the research was conducted. The rectangles represent online institutions, and the arrows depict the connections between institutions and the direction of process flow, with letters that correspond to descriptions of each arrow: *a*: After each transaction on Taobao, the seller and buyer leave public reviews of each other. *b*: For each transaction, the online payment system Alipay provides payment and escrow services to enforce contracts between the seller and the buyer. *c*: When a dispute occurs during a transaction, users can ask Taobao employees or "public assessors" to arbitrate. *d, e, f*: Alibaba gathers data from its online rating system (reputation and feedback data); Alipay (payment data); its dispute resolution system (dispute data); and other sources. *g*: Taobao uses big data to provide a credit-scoring service for each user. *h*: Taobao leverages big data to monitor, analyze, and contain fraud through a multilayer fraud risk management framework. *i*: The deposit kept by Alipay forces feuding parties to enter Taobao's dispute resolution system and comply with its decision. *j*: Taobao uses jurors (called "public assessors") to manually review suspicious fraud cases. *k*: Taobao uses credit scores to select candidates for jurors from among all users. *l*: Taobao uses credit scores to select candidates from all users to vote in the House of Representatives for Rules. *m*: Representatives can vote to change certain platform rules and influence future transactions.

a self-reinforcing system that has improved its capacity to identify and punish market rule violations over time.

This section presents how Taobao's core institutions effectively address three critical trade-related issues: contract enforcement, fraud prevention, and dispute resolution. Additionally, I explore how various supporting institutions enhance the core institutions' stability, effectiveness, and adaptability.[25]

CONTRACT ENFORCEMENT THROUGH ESCROW AND REPUTATION MECHANISMS: ALIPAY AND ONLINE RATING SYSTEM

Throughout history, traders have faced a similar problem regarding contract enforcement: the assurance problem. When trading parties strike a deal, how do they ensure that each party honors the agreed-upon terms? This problem is especially acute in the online market for two reasons. The first is information asymmetry. Since the buyer cannot inspect a product before delivery in online transactions, the seller has an incentive to misrepresent the product, for example, by exaggerating the quality or quantity. Anticipating this behavior, the buyer may not engage in trade. The second reason is the difficulty in committing. The buyer cannot commit to pay if the seller has already shipped the product. Likewise, if the buyer has already made the payment, the seller has an incentive not to provide the product. Knowing each other's incentive to dishonor the contract, neither party will take the lead to proceed with the transaction, and trade fails.

Taobao has created two major institutions to enforce contracts. The first is the online payment system Alipay, which has a compulsory escrow component for most online transactions on Taobao. Failure by one of the parties to follow the rules results in sanctions, such as the loss of money in escrow, a change in reputation rating, or being banished from the platform.

Alipay's escrow service enhances Taobao's enforcement capability in both direct and indirect ways. Alipay can directly freeze or deduct from the money in a user's account if they violate the platform rules. Also, Alipay indirectly improves the platform's rule enforcement by collecting valuable data to identify potential rule violators. For instance, the payment data collected from each Alipay transaction provides objective information about Taobao users that Alibaba can use to detect fraud (as discussed in the next section) and to evaluate each user's trustworthiness and creditworthiness. Most importantly, knowing that Alipay makes rules/contracts enforceable incentivizes users to respect them. This produces a positive feedback loop that improves contract performance.

The second institution that strengthens contract enforcement is the online rating and feedback system. By maintaining the public reputations of all traders, Taobao's rating system creates positive incentives to honor contracts, gather information, and report disputes. Historically, many trade institutions relied on a homogenous social group to operate. For example, the Maghribi traders' coalition enabled a distinct group of Jewish traders to employ overseas agents in the eleventh century, despite the commitment problems and other trust issues. Taobao's rating system, on the contrary, does not rely on such homogenous social groups and can sustain a much larger market. This is an example of how the internet can expand the size of reputation networks and act as a powerful tool to share and track traders' previous histories.

Taobao's rating system consists of credit ratings and store ratings. Both ratings are sums of user reviews from each transaction that are displayed publicly on buyers' and sellers' profiles. Credit ratings reflect the overall reliability of sellers and buyers over their entire histories.[26] This rating is cumulative and can disadvantage new sellers and buyers since they do not have a long history of trading. Store ratings indicate sellers' reputations over the previous six months to better capture the changing dynamics of service quality. These ratings are based on buyers' reviews of the seller's accuracy of product descriptions, customer service, and shipping time.[27] Buyers can also check past reviews of all products. Customers can rate, write reviews about, and take photos of the products they purchase. Taobao can then use text analysis to summarize individual comments and help users internalize product reviews.

It is essential to acknowledge that Western platforms also utilize online rating systems to enforce contracts. However, as discussed later in this chapter, Taobao made refinements to eBay's online rating system, and these changes played a role in its success over eBay. This serves as a compelling demonstration of how online institutions can be main drivers of growth.

FRAUD PREVENTION THROUGH RISK FRAMEWORK: BIG DATA, MANUAL REVIEW, AND STATE'S COERCIVE POWER

Fraud must be contained to facilitate trade. Despite some overlaps, fraud is conceptually distinct from contract enforcement problems. Fraud generally involves purposeful deception to pursue unlawful gains, and it is not necessarily related to specific contracts. Common types of fraud in the online market include online payment fraud, account hacking, attempts to manipulate online reviews, and selling counterfeit products.

Taobao uses five layers of checks to detect online payment fraud.[28] The first four layers involve automatic classifications of cases and auto-decisions. The first layer, "account check," examines whether the accounts have exhibited suspicious activity. Obvious fraud cases will be sent for automatic decisions, which include declining the transactions or requiring the user to complete additional authentication processes. Cases that pass the first check will enter the next three layers: device check, activity check, and risk strategy. The fraud risk management system checks different information about a transaction in each layer, sending obvious fraud cases to auto-decision and nonobvious ones to the next level of checks. Data and machine learning play a central role at each step. Taobao's platform collects a large, diverse volume of proprietary data—including user behavioral data, network data, delivery details, and IP addresses—which it analyzes using big data models to detect suspicious activity and counter fraud risks.

After four layers of checks and auto-decisions, cases that are still considered borderline will be sent to the final layer: manual review. Taobao employees may contact the parties involved to obtain additional information. The platform has also experimented with inviting users to act as jurors and vote on whether a case involves counterfeiting (discussed below).

After identifying a case of fraud, Taobao can inflict punishment through either online or offline means. The online sanctions include lowering a user's rating, making a fraudulent store unsearchable for a certain period, or, in extreme cases, banning accounts (for repeat offenders). If a user believes the judgment is unfair, they can appeal to Taobao with evidence to support their claim and the case will be reexamined. The online sanctions, however, have limited coercive power. For example, sellers who have their store banned can use someone else's identity to start a new one, which is difficult for the platform to detect. This calls for offline punishment to combat fraud at the source to raise the cost of rule violations.

Taobao has extended its coercive power offline by collaborating with police and local courts. Such collaboration also benefits the state's coercive apparatus since the state often lacks information to address market fraud. Taobao compiles rich data—including chats, product return/delivery addresses, and shared phone numbers—that it can use to identify the physical locations of fraudulent online stores. It can even map the entire network of offline businesses linked to these problematic online stores. Taobao supplies this information to the police to help track suspects who produce and sell counterfeit products. In 2014 alone, Alibaba's collaboration with state enforcement agencies in over one thousand counterfeiting cases led to the arrest of four hundred suspects and the shutdown of two hundred brick-and-mortar stores, warehouses, and factories.[29]

DISPUTE RESOLUTION THROUGH CROWDSOURCING JUSTICE: AN ONLINE PUBLIC JURY SYSTEM

When disputes occur, Taobao encourages buyers and sellers to negotiate with each other first. If the feuding parties cannot reach an agreement and do not want to go to court, they can use one of Taobao's two judicial channels: asking a Taobao employee to adjudicate or using an online jury panel to arbitrate. The rest of the section discusses the second channel, a unique Chinese institutional innovation.

Alibaba's Public Jury (pan.taobao.com) was established in 2012 to crowdsource justice. It uses a Western-style jury-voting mechanism to solve online disputes and controversial issues. These jurors are termed "public assessors" (大众评审) by Taobao. Interestingly, the name "public assessor" was drawn from the Chinese talent show *Super Girl* (超级女声, similar to *American Idol*), which, after the government shut down its mass voting system, transitioned to using a small panel of audience representatives (or "public assessors") to vote for the show's winner.[30] The public jury was widely used by the main Taobao site by 2020 and is now frequently used by Xianyu, Taobao's used-goods market.

Why did Taobao introduce the jury system? Certainly, as Taobao expanded, the volume of online disputes surged, posing challenges for the platform to handle all disputes by itself. However, according to a former platform employee responsible for designing this institution, the primary motivation was not the caseload. Instead, it was propelled by the complexity of online disputes that proved challenging for the platform to resolve alone. Consequently, they opted to involve users in adjudicating these cases to ensure a fairer process rather than solely relying on platform intervention.[31]

To form a jury, Taobao randomly chooses each panel of thirteen jurors[32] from four million volunteer candidates; each juror may participate in up to forty cases per day.[33] The candidate needs to be an experienced Taobao user (i.e., those who have registered for more than a year) with a good online reputation (i.e., those who have a sufficiently high credit rating, as discussed below). This requirement is high enough to prevent most dishonest traders from manipulating votes, but low enough to be inclusive and keep the juror pool large. These jurors are unpaid yet motivated to participate. They gain experience points that can translate into different virtual titles or that can be donated to charity by Taobao as real money.

The jurors review evidence presented by the feuding parties, including product photos, parcel delivery receipts, and chat histories between the seller and buyer. All participants are anonymized in the trial to reduce bias. To ensure justice, no communication is permitted between disputing parties and the jurors, or among jurors. The jurors cast votes within forty-eight hours and can provide written comments on the trial. The party that secures a simple majority vote wins the case.

Up to date, 1.72 million jurors have resolved sixteen million case trials, and collectively cast over one hundred million votes.[34] Most cases consist of buyer-seller disputes regarding contract violations, such as complaints that the items received do not match the store descriptions. Other cases involve platform-seller disputes in which sellers believe Taobao has unfairly penalized them for violating certain rules. These jury trials not only ease the judicial burden for Taobao; they also help refine the platform's rules. In 2013 alone, feedback from jurors led to adjustments of more than 140 policies governing users.[35]

In recent years, Taobao has even experimented with panels of eight hundred to one thousand jurors to address complicated issues in market governance. For example, it used to host two brands of baby bottles with similar names: "Doctor Betta" and "Betta." The former is an internationally renowned Japanese brand, while the latter is an inferior Chinese copycat that has been legally registered in China. Taobao faced a dilemma: keeping both brands could mislead customers, but removing a legal brand might hurt its reputation as a fair market. It thus opened the case to jury trial. The jurors voted to remove the Chinese copycat from the market.[36]

Importantly, jury decisions are enforceable. Taobao can freeze the payment in a dispute, take money from the store deposit (for sellers only), lower the ratings of the users involved, or deny the losing party's privilege to use the platform. If a party is unsatisfied with the jury decision, it can request that Taobao employees intervene and reexamine the case.

SUPPORTING INSTITUTIONS: CREDIT SCORING AND DEMOCRATIC RULEMAKING

Two supporting institutions contribute to making Taobao's private institutions work. The first is Taobao's credit-scoring service, Sesame Credit (芝麻信用), provided by Ant Financial, which is affiliated with the Alibaba group. This credit-scoring service evaluates users' trustworthiness and creditworthiness and screens out those deemed to be dishonest or untrustworthy.

China has a much lower rate of credit card usage than developed markets and thus lacks the associated credit reports. By late 2013, fewer than 25 percent of the country's population had credit records with China's central bank, while the United States had 85 percent coverage at the time.[37] Sesame Credit thus intends to leverage online big data to reach the population traditionally underserved by state-owned banks.

Sesame Credit, established in 2015, was China's first credit-scoring system. It initially used transaction data from 300 million registered shoppers and thirty-seven million vendors who were trading on Alibaba-owned platforms (e.g., Taobao.com, Tmall.com, and Alibaba.com). The system assigns each user or business a credit score ranging from 350 to 950. The idea, in the US context, parallels an individual's FICO score determined by his/her eBay rating or Amazon feedback. Private credit-scoring services are for commercial use only in China; they are not currently related to the government's social credit score, which serves mainly political ends.[38]

Sesame Credit plays an important role in assisting and reinforcing Taobao's online institutions. It gives users a strong incentive to maintain a positive reputation by honoring online institutions. A higher credit score renders competitive advantages on Taobao, such as larger microloans from Alibaba. It also brings benefits outside the platform, such as waiving deposits when booking hotels or renting bicycles at businesses partnered with Alipay.[39] These additional incentives to honor contracts on the platform have paved the way to microfinance for sellers. Sesame Credit also protects Taobao's voting systems from acts of manipulation and fraud, such as the creation of fake user identities and voting bots. Only users with a high score can become jurors and adjudicate user disputes, or voters in the House of Representatives for Taobao Rules.

House of Representatives for Taobao Rules (规则众议院) is the other supporting institution launched in 2015. It gives Taobao users a voice in rulemaking by holding hearings, collecting user feedback before enacting rules, and even opening up certain nonessential platform rules to voting. This institution helps platform rules adapt to users' changing demands. According to an interview with a Taobao employee, the institution was established to preempt seller revolt associated with rule changes, a recurrent problem for Taobao. This institutional innovation has proven effective, and the employee explained that "no large-scale user protests have taken place since then."[40] Interestingly, to encourage users to vote, Taobao incorporated an image of a cartoon representation of the US Capitol building into the advertisement, along with the slogan "to shape rules, you have a voice" (规则制定, 你有话语权).[41]

When Taobao proposes a rule change or a new rule in the House of Representatives, all buyers and sellers with a decent Sesame Credit score can vote and express their opinions on the rule.[42] In addition to ordinary representatives, Taobao also invites professionals and scholars who specialize in the rule-related issue area to evaluate the issue and inform ordinary voters. For a certain period after each vote, Taobao makes the results public and adjusts the rule accordingly. From June 2015 to February 2017, the House of Representatives voted on forty-two rules. Each case involved over ten thousand votes.

For example, on September 9, 2015, Taobao proposed raising the buyer compensation that sellers would pay if they missed the agreed shipping deadline. On the voting page, Taobao outlined the key points and the reasons for the rule change.[43] Users had a week to post their comments and vote (October 16–22). On October 28, Taobao announced the results: the majority of users supported the new seller compensation scheme, and the new rule passed. In the same announcement, Taobao also acknowledged some concerns raised by the minority who voted against the change, such as the idea that an increase in buyer compensation would only increase buyers' incentives to abuse the right. In response, Taobao listed the existing constraints on buyers to prevent this from occurring.[44]

Interestingly, Taobao's House of Representatives shares characteristics with the mixed government that Aristotle and Polybius (as well as Machiavelli, Harrington, and Montesquieu) thought necessary for a republic's long-term stability. This structure is sometimes identified as "the one, the few, and the many"—that is, an executive, such as a king; the nobility (sometimes mixed with ecclesiastic lords); and the commons (for example, the non-nobility with a certain level of wealth). Under mixed government, the nobles (like Taobao) were often granted the power to make proposals, and the commons (like the platform's users) had the power to accept or reject them.

However, Taobao's House of Representatives is only quasi-democratic. The platform retains exclusive power to choose what rules will be voted upon; only changes to nonessential rules (e.g., those governing user-user rather than user-platform relations) can be proposed. But as a private institution, Taobao's House made it possible to introduce mass voting into the making of market rules. It would be substantially harder for an authoritarian state to do the same with formal market institutions. Too often, the state is reluctant to formally grant citizens any type of voting rights, due to fears of increasing civic demands for further political reforms. Acquiescence to the private voting mechanism allows the state to facilitate market development while bearing fewer political risks.

LIMITATIONS

It is important to note that platform institutions have many limitations. The fact that Taobao's institutions fill the gap left by the state does *not* mean that they are perfect substitutes for state institutions.

To begin with, there is no perfect institutional design. I had a conversation with a rule designer at Taobao who highlighted an issue in a specific market segment—the sale of seeds. This market faced a downfall because the Alipay escrow system only held the product payment in escrow for up to fifteen days.[45] Although the fifteen-day window is adequate for most transactions where buyers can promptly inspect product quality, it presents a problem for seeds. The authenticity of rose seeds, for example, can only be verified several months later. This resulted in a market flooded with counterfeit seeds, ultimately leading to its collapse.[46]

Second, the enforcement capabilities of digital platforms are inherently limited. Certain counterfeit products can evade detection by online platforms. For instance, I once visited a popular Taobao store selling Yangcheng Lake hairy crabs. These crabs, known for their exceptional quality, command significantly higher prices compared to crabs from other regions. However, a discrepancy caught my attention during my conversation with the store owner. The store owner provided information about the size of their cultivation base in Yangcheng Lake and the yield of hairy crabs per acre. Yet a basic multiplication exercise revealed a glaring mismatch—the total number of crabs they claimed to cultivate was far less than the number they reportedly sold. A local industry expert later told me that the discrepancy is likely due to the sale of both genuine Yangcheng Lake crabs and deceptive "bathing crabs" (洗澡蟹)—crabs sourced from elsewhere that had been briefly immersed in the lake before being sold as genuine Yangcheng Lake crabs. This fraudulent practice is widespread in the region and occurs in both online and offline stores. This instance underscores the limitations of online systems in addressing complex quality issues unless more stringent certification processes are introduced.[47]

Even if platforms can identify violations of their rules, the resulting penalties may not be severe enough to deter future instances of fraud. When a user violates a rule, the typical consequences include a reduction in their rating, freezing of funds in escrow, or, in extreme cases, the suspension of their account. It's worth noting that while a Taobao account is linked to the user's national ID, there are ways for the same person to create a new store using someone else's ID, as acknowledged by a platform employee.[48] Such behaviors are difficult to detect as platforms lack offline enforcement power unless they collaborate with the police. This situation helps to explain why counterfeits and cybercrimes persist in the online marketplace.

Moreover, wherever there are rules, there are people who game them. For example, Taobao's online rating system has become a victim of its own success. Ratings make sellers value their online reputation so dearly that it has generated a large industry of fake reviews. A platform employee admitted the difficulty of identifying fake reviews: "As we improve our system to identify 'brushers' (aka 'fake reviewers'), the 'brushers' also become smarter and try their best to imitate real customers . . . This is a game of 'catch me if you can' (猫捉老鼠)."[49]

Interestingly, having more rules does not necessarily improve the quality of institutions. To prevent users from gaming the system (such as by faking reviews), Taobao needs to introduce new rules to fix the loopholes. However, interviews show that frequent rule changes confuse users, and having too many rules leads to inadvertent rule violations.[50] This particularly hurts small sellers or rural sellers who do not follow rule changes as closely as large sellers.

All of the examples above highlight the limitations of platform regulations. In fact, the governance model of platforms is inherently plagued by various other issues, including the excessive collection of personal data, algorithmic bias, and antitrust concerns. In chapter 6, I will delve further into these matters concerning the drawbacks of digital governance and how the Chinese government attempted to tackle these problems through a campaign-style regulatory crackdown on Big Tech companies in 2020.

Institutions as an Important Driver of Taobao's Growth

The preceding section analyzes Taobao's ecosystem of institutions and their significance in sustaining the online market. To demonstrate that institutions are indeed a significant driver of Taobao's growth, it is necessary to address two potential concerns. First, there might be alternative explanations for Taobao's market development, such as China's large domestic market and consumption potential. After controlling for these other factors, institutions might no longer emerge as a crucial driver of e-commerce development. Second, there is a potential issue of reverse causality. Establishing causality through descriptive analysis, as done with Taobao's institutions, can be challenging. This raises doubts about whether Taobao's institutions are simply *outcomes* rather than the *cause* of e-commerce development.

Let's first discuss common alternative explanations. Indeed, institutions are not the sole contributor to Taobao's growth. China possesses numerous favorable conditions for e-commerce development. For instance, it boasts a large population and substantial potential demand for online products. As the world's largest manufacturing hub, it is relatively easy for online merchants to source products domestically. Additionally, the government has made significant investments in infrastructure conducive to e-commerce growth, including road construction and internet access.

However, it would be inaccurate to ignore the significance of online institutions and attribute Taobao's success solely to these country-level factors. For instance, while other countries may possess a large population (e.g., India) or robust infrastructure (e.g., developed countries), not all have a thriving e-commerce sector. Moreover, if national conditions were the primary determinant, it fails to elucidate why Taobao outperformed eBay in the same Chinese market under similar circumstances.

Another commonly cited alternative explanation for Taobao's rise is its adoption of a no-fee policy at the early development stage. The argument posits that many eBay sellers migrated to Taobao to avoid eBay's commission and product listing fees, which eventually contributed to Taobao's rise. This assertion, however, was challenged by an interviewee, a veteran e-commerce seller who emphasized institutional factors. She said that many early sellers "ditched eBay for Taobao because Taobao's system is more localized and easier to use."[51] Consistently, survey data also finds that fees were not among the top five reasons why consumers preferred Taobao over eBay, and that "even after eBay offered free listings in early 2006, they still lost customers to Taobao."[52] Instead, the primary reason cited was eBay's poor service and its failure to "focus on building up trust."[53] This also points to institutions as an important driver for Taobao's expansion.

The second concern is that Taobao's institutions may be the outcome, rather than the cause, of its market growth. In fact, institutions and growth always coevolve and influence each other, akin to the conundrum of the chicken and the egg (as argued by Ang, 2016). Moreover, the history of the Taobao-eBay battle provides evidence that institutions can indeed cause e-commerce development, rather than merely being a result of it.

At the time, both companies competed in the same Chinese market, targeting the same group of customers, and many factors influencing e-commerce development remained constant (e.g., internet penetration, culture, user characteristics). The critical difference lay in the adoption of different institutions: eBay China imported institutions largely from their American model, which proved inadequate in addressing trust concerns among Chinese users, while Taobao built institutions specifically to foster trust and ended up winning the battle.

The historical records illustrate how institutional disparities result in distinct growth outcomes. As mentioned earlier, Taobao's Alipay emerged as a key institution that fueled the rapid expansion of trade. Its escrow system significantly increased the prevalence of long-distance e-commerce trade by alleviating traders' concerns about contract enforcement issues. In contrast, eBay's delay in seamlessly incorporating the escrow system hampered its ability to regain lost ground.

Another notable example is Taobao's instant messaging system, known as Aliwangwang. This system facilitates direct communication between sellers and buyers to build trust, in which sellers could even provide their phone numbers and other contact information on their storefronts. In contrast, eBay prohibited any direct conversations, fearing that traders might bypass the transaction fee by striking deals outside the platform. Taobao, being a free-to-use platform, did not have the same concern.[54] The direct communication feature provided by Taobao was instrumental in expanding its user base.[55] Within an environment characterized by a weak rule of law, personal communication allowed low-trust buyers to gather extra information about products, thereby providing assurance and facilitating smooth transactions.

Even subtle differences in institutional designs can lead to different outcomes. For instance, both eBay and Taobao employ online rating systems as reputation mechanisms to enforce contracts. However, Taobao's online rating system was specifically tailored to suit the Chinese market and at the time was more comprehensive compared to eBay's approach. An article attributes Taobao's triumph over eBay to the design of its online rating system, stating:

> Instead of using a simple percentage-based rating system like eBay China, Taobao introduced a tiered system of stars, diamonds, and crowns (later including gold crowns). This pyramid-like grading system creates a clear hierarchy, putting pressure and providing motivation for sellers to improve their ratings. As a result, buyers not only prefer merchants with high positive ratings but also value merchants with a proven sales history. The underlying principle is simple: when the positive ratings are similar, the credibility of a merchant with only a few records differs from that of a merchant with a substantial transaction history.[56]

In conclusion, Taobao's triumph over eBay demonstrates that institutions are causal factors in e-commerce development. It also illustrates that well-designed institutions can have substantial effects, effectively offsetting significant advantages held by competitors like eBay, such as greater resources and a first-mover advantage.

Why (and How) the Chinese State Outsources Institutional Functions to Platforms

Having examined how e-commerce platforms serve as private regulatory intermediaries (PRIs) in China's e-commerce market, we now turn to the second condition of institutional outsourcing: given that PRIs exist, the developing state must either acquiesce to or actively encourage PRIs to serve as private suppliers of market institutions. In the following, I first discuss how the broad political and economic contexts in China—economic rebalancing—make the authoritarian government open to private institutional developments by e-commerce platforms. I then present concrete examples of institutional outsourcing from the state to platforms and demonstrate that the practice has become more explicit and institutionalized over time.

The Political Economic Contexts of China's E-Commerce Boom

As in many other countries, e-commerce in China began as an exogenous shock of technology innovation. However, its burgeoning prominence is endogenous to the country's economic transition.

As early as the mid-2000s, China began to pursue economic rebalancing—a structural reform to shift the economy from an investment- and export-led model to one focused on consumption and services. This strategic shift was prompted by the leadership's acknowledgment that the previous growth model was "unstable, unbalanced, uncoordinated, and unsustainable."[57] Specifically, two key growth drivers had begun to falter: investments and exports. State-led investments not only yielded diminishing returns but also contributed to issues such as industrial overcapacity, severe pollution, and nonperforming debt. China's excessive reliance on exports rendered the country susceptible to foreign demand shocks. For instance, the 2007–8 global financial crisis led to an export slump in China and the loss of twenty million jobs in the manufacturing sector.[58] Furthermore, China's burgeoning trade surplus from exports also exposed it to trade disputes with other major economies.[59]

Consequently, the government began to identify new growth drivers, focusing on promoting domestic consumption and indigenous innovation to sustain long-term growth. China's domestic consumption, in particular, had ample room to grow. In 2010, household spending accounted for merely 33.8 percent of GDP, "a record low for a major economy in peacetime."[60]

Yet, until 2008, the government had achieved remarkably little by shifting the growth model.[61] It proved easier for the state to enhance GDP through investments in infrastructure projects than to encourage private consumption. Chinese citizens were reluctant spenders due to factors such as low average household income, soaring housing prices, and the absence of broad-based social security and health insurance coverage, which led to significant savings to mitigate life's uncertainties. The global financial crisis of 2007 and 2008 further hampered the government's ability to rebalance the economy. China's implementation of a 4 trillion RMB stimulus package increased the share of state investment in the overall economy,[62] pushing the country further away from its rebalancing objective.

Following the global financial crisis, however, e-commerce emerged as an unexpected driver of domestic consumption.[63] Both the demand for and supply of online products increased. On the demand side, China's real estate bubble and surging rents made brick-and-mortar stores costly to operate.

More customers found offline products unaffordable and started looking for cheap online alternatives.

On the supply side, due to the global financial crisis and the diminished demand from Western markets, Chinese manufacturers had to pivot toward the domestic market. To save overhead and operational costs, many manufacturers turned to online marketing channels by either creating their own brands or providing products to online merchants. One online merchant told me, "Previously, it was challenging for online merchants to procure goods from local manufacturers, as their products were primarily intended for export and sold in bulk. However, in the wake of the financial crisis and sluggish exports, these local factories adapted by accepting smaller orders from online merchants. After all, half a loaf is better than none (苍蝇也是肉)!"[64] This shift sparked a proliferation in the quantity and diversity of online products, rendering e-commerce an increasingly attractive shopping option. In 2008 alone, China's online retail sales saw a staggering twenty-one-fold increase.[65]

Since the mid-2000s, the government has embraced e-commerce for its potential to support economic rebalancing goals, especially by promoting domestic consumption, innovation, and entrepreneurship. In the 2011 Government Work Report of the Two Sessions, Premier Wen Jiabao expressed strong support for e-commerce, citing its potential to expand domestic consumption.[66] This support continued under the subsequent Xi-Li administration. E-commerce constituted an integral part of China's "Internet Plus" strategy unveiled in 2015, aiming to utilize the internet to upgrade the Chinese economy. As e-commerce lowers the barriers of starting a business, it was also viewed as a critical driver of Premier Li Keqiang's landmark policy, known as "mass entrepreneurship and innovation" (大众创新, 万众创业), which sought to explore fresh avenues of economic growth as traditional models lost traction. In the latest developments, e-commerce and other components of the digital economy align with China's national "Big Data" strategy, which aims to harness data to improve economic and political governance.[67]

The Chinese government's backing of e-commerce extended beyond traditional measures of industrial policy, such as financial support for e-commerce-related projects and tax incentives for platform companies. The key is that the government provided ample room for these companies to innovate and operate, even in legally ambiguous areas, especially before 2020.

There are several reasons why the government chose not to impose strict regulations in this domain. First, the government acknowledged the positive impact of e-commerce on employment and feared that overly strict regulations could lead to job losses. Premier Li Keqiang said in 2015 that "despite the slowdown in economic growth, employment did not decrease but increased . . . e-commerce has played a great role in promoting this."[68] Second, e-commerce and other digital economies are relatively new industries, prompting the government to adopt a "development first and regulate later" approach. This strategy entailed purposefully avoiding or deferring strict regulations to nurture the development of a new industry. Furthermore, the decision to provide platforms with greater autonomy in governing the online market can be contextualized within two relevant policies. One is "streamlining administration and delegating power" (简政放权), a key administrative reform under the Xi-Li administration. This reform aimed at decentralizing authority to lower-level governments and society to preserve market vitality. The other is a government-supported concept called "collaborative governance" (协同治理). It involves the sharing of governing power and responsibilities between the public and private sectors to enhance the state's governance capacity. These policies justified giving platforms regulatory discretion in the e-commerce sector and the government's hands-off approach for nearly two decades before 2020. It also sheds light on why authoritarian states are willing to delegate some governing functions to digital platforms.

In summary, the Chinese government has strived to rebalance the economy, motivating it to tolerate the disruptive growth of e-commerce. A caveat is that, in hindsight, these policy efforts have had limited effects on balancing the Chinese economy. Factors such as the US-China trade war and the COVID-19 pandemic have compelled China to stick to traditional economic stimulus measures like state-led investments.[69] Additionally, e-commerce's impact has been mostly limited to retail consumption, which is a small part of overall expenditures compared to essential costs like housing and education. Despite the gap between policy goals and outcomes, the government's intention of economic rebalancing has indeed granted internet platforms significant autonomy for decades, laying the foundation for the e-commerce boom.

From De Facto to De Jure Outsourcing

To recap, the book's main argument is that the Chinese government has outsourced certain institutional functions to e-commerce platforms. While both de jure and de facto outsourcing are important, such outsourcing has become more explicit and institutionalized in recent years. There are at least three types of de jure outsourcing.

(1) *Official recognition*: The E-Commerce Law passed in 2018 recognized the role of platforms as important market entities. It stipulated their legal obligation to regulate online businesses and buyers. The implementation of the law follows the principle that "the state regulates the platforms, and the platforms regulate online businesses" (监管抓平台, 平台抓商家).[70] In other words, platforms have become proxies of the state to regulate the online market.[71] At

the same time, platforms still maintain substantial autonomy to regulate the market. For example, the law encourages platforms to establish online dispute resolution systems and other online institutions (Articles 58–63).[72] It stipulates that the "the state shall establish a collaborative administration system" jointly participated in by e-commerce industry associations, e-commerce businesses (including online businesses and platforms), and consumers, among others (Article 7).[73]

(2) *Official outsourcing of law enforcement authority*: The central government has started to collaborate with private platforms to enforce several main legal functions that the state apparatus finds difficult to fully enforce. The first is curbing commercial bribery. In May 2017, the Anti-Corruption and Bribery Bureau affiliated with the Supreme People's Procuratorate signed a memorandum with Alibaba "to create a clean, credible, rule-of-law market environment."[74] It provided Alibaba with fast and convenient access to criminal records related to bribery. On the other hand, Alibaba and Ant Group will conduct queries into criminal records of bribery in various aspects, including during the online bidding and procurement processes, during the verification of Taobao sellers, and in their involvement in anti–money laundering initiatives and financial risk control. Subsequently, they will take necessary actions in accordance with the law against any companies or individuals found to have engaged in bribery crimes.

Another legal function the central government collaborates with private platforms to provide is enforcing debt payment. To improve the enforcement of court orders, the Supreme People's Court has teamed up with major platforms (e.g., Alibaba, JD, WeChat) since 2015. The platforms punish those who fail to repay their debts by lowering their credit ratings and restricting them from buying high-priced items online. As of 2017, Alibaba alone had punished 730,000 debtors, fifty thousand of whom have since repaid their debts.[75]

(3) *Formal institutional development through formalizing platform rules*: The state has incorporated some components of platform rules into its own regulations on e-commerce. One example is a return policy stipulating that consumers shall have the right to return the commodities within seven days of receipt without cause (七天无条件退货). This policy was first made and enforced by Taobao in 2008 on clothes sold on the platform. In 2014, this regulation was recognized as an industry standard and was written into Article 16 of the Administrative Measures for Online Trading released by the State Administration for Industry and Commerce.[76] Many local governments have since encouraged offline stores to implement the same return policy.[77]

The platforms' rules and inputs also strongly influenced the development of the formal institution: the E-Commerce Law. In a very unusual practice for

China, the government invited four groups to propose draft versions of the law—the China Electronic Commerce Association (a business alliance representing the interests of e-commerce companies), academics, central government ministries, and local governments. The final version synthesizes elements of each.[78]

In summary, institutional outsourcing has become increasingly explicit. Not only do platforms assist the state in *enforcing* economic and legal functions; they also help the state *create and reform* formal institutions by experimenting with the nature and content of the rules. Institutional outsourcing fosters institutional innovation in market regulations. Chapter 4 discusses platform-government relations and presents more examples of government agencies' involvement in institutional outsourcing.

Institutional Spillover to Other Platforms

One might ponder whether these functions unique to Taobao transcend the boundaries of a single platform. Instances of institutional diffusion across platforms are prevalent, fueled by fierce competition that compels platforms to imitate and gather insights from one another, leading to the dissemination of platform regulations. Additionally, given Taobao's market influence, many other platforms have enlisted members from Taobao's rulemaking teams, acquiring knowledge and emulating their practices.[79]

Examples of institutional diffusion are abundant. Beyond the previously mentioned example of the seven-day return policy, which has been incorporated into state regulations and embraced as an industry-wide standard, Taobao's practices such as escrow, specific designs of online ratings, return shipping insurance, and terms of consumer protection are widely adopted.[80]

In particular, other platforms have widely adopted Taobao's public jury system, where a panel of ordinary users is randomly selected to settle online disputes through virtual voting. Tencent launched a similar system to judge "article laundering" (洗稿), a difficult-to-detect, nonliteral form of plagiarism that copies only the storylines or ideas of other works.[81] Likewise, the ride-hailing company Didi (the Chinese counterpart to Uber) adopted a user voting system to resolve disputes between drivers and passengers and to determine sensitive policies regarding sexual harassment prevention and teenager passenger safety.[82] Meituan, China's leading food delivery platform, boasts a volunteer base of six million individuals who arbitrate disputes between customers and restaurants. The public has the collective authority to decide whether negative reviews should be removed from a restaurant's page.[83] Douyin, TikTok's Chinese version, also adopted this jury institution to determine whether certain comments or controversial videos have violated its rules.[84]

The US E-Commerce Platforms and E-Commerce Market

The above analysis demonstrates that China's e-commerce market has both of the enabling conditions for institutional outsourcing: (1) PRIs must exist, and (2) the state must acquiesce to or explicitly endorse them. Below I compare Taobao with its US counterparts, Amazon and eBay, and find that, judging by the two enabling conditions, institutional outsourcing seems much weaker in the US e-commerce market.

First, although Amazon and eBay have also developed private institutions to regulate online transactions, such as online rating systems and antifraud measures, their institutional development doesn't match that of their Chinese counterparts. For instance, Amazon and eBay do not offer compulsory escrow services, have not developed a public jury system like Taobao, and do not allow users to vote on changing rules.

This disparity is not indicative of the capabilities of American platforms; rather, it results from the presence of more robust preexisting market institutions in the United States. For instance, although US platforms also grapple with counterfeit issues, the problem is less severe due to stricter legal regulations against counterfeits. Consequently, US platforms do not need to establish exceptionally strong institutions to combat counterfeiting, as is necessary for their Chinese counterparts. Essentially, the formal institutional gaps in the United States are less pressing, rendering it less necessary for US platforms to develop comprehensive institutions.

Second, the extent of state-level outsourcing to platforms is significantly lower in the United States. Although US e-commerce platforms also enjoy substantial market autonomy and work with the government on occasion, the public and private regulatory powers lean more toward competition than collaboration. Moreover, the US system of an independent judiciary allows these platform companies to openly and legally challenge state authority. On the contrary, Chinese digital platforms proactively enter into strategic collaboration agreements with different levels of government, actively supporting the state in achieving its economic and political goals.

While the US e-commerce market is not a strong case for institutional outsourcing, there are other non-China cases that fit the framework. I will present these ancillary cases in the concluding chapter when discussing the possibility of generalizing beyond the Chinese e-commerce market.

Conclusion

This chapter fills in specifics of the broader political economy argument introduced in the previous chapter. I demonstrate that Taobao—which has over 800 million users and ten million vendors—serves as a PRI. It supplies market

institutions where state institutions fall short. This private set of market institutions is highly developed: it features a complex reputation mechanism, a
credit score, a fraud detection program, and even a jury system that allows
ordinary users to adjudicate cases or change platform rules. As these digital
institutions can be scaled up and evolve rapidly, Taobao and other platforms
have established a national common market with large-scale impersonal exchange, which is difficult to cultivate offline.

The Chinese government has opportunistically, if subtly, embraced platforms' development of market institutions. This chapter shows that the state's
outsourcing to platforms has become more explicit and institutionalized over
time. The state uses platform institutions to strengthen its enforcement of existing policies and occasionally reforms formal institutions based on the rule
experiments conducted by private platforms.

An interesting question is whether experience with online private
institutions—especially mass voting on platforms—will motivate consumers
to demand political rights in other aspects of their lives, such as increased
demands for national elections. While it is difficult to directly test this question, empirical evidence presented in chapter 4 indicates that e-commerce
participation is not associated with more offline political participation. This
suggests that voting on commercial platforms does not seem to carry broader
democratic implications, at least for the time being.

The findings of this chapter shed light on other major developments in
Chinese politics. Beyond legal and economic institutions, Beijing has also outsourced political and coercive functions to private actors such as tech companies. For instance, censorship is largely carried out by private social media
platforms rather than the state.[85] The Chinese state has also increasingly outsourced social functions. During the battle with the coronavirus, the Ministry
of Civil Affairs openly requested that tech companies such as Tencent and Alibaba develop community epidemic control apps, and the companies quickly
did so.[86] The parallel state outsourcing activities in different realms indicate a
crucial change in China's state-private sector relations. Experimentation by
internet platforms appears to be changing the country's legal, political, and
economic foundations. In the next two chapters, I will discuss what specific
changes are associated with e-commerce adoption.

4

The Invisible State?

HOW E-COMMERCE TRANSFORMS STATE-BUSINESS RELATIONS

Reversal of Fortune

Built from Scratch

Dongfeng, an impoverished village in Suining County of Jiangsu Province, was once characterized as a mere "dumping ground," with its economy heavily reliant on plastic waste recycling. This bleak situation led to an exodus of young adults seeking employment opportunities in cities, to the extent that one villager expressed concern, stating that "if an elderly person died, the village would not be able to muster four able-bodied men to carry the coffin."[1]

Han Sun, born in 1982, was among the youths who left their hometown for cities to pursue a better life. After dropping out of college, Sun attempted various occupations—gatekeeper, mover, and even background actor in Hengdian (known as "China's Hollywood")—but struggled to find the right fit.

During a casual visit to IKEA's Shanghai store in 2007, Sun was inspired by the idea of producing and selling furniture similar to IKEA's offerings. Leveraging his prior experience in e-commerce from selling prepaid phone cards, he decided to return to Dongfeng Village and embark on this new online venture.[2] Given the absence of a furniture industry or skilled carpenters in the village, he had to recruit several coffin makers to manufacture furniture, which he subsequently sold on Taobao.com. The online business immediately took off, with furniture sales exceeding 100,000 RMB ($13,700) within the first month alone, and the momentum continued to grow.

Sun's fellow villagers soon discovered his money-making formula after observing a truck routinely picking up packages from his backyard. Since Chinese rural villages are ungated communities where everyone knows each other, gossip travels fast. This soon led to a mix of envy and a herd mentality, prompting other villagers to copy Sun's lucrative business model.[3] As more households joined the e-commerce frenzy, Dongfeng Village soon blossomed into a bustling hub for online furniture sales.

I first visited Dongfeng Village in 2014. This village of 1,180 households surprisingly hosted over two thousand online stores, surpassing its own household count. Its online furniture sales alone raked in an impressive annual revenue of more than 1.3 billion RMB ($210 million).[4] I strolled along several roads that were aptly named to commemorate the village's remarkable rise in e-commerce, including "Taobao Avenue" and "Ma Yun Avenue," paying tribute to the Chinese name of Jack Ma (Ma Yun), the founder of Alibaba. Interestingly, during my visit, "Ma Yun Avenue" had already been renamed "Yun Avenue," with Ma's family name removed from the street sign to give it a more ordinary appearance. A village cadre informed me that this alteration was done according to Jack Ma's own wish to maintain a low profile.[5] Little did Jack Ma know at the time that several years later, in 2020, he would face significant consequences for his remarks challenging financial regulators in a speech, leading to the halt of the Ant Financial IPO and the initiation of a two-year government crackdown on all tech firms (see chapter 6).

Online traders I interviewed told me that e-commerce not only brought wealth to the village; it also triggered a social transformation[6] by reversing the village's earlier labor drain. Youths are now much more likely to stay in the village or to return after they graduate from college. Elderly members of the community often help with their children's online businesses, leading to a richer labor force and feelings of self-worth. "There was even a drop in how frequently villagers wrangle over trivial matters," said a village cadre, "as everyone is busy with e-commerce now, even neighbors don't necessarily have time to visit each other."[7]

The Puzzles

I went to Dongfeng Village with a series of research questions in mind. Yet, upon departure, I realized that I had not found the answers because I had been asking the wrong questions.

My initial research question revolved around how local governments helped foster the e-commerce industry. Prior research on transitional economies like China has depicted governments as either a "helping hand" or a "grabbing hand," depending on whether they support or expropriate private firms.[8] The Chinese government has historically been perceived as closer to a helping hand when compared to Russia and Ukraine. This is because local Chinese officials directly benefit from the success of the local economy, whether through increased tax revenues or personal rewards such as promotion opportunities.[9] Meanwhile, more recent studies find that the grabbing hand phenomenon also exists in China and has intensified since the 1990s, particularly at government-controlled firms.[10] In a nutshell, whether support-ive or exploitative, the Chinese government has always been perceived as a *visible* hand, wielding significant influence over the economy.

However, my fieldwork in Dongfeng Village and other locations revealed that local governments played a much less significant role in e-commerce than antici-pated. Although local governments engaged in various collaborations with e-commerce platforms, they appeared to have limited interactions with online merchants operating on these platforms. Many e-commerce merchants chose not to register officially with the local government or fulfill their tax obligations. For those who did register, their tax payments were often merely symbolic.[11] While the Chinese government is known for its extensive use of industrial policies, in-cluding subsidies and tax breaks to support various industries, most merchants expressed disinterest in receiving any government support. One merchant even strongly asserted, "No regulation is the best support (不管就是最大的扶持)."[12]

To be sure, local governments were not irrelevant. They provided the neces-sary infrastructure for e-commerce to thrive, from internet connectivity to roads. Their endorsement of e-commerce also lent credibility to the industry in the eyes of citizens. However, given e-commerce's prominent status and the government's history of active intervention in the economy, the level of gov-ernment involvement seemed intriguingly limited.

Indeed, "e-commerce villages" like Dongfeng emerged organically with minimal government assistance. A common issue is that local governments lack detailed information about the online stores operating in their areas and the sales data of online merchants. In one instance, a local official asked an Ali-baba employee, who was traveling with several researchers (including myself), if the platform could share user-level information with the local government. The employee declined. As we became more acquainted, the local official openly shared her frustration:

> E-commerce makes Alibaba and peasants rich, but the local government gets nothing. The [local] government loses. While the e-commerce industry makes our locality nationally well known, our government does not benefit financially. The merchants do not pay taxes, and the logistics companies located in our village only pay taxes in Shanghai, where their headquarters are located . . . I envy those online merchants. Before, being a local cadre at least brought some sense of status. Now, seeing all the peasants making a big fortune and my own monthly salary lower than 3,000 RMB, I even thought about resigning.[13]

Some local governments tried to take a more visible role in the local e-commerce industry by using typical industrial policy measures, but their efforts did not yield significant results. Many governments attempted to create their own platforms, but the dominance of private platforms discouraged users from switching.[14] Subsidies were offered to online merchants, but few applied. According to two industry experts, in 2013, a district in Suzhou City allocated 20 million RMB to support e-commerce, but only 15 percent of it was utilized. Similarly, in Shanxi Province, 10 million RMB remained unused and had to be returned to the government.[15] The tepid response from online merchants stemmed from their deliberate avoidance of interactions with the government, fearing tax obligations and potential expropriation.[16] Additionally, many merchants did not need subsidies because of sufficient cash flow from e-commerce.[17]

As my fieldtrip progressed, I switched my research focus from "how local governments supported online merchants to succeed" to "how online merchants achieved their success *without* substantial government support." This shift in perspective allowed all the disparate pieces to come together into a coherent narrative, which I will elaborate on in this chapter.

Preview of the Chapter

This chapter examines the dynamics of state-business relations in the e-commerce sector. My analysis encompasses two governmental tiers—central and local—and two categories of businesses—merchants operating on platforms, and the platforms themselves. I focus on three dyadic relationships: merchant vs. local government, platform vs. local government, and platform vs. central government.[18]

Beginning with merchant-local government relations, a key question arises: Does private entrepreneurs' involvement in e-commerce increase their autonomy from local governments, and if so, how?

Drawing from a synthesis of interviews, web-scraped data gathered from 1.76 million online stores, and an original national survey, I find that online merchants indeed enjoy greater autonomy from local governments compared to their offline counterparts. This is evidenced by online merchants' reduced interaction with local authorities, decreased investment in maintaining political connections with local officials, and a diminished perceived value of such connections.

The increased autonomy of online merchants can be attributed to two factors. First, the rise of e-commerce has provided cheap access to the national market, thereby alleviating geographic and resource constraints imposed by localized markets. Second, e-commerce has transformed the nature of resources crucial for business success. Unlike brick-and-mortar stores, online businesses rely less on resources such as land, permits, and bank loans, which were traditionally controlled by local governments.

The perceived liberation of private merchants from local governments via e-commerce prompts a question: Does e-commerce foster an independent business class, thereby diminishing the importance of state-business relations? This question is important because once a business class becomes autonomous, they may begin to demand political rights from the government, a pattern observed in the historical development of Western countries.

I find no evidence that e-commerce generates a business class independent of the state. Although individual merchants may gain autonomy from local governments, they have redirected their dependence toward e-commerce platforms, which now regulate them. These platforms, in turn, have cultivated close connections with both central and local governments.

In an authoritarian regime, these platform-government connections are vital for the survival of the platforms. Research on democracies has shown that platforms can derive political power from their vast user base and potentially challenge the state.[19] However, in autocracies, such latent political power can become a liability. The more individual merchants a platform hosts, the higher the likelihood of attracting suspicion from the Communist Party. Consequently, platforms deem it imperative to establish strong connections with the authoritarian government as they expand their business.

As documented in this chapter, platforms have forged extensive strategic collaborations with various levels of government. Moreover, major platforms have established informal political ties by accepting investments from government-backed funds or hiring ex-regulators, known as the government-business "revolving door." Notably, relationships with the central government are of paramount importance for platforms, given the central government's substantially greater bargaining power in comparison to local governments. This presents the central government with an opportunity to utilize platforms as proxies of state power, rather than relying solely on local governments to execute economic and political functions.

In light of the above findings, the rise of e-commerce does not eliminate state-business connections. Instead, e-commerce serves to *centralize* these ties, *shifting the locus of connections from the individual merchant level to the platform level*. This also means that the e-commerce revolution does not create an independent merchant class, as platforms on which merchants now rely remain susceptible to the influence of the powerful authoritarian government.

Merchant-Local Government Relations

To comprehend the impact of e-commerce on state-business relations, the first step is to examine the interactions between individual merchants and their respective local governments.

How E-Commerce Transforms Localized State-Business Relations

State-business relations are crucial in determining a country's economic performance and political development.[20] State-business relations include regular interactions like tax inspections and business license applications. In countries like China, political connections pursued by private businesses are also a key aspect of these relations.

A key characteristic of China's state-business relations is the localization of most interactions.[21] Unlike in centralized political systems, such as Suharto's Indonesia, where business success relies on fostering relationships with top leaders, China's economic structure is highly decentralized.[22] This decentralization affords considerable authority to local governments in directing the local economy and distributing business resources.[23] In this context, the relationship between private businesses and the local government is crucial.

Private entrepreneurs in China frequently interact with local governments to obtain critical business resources such as land, loans, and business licenses.[24] They also strive to build good personal relationships with local officials in the hope of establishing political connections. Such political ties serve to compensate for the inadequacies of formal institutional support, helping private businesses to secure their property rights, enforce contracts, and ensure equitable access to market resources.[25]

It's noteworthy that not only large enterprises, but also small- and medium-sized enterprises (SMEs)—which comprise the majority of private merchants—actively pursue political connections. While larger firms may find it easier to establish political ties due to their prominent status, they can also leverage their resources and scale to reduce their dependence on such connections. In contrast, SMEs tend to derive more benefits from political connections and are therefore more enthusiastic about establishing them.[26]

In a nutshell, in traditional business settings, regular and positive interactions with the local governments are essential for achieving business success. E-commerce, however, diminishes the interactions between the local governments and private merchants by lifting the geographic and institutional constraints on doing business.

Without e-commerce, most private merchants would be confined to local markets with strict regulations from local authorities in China. The local governments control crucial business assets like land, loans, and business permits and play roles as resource allocators, contract enforcers, and dispute mediators. Only a small fraction of private enterprises, typically larger ones or those with mobile assets, could engage in national trade or negotiate with local governments.

E-commerce changes this dynamic by providing a gateway to the national market, breaking down geographical barriers for businesses of all sizes. In the following, I show how e-commerce access reduces merchants' reliance on local government-controlled resources and diminishes regular interactions with the state.

LAND USE

In China, land is a critical business resource controlled by the state. There is no private ownership of land. Individuals can only obtain transferable land-use rights from the state for certain years. To establish a brick-and-mortar store, it is necessary to obtain certification for land use rights and ownership of buildings attached to the land.

E-commerce, however, has reduced the demand for physical space among private merchants. It is no longer necessary to establish a brick-and-mortar store or secure an expensive location to attract customers. Many online entrepreneurs even conduct business from home. While the use of residential properties for commercial purposes was prohibited by law,[27] local governments had long acquiesced to this practice in e-commerce. In 2019, the national-level E-Commerce Law legalized this practice and allowed individual merchants, who comprise the largest group of online merchants, to utilize a virtual address as their business location.[28]

Inventory management further diminishes the need for physical space in e-commerce. Unlike brick-and-mortar stores, which must maintain extensive inventories for immediate product availability in face-to-face transactions, online merchants typically maintain limited or no stock. Many online retailers rely on drop-shipping, wherein upon receiving an order, they forward consumer details to a supplier, who then ships the products directly to the customer.[29] This process minimizes the burden of managing large inventories and reduces the demand for storage space.

Therefore, government incentives like free workspace and rent subsidies lack appeal for online merchants. During my fieldwork in a northern city, I found a government-sponsored e-commerce incubator that was impressively built but mostly vacant. Despite offering a year of free office space and storage, online merchants showed little interest in relocating. One merchant explained, "The incubator is far from where we live and work, and most of us operate without inventory, relying on direct drop-shipping from factories. Therefore, there is no need for us to move into the incubator."[30]

CAPITAL AND LOANS

Compared to traditional merchants, online merchants also have less demand for bank loans, which are often controlled by local governments through state-owned banks. E-commerce alleviates the financial constraints on private entrepreneurs by decreasing costs, speeding up cash flow, and offering financing alternatives.

First, online entrepreneurs save on real estate and overhead costs. As mentioned above, online merchants do not need a physical storefront, a prominent location, or large storage space. On certain consumer-to-consumer (C2C) platforms like Taobao.com, there are no charges for setting up and managing an online store, and no commissions on transactions. Even fees for store hosting and promotion on business-to-consumer (B2C) platforms are usually lower than the costs of running a traditional brick-and-mortar store. While online merchants do incur additional expenses like online advertising and restocking returned items, running an online store remains cheaper than an offline one in most cases.

The second financial benefit, as noted by several interviewees, is accelerated cash flow. Unlike the common practice of using IOUs in offline commerce,[31] e-commerce guarantees that private entrepreneurs promptly receive a cash payment for each transaction.[32] Additionally, online entrepreneurs can accept preorders, allowing them to receive cash in advance. This approach reduces the need for significant working capital, which is the amount of money required to cover the gap between payments made to suppliers and payments received from customers.

Lastly, e-commerce platforms like Alibaba and JD have established their own loan services for online entrepreneurs. Small businesses often face challenges in obtaining bank loans due to inadequate collateral and complicated paperwork. In contrast to traditional banks, e-commerce platforms leverage a store's history of online transactions and overall reputation to determine its eligibility for a loan. The process requires no complex paperwork and can be completed within minutes. In 2015, I came across a discussion between two online entrepreneurs situated in Shandong Province. One rural merchant expressed frustration about the difficulty of obtaining bank loans: "The process is too complicated and time-consuming; in addition, I don't have enough collateral."[33] Another entrepreneur suggested trying loan services provided by e-commerce platforms: "Check the system, and you can see immediately how much they can loan you. I can get 700k-ish RMB."[34]

BUSINESS LICENSES AND OFFICIAL REGISTRATION

Business permits are another essential resource that local governments control. At e-commerce's takeoff stage (prior to the mid-2010s), China ranked among the bottom 30 percent of global economies in terms of the ease of starting a business, according to the World Bank Doing Business Indicator. It took on average close to thirty days to complete the necessary procedures to start a business, during which time private entrepreneurs have no choice but to interact with multiple local state agencies.[35]

There are two types of online sellers: enterprise sellers and individual sellers. Enterprise sellers typically register officially because they already have a business organization or plan to operate on B2C marketplaces like Tmall or JD, which require it.

The vast majority of online sellers are individual sellers. For two decades, they were not required to undergo official registration. To launch an online store, they only needed to upload a photo of their national ID, provide bank account information, and create an online payment account. After the e-commere platform verified the identity of the owner, typically within several days, the store could be promptly launched. It is noteworthy that certain individual sellers operate on a significant scale, with their stores generating sales in the tens of millions of RMB. Despite achieving comparable or even higher sales than enterprise sellers, these individual sellers have opted not to switch to enterprise status to avoid the obligation of government registration.

Ultimately, the 2018 E-Commerce Law mandated official registration for all online sellers.[36] Nevertheless, exceptions were still incorporated into the law to accommodate specific cases, such as "individuals selling self-produced agricultural products and byproducts, or family handicrafts, individuals using their own skills to engage in labor activities for the convenience of people and few small-amount transaction activities that do not require any license under the law, and other circumstances under which no registration is required under laws and administrative regulations."[37] These criteria, in seeking to preserve the jobs in the e-commerce industry, exempt numerous individual merchants from the registration requirement.

TAXATION

Tax collection constitutes a major interaction between private businesses and local governments. However, in the mid-2010s, during my fieldwork, there were few such interactions in the realm of e-commerce.

In theory, e-commerce stores should pay taxes just as traditional offline businesses do, since they are subject to the same tax system.[38] However, most online stores are small, do not meet the revenue threshold, and are thus tax-exempt—a benefit designed to protect small businesses. Consequently, many online merchants do not need to interact with local officials for tax purposes.

Meanwhile, tax evasion is common among online merchants who have exceeded the revenue threshold and should pay taxes. In my interviews, online merchants frequently dodged questions regarding taxes, or called it "a sensitive issue."[39] After getting familiar with them, some merchants admitted that they paid no taxes, or merely paid "a symbolic amount" (象征性交一点).[40]

Tax compliance among online stores varies depending on their size and official registration status. Larger e-commerce stores on B2C platforms like Tmall, Suning, and JD are more inclined to pay at least some taxes, as these platforms require them to undergo official registration. Moreover, these B2C stores are also obligated to provide tax payment invoices (发票) to customers upon request. Even so, one seller estimated in 2015 that "90 percent of the Tmall stores are paying taxes," but "not for every transaction."[41] In contrast, C2C stores on platforms such as Taobao or PDD are generally small in scale and qualify for tax exemptions. However, some highly profitable C2C stores have taken advantage of lenient regulations to evade taxes. It is estimated that C2C stores evaded between 53.2 and 74.8 billion RMB in tax revenue in 2016.[42]

Local governments face challenges in levying taxes on e-commerce. They often cannot identify who or where to tax because platforms don't share individual sales information. Even when officials do identify successful e-commerce stores, merchants frequently underreport their revenue to avoid taxes. A local official once told an anecdote: "An online store achieved annual sales of over 20 million RMB, but the owners did not dare to admit it. When the officials visited, the owners coordinated their statements (统一口径), all claiming that the business was not profitable."[43] An official from a different province concurred that successful online merchants were "surprisingly consistent in public statements" about how e-commerce was unprofitable for them.[44] Besides lacking sales information, some officials fear that taxing e-commerce stores would lead to strong resistance and social instability. As a result, many governments turn a blind eye to tax evasion.

Considering these factors, online merchants interact less with local authorities regarding tax collection compared to their offline counterparts.

Data and Empirical Tests

Considering the factors mentioned, online merchants should have less need to directly interact with local governments and may find political ties with local officials less important compared to their offline counterparts, all else being equal. A caveat is that, the fact that online merchants interact less with local officials does not mean there are no interactions at all. Some online merchants still need to interact with local governments, particularly those who run physical stores simultaneously or have factories.[45]

To test this hypothesis, I employ a multi-method approach that draws on semi-structured interviews, data scraped from 1.76 million Taobao stores collected in December 2014, and an original national survey called the China

Entrepreneurs Survey (CES). The comprehensive data notes can be found in the appendix of chapter 4.

The core dataset for my analysis, CES, was implemented in February 2016.[46] The survey's main objective is to estimate how the use of online channels affects private merchants' interactions with local governments, as well as their political beliefs and participation. The sample includes both online and offline merchants. The offline merchants constitute a comparison group, based on which I use statistical tools to construct a counterfactual to compare against the situation of online merchants. All the merchants are private business owners[47] and can be distinguished by a unique identifier indicating whether their major business income comes from online or offline sales.[48]

The sample consisted of 3,280 business owners, with 1,920 being online merchants and 1,360 being brick-and-mortar merchants. The online merchants are oversampled and asked extra questions to better understand their business operations while retaining statistical power. The survey's online execution was essential—it's the only viable method to engage with online merchants due to the flexible nature of their work. These entrepreneurs frequently conduct business from residential or noncommercial addresses, where a physical door-to-door survey approach would likely yield minimal participation.[49]

Online surveys, however, often face data quality challenges. To mitigate these, I collaborated with a premier Chinese survey firm and implemented a series of strategies to address problems such as survey satisficing (i.e., when respondents do not fully engage with the questions and only choose the answers that require the least cognitive effort) and the self-selection bias of respondents (i.e., respondents can self-select into a survey, hence skewing the sample toward entrepreneurs who have strong opinions on the subject). Details of the sampling frame and strategies to ensure data quality are provided in Appendix A.1 of chapter 4.

Another concern is the risk of coverage error, stemming from the non-probabilistic sampling strategy the survey had to adopt. This is because online merchants constitute a group that is not easily defined or contacted, given their presence on multiple digital platforms, their mobile operations, and often the lack of official registration. The important question is: To what extent does the CES sample accurately reflect the general online merchant demographic? A significant discrepancy would jeopardize the external validity of the findings.

To ascertain the representativeness of the CES sample, I conducted a comparative analysis with a benchmark survey—the Taobao Online Merchant Survey (TOMS), which I obtained unique access to from Alibaba.[50] TOMS provides a good benchmark for two reasons. First, it represents a comprehensive, platform-conducted survey that was nationally representative of all online merchants on Taobao.com in 2012. At that time, Taobao was the premier e-commerce platform in China, hosting an overwhelming majority of the country's online merchants.[51] Second, the high quality of TOMS is evident in its rigorous two-stage sampling design with stratified random sampling at each stage.[52] The survey questionnaires were sent directly to storeowners' accounts, which ensured that the respondents were real online merchants. In addition to the self-reported data, TOMS also includes account and sales information for each store owner, as verified by Taobao. This positions TOMS as the most reliable benchmark to compare and validate my survey sample.

Table 4.1 shows that the CES sample is broadly representative of the general online merchant population in basic demographic and business-level characteristics, as evidenced by a comparison with the full TOMS sample and the subset that received the questionnaire. The CES has slightly more females than the benchmark, but the discrepancy is negligible. The CES also aligns well with the benchmark in the distribution of store owners' years of birth, except that the CES includes fewer merchants born before 1970 and more born after 1990. This is not surprising, given that the surveys were conducted four years apart and that online entrepreneurs tend to be younger. In addition, except for the "Leisure and Culture" product category, the samples exhibit a similar distribution of products sold.

One should not expect the CES sample and the TOMS subsample to fully resemble each other. Even the full TOMS sample does not perfectly match the TOMS subsample in demographic and store-level characteristics. Additionally, China's e-commerce retail sales almost tripled during the four-year gap between the surveys, which would have introduced more differences. Although one should exercise caution with a nonrepresentative sample, the relatively small divergence between the CES and TOMS samples enhances the credibility of my survey data.

Who Are the Online Merchants?

Table 4.2 draws upon the China Entrepreneurs Survey (CES) data and presents the demographic characteristics of online merchants as of 2016. It indicates that they tend to be younger and have higher levels of education, with a higher representation of females compared to China's general population. Among the online merchants, 58.18 percent fall within the age range of twenty-five to thirty-five years, and 66.92 percent possess a college degree or higher. The most popular categories of products that they sell online are Apparel, Shoes, Accessories and Beauty Products (42.29 percent), Household Products (10.99 percent), Food and Health Care Products (9.17 percent), and Mother and Baby Products (6.67 percent), and Electronics and Appliances (5.68 percent).

TABLE 4.1. Checks on the Representativeness of Online Merchants in CES

	CES sample	TOMS subpopulation	TOMS sample	Comparison
	(1) (self-reported data)	(2) (account information)	(3) (self-reported data)	(1)–(2)
Year of Birth				
Before 1950	0.16%	1.88%	1.51%	(−1.72%)
1950–1954	0.16%	1.48%	1.03%	(−1.32%)
1955–1959	0.26%	2.22%	1.72%	(−1.96%)
1960–1964	0.73%	2.66%	1.37%	(−1.93%)
1965–1969	2.34%	3.58%	2.26%	(−1.24%)
1970–1974	6.61%	6.57%	5.83%	(0.04%)
1975–1979	12.55%	13.26%	10.78%	(−0.71%)
1980–1984	26.30%	27.40%	26.97%	(−1.10%)
1985–1989	31.88%	31.45%	36.03%	(−0.43%)
1990–	19.01%	9.50%	12.49%	(9.51%)
Gender				
Male	48.23%	51.77%	54.02%	(−3.54%)
Female	51.77%	48.23%	45.98%	(3.54%)
Major Product Category				
Secondhand & Used Products	4.06%	2.62%	2.47%	(1.44)%
Apparel, Shoes, Accessories & Beauty Products	42.29%	36.35%	42.55%	(5.94%)
Personalized Products & Creative Design	5.99%	0.95%	1.10%	(5.04%)
Household Products	10.99%	9.98%	9.81%	(1.01%)
Mother & Baby Products	6.67%	7.11%	6.73%	(−0.44%)
Auto Parts & Accessories	1.56%	1.95%	1.10%	(−0.39%)
Domestic Services	7.19%	5.92%	6.59%	(1.27%)
Food & Health Care Products	9.17%	5.34%	5.15%	(3.83%)
Electronics & Appliances	5.68%	9.22%	7.14%	(−3.54%)
Investment Goods & Collectibles	0.94%	2.2%	2.2%	(−1.26%)
Leisure & Culture	1.88%	15.31%	13.45%	(−13.44%)
Other	3.59%	3.04%	1.72%	(0.55%)
N	1,920	58,793	1,457	
Survey Year	Feb. 2016	March 2012	March 2012	

Note: The TOMS subsample is a nationally representative sample of all online merchants on Taobao in March 2012. The demographics and store characteristics of these merchants were extracted from their actual account information, such as national ID and store sales. Unlike the TOMS subsample data, all the information in the TOMS sample and the CES sample was self-reported.

TABLE 4.2. Comparing Online Merchants with the General Chinese Population

		Online Merchants	General Population
		CES (2016)	Census (2015)
Gender	Female	51.80%	48.78%
	Male	48.20%	51.22%
Education Level	Elementary School or Below	0.48%	36.57%
	Junior High School	10.26%	35.63%
	Senior High School*	22.34%	15.35%
	College or Graduate School*	66.92%	12.44%
Decade Born	Before 1970s	3.65%	38.35%
	1970s	19.17%	15.64%
	1980s	58.18%	16.73%
	1990s and After	19.00%	29.29%
Living Area	Rural	12.97%	44.12%
	Nonrural	87.03%	55.88%

Note: The 2015 census data is based on a 1% national sample, covering a population of about 14 million in China. "Senior High School" covers academic senior secondary schools, vocational senior secondary schools, and technical secondary schools. "College or Graduate School" includes national general colleges and universities, adult higher education institutions, and higher vocational colleges. It is important to note that online survey panels tend to have respondents with a notably higher average education level compared to the general population. Consequently, the notable disparity in education levels between the CES sample and the census data could be attributed to factors such as the characteristics of online merchants, the overall composition of the online survey population, or a combination of both.

Gender balance. Traditionally, women encounter various barriers in business and own only one-third of businesses worldwide.[53] However, the CES data paints a different picture, with 51.80 percent of online store owners being female. This aligns with Alibaba's official data, indicating that women owned 50.1 percent of active Taobao stores in 2015, as recorded during store registration using national IDs.[54] The true number of female owners could be even higher, as suggested by a top executive at Alibaba, who mentioned that some married women might have used their spouses' ID cards due to implicit gender bias.[55] It is essential to emphasize that e-commerce's empowering impact on women extends beyond Chinese platforms. On global platforms like Shopify, women also make up 53 percent of the store owners.[56]

The substantial presence of female entrepreneurs in the online market may be attributed to several factors. First, women tend to have extensive knowledge on product categories highly popular in the e-commerce landscape, such as clothing, accessories, household items, and beauty products. Meanwhile, the percentage of women-owned businesses in traditionally male-dominated sectors such as digital products and furniture has also seen a substantial increase over time.[57] Second, the anonymity of online platforms may reduce gender bias and discrimination found in traditional markets, such as the pressure to engage in heavy drinking to seal business deals in China. This creates a level playing field where women can compete on merit. Lastly, the flexible hours and remote work opportunities offered by e-commerce are appealing to women with childcare responsibilities, enabling them to balance family commitments and entrepreneurial aspirations.

Geographical distribution. Online merchants are significantly more likely to reside in nonrural areas, with 87.03 percent of the sampled merchants living in cities or townships, including some rural migrants. Despite the potential of e-commerce to grant rural regions equal national market access, there remains a persistent urban-rural disparity in online entrepreneurship. This suggests that the urban-rural divide is not primarily caused by the lack of market access in rural areas, but rather that it stems from underlying disparities, such as differences in human capital and the availability of various services. Interviews with online merchants further support this notion, as even those who initially establish their businesses in rural villages tend to relocate to urban areas once they accumulate some wealth. This trend is mainly driven by the availability of better service industries and improved educational opportunities for their children in urban settings.[58] The implication here is that while some people believe the internet flattens the world and diminishes the importance of physical space, the truth is more nuanced. Geographical differences and access to resources continue to play a crucial role in shaping the rural-urban divide, and addressing these disparities necessitates comprehensive approaches that go beyond solely improving digital connectivity.

Regional distribution. To ascertain the geographical distribution of online merchants, I used geocoded data from 1.76 million active online stores, providing a nationally representative sample of all active stores on Taobao.com in December 2014 (see Appendix B of chapter 4).[59] The findings reveal that online stores are widely dispersed throughout China, with a higher concentration in developed, coastal areas. All mainland Chinese prefectures had hosted online stores at that time, with the exception of Ngari Prefecture in Tibet, a disputed area with India (see Figure 4.1). Although the number of online stores has a strong correlation with the prefecture's GDP level (see Figure 4.2), some regions benefit disproportionately from the rise of e-commerce.

To assess the extent to which a region is benefiting from e-commerce development or lagging behind, I followed a method first used by a research institute

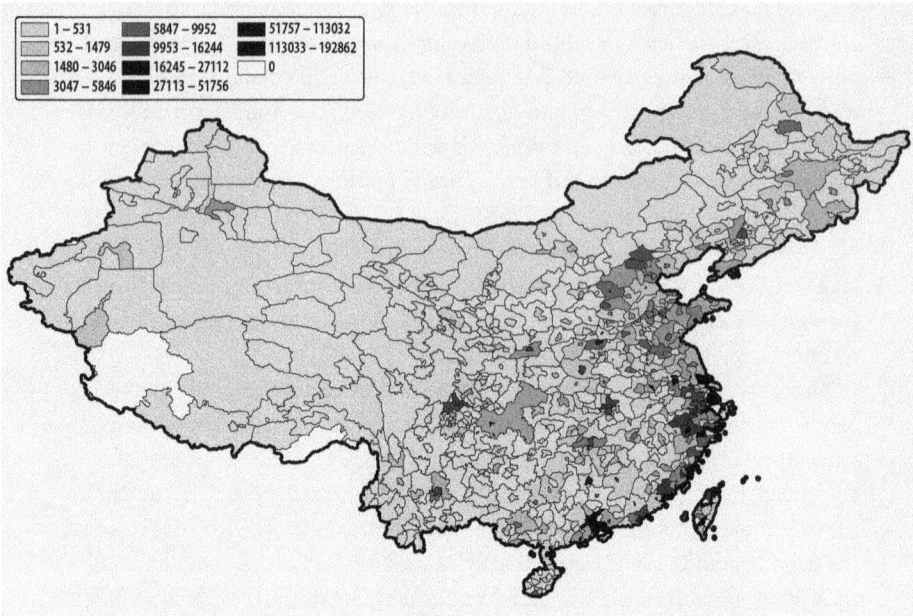

FIGURE 4.1. Regional Distribution of Online Merchants on Taobao.com as of December 2014. *Notes*: The raw dataset includes Python-scraped information on 1.76 million stores that were active on Taobao.com in December 2014, based on which the number of Taobao stores is aggregated to the prefecture/city level visualized with GIS. Two regions are depicted in white because they lack online store records: Ngari Prefecture of Tibet and China's disputed area with India.

MetroData. It involves first creating a prefecture/city-level e-commerce/GDP ratio: dividing the number of online stores in a region by the region's GDP in 2013 (per billion RMB). All prefectures were then ranked based on this ratio and their GDP.[60] If the two ranks were comparable, it indicated that the region's e-commerce development matched its overall economic development level, with no disproportionate gains or losses from e-commerce.

For instance, both Beijing and Shanghai ranked among the largest holders of online stores and had high e-commerce/GDP ratios, but they also held top positions in overall GDP. This implied that these cities did not disproportionately benefit from e-commerce; rather, they were following the overall trend. On the contrary, some regions experienced disproportionate benefits from e-commerce, as evident from significantly higher e-commerce/GDP ratio rankings compared to their GDP rankings. Jieyang in Guangdong Province, for example, hosted 14,946 online stores and had an e-commerce/GDP ratio higher than both Beijing and Shanghai. However, its GDP rank did not even

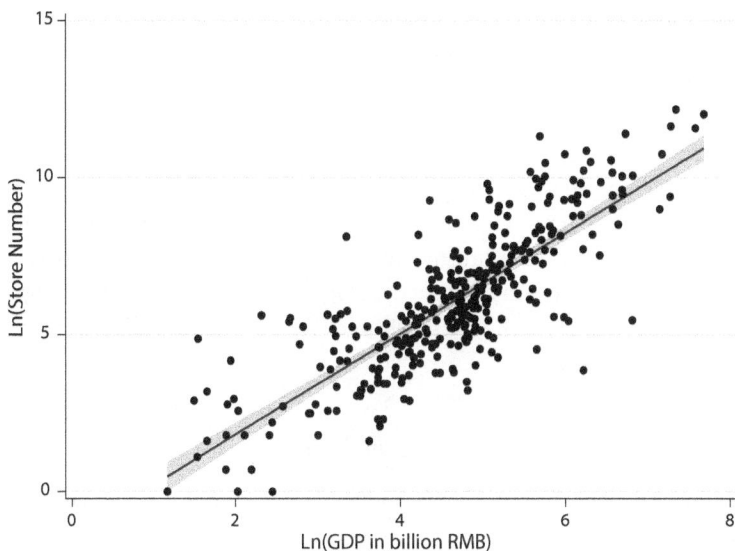

FIGURE 4.2. Number of Online Stores vs. Prefecture-Level GDP. *Notes:* The graph illustrates the relationship between the level of e-commerce development (proxied by the number of online stores in 2014) and the level of overall economic development (proxied by GDP level in billion RMB the year before (2013)) across Chinese prefectures. Both numbers are in natural log forms before plotting.

place it among the top 150 Chinese cities/prefectures, highlighting substantial benefits from e-commerce. Other examples of cities/prefectures that greatly benefited from e-commerce include Jinhua, Shantou, and Hotan. Interestingly, in terms of regions losing from e-commerce, indicated by a large difference between a high GDP rank and a low e-commerce/GDP ratio rank, a clear pattern of the "resource curse" emerged. Cities like Yulin, Daqing, and Erdos, which heavily relied on resource windfalls such as oil and coal to drive their GDP, ranked among the lowest in e-commerce development, raising concerns about their ability to diversify their economies.

The CES data confirms that China's e-commerce market is largely based on digital platforms rather than independent company websites. The CES data shows that only 5.4 percent of the merchants use non-top-ten platforms or sell through their own independent websites. The three most popular platforms in 2016, measured by the percentage of sampled merchants who own at least one store on a particular site, are Taobao (87.7 percent), Tmall (17.8 percent), and JD (14.8 percent). Almost half of the merchants (47.1 percent) operate two or more online stores simultaneously, employing a risk-pooling strategy of not putting all their eggs in one basket.[61] This approach serves as a safeguard in case one store does not perform well or faces platform penalties. On the other hand, only 19.6 percent of the sampled online merchants simultaneously manage physical stores.

In brief, online merchants constitute a demographic of young, urban, and educated adults engaged in small- and medium-sized retail and wholesale businesses. Their presence is widespread across China, and they primarily rely on online platforms for conducting business. To establish a comparison group, I also enlisted a group of offline merchants from the same online panel, resembling online merchants in all aspects except for the mode of business operation. Statistical tools will be utilized to ensure a fair and valid comparison between the two groups.

Regression Analysis

Drawing upon the CES data, the main test focuses on whether e-commerce participation is associated with greater autonomy of private merchants from the local government.

VARIABLES AND MODELS

There are four outcome variables used to operationalize the concept of a private merchant's autonomy from the local government. The first two measure the frequency of the interactions between private merchants and local governments:

- *RegulatoryIntensity*: an eight-level ordinal variable[62] that measures the time the merchant spends each month dealing with the requirements imposed by government regulations, e.g., taxes, customs, licensing, and registration.
- *NumOfficialInspec*: a four-level ordinal variable[63] that measures the frequency of visits by local officials or the number of meetings required.

The other two outcome variables measure the merchant's perceived value of informal ties with local officials:

- *TimeGovRelations*: a count variable that indicates the average number of hours per day the merchant spends maintaining and improving local government relations.
- *ValuePC*: a five-level ordinal variable[64] that measures the merchant's subjective assessment of the economic value of localized political connections.

As the four dependent variables differ in types, I employ two different estimation models. Since *TimeGovRelations* is a count variable (number of hours) rather than a continuous random variable, the use of standard ordinary least squares techniques cannot be justified. The data of *TimeGovRelations* also exhibits over-dispersion:[65] its conditional variance is several times larger than the conditional mean. This also precludes the use of a standard Poisson regression, as it may cause standard error estimates to be biased downward. I instead use a negative binomial regression that generalizes the Poisson regression by adding a parameter σ^2 to model over-dispersion. More specifically, merchant i's number of daily hours invested in maintaining political relations, Y_i, is modeled as drawn from a negative binomial distribution. The baseline estimation equation is the following:

$$Y_i \sim NB\left(y_i \left| e^{\left(\alpha + \beta Online_i + X_i'r + Z_i'\delta + \epsilon_i\right)}, \sigma^2\right.\right)$$

The other three outcome variables, *RegulatoryIntensity*, *NumOfficialInspec*, and *ValuePC*, are ordinal variables that are estimated using ordered logit models. The following is the model expression with a hypothetical latent continuous response variable Y_i^*, and the observed categories of response Y_i:

$$Y_i^* = \beta Online_i + X_i'r + Z_i'\delta + \epsilon_i$$

$$Y_i = \begin{cases} 0 & \text{if } Y_i^* \leq \mu_1, \\ 1 & \text{if } \mu_1 < Y_i^* \leq \mu_2, \\ 2 & \text{if } \mu_2 < Y_i^* \leq \mu_3, \\ \vdots \\ N & \text{if } \mu_N < Y_i^* \end{cases}$$

The negative binomial model and ordered logit model use the same set of independent and control variables. The independent variable, $Online_i$, is a dichotomous variable indicating whether merchant i trades online ($Online = 1$) or offline ($Online = 0$), as identified by the main source of his or her business income. The quantity of interest throughout the paper is β, the effect of online business status on localized state-business ties.

The vector X_i denotes a set of individual-level covariates, including Gender, Age, Education, CCP (membership in the Chinese Communist Party), PCorPCC (membership of the People's Congress or Chinese People's Political Consultative Conference at any level), and YearOfBiz (the number of years working as an offline/online merchant). The vector Z_i indicates a set of business-level controls including Sales (annual sales in 2015), Employment (number of employees at the end of 2015), Area (the type of geographical area where the merchant mainly operates his/her business, e.g., city, suburb, county/township, or countryside). Appendix Table A4.1 summarizes the descriptive statistics of the variables.

MAIN RESULTS

Table 4.3 reports the baseline estimates of the impact of e-commerce participation on localized state-business relations, and more specifically on private merchants' autonomy from the local government. All models include province fixed effects to control for province-specific factors that are constant over time. Standard errors are clustered at the provincial level to account for within-province heteroskedasticity.[66]

Columns (1)–(4) in Table 4.3 use the ordered logit model to evaluate how e-commerce participation changes the passive interactions imposed by the state on private merchants. The only differences between models (1) and (2), and between models (3) and (4), are that the latter models control for all the individual- and business-level covariates specified in the previous section. Table 4.3 shows that being an online merchant is associated with fewer interactions with the local government. After controlling for a variety of individual- and business-level covariates, being an online merchant is associated with a 0.317-unit decrease in the ordered log odds of spending more time dealing with government regulations, and a 0.198-unit decrease in the ordered log odds of experiencing more visits or inspections by local officials or tax bureaus.

Being an online merchant is also associated with a lower perceived value of being politically connected to the local government. Columns (5) and (6) share the same dependent variable, *TimeGovRelations*—the average number of hours per day the subject spends maintaining and improving local government relations. Here I adopt the negative binomial regression model. Both models demonstrate a highly significant relationship between a merchant's online status and the time spent managing local government relations. In the full model, model (6), the difference in the logs of the expected number of hours spent managing local government relations is 0.607 units lower for online merchants than offline merchants, holding the other variables constant. Columns (7) and (8) also use an ordered logit model to estimate the effect of e-commerce participation on subjective assessments of the value of localized political connections. A higher level of DV means a stronger disagreement with the statement "making acquaintance with local officials is helpful for my business"—i.e., a lower perceived value of political connections. Models (7) and (8) both indicate a positive and significant treatment effect of online business status. As shown by model (8), relative to offline merchants, online merchants

TABLE 4.3. The Effects of E-Commerce Participation on State-Business Relations

	RegulatoryIntensity		NumOfficialInspec		TimeGovRelations		ValuePC	
	(1)	(2)	(3)	(4)	(5)	(6)	(7)	(8)
Online	−0.711***	−0.317***	−0.588***	−0.198***	−0.690***	−0.607***	0.641***	0.394***
	(0.058)	(0.074)	(0.083)	(0.070)	(0.075)	(0.076)	(0.090)	(0.115)
Individual-level Covariates		✓		✓		✓		✓
Business-level Covariates		✓		✓		✓		✓
Province FE	✓	✓	✓	✓	✓	✓	✓	✓
Model	Ordered Logit	Ordered Logit	Ordered Logit	Ordered Logit	Neg. Binom.	Neg. Binom.	Ordered Logit	Ordered Logit
N	3,269	3,249	3,251	3,231	2,941	2,926	3,280	3,260
Pseudo R-squared	0.013	0.069	0.015	0.074	0.027	0.074	0.015	0.039

Note: * $p < 0.1$; ** $p < 0.05$; *** $p < 0.01$. Standard errors are clustered at the provincial level and reported in parentheses.

are, on average, 0.394 units higher in the ordered log odds of disagreeing with
the value of local political ties.

Overall, the results reported in Table 4.3 indicate that online merchants
spend less time than their offline counterparts maintaining and improving
relations with the local government; they do not adhere to all the necessary
requirements imposed by the government; carry out fewer visits and required
meetings with local officials; and have a lower perceived value of maintaining
local government connections.

SUGGESTIVE EVIDENCE ON CAUSALITY

The initial estimation suggests that online merchants have more autonomy
from local governments than their offline counterparts. However, correlation
does not imply causation. To establish a causal claim, it is crucial to consider
that becoming an online merchant is not random. E-commerce may have
an inclusive impact, allowing individuals with limited political capital or minimal state interactions to conduct business online, thereby self-selecting into
the group of online merchants. This raises the question of whether the observed autonomy among online merchants is due to this selection effect or if
e-commerce genuinely reduces the need for strong connections with the state.

I employ three approaches to attenuate concerns about causality: matching
online and offline merchants, controlling for potential confounders, and per-
forming subsample analysis. All three approaches provide evidence that the
effect of e-commerce participation on state-business ties is likely to be causal.

Matching Online and Offline Merchants. The survey data reveals that online
merchants tend to be younger and more educated than their offline counterparts, and online businesses are generally newer and smaller. Although this
type of selection may create biases *against* my findings,[67] I use matching to rule
out concerns that my results rely on model-specific parametric assumptions.

I employ two matching techniques to maximize covariate balance between
the online and offline merchants in my sample: Mahalanobis Distance Matching (MDM) and Coarsened Exact Matching (CEM).[68] For MDM, I employ
both 1-to-1 and 2-to-1 matching within propensity score calipers (0.10). Tests
for post-matching balance indicate no significant imbalance on covariates
across the treated and control groups after matching, regardless of which approach is used. Figures 4.3–4.4 and Appendix Table A4.9 show the covariate
balance before and after each matching procedure. After obtaining matched
pairs of online and offline merchants, I compare the pre- and post-matching
regression results by fitting the same statistical models, adding province fixed
effects and cluster-robust standard errors. Figure 4.4 displays the results of the

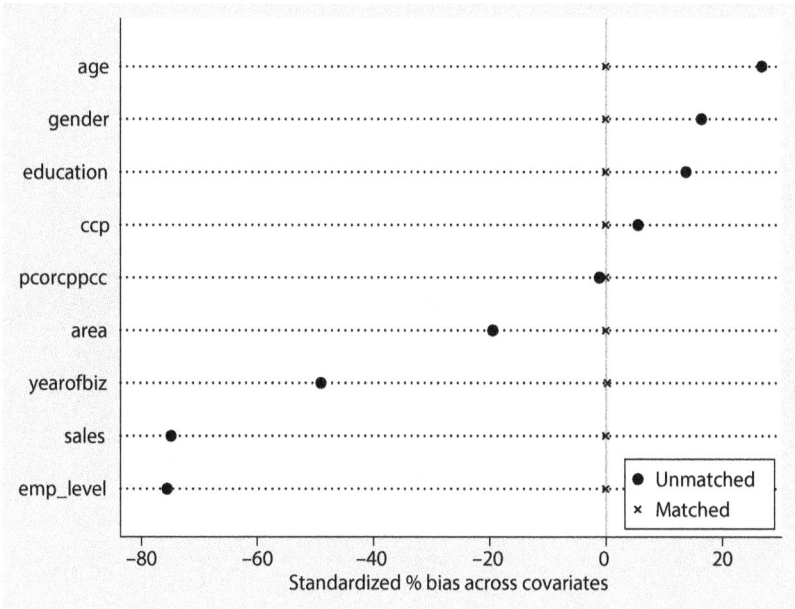

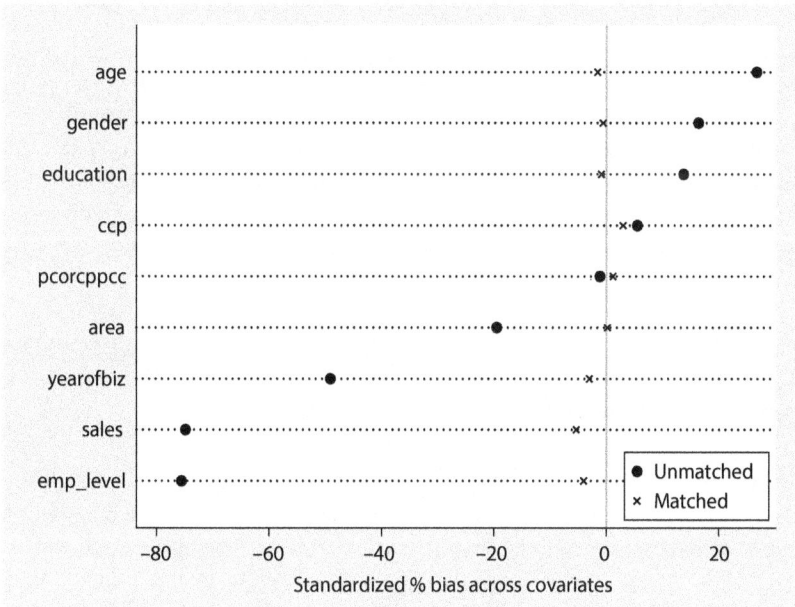

FIGURE 4.3. Covariate Balance Plots: (*top*) 1:1 Mahalanobis Distance Matching with Calipers (0.10); (*bottom*) 2:1 Mahalanobis Distance Matching with Calipers (0.10).

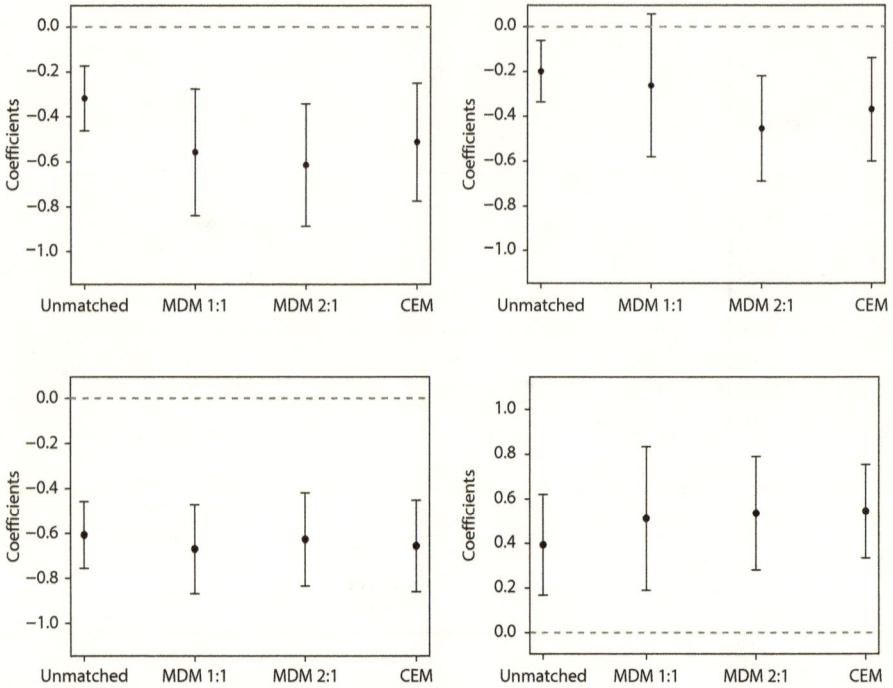

FIGURE 4.4. The Effects of E-Commerce Participation before and after Matching. *Notes*: The graphs present the effects of e-commerce participation on different outcome variables using both unmatched and matched data. The matched data are generated using three different matching procedures: 1-to-1 Mahalanobis Distance Matching (1:1 MDM); 2-to-1 Mahalanobis Distance Matching (2:1 MDM); and Coarsened Exact Matching (CEM). The graphs use dots to represent coefficients and bars to denote 95 percent confidence intervals.

matching analysis. It shows that matching does not change the direction or significance of the treatment effect.[69] If anything, the effect of e-commerce participation becomes stronger after matching.

Controlling for Potential Confounders. The second strategy for addressing causality concerns is to control for additional variables that may influence both the choice to engage in e-commerce participation and the outcome variable. To do this, I control for five potential confounders. First, it is possible that people devoid of political ties or strong family backgrounds opt to engage in e-commerce; thus their political backgrounds will also affect their subsequent interactions with the local government. To control for prior political ties, I code where a respondent's parents worked before he or she became an offline or online merchant. If the respondent's father or mother worked for the party or government organs, I code the respondent as having prior political ties. Appendix Table A4.2 shows that including the new variable *Prior Political Ties* does not change the direction or significance of the effect of e-commerce participation on the outcome variables.

The next four potential confounders are coded using a five-level ordinal scale that indicates whether the respondent tends to (1) strongly agree, (2) somewhat agree, (3) neither agree nor disagree, (4) somewhat disagree, or (5) strongly disagree with a particular statement. One caveat is that all these attitudinal variables are posttreatment variables. This means they reflect the respondent's current attitudes rather than their attitudes before they decided to open an online store. Because the CES data is by nature cross-sectional, it is difficult to trace a respondent's historical attitudinal data. Thus, the key assumption here is that respondents' attitudes are sticky and tend to change slowly over time.

The second variable I control for is sociability. Social skills may determine both the respondent's choice to trade online and his/her desire to interact with local officials. I code the variable *Sociability* based on the respondent's attitude toward the statement "I do not feel nervous about interacting with strangers." Appendix Table A4.3 shows that the inclusion of this potential confounder does not change the significance of the coefficients.

The third potential confounder is the *Respondent's Interest in Politics,* based on their assessment of the statement "I am very interested in public affairs." Again, the results reported in Appendix Table A4.4 illustrate little change in the treatment effects before and after the inclusion of the variable.

I also control for the respondent's antiauthority attitude by coding two variables that correspond to the degree with which the respondent agrees with the statements "There is no need to be timid in front of people of status and authority" (Anti-Authority Attitude_Var1) and "Government leaders are like the head of a family; we should all follow their decisions" (Anti-Authority Attitude_Var2). Similar to the inclusion of other potential confounders, Appendix Tables A4.5 and A4.6 show that controlling for "antiauthority attitude" does not affect the results.

Lastly, I control for the respondent's risk preference. A risk-taking respondent may be more likely to adopt new technologies (including e-commerce) and be less likely to seek protection from local officials. I code risk preference based on the respondent's evaluation of the statement "As long as my job is stable, it does not matter how much money I can earn from the job." Appendix Table A4.7 reports the results, which are similar across the board.

Overall, I find that my results change remarkably little with the inclusion of potential confounders, which reduces concerns that the results are mainly driven by omitted variable bias.

Subsample Analysis. Matching techniques and including additional control variables still cannot control for selection bias arising from unobserved variables that affect both the independent variable and outcome at the same time. Subsample analysis can help reduce concerns about unobservables. I examine the temporal change in state-business connections within a particular subgroup of online merchants—those who *switched* from offline to online commerce. This group of merchants is identified by survey questions about their occupations prior to engaging in e-commerce.

Because all the merchants in this subset already participate in e-commerce, I do not need to worry about the unobservables that determine their decision to become an online merchant. To measure the change in state-business ties experienced by this subgroup, subjects were asked to evaluate the following statement: "My interaction with the local government (e.g., with local administrations for taxation, industry, and commerce) decreased after I switched to e-commerce business" (1 = strongly agree; 5 = strongly disagree). To avoid left-side bias—the tendency to choose responses listed first on a horizontally organized scale[70]—I randomly assigned half of the subgroup to answer the question with "strongly agree" on the left, and the other half on the right. The distribution of responses in Appendix Table A4.8 directly supports the argument.

According to the survey, 60.0 percent of the merchants strongly or somewhat agree that they interact less with local officials after switching from offline to online business. Of the respondents, 20.9 percent neither agreed nor disagreed with the statement. Only 19.1 percent disagreed with that statement, meaning that their interactions with local government did not decrease. This may be because some e-commerce businesses are large and registered in the same area as their previous offline business; in some places, ties with the local government are not easily cut. While this analysis cannot fully resolve the issue of causality due to the cross-sectional nature of the data, it does offer some indication that the increased autonomy enjoyed by online merchants is not solely attributable to selection bias.

Challenges for Local Governments
in Closing the Regulatory Gap

Despite the caveats about causality, the above analysis suggests that e-commerce participation makes private merchants more autonomous from local governments. However, some may argue that this autonomy is temporary, expecting local governments to eventually exert the same control over online merchants as they do over offline ones.

Indeed, some local governments intentionally postponed implementing regulations on e-commerce. Officials in a rich southern city shared that they refrained from collecting taxes from the local e-commerce industry to foster a more conducive environment (放水养鱼) for online entrepreneurship and job creation.[71] Their logic is that by forgoing the tax revenue from the small and emerging e-commerce industry, they could stimulate growth in related industries like logistics and local manufacturing, thus enlarging the tax base elsewhere.

However, if local governments attempt to regulate e-commerce, they would face structural problems that are difficult to overcome, such as information gaps and coordination issues among the local governments themselves. Therefore, bridging the regulatory gap is challenging, if not impossible.

Information Problem

Local governments have very limited information about online merchants, many of whom have not registered officially. The platforms control merchants' account information and sales data, which are not accessible to most local governments.

Field interviews with local officials reveal a common grievance: they do not know, even within their own jurisdictions, who is selling or buying what, and where these transactions are occurring.[72] A government official in a township that hosts a nationally well-known e-commerce village told me, "The township government was not even aware of this e-commerce phenomenon until 2009, when many logistics companies started to come into the township to set up their branches. At the time, the township's online furniture trading industry had already reached 300 million RMB in annual sales."[73] A similar case happened to another e-commerce village I visited. The county mayor was unaware of the e-commerce village in their jurisdiction until the provincial governor paid a surprise visit to the village after reading a news report about its e-commerce industry.[74]

Coordination Problem

Local governments also face problems of coordination among themselves in e-commerce regulation.

Take, for example, tax collection by local governments. As the existing tax system was designed for the traditional economy, taxes are mainly collected based on territorial and physical principles: namely, where the business is registered or operated.[75] For brick-and-mortar stores, these two locations are often fixed and equivalent, and whether a local government has tax jurisdiction over a firm is clearcut. However, e-commerce operates differently. It does not require a physical establishment; instead, it often has separate locations for registration, business operations, and sales. Interviews indicate that many rural e-stores chose to register in the nearby city to raise the credibility of their store.[76] Some e-stores even lack fixed operational locations; with just the internet and a cell phone, the owner can manage the store anywhere. In such cases, it is difficult to determine which local government should claim tax jurisdiction, and how tax revenues should be distributed. Without a coordination device among local governments, it is also easy for the e-store to underpay or evade taxes.

In addition to taxation, another area rife with coordination problems is the adjudication of online disputes. Suppose a consumer in Shanghai feuds with an online seller in Beijing over the quality of a product sold on Taobao, a platform headquartered in Hangzhou City. If the consumer wants to sue the seller and the platform, it remains controversial as to which local court should have jurisdiction.

As an online dispute can be viewed as a contract dispute, according to the Civil Procedure Law, it shall be "under the jurisdiction of the people's court of the place where the defendant has his domicile or where the contract is performed."[77] However, similar cases in the past received different rulings, depending on how local judges interpreted the law.[78]

Some rulings claim that the court of the defendant's domicile—where the seller or the platform is located—shall have the jurisdiction. They deem that the contract is performed when the seller gives the product to the courier company. Therefore, where the seller resides is not only the defendant's domicile but also "where the contract is performed."[79] Additionally, consumers have signed user agreements with the platforms (e.g., PDD, Taobao), which usually state that the court of the defendant's domicile shall have the jurisdiction for the first instance.[80]

Other rulings support the jurisdiction of the court at the plaintiff's domicile— where the customer resides and the product is delivered.[81] E-commerce by nature involves trading parties who reside in different areas. If the consumer needs to travel afar to sue in the seller's district, it prevents her from protecting consumer rights. Judges also cite the Civil Procedure Law but contend that where the product is delivered should be "where the contract is performed" and the corresponding local court should have jurisdiction.[82]

———

The preceding analysis suggests that the limited interactions between local governments and online merchants are not transient but result from persistent information and coordination challenges faced by local governments. Essentially, e-commerce creates a national common market with problems beyond the reach of individual local governments, necessitating national solutions. These solutions can be provided either by the central government or through collaboration between the central government and national platforms. For instance, since 2017, the central government has established three specialized cyber courts to deal with internet-related disputes, where defendants, plaintiffs, and judges meet over video conference. Another example is the potential collaboration between the central government and major platforms in tax collection. For example, the platforms can withhold taxes from platform users to help collect taxes for the central and local governments.

Merchants' Shifted Dependency toward Platforms

If online merchants indeed enjoy greater autonomy from local governments relative to their offline counterparts, does this mean that e-commerce has created an independent business class? Not exactly. While e-commerce gives private merchants more autonomy from local governments, it also makes them dependent on e-commerce platforms.

Merchants rely on platforms for national connectivity and institutional support. As I show in earlier chapters, platforms partially substitute for the state's role as an institutional provider. For instance, online merchants rely on the platform's online rating system for contract enforcement, the fraud detection program to hedge risks, and the dispute resolution system to address conflicts. The platform rules—rather than state regulations—directly determine an online store's economic success. Indeed, the CES survey finds that online merchants generally care more about platform rule changes than changes in state policies. Specifically, when asked to rank the importance of three types of policies to them, the vast majority of merchants chose "rule changes on Taobao and other e-commerce platforms," followed by "changes in national-level e-commerce policies," and lastly, "changes in local-level e-commerce policies."

Moreover, online merchants depend on platforms for a key business resource: web traffic (流量). Chinese online merchants often say, "traffic is king" (流量为王). Just as location is crucial to a brick-and-mortar store, more web traffic means more consumer visits for an online store. Platforms distribute web traffic across stores in three main ways. First, search rank algorithms determine the rank of a store/product based on a mix of variables, including online ratings, historical sales, and customer service. As most online shoppers have no store loyalty, higher rankings bring more customer visits. The top-three ranked results (dubbed "the tofu cube" (豆腐块)) on Taobao usually account for 70 percent of the total click-throughs for a product search.[83] Second, platforms occasionally use web traffic to subsidize certain sellers. For instance, new sellers often receive free traffic to help launch their business.

FIGURE 4.5. Online Merchants Pray to Alibaba Founder Jack Ma during the Singles' Day Online Shopping Festival in 2016. *Source*: Zhong Zhenbin/Anadolu Agency/Getty Images.

Lastly, many online merchants purchase traffic from the platform, usually by auctioning for advertisement spots.

Online merchants are well aware of their dependency on platforms. An online merchant once complained: "One problem is that platforms like Alibaba and JD are too powerful (强势) ... They charge a high price on promotional ads. I have to fight a rat race with other merchants just to increase my store ranking. This leaves me little choice but buying ads for my product listings ... Each day, I pay a fixed cost to the platform for promotion, but my daily sales are uncertain. This is why many online shops like mine cannot make money." He said that some merchants have attempted to reduce their dependency on platforms by using social media (e.g., WeChat) to attract customers, but it remained difficult to go fully independent of platforms.[84]

Many merchants have embraced their reliance on platforms with a light-hearted perspective. Ahead of major online sales events, some merchants engage in playful worship of the founders of major e-commerce platforms such as Jack Ma (Alibaba), Richard Liu (JD), and Colin Huang (Pinduoduo), revering them as Gods of Wealth and praying for successful trading days.[85] For example, Figure 4.5 depicts a scene captured in Guangzhou City before the 2016 Singles' Day Online Shopping Carnival. In this event, Jack Ma was creatively portrayed as "Lord Guan" (Guan Gong), a Chinese deity traditionally revered by merchants for prosperity and fair business practices. Merchants would bow or even kneel before posters of the e-commerce tycoon to wish for a great fortune, offering items such as drinks, snacks, and other tributes.

Thus, e-commerce has not created an independent merchant class but rather a merchant class heavily dependent on e-commerce platforms. Therefore, we must also examine another aspect of state-business relations: the interactions between the state and platforms.

From Merchant-Government to Platform-Government Relations

As ties between individual merchants and local governments weaken and merchants increasingly rely on platforms, platforms have established extensive connections with both central and local governments. These platform-government relationships are crucial for a platform's survival in an authoritarian country, particularly its collaborations with the central government.

Platform-Local Government Relations

Overall, local governments have a complicated relationship with platforms. For one thing, there is economic competition: platforms take away some of the regulatory power of local governments by creating a national trading network supported by digital governance tools. For another, local governments also seek strategic collaborations with platforms to implement national development strategies, such as the Internet Plus Strategy, aimed at upgrading the Chinese economy and government services through digital means.

There is considerable heterogeneity among local governments regarding their bargaining power vis-à-vis platforms, leading to variations in their relationships.

Platform companies have formed close and mutually beneficial relationships with their home local governments, where their headquarters are located. In this symbiotic relationship, the home local government offers the platform economic incentives, and the company provides jobs, tax revenue, and industry upgrades in local economies in return. For example, Alibaba, headquartered in Hangzhou, has received significant land and tax benefits from its home city. In return, Alibaba's rapid growth has spurred Hangzhou's transformation into China's innovation and entrepreneurship hub. By 2013, Alibaba was paying 7 billion RMB in taxes, second only to tobacco companies in its home province of Zhejiang. For years, it worked closely with the city government to build a cashless society, the "Smart City" initiative, and other projects to digitize the local economy. The same dynamics exist between another internet giant, Tencent, and its home city of Shenzhen.

Home local governments also provide political protection, including home court advantage. As China does not have an independent judiciary, past research has found that local governments can influence local courts to favor firms within their jurisdiction.[86] For example, netizens have nicknamed Tencent "Nanshan Indominables" (南山必胜客) for its exceptionally high winning rate in the Nanshan People's Court in Shenzhen City. The home turf advantage is so important that when ByteDance sued Tencent for monopolistic practices in 2019, ByteDance filed the case in Fujian, the home province of its founder, Yiming Zhang. Tencent challenged this jurisdictional decision and had the case transferred to its home court in Shenzhen. After an unsuccessful appeal to stop the transfer, ByteDance dropped the lawsuit in 2021.[87]

Beyond home local governments, platforms have also established connections with other provincial, city, and lower-tier governments. Take Alibaba as an example. Table 4.4 only lists major collaborations at the provincial level, as there are too many platform engagements with lower-tier governments to document. As of 2020, almost all provincial-level governments in mainland China had signed strategic collaboration agreements with Alibaba in areas such as cloud computing, big data, rural e-commerce, and Smart City initiative.[88] Note that the table only includes the first major agreement signed; many provinces signed subsequent agreements to deepen the relationship. Tencent, JD, Suning, Didi, Meituan, Baidu, Sina Weibo, and other platform companies have also forged similar formal collaborations with various local governments since the mid-2010s.

Compared to their home local governments, other local governments have less bargaining power with platforms. Platforms can exploit interjurisdictional competition to demand favorable terms, and the lower the level of government, the weaker its bargaining power. Theories of exit threats and asset mobility explain this dynamic, indicating that corporations can enhance their bargaining position by threatening to move assets elsewhere.[89] Since platform companies largely operate virtually and make asset-light investments, they are much more mobile than other private firms, such as brick-and-mortar stores, real estate developers, and manufacturers. This gives platforms an advantageous bargaining position rarely seen for private firms in China.

I obtained a firsthand view of platforms' bargaining power against local governments during my fieldwork between 2014 and 2016. Western analysts often assume the Chinese state has unlimited access to tech firms' data. Yet the Chinese state is not a monolithic entity. In contrast to the central government, local governments hold far less bargaining power against platforms with regard to data; and such power diminishes further as one moves down to lower levels of government.[90] Local governments often do not have access to local merchants' user-level information held by platforms, which has restricted the government's regulatory capacity. In my field visits, local officials would occasionally complain about the lack of information; some even directly asked platform employees for it. Such data requests were always politely declined. Alibaba even organized an event called "Data Goes Rural" (数据下乡), inviting local governments to apply and compete for Alibaba's data support to rural merchants in their jurisdiction. A total of fourteen county-level governments spanning eight provinces applied, and two won the competition. I was invited to join an expert panel of e-commerce researchers tasked with reviewing and scoring the applications submitted by these local governments. It was notable how seriously these local authorities viewed the competition, evident in their detailed and carefully crafted application documents.

Another indication of platforms' bargaining positions is how the strategic collaboration is carried out. My onsite experience with rural e-commerce, a major area of platform-government partnership, reveals that local governments and platforms behave like business partners rather than patron and client: hard bargains are involved and clear expectations are laid out in contractual terms. As described by a local official from Sichuan Province, "The platform takes a very strong stance (强势) during negotiations; they only start a project in places where the local government has already met their specified requirements; otherwise, they go elsewhere."[91] For the platform, having hard bargains reflects lessons drawn from past failures, where projects routinely encountered difficulties due to some local governments offering empty promises instead of concrete investments.[92]

For example, to ensure the smooth implementation of the Rural Taobao Initiative (see chapter 5 for detailed information), Alibaba set three preconditions for county governments that collaborated with the firm. First, Alibaba required that the county's top official—either the governor or party secretary—take direct charge of the collaboration. Second, the county government must prepare five things before the firm's local team arrived. As illustrated in Appendix C of chapter 4, the five requirements are detailed, bold, and fairly standard for all counties. These requirements include preparations on the government side in terms of land and buildings (to be used to establish the program's county operations center and e-commerce terminals), capital (to stimulate terminal managers and subsidize the costs of shipping from the county center to the village), and multichannel promotion (to increase e-commerce awareness in rural areas). More surprisingly, Alibaba required the county government to establish a "leading small group" (领导小组) and an "implementation small group" (执行小组), including key officials, to support the

TABLE 4.4. The First Agreement of Strategic Collaboration Signed between a Provincial-Level Government and Alibaba

Provincial-level Government	Date of First Agreement	Major Areas of Collaboration
Zhejiang (home province)	April 2014	E-commerce platforms, logistics network, cloud computing, big data, sales of local products, cross-border e-commerce, rural e-commerce, establishing centers of innovation and financial services, smart services for people's daily lives, smart logistics, government e-procurement, social credit system
Guangxi	April 2014	Cloud computing, big data
Ningxia	May 2014	Establishing Ningxia Cloud Computing Data Center, Smart City, O2O
Henan	June 2014	Cloud computing, big data
Hebei	June 2014	Health care, culture, e-commerce, cloud computing
Xinjiang	Nov. 2014	O2O, fresh fruit e-commerce, cloud computing, big data, human capital development
Gansu	Nov. 2014	E-commerce, e-government, cloud computing, big data, O2O
Guangdong	Dec. 2014	Industrial upgrading (for the manufacturing sector)
Jilin	Dec. 2014	Cloud computing, cross-border e-commerce
Tianjin	Jan. 2015	E-commerce, cloud computing
Yunnan	April 2015	E-commerce, poverty reduction, services to improve people's livelihoods
Fujian	May 2015	Cross-border e-commerce, rural e-commerce, sales of local products, e-commerce personnel training, cloud computing, big data, internet + people's livelihoods, internet + health care, internet + tourism, social credit system
Shanghai	May 2015	Cloud computing, big data, smart city, e-commerce, internet finance, smart health care, social credit system
Shandong	July 2015	Cross-border e-commerce, rural e-commerce, internet finance, business logistics, cloud computing, big data
Shaanxi	July 2015	Cross-border e-commerce, internet applications, smart logistics, social credit system
Hunan	Nov. 2015	Cloud computing, big data, smart city, e-commerce, internet finance
Hubei	Nov. 2015	Intelligent transportation system, Alibaba cloud + entrepreneurship, rural e-commerce, cross-border B2B, YunOS, Smart logistics
Guizhou	Aug. 2016	Big data, cloud platform lab, Guizhou education cloud, smart manufacturing, smart logistics, intelligent transportation system, smart government affairs, smart police, smart health care, big data and social credit system, internet finance, cross-border e-commerce, rural e-commerce, big data and smart corporate services, talents and personnel training programs

TABLE 4.4. (*continued*)

Provincial-level Government	Date of First Agreement	Major Areas of Collaboration
Jiangsu	Oct. 2016	Smart city
Hainan	Dec. 2016	Culture and entrainment, internet + tourism, industry upgrading, rural e-commerce
Sichuan	Feb. 2017	Cloud computing, big data, e-commerce, logistics, upgrading the tourism industry through e-commerce
Shanxi	April 2017	Big data, cloud computing, internet finance, smart logistics, intelligent transportation system, poverty reduction through e-commerce, rural Taobao
Chongqing	Jan. 2018	Smart city (Smart Chongqing initiative based on "city brain" projects)
Jiangxi	June 2018	E-government and services, social governance, welfare and social security, industrial upgrading, e-commerce, financial services, smart logistics, smart tourism, culture and education, personnel training
Heilongjiang	July 2019	Digital agriculture, inclusive finance, stimulating domestic consumption, cloud computing for corporations, e-government
Anhui	June 2020	Internet of things, big data, AI, blockchain

Notes: Provincial-level governments include governments of provinces, autonomous regions, municipalities, and special administrative regions. The information about strategic collaboration agreements is compiled from multiple media reports.

collaboration.[93] Lastly, Alibaba required high-ranking officials, preferably the firsthand official, to participate in the e-commerce training program offered by Taobao University (淘宝大学), the company's training facility in Hangzhou.[94]

In less than two years (December 2014 to May 2016), Taobao University conducted training for a remarkable total of 2,180 local officials, spanning two-thirds of all prefectural divisions. Most of the officials worked at the county-level governments, with half of them holding important positions at the deputy county-level or above.[95] It is rare, perhaps unprecedented, for private companies in China to organize training sessions for government officials. Yet platform companies like Alibaba and JD have offered courses to educate local officials about e-commerce.

I had the opportunity to participate as an auditor in a four-day training program with local officials from Jilin Province. Notably, the program strongly reflected the so-called internet culture. As an effort to flatten the hierarchy among the officials, the first day began with team-building activities, including games and spirited singing with participants raising their hands high (see

FIGURE 4.6. County Governors Training Program at Alibaba's Taobao University: Team-building Activities before the Classes. *Source*: Picture taken by the author in July 2016.

Figure 4.6). The organizers also assigned seats based on randomly formed groups rather than following the government norm, which is to arrange seats by officials' ranks. The program's instructors comprised e-commerce experts, Alibaba staff, and local officials specializing in e-commerce-related fields. They covered a wide range of topics, including e-commerce trends and the interpretation of government policies.

What stood out was the discussion on the government's role in e-commerce development, which conveyed a strong "promarket" message. One instructor, a provincial-level official, remarked that to promote the growth of e-commerce, the government's role is to "cultivate fertile ground" (松土壤) rather than dictate what crops should be planted.[96] He also emphasized government responsiveness, stating, "Whatever services that e-commerce requests, the government should provide them; whatever reforms that e-commerce requires to take place, the government should make them" (电商需要什么服务, 政府就提供什么服务; 电商需要政府如何改革, 政府就应该如何改革).[97] Another instructor defined the limits of government power, asserting that the government's proper role should be one of "guiding, not dictating; supporting, but not interfering (引导不主导, 扶持不干涉)."[98]

To sum up, local governments across China collaborate extensively with powerful platforms despite economic competition. Such collaborations are driven by the central government's directives to digitize the economy, develop e-government, and spur innovation and entrepreneurship.

Platform-Central Government Relations

Platforms establish ties with both central and local levels of government, but central government ties are far more important. At the local level, a geographically transcendent platform can exploit competition among local governments to negotiate favorable terms. However, such maneuvering is not feasible with the Chinese central government, which maintains the upper hand in its relationship with platforms due to its control over the nation's internet access and other regulatory mechanisms.

The first type of platform-central government connections is contractual or ad hoc collaboration. Table 4.5 shows examples of collaborations between major platform companies (e.g., Alibaba, JD, Baidu, Didi, and Tencent) and central government agencies under the State Council, China's executive branch. While far from an exhaustive list, it reveals the prevalence of formal connections between platforms and central ministries. Over two-thirds of the constituent departments of the State Council have collaborated with platforms. Some have even signed strategic collaboration agreements in a range of areas, including economic governance (e.g., digital yuan, credit system, rural development), transportation (e.g., connected and automated vehicles), health (e.g., pandemic control, child care), public security (e.g., anti–child trafficking; combating online crimes, fraud, and counterfeits), and emergency management (e.g., natural disaster early warning system). Such collaborations have continued even during a period of increased government scrutiny and crackdown on tech after 2020. For instance, to experiment with rolling out a digital currency (digital yuan), China's central bank partnered with both state-owned banks and platform companies like Alibaba, Meituan, and Tencent in 2021.

More collaborations exist beyond those listed on Table 4.5. For example, since 2015, the Supreme People's Court has shared debtor information with platforms (e.g., Taobao, JD, Tencent) and authorized the latter to enforce court rulings on debt collection. Deadbeat debtors (老赖) are denied access to online services if they do not repay their debt.[99] Another prominent area of collaboration is the data front. As early as 2013, the National Bureau of Statistics

TABLE 4.5. Selected Ministry-level Collaborations with Major Platform Companies

Constituent Ministries and Commissions of the State Council	Examples of Collaboration
Ministry of Education	• Tencent (2018: "Cloud + Campus" initiative, offered online courses) • Alibaba (2021: Held online recruitment sessions to help college graduates find digital economy–related jobs)
Ministry of Agriculture and Rural Affairs	• Tencent (2021: Strategic cooperation on the "Cultivator" Rural Revitalization Plan) • Alibaba (2020: Strategic collaboration on revitalization strategies for rural areas)
National Development and Reform Commission	• Alibaba & JD (2016, 2017: Jointly constructed a system of corporate creditworthiness, especially in e-commerce, data sharing) • Alibaba & JD (2016: Helped rural migrant workers return home and start businesses in rural areas)
Ministry of Industry and Information Technology	• JD & Tencent (2017, 2019: Strategic collaboration on product traceability, consumption upgrade, and brand marketing) • Alibaba (2013: Cracked down on counterfeit products; 2016: Tuanyuan platform, an anti–child trafficking system to recover missing children)
Ministry of Public Security	• Baidu (2020: Strategic collaboration agreement signed to jointly develop the management system of connected and automated vehicles) • Baidu & Tencent (2015–2016: Combatted crimes related to pseudo base stations) • Alibaba, JD & other tech firms (2019: Antifraud early warning system)
Ministry of Human Resources and Social Security	• Alibaba's Ant Group & Tencent (2019: Innovation and services for National Social Security Card)
Ministry of Ecology and Environment	• Tencent (2017: Air quality inquiry service; 2019: WeChat-based national electronic health card; 2021: Vaccination map) • Alibaba (2020: Provided baby and child care in poor areas)
Ministry of Transport	• Alibaba (2018: Joint research lab on connected and automated vehicles) • Tencent (2020: Big data platform for public transportation) • Baidu (2016: Big data open-cloud platform for transportation and travel)
Ministry of Culture and Tourism	• Alibaba, JD & Pinduoduo (2020–2021: Online shopping festival to promote the sales of products related to Intangible Cultural Heritage)
Ministry of Veterans Affairs	• Didi, JD & Alibaba (2020: Created job opportunities for veterans)

TABLE 4.5. (*continued*)

Constituent Ministries and Commissions of the State Council	Examples of Collaboration
People's Bank of China	• Alibaba's Ant Group (2021: Jointly built the technology platform for China's e-currency (digital yuan)) • Tencent, Alibaba, Didi, Meituan & Bilibili (2021: Digital yuan pilot program)
Ministry of Civil Affairs	• Alibaba, Tencent & ByteDance (2020: Developed apps for community-based epidemic prevention and control)
Ministry of Natural Resources	• Alibaba (2018: Cloud computing support to data management and applications related to natural resources)
Ministry of Housing and Urban-Rural Development	• Alibaba (2014: Joint launch of a virtual transportation card)
Ministry of Water Resources	• Alibaba (2020: Flood monitoring and warning system on Alibaba Cloud) • Tencent (2020: Smart Water Resources Management)
Ministry of Commerce	• JD (2016: Strategic collaboration agreement signed with the ministry's Foreign Trade Development Bureau) • JD (2017: Cooperation agreement on promoting the development of digital commerce signed with the ministry)
National Health Commission	• Tencent (2019: WeChat-based national electronic health card; 2021: Vaccination map); • Alibaba (2020: Provided baby and child care in poor areas)
Ministry of Emergency Management	• Alibaba (2020: Built emergency management information systems) • Baidu (2019: AI applications in emergency management) • JD (2020: Built a national emergency resource management platform, disaster logistics, etc.)

Notes: Alibaba, JD, and Pinduoduo are China's three e-commerce giants. Didi is China's largest ride-hailing company. Tencent owns several social media platforms, including WeChat and QQ. Meituan is China's largest lifestyle online-to-offline service provider. Baidu is its largest search engine. Bilibili is a prominent video-sharing platform that is particularly popular among the young generation. ByteDance owns several short-video-sharing platforms such as TikTok and Douyin. The information about platform-government collaboration is compiled from multiple media reports.

had signed collaboration agreements with major platforms, using real-time, online big data to improve and complement official data.[100] There are also ad hoc and unpublicized collaborations, particularly in sensitive or national security areas, including tracking the online footprint of terrorist suspects.[101]

There are also informal ties between the platforms and the central government. As discussed in chapter 2, the major platforms have established political ties by accepting investments from funds that are government backed or run by the scions of Chinese leaders. Another channel is through the "revolving door." As China's digital economy booms and the anti-corruption campaign since 2013 has reduced the allure of public office, many bureaucrats have "plunged into the private sector" (下海), joining internet firms.[102] Alibaba, Tencent, ByteDance, and Meituan have all hired former central government officials to serve as legal counsels and policy research fellows (see Table 4.6). Some of them previously worked in the direct regulatory agencies for private firms, such as the antimonopoly department of the Ministry of Commerce or the National Development and Reform Commission. Leveraging insider knowledge and informal networks, these former officials have helped internet firms navigate China's regulatory uncertainties.

Given the platforms' formal and informal connections to central government agencies, is there a possibility of state capture, namely, corporate interests strongly shaping the state's policies to their own advantage? Or will powerful platforms end up challenging the central authority?

According to research by Pepper Culpepper and Kathleen Thelen (2020), tech platforms in rich democracies can exploit consumers' allegiance, using it as political power to fight government regulations that threaten these platforms.[103] In China, platforms also seek to influence policy, commonly framing themselves as representing the broad interests of consumers and the SMEs they host. Occasionally, platforms even bargain for favorable policies on behalf of their users. For instance, in a meeting with officials from the State Taxation Administration in 2017, e-commerce platform founders Jack Ma and Richard Liu suggested lowering taxes for small businesses and microbusinesses.[104]

However, this does not mean that Chinese platforms will mobilize their users to act collectively against the central government or possess the same level of influence on policies as large corporations in the West. While a platform's popularity may mitigate the risk of a severe outcome like a forced shutdown, it doesn't render it immune to government regulation.

In China, a large user base represents more of a liability than a shield against regulation. For an authoritarian government, the primary concern isn't the potential for a private firm to become "too big to fail," but rather "too big to control." As a big platform accumulates more users, it gains greater political clout with the central government—and it is more likely to raise government suspicions and risk a regulatory crackdown.

As shown in chapter 6, the Chinese central government retains a wide range of regulatory means to rein in platforms, if needed. Since 2020, the Chinese government has carried out a series of regulatory crackdowns on platform companies, including the suspension of Ant Group IPO, antitrust investigations of big platforms, and strengthening the regulations on algorithms and

TABLE 4.6. China's Tech "Revolving Door"

Employee	Current Employer	Current Job Title	Formal Government Position
1	Alibaba	Director of Competition Policy Research Centre, Alibaba Research Institute	Former deputy director, antimonopoly department, Ministry of Commerce
2	Alibaba	Head of Alibaba Research Institute	Former director, policy and legal department, State Council Information Office
3	Alibaba	Legal counsel	Former official, antimonopoly department, National Development and Reform Commission
4	Ant Group	Legal director	Former judge, Hangzhou Intermediate People's Court
5	ByteDance	Chief antimonopoly legal counsel	Former deputy director, antimonopoly department, Ministry of Commerce
6	ByteDance	Senior security specialist	Former deputy director, antimonopoly department, Industry and Commerce Bureau
7	Didi Chuxing	Vice president	Former deputy director, Ministry of Transportation
8	Didi Chuxing	Chief safety officer	Former deputy director, Ministry of Emergency Management
9	Meituan	Senior vice president	Former deputy director, antimonopoly department, Ministry of Commerce
10	Tencent	Vice president for legal affairs	Former judge, Nanzhou District Court
11	Tencent	Director of Policy and Regulation Centre, Tencent Music	Former director, antimonopoly bureau, Ministry of Commerce

Source: Yu Sun, "China Tech Groups Hire Ex-regulators to Fend Off Beijing's Crackdown," *Financial Times*, April 20, 2021, https://www.ft.com/content/71daa106-259e-4dc2-b267-b0289177de1f.

data. These moves prove that China's central government has the upper hand in its relations with platforms, rather than the other way around.

This highlights a key difference in central and local governments' bargaining positions with platforms. The central government has far greater resources and regulatory capacity than local governments. Consequently, establishing ties with the central government is more important for platforms to ensure their survival within the authoritarian regime. By closely collaborating with the state, powerful platforms seek to preempt strict regulations and reassure political elites that they pose no threat.

Centralization of State-Business Relations

Considering the analysis above, e-commerce transforms rather than eliminates state-business relations. While it provides online merchants with some autonomy from local governments, it does not create an independent merchant class. Instead, merchants become dependent on platforms, which are in turn regulated by the government. Thus, the state still exerts control over individual merchants, albeit indirectly, through these platforms.

In fact, the more merchants a platform hosts and "liberates" from local governments, the higher the political risk it faces in an authoritarian regime. Consequently, it becomes crucial for the platform to build strong ties with the government, particularly the central government. Instead of eliminating state-business relations, the rise of platform-based e-commerce *centralizes* these ties, shifting the locus of interactions and political connections from the merchant level to the platform level.

Concluding Remarks

Based on a national online survey, web-scraped information, and qualitative evidence, this chapter shows that platform-based e-commerce centralizes state-business interactions from the individual merchant level to the platform level. The findings have several important implications.

First, the rise of e-commerce will not generate an independent merchant class. Rather, online merchants operate within a system of nested authority: merchants are directly regulated by platforms, while these platforms, in turn, are subject to direct regulation by the government.

Second, while further research is warranted, e-commerce may have generated efficiency gains by centralizing state-business interactions. In China, where the state wields substantial business resources, state-business interactions create opportunities for corruption. Andrei Shleifer and Robert Vishny (1993) suggest that a centralized economic system tends to exhibit less corruption compared to a decentralized one. In a decentralized system, various governmental agencies can independently demand bribes, leading to uncoordinated rent-seeking behaviors. Similarly, by curtailing decentralized interactions between local governments and tens of millions of individual merchants, e-commerce might hold the potential to reduce the overall deadweight loss in the economy.

Third, the rise of large platforms may help the central government recentralize its power vis-à-vis local governments. These platforms form ties with both central and local governments but prioritize the central government. For example, a platform can decline an information-sharing request from one local government, knowing it can collaborate with another. However, refusing a similar request from the central government is more challenging. Consequently, the central government is better able to recruit platforms to augment its power. As centralized tools for collecting market information, platforms can mitigate the central government's information disadvantage relative to local governments. Moreover, by breaking down internal trade barriers, platforms further weaken local governments' authority, revenues, and rent creation.[105] In this manner, platforms hold the potential to tilt the power balance toward the central government.

Overall, this chapter suggests that the proliferation of e-commerce is not merely a technological phenomenon. Rather, it fundamentally restructures the relations among local governments, the central government, and private economic agents, including the platforms and their users.

5

Digital Path to Prosperity or Road to Nowhere?

THE ECONOMIC EFFECTS OF E-COMMERCE ACCESS

The Anti-Valentine's Day

In the 1990s, a group of college students decided to celebrate rather than lament their singlehood. They jokingly picked November 11 for their anti-Valentine's celebration, since the date 11/11 represents four singles. Singles' Day quickly became an unofficial holiday, a fun excuse for the unpartnered to splurge on fancy products they wouldn't otherwise purchase. In 2009, Alibaba popularized the concept by rebranding it into an online sales day for everyone. Other Chinese platforms such as JD.com and Suning.com later joined the fad by simultaneously running online deals. This sales holiday even has an international reach: more than 200,000 brands from seventy-eight countries participated in 2019.[1]

Singles' Day has become the world's biggest shopping bonanza, starting with a four-hour nationally broadcast gala featuring international celebrities to kick off the "Super Bowl of Shopping." In 2020, the two largest e-commerce companies, Alibaba and JD.com, sold $74 billion and $41 billion worth of products, respectively. Together they eclipsed the combined sales of US Thanksgiving, Black Friday, and Cyber Monday.[2] In fact, in just thirty minutes of presales, Alibaba achieved the sales number of Amazon's forty-eight-hour Prime Day,[3] with a peak number of 544,000 orders per second.

To many, the stunning success of Singles' Day demonstrated the revolutionary effects of e-commerce: empowering producers nationwide, incubating domestic brands, and stimulating domestic consumption. A 2013 McKinsey report contends that e-commerce would have a leapfrog effect, allowing China to "forgo the national expansion of physical stores commonly seen in Western nations and move directly to a more digital retail environment."[4] There are also signs that e-commerce has begun to trigger broad ripple effects beyond retail. For example, the rise of e-commerce has spurred the growth of flexible manufacturing, enabling the fulfillment of small-batch and highly customized orders while maintaining short production cycles and cost-effectiveness.

However, skeptics argue that e-commerce has marginal or harmful effects on the economy, causing physical store closures and unemployment. They also claim that e-commerce facilitates counterfeit sales, harms brands, and intensifies price competition, pressuring manufacturers to compromise on quality. These criticisms sparked a heated debate in 2016–17 about whether e-commerce strengthens or weakens China's pillar industry, the manufacturing sector. Although the e-commerce sector came out on top in this debate, especially after the endorsement of Premier Li Keqiang, skepticism about its true impacts still occasionally resurfaces.

Despite a divergence of opinions, surprisingly little research rigorously evaluates the impacts of e-commerce. There is scant empirical evidence beyond anecdotes and case studies. To help fill this gap, this chapter investigates a simple question: What are the economic effects of e-commerce?

Preview of the Chapter

Assessing the causal effects of e-commerce is challenging due to the nonrandom distribution of e-commerce access. For instance, evaluating whether e-commerce access increases a region's wealth is complicated by the "digital divide" thesis, which suggests e-commerce is more accessible in affluent regions. Thus, observed wealth disparities between regions may stem from preexisting economic differences rather than unequal e-commerce access.

To identify the causal effects of e-commerce, we would ideally have two groups of regions with comparable preexisting conditions. We would then randomly introduce e-commerce to one group of regions (the treatment group), while the other remains unconnected (the control group). After a certain period of e-commerce treatment, if the treatment and control groups start to diverge in certain socioeconomic outcomes, we could confidently determine that this change is attributed to e-commerce rather than the preexisting differences between the groups. This is the philosophy underlying the main research method used in this chapter: the *randomized controlled trial (RCT)*, also known as a field experiment.

In 2015–17, my coauthors and I seized a rare opportunity to conduct an RCT that randomized first-time e-commerce access across regions with similar preexisting conditions.[5] As most urban areas in China already had e-commerce access during the research period, we specifically focused our RCT on *rural* areas where the majority of villages had yet to be covered by e-commerce services. Our RCT took advantage of China's policy to introduce e-commerce in rural regions as a means of poverty alleviation. This policy was implemented through a collaborative effort between the government and major e-commerce platforms. We implemented our experiment as part of Alibaba's rural e-commerce program, which aimed to provide e-commerce access to 100,000 administrative villages, representing approximately one-sixth of the total villages in the country.

Our experiment randomly assigned e-commerce access to one hundred villages across three provinces of China: Anhui, Henan, and Guizhou. The field experiment was combined with a novel collection of microlevel data, including Alibaba's transaction records, which are rarely provided to external researchers. The three sets of data are: (1) survey data on 2,800 (baseline survey) and 3,800 (endline survey) households; (2) two rounds of local retail price surveys with 11,500 price quotes per round; and (3) 27.8 million anonymized buying and selling records provided by Alibaba, which cover approximately twelve thousand villages in five provinces over an eighteen-month period.

The RCT research is the first study to causally identify e-commerce's effects on rural household welfare. The results suggest that for the average rural household, e-commerce generates economic gains, mainly through consumption effects (i.e., increasing the household's purchasing power by reducing the cost of living) rather than production effects (i.e., increasing the nominal income or stimulating entrepreneurship).

Although the RCT provides a solid foundation for establishing causality, it is far from an exhaustive assessment of the impact of e-commerce across China. I acknowledge several limitations associated with the study. First, rural e-commerce programs vary in their settings and evolve over time. Although the study finds that the RCT results are driven by the general conditions of rural areas rather than the implementation of the program, it is possible that the effects of e-commerce may be altered as the underlying conditions of rural areas evolve. Additionally, the RCT primarily focuses on short- to medium-term effects, making it challenging to predict the long-term consequences. In the chapter, I delve into the extent to which the RCT can inform us about other e-commerce programs and subsequent developments.

Second, because our RCT is rural based, its results cannot be directly applied to urban areas where e-commerce development is far more advanced. As discussed in the chapter, the RCT results likely represent the lower bound of e-commerce's effects in urban areas, and some of the insignificant results obtained in the experiment may actually turn significant in urban settings. Another limitation is that the RCT only captures a subset of e-commerce's effects. In light of this, I dedicate a section of discussion to the effects of e-commerce beyond the scope of RCT. These effects are challenging to quantify, but they merit investigation in future research.

Research Context of the RCT Study

E-Commerce Goes Rural

China's e-commerce development was initially limited to urban areas. However, in 2009, the media discovered three "Taobao villages" that experienced stellar income growth by selling products on Taobao.com. A Taobao village was later officially defined as an administrative village in which at least 10 percent of households actively engage in online business, with total annual e-commerce sales exceeding 10 million RMB ($1.6 million). By June 2020 there were 5,425 such villages spanning twenty-eight provinces, selling a wide range of products including crabs, food, handicrafts, clothing, and furniture.

These prosperous e-commerce villages have garnered attention from international organizations and policymakers worldwide, prompting them to endorse e-commerce as a potential strategy for rural development and poverty alleviation.[6] The rationale is that e-commerce serves as a digital highway that connects previously isolated rural markets, enabling a *two-way* flow of goods and services.

Inward bound ("Buy"): E-commerce improves the sale of consumer goods and agricultural/business inputs into rural areas. In this way, it improves the *consumption side* of rural livelihoods by offering direct access to cheaper, higher-quality products, as well as a wider variety of products, than physical stores can provide. Rural residents can thus enjoy greater purchasing power and similar shopping amenities as their urban counterparts.

Outward bound ("Sell"): E-commerce can help rural households sell products from their village, sparking rural entrepreneurship and raising household income levels. Such *production-side* welfare improvement can be generated by reducing the market entry and business operation costs. E-commerce also has a disintermediation effect: it cuts out the intermediaries (who otherwise enjoy a large share of the profits) and enables direct transactions between rural producers and urban consumers. As e-commerce in principle widens market access, policymakers believe it can improve livelihoods not through "giving a man a fish"—as traditional measures such as aid and subsidies do—but by "teaching him how to fish."

Recognizing e-commerce's potential for development, China has proactively introduced e-commerce access to rural areas since the mid-2010s. Rural e-commerce has been embraced as a national-level strategy, and it has been included in the Chinese Communist Party's annual "No. 1 Central Document" each year since 2014, reflecting the strategic importance of this endeavor.[7] Numerous central and local policies have provided generous financial support for e-commerce-related training, logistics, and operations. In 2015, the Ministry of Finance allocated 2 billion RMB to two hundred counties to equip some of China's most impoverished areas with e-commerce facilities by 2020. This proactive approach has inspired other developing countries, such as Egypt, India, and Vietnam, to design their own policies aimed at introducing e-commerce to unconnected rural villages.[8] How to enable rural e-commerce access?

Unpacking Rural E-Commerce Access

Bringing e-commerce to rural areas in developing countries requires more than just road accessibility and internet access. By 2010, nearly all administrative villages in China had been connected to the public road system and phone networks through infrastructure projects like Connecting All Villages (村村通).[9] Similarly, before the advent of e-commerce, the internet was already available in most of the Chinese countryside thanks to dial-up internet services via phone networks, smartphones, and expanding broadband access.

Instead, e-commerce access means overcoming two formidable hurdles to e-commerce trading, which we refer to as the logistical and transactional barriers.

The *logistical barrier* arises due to limited logistics networks at the village level, especially for express parcel delivery. According to interviews with two industry experts, prior to the mid-2010s, parcel deliveries were mostly limited to administrative levels higher than townships or counties.[10] Village households could not receive direct package deliveries and instead received (bi)monthly paper notifications to collect packages from nearby townships or counties.[11]

The lack of logistics coverage is due to the "last mile" challenge, where the final phase of delivery from a transportation hub to individual households incurs high costs. This issue is exacerbated in rural areas due to the scattered population and low demand, making rural delivery economically unviable for logistics companies. This creates a vicious cycle: inadequate rural delivery reduces e-commerce demand, and the low demand makes it financially impractical to extend delivery networks to villages.

Another bottleneck to e-commerce is the *transactional barrier*. Rural households often lack the technical know-how to navigate online platforms or use online payment methods. Additionally, villagers may not trust online transactions without first inspecting the product or interacting with sellers in person.

Therefore, rural e-commerce access requires a bundled solution to overcome both logistical and transactional barriers in the rural area.

FIGURE 5.1. The Signing Ceremony for the Collaboration between the Communist Youth League and Alibaba. *Notes*: This collaboration started in March 2016 and focused on promoting online entrepreneurship among rural youths. In addition to the collaboration with the Communist Youth League, Alibaba has signed agreements of collaboration with the National Development and Reform Commission (February 2016), the Ministry of Agriculture (September 2016), and every local government that participates in its rural expansion program. The picture was provided by an Alibaba employee.

The Rural E-Commerce Program

In the mid-2010s, the Chinese state started to collaborate with various companies to expand rural e-commerce (see Figure 5.1). In 2014, it partnered with Alibaba to launch a rural expansion program called Rural Taobao, one of the earliest and largest programs of its type.[12]

The program has two missions: providing rural households with the same level of access to consumer goods and business inputs as urban residents ("buy"), as well as helping rural households sell agricultural products from their village ("sell"). The program initially aimed to invest 10 billion RMB ($1.6 billion) over the next three to five years to extend e-commerce services to 100,000 administrative villages, encompassing roughly one-sixth of all villages in China. In 2015–17, when our research was conducted, the program was in rapid expansion, covering approximately 16,500 Chinese villages across 333 counties in twenty-seven provincial-level divisions.[13]

It is important to differentiate between Rural Taobao Villages and the previously discussed Taobao Villages. Taobao Villages are rural e-commerce centers that arose spontaneously, numbering about five thousand by mid-2020, mostly in developed coastal regions. In contrast, the Rural Taobao program is a government-firm collaboration aimed at introducing e-commerce to a broader rural area, seeking to replicate the success of Taobao Villages. Rural Taobao Villages are more representative of the general countryside: many are located in poorer inland areas and do not necessarily have the favorable conditions found in Taobao Villages. Therefore, Rural Taobao Villages provide a more suitable context for studying the impact of first-time e-commerce connectivity on an average village.

To enable rural e-commerce access, the Rural Taobao program has two key elements to overcome the logistical and transactional barriers to e-commerce mentioned in the previous section.

LOGISTICAL ELEMENT

The program aims to extend the logistics network to the village level and make e-commerce shipping costs in villages as affordable as those in the main urban centers of counties. To this end, in the urban center of each participating county, the program sets up a logistical hub comprising a warehouse, distribution center, and sorting rooms to process all e-commerce-related packages to/from the participating villages (see Figure 5.2 (top)). Importantly, Alibaba and sometimes the local governments fully subsidize the additional costs associated with shipments between the county center and the villages. This allows villagers to enjoy the same low shipping costs as their urban counterparts. It is worth noting that Alibaba and the government do not intend to provide perpetual subsidies. The expectation is that as more rural households adopt e-commerce, economies of scale will come into effect. With the increase of rural e-commerce orders, it is anticipated that the transportation costs per order will decrease to a more affordable level, eventually eliminating the need for subsidies.[14]

TRANSACTIONAL ELEMENT

To recap, the transaction barriers to e-commerce adoption among rural households are rooted in their limited knowledge of technology, lack of online payment methods, and distrust of online platforms. To tackle this issue, the

FIGURE 5.2. The County-Village Structure. *Notes*: (*top*) A county-level operation center: the distribution and sorting room. (*bottom left*) Exterior and (*bottom right*) interior of a village-level store with e-commerce terminal. These pictures were taken during a field visit to Mengzhou (a county-level city) in Henan Province, August 8, 2015. (*overleaf*) The plastic-packed corn cob to be sold through the e-commerce terminal.

FIGURE 5.2. (*continued*)

program sets up an e-commerce terminal at a central location in each participating village, where a terminal manager helps rural households buy and sell
products via e-commerce. The e-commerce terminal is equipped with a computer and a large screen, so village shoppers can see the store manager placing
orders on Alibaba's platform. The store manager plays a crucial role and is typically a young, tech-savvy villager recruited from the local community. They have
to pass a competitive test to demonstrate their proficiency in e-commerce.[15] The
store manager assists rural households in purchasing and selling products
through the e-commerce terminal. Rural residents can place orders using the
store manager's online account and pay in cash when the product is delivered.
This approach allows villagers without online accounts or shopping experience
to engage in e-commerce and gain knowledge about product prices beyond their
local market.

While there are other rural e-commerce programs, Rural Taobao provides
an ideal setting for our research purposes. The program does not improve internet infrastructure or road conditions, nor does it directly reduce transport
costs beyond e-commerce or in nonparticipating villages. This enables us to
separate the effects of e-commerce from those of internet access or general
improvements in offline trade access. In addition to evaluating the program's
overall impact, we can also leverage the features of this setting to examine the
relative importance of trade cost reductions (logistical barrier) and additional
investments targeted at adapting e-commerce to the rural population (transactional barrier).

Fieldwork and the RCT Opportunity

The research opportunity arose in February 2015, when my fieldwork led me to Wantou, a Taobao Village where e-commerce was hailed as a silver bullet against poverty. However, I observed that many neighboring villages encountered obstacles in adopting e-commerce, such as the absence of suitable products and limited technical skills related to e-commerce. One villager mentioned that their own village struggled to become an e-commerce hub because it "lacked a leader to initiate the transformation" (没有带头人).[16]

Scaling up rural e-commerce was a widespread challenge across China. Less than 1 percent of Chinese villages had organically developed into e-commerce hubs, known as Taobao Villages. Government officials were keen to expand rural e-commerce, turning more villages into e-commerce centers. E-commerce companies were equally eager to tap into the potential of the rural areas, eyeing the vast "next trillion-RMB market." A platform manager explained to me, "The urban market is nearing saturation, with limited growth potential for e-commerce. However, half of the Chinese population has yet to experience e-commerce, and the majority of them reside in rural areas."[17] This powerful business incentive, combined with unwavering government support, gave birth to various rural e-commerce initiatives, including Rural Taobao.

During my visit to Wantou Village, I learned about the Rural Taobao program. A local Alibaba manager informed me that a neighboring village was among the first to receive an e-commerce terminal under the program.

Intrigued, I decided to visit the site, a mom-and-pop store managed by a tech-savvy young villager who adeptly handled the digital intricacies, such as online orders and communication with the e-commerce platform.[18] Meanwhile, his father, aged in the sixties or seventies, took the responsibility of persuading other village seniors to shop at their e-commerce terminal. His advertising pitch was, "My store may look small, but you can buy everything here!" On the launch day of their e-commerce terminal, they spent 2,000 RMB (around $400) in store decoration and even celebrated by beating gongs and drums, a customary practice in Chinese villages to mark the beginning of festivals and ceremonies. They achieved an impressive total of 620 orders on their first day, including presales, which included high-value items like refrigerators and televisions. For each transaction, they receive a 5 percent commission from the seller. The family believed in the potential of rural e-commerce: "Online products are so cheap—and everyone would know it after the first purchase . . . Look, this well-packed dried jujube only costs 9.9 RMB ($1.50)—and shipping is free!"[19]

Upon learning about the phased rollout of the Rural Taobao program, I recognized a unique opportunity to conduct a randomized controlled trial

(RCT) to examine the causal effects of e-commerce. This research could have significant implications for China's rural development by exploring whether e-commerce can bridge the urban-rural divide and drive transformative change. To undertake this ambitious project, I collaborated with scholars Victor Couture, Benjamin Faber, and Yizhen Gu.

After a series of negotiations, we successfully garnered the support of Alibaba to execute the RCT. The company exhibited a genuine eagerness to glean insights from our research. At that time, rural e-commerce remained an uncharted territory, with substantial uncertainties and an unclear path to success. Our research had the potential to guide the future operations of Rural Taobao, highlighting the areas where it could yield the greatest welfare, its limitations, and the underlying mechanisms driving welfare generation. The shared interest in uncovering the true effects of e-commerce fostered a commitment from Alibaba to diligently adhere to our research protocol, demonstrating full cooperation and refraining from any interference throughout the course of our study.

To create a realistic experimental design, our entire team took a trip to Mengzhou, Henan Province, immersing ourselves in the day-to-day operations of the program. We had the opportunity to visit village e-commerce terminals and an agricultural business that utilized these terminals to sell vacuum-sealed corn cobs. The fieldwork helped us design the RCT and finalize the research collaboration. We developed two additional sets of in-person surveys related to the RCT and recruited a team of over eighty surveyors. Conducting these surveys cost approximately $300,000. To ensure research independence and avoid any potential conflicts of interest, we raised the necessary funds from various independent research institutes, separate from Alibaba.[20]

Experimental Setting and Data Collection

Experimental Design and Overview of Datasets

The RCT was administered in eight counties located in Anhui, Henan, and Guizhou provinces (see figures 5.3 and 5.4),[21] where the research team randomly introduced e-commerce access across one hundred villages.

In terms of experimental design, for each county, we obtained a list of villages in which Alibaba planned to introduce the e-commerce program. We asked the firm to extend this list by adding the next five most suitable village candidates in the county (see Appendix F.2 for details). We then had two to three weeks to run the stratified randomization, randomly selected five control villages and seven to eight treatment villages for each county from this expanded list, and sent our surveyors to all treatment and control villages to collect

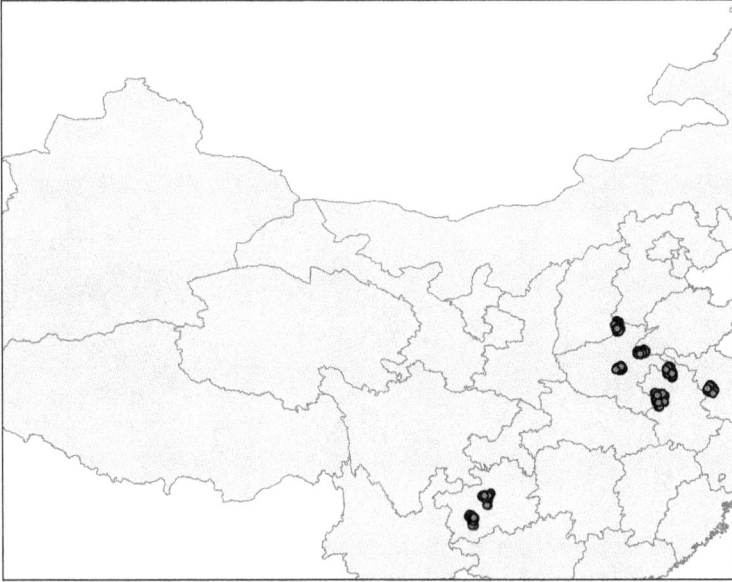

FIGURE 5.3. Provinces and Counties Where the RCT Was Implemented. *Notes*: The boundaries indicate provinces of mainland China. The dots indicate the RCT villages in eight counties. *Source*: Victor Couture, Benjamin Faber, Yizhen Gu, and Lizhi Liu, 2021. "Connecting the Countryside via E-Commerce: Evidence from China," *American Economic Review: Insights* 3, no. 1: 35–50. Copyright American Economic Association; reproduced with permission of the *American Economic Review: Insights*.

baseline survey data. After that, the firm's local teams installed the e-commerce terminals in the treatment villages while the control villages remained unconnected; the villages on the list that are neither treatment nor control villages also received the e-commerce program as planned. One year later we dispatched surveyors to collect endline survey data for both treatment and control villages.

The full sample in which we collected survey data thus includes forty control villages and sixty treatment villages, randomly selected from 432 candidate villages. Compliance with our assignments was not complete: the program was rolled out in thirty-eight of the sixty treatment villages and five of the forty control villages. We therefore report both intent-to-treat (ITT) and treatment-on-treated (TOT) effects. The main reason for imperfect compliance is that some of the store manager applicants ended up rejecting the job offers to run the e-commerce terminal, or they found other jobs before we could finish the

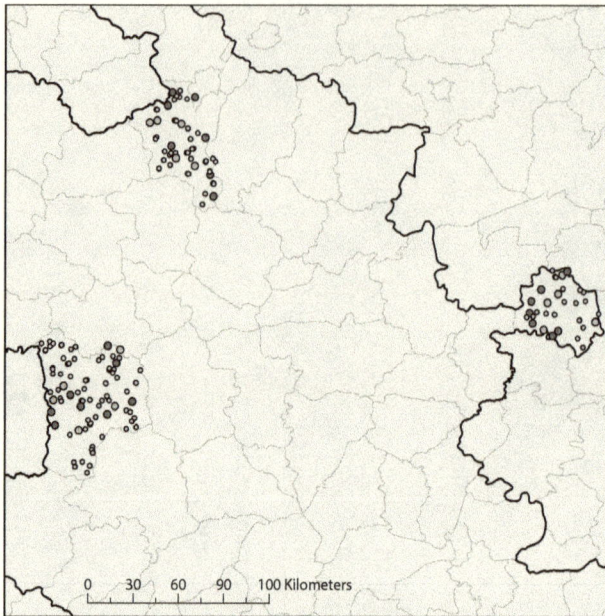

FIGURE 5.4. Counties and Villages in Anhui Province Where the RCT Was Implemented. *Notes*: The RCT was implemented in three counties in Anhui Province. The large, light gray dots represent treatment villages that received a terminal, the large, dark gray dots denote control villages that did not have a terminal, and the small dots represent other program villages that received terminals. In Guizhou and Henan provinces, the RCT was implemented in a similar manner. *Source*: Victor Couture, Benjamin Faber, Yizhen Gu, and Lizhi Liu, 2021. "Connecting the Countryside via E-Commerce: Evidence from China," *American Economic Review: Insights* 3, no. 1: 35–50. Copyright American Economic Association; reproduced with permission of the *American Economic Review: Insights*.

randomization process and baseline data collection (which took two to three weeks to complete).[22] In one county, the local government suspended our data collection for unknown reasons, leaving four of the one hundred villages without endline data.[23] The appendix provides details on the experimental design, including the stratification and randomization process for selecting the RCT locations.

We draw on three unique datasets. The first two are survey datasets collected in conjunction with the RCT: the household survey and price survey. Both were administered in baseline and endline rounds, capturing changes in the outcomes of interest over a period of one year. The third dataset is the firm's internal dataset on a total of 27.8 million transactions/shipments over an eighteen-month period. We used this proprietary dataset to test the representativeness of our one hundred survey villages relative to the general program villages (twelve thousand villages in five provinces) and to test whether our results hold for a longer period of time beyond the RCT timeframe.

Household Survey Data

The longitudinal household survey is the primary dataset of analysis. It consists of two rounds. For the baseline survey conducted in late 2015 and early 2016, we collected data from twenty-eight households per village. Half of those households were randomly sampled within a three-hundred-meter radius of the planned terminal location ("inner zone"), and the other half were randomly sampled from other parts of the village ("outer zone"). The endline survey took place one year after the baseline.[24] We collected data from the same households as in the first round, and we were also able to extend the original sample by ten randomly sampled households within the inner zone (i.e., in total thirty-eight households per village for the endline survey).[25] The respondent in each sampled household was the household member who had the most knowledge about household consumption and income.[26]

Each survey interview took at least an hour to complete. It provided detailed information in four categories: (1) *Consumption*: we documented every retail purchase—both online and offline—made by the household in the recent period[27] prior to the survey interview. The purchased products were classified into nine major categories[28] and production inputs. For each purchase, we collected fine-grained, bar-code-level information, including product category, quantity, description, price, brand, and packaging details. (2) *Income*: we collected information on every possible source of household income (e.g., salaries, government subsidies, and remittances), each household member's work hours, occupation (e.g., farmer, manual worker), and sector (agricultural, manufacturing, and services). (3) *Sociopolitical beliefs*: we surveyed the sociopolitical beliefs of rural households, including whether they intend to migrate, their life satisfaction, attitudes toward local affairs, and level of generalized trust. (4) *Other variables*: we also collected information about internet use, asset ownership, and the financial accounts of rural households, which helped us control for confounding variables.

Local Retail Price Survey Data

We also sought to understand the effects of e-commerce on brick-and-mortar stores, which indirectly affects rural households' welfare. For each village in each survey round, we gathered 115 price quotes from a representative sample of local retail outlets, including physical stores and market stalls.[29] Of these 115 price quotes, fifteen were for business or agricultural inputs, and one hundred were from the nine product categories included in the household survey. To decide how many products to sample in each category, we used rural households' expenditure shares in our primary RCT locations—Anhui and Henan provinces—from the 2012 China Family Panel Study.[30] For each price quote, we collected barcode-equivalent information (e.g., product name, brand, packing type, size, and flavor, if applicable). The whole research protocol closely followed the standards that central banks and international organizations use to compute consumer price indices. Similar to the household survey, we also conducted an endline price survey one year after the baseline survey. In the endline, the surveyors were instructed to record the prices for the identical products at the same stores.[31] This allows us to measure the changes in price quotes over one year.

Alibaba's Administrative Database

Alibaba's administrative database helps answer questions outside the scope of the RCT. It contains two types of information. (1) *Consumption data*: the dataset covers the universe of transaction data for five provinces (the three RCT provinces and two additional provinces, Yunnan and Guangxi, that have high proportions of rural populations) during the research period (November 2015 to April 2017). The dataset contains all online purchases from every village covered by this program in the five provinces,[32] including 27.3 million transactions made at twelve thousand village terminals over a period of eighteen months. For each purchase, the dataset provides information about the village where the terminal was installed, the unique buyer, the product category (three levels from the most general to the most detailed), the number of units purchased, and the amount paid. (2) *Outward shipment data*: the dataset covers the five provinces' universe of external sales from the program villages between January 2016 and April 2017, including information on the village name and the weight of shipments in kilograms. This dataset includes approximately 500,000 observations.

Descriptive Statistics

Appendix Tables A5.1.A–A5.1.C and Tables A5.2–A5.4 present descriptive statistics of the baseline survey data. These tables indicate that the randomization successfully created treatment and control groups that are on average balanced in preexisting baseline outcomes. The discussion below summarizes the key baseline characteristics of the sampled households and local retailers.

FIGURE 5.5. Two RCT Villages

FIGURE 5.6. Satellite Image of a Sampled Village in Guizhou
Province

Individual and Household Characteristics

Our sample of rural households is demographically similar to nationally representative rural household samples from the China Family Panel Study as well as the most recent Chinese Agricultural Census for the year 2016. In the baseline survey, the median household size was three, and the median age of all household members was forty-four. Over half (60 percent) of the households reported that their primary earner was a peasant, and 82 percent reported that the primary earner had at least a primary school education. Rural households in the sample were significantly poorer than the average urban Chinese households: mean monthly per capita income and per capita retail expenditure were approximately 876 RMB and 732 RMB (both lower than $150).

At baseline, households spent on average half of their retail expenditure outside the village (usually in the nearest township center) at a median round-trip distance of forty minutes, and 80 percent of the primary earners worked in the village. Many households reported accessing the internet via smartphones or other devices at baseline: close to 40 percent reported having used the internet; more than 50 percent owned smartphones; and close to 30 percent said they owned a laptop or personal computer. Almost all households owned a television before the project began.

Yet e-commerce penetration was very limited compared to urban areas at baseline: the average share of household retail expenditure on local e-commerce deliveries was less than 1 percent, and this did not change over time for the endline survey in the control villages. Similarly, online selling accounted for less than 0.5 percent of monthly household income at baseline, which remained constant at the endline for the control villages. By comparison, a survey conducted by McKinsey in 2016 found that urban households in China spent, on average, up to 20–30 percent of their total retail consumption on e-commerce deliveries. This indicates a significant rural-urban gap in e-commerce penetration, at least in the short to medium term.

E-Commerce vs. Preexisting Market Channels

The local retail surveys indicate the characteristics of local physical stores before the launch of e-commerce. The median number of physical stores per village was three at baseline. These stores were small, with a median floor space of 50 m^2, and the median store had not added any new products within the previous month (Appendix Table A5.4). The surveys show that durable goods (furniture and appliances, electronics, and transport equipment) were more expensive than nondurable goods.

The e-commerce option compared favorably with the preexisting market channels in terms of accessibility, product variety, and value for money. In terms of accessibility, rural households sourced more than half of their total retail consumption and almost 70 percent of their durable goods consumption outside their villages at baseline (Appendix Table A5.3). This is not surprising, given that our surveyors could not find any durable goods in local stores in about half of the sample villages. Households' main reported shopping destination outside the village was a median roundtrip distance of 10 kilometers, representing a forty-minute round-trip journey at a median cost of 4 RMB (60 cents). In contrast, the e-commerce terminals were much closer to our sampled households, with a median distance of 230 meters.

The terminal also offered cheaper products, and a greater variety of products, than those available in local physical stores. Sixty-two percent of all goods (and 84 percent of durable goods) bought through the e-commerce terminal were previously unavailable in the village. When goods were available at both the terminal and in the village, the terminal was cheaper by a median price reduction of 15 percent.[33] The nearest main shopping destination outside the village generally offered more variety (80 percent of goods purchased on the terminal are available there), but the terminal remained cheaper by a median of 18 percent, even before accounting for transport costs. Given the fast turnaround at the warehouse locations, e-commerce delivery times in the program villages were almost as fast as those in urban regions within the county.

Analyzing the Welfare Impacts of E-Commerce Access

This section empirically investigates the economic effects of e-commerce access on rural household welfare, including the average program effects on consumption and production, the program's heterogeneous economic effects across households and villages, and the spillover effects across villages. After considering all of these effects, we quantify total household welfare upon the arrival of e-commerce.

Average Program Effects

We run regressions of the following form:

$$y_{hv}^{Post} = \alpha + \beta_1 Treat_v + \gamma y_{hv}^{Pre} + \epsilon_{hv}, \tag{1}$$

where y_{hv} is the outcome of interest for household h living in village v.[34] For outcomes from the retail price data, h indexes individual price quotes or store-level outcomes instead. $Treat_v$ is either an indicator of randomly assigned treatment status when estimating the intent-to-treat effect (ITT) or actual treatment status when estimating the treatment-on-the-treated effect (TOT) and instrumenting with intended treatment. We cluster standard errors at the treatment (village) level and report point estimates both individually and after combining outcomes into category indices following Kling et al. (2007) (KLK).

Table 5.1 presents the estimation results from the average effects on household consumption (Panel A), incomes (Panel B), and local retail prices (Panel C). Our discussion here focuses on the TOT results.

HOUSEHOLD CONSUMPTION

On average, the program led to a 9 percent increase in the number of households using the new e-commerce option in treatment villages compared to control villages. As documented by the nonzero mean among control villages, this effect masks additional uptake due to users in nearby control villages, which increases the effect on uptake to about 14 percent of village households. We further investigate such spillovers at the end of this section. The treatment effect on e-commerce's share of total household retail expenditures is 1.24 percent for the average village household. Thus, households that report having engaged in e-commerce spent, on average, 0.0124 / 0.089 = 14.1 percent of their retail consumption online during the past month.

We find stronger effects for durables than nondurables. The average household spends 6.9 percent of its total household expenditure on durables online, indicating a 45 percent shift in durable consumption to the new e-commerce option among uptaking households.[35] For nondurables, the treatment effect on the share of household retail expenditure is 1 percent for the average household, indicating that ever-users spend on average about 11 percent of their total nondurables expenditure online. While households do shift part of their expenditures to e-commerce, there are no significant treatment effects on total monthly retail expenditures. The last column of Table 5.1, Panel A, combines eleven outcomes related to substitution into e-commerce into a single index, defined as the equally weighted average of z-scores that are calculated by subtracting the mean and dividing by the standard deviation of the control group. The treatment effect on this index is 0.89 and is significant at the 1 percent level.[36]

INCOMES

Table 5.1, Panel B, reports point estimates on per capita incomes that are close to zero and not statistically significant. As above, we also report a single index combining fourteen outcomes related to income generation. We find no effects

TABLE 5.1. Average Effects on Household Welfare

—Panel A: Consumption—

	Monthly Retail Expenditure Per Capita in RMB		Has Bought Something through E-Comm Option (Yes = 1)		Share of E-Comm Option in Monthly Total Retail Expenditure		Share of E-Comm Option in Monthly Durables Expenditure		Share of E-Comm Option in Monthly Nondurables Expenditure		Consumption Effects (K-L-K Index)	
	ITT	TOT	ITT	TOT	ITT	TOT	ITT	TOT	ITT	TOT	ITT	TOT
Treat	−22.09	−41.20	0.0484[a]	0.0894[a]	0.00668[a]	0.0124[a]	0.0408[b]	0.0686[a]	0.00538[a]	0.01[a]	0.478[a]	0.885[a]
	(31.99)	(60.22)	(0.0167)	(0.0268)	(0.00239)	(0.00435)	(0.0160)	(0.0263)	(0.00196)	(0.00356)	(0.0336)	(0.126)
R-Squared	0.038		0.008		0.006		0.012		0.003		0.118	
Control Mean	592.21		0.0501		0.00277		0.0152		0.0027		0.00	
1st Stage F		44.01		45.31		44.03		52.43		44.11		44.94
Obs	3,436	3,436	3,518	3,518	3,434	3,434	768	768	3,433	3,433	3,539	3,539

—Panel B: Nominal Incomes—

	Monthly Income Per Capita in RMB		Income Effects (K-L-K Index)	
	ITT	TOT	ITT	TOT
Treat	−7.864	−14.53	−0.0309	−0.0572
	(70.78)	(129.9)	(0.0349)	(0.0646)
R-Squared	0.038		0.002	
Control Mean	915.51		0.00	
1st Stage F		45.33		45.01
Obs	3,437	3,437	3,538	3,538

—Panel C: Local Retail Prices—

	Log Prices		Product Replacement Dummy		Production Addition Dummy		Price Effects (K-L-K Index)	
	ITT	TOT	ITT	TOT	ITT	TOT	ITT	TOT
Treat	0.0189	0.0352	−0.00392	−0.00747	2.194[b]	4.020[c]	−0.217	−0.389
	(0.0142)	(0.0263)	(0.0300)	(0.0569)	(1.073)	(2.278)	(0.134)	(0.260)
R-Squared	0.893		0.00		0.277		0.010	
Control Mean	1.9813		0.0828		0.626		0.00	
1st Stage F		41.66		39.82		19.69		24.05
Obs	6,877	6,877	8,956	8,956	312	312	343	343

Notes: Table reports point estimates from specification (1). Outcomes in panels A and B are at the household level. KLK consumption index based on 11 variables related to substitution into e-commerce, all entering positively (reducing price index). KLK income index based on 14 variables related to income generation, 13 entering positively and one negatively. In panel C, the first four columns are at the individual product item level. The final four columns are at the store level. KLK retail index based on four store-level variables, with two entering positively (reducing price index) and two negatively. Standard errors are clustered at the level of villages: a 1%, b 5%, c 10% significance levels. *Source:* Victor Couture, Benjamin Faber, Yizhen Gu, and Lizhi Liu. 2021. "Connecting the Countryside via E-Commerce: Evidence from China." *American Economic Review: Insights* 3, no. 1: 35–50.

on annual or monthly incomes, from agricultural or nonagricultural sources, on labor supply as measured by hours worked by the primary (or secondary) earner or on online selling activity, online revenues, sourcing of business inputs, or business creation (offline or online). In terms of precision, the ITT point estimate on the income index indicates detectable positive effects down to about 2.6 percent of a standard deviation (one-sided 95 percent CI).

LOCAL RETAIL PRICES

In Table 5.1, Panel C, we find no significant reduction in local store prices for products that we observe for sale at the same local retailer at both baseline and endline. The point estimate is close to zero and positive, and not statistically significant. Given our sampling framework, the unweighted average effect on local retail prices is akin to the Laspeyres price index for local retail consumption. We also find no effect when combining four outcomes related to local retail prices and product exit/additions into a single index. We find one piece of evidence that suggests knock-on effects on preexisting local stores: the effect on the number of new products per store over the past month is four goods and is significant at the 10 percent level.

Heterogeneity across Households and Villages

In Table 5.2, we turn to the heterogeneity of the effects: which types of households and villages benefit the most from e-commerce. We begin by investigating the effect of the program as a function of preexisting availability of commercial parcel delivery at the village level. Villages serviced by commercial parcel delivery operators during our baseline survey already had access to local e-commerce deliveries. Interacting the treatment with preexisting parcel delivery status therefore allows us to shed light on the combined effect of removing both logistical and transactional barriers (among villages *without* preexisting parcel delivery) from the effect of removing only the transactional barrier (adding a terminal interface in villages *with* preexisting parcel delivery).[37] Next, we investigate heterogeneity across a basic set of household demographics that have been documented in recent studies of internet and e-commerce use in China (respondent age, education, and income per capita).[38] We also consider residential distance to the planned terminal location and a measure of village remoteness (motivated by Fan et al. 2018) based on road travel distance to the nearest township center. One should note that these interaction terms are not causally identified by experimental variation and provide additional suggestive evidence.

We estimated regressions of the following form:

$$y_{hv}^{Post} = \alpha + \beta_1 \text{Treat}_v + \beta_2 X_{hv} + \beta_3 \text{Treat}_v \times X_{hv} + \gamma y_{hv}^{Pre} + \epsilon_{hv}, \qquad (2)$$

where X_{hv} indicates various preexisting household or village characteristics. As before, we report the regression results for both ITT and TOT and after replacing the binary treatment variable with log household residential distance from the nearest terminal location (again using intended treatment status as an instrumental variable (IV)). We first run regressions in which one characteristic at a time is interacted with the treatment, and then a combined regression with all interactions included jointly.

On the consumption side, the effect on program uptake is driven by villages that were not initially connected to commercial parcel delivery services. The treatment effect is 10.6 percent among the roughly 85 percent of villages not previously connected to commercial parcel delivery, but it is a relatively precise zero for villages with preexisting parcel delivery. On the production and local retail sides, we find no significant effects in either group of villages, confirming the earlier pooled results. Turning to other potential sources of heterogeneity, we find that younger, richer households that live closer to the planned terminal and those in more remote villages experience a sharper increase in consumption. For example, consumption uptake would close to double if average incomes were to double and primary earners were on average ten years younger. Somewhat surprisingly, we find no significant heterogeneity with respect to the years of education.

Spillovers

We investigate the role of spillovers that could bias our findings from the survey data. For example, if trade linkages with surrounding villages are an important driver of the local economy, then the comparison between treated and control villages could miss income or retail price effects. More simply, residents in control villages could use e-commerce terminals in a nearby treated village. To investigate these forces, we follow Miguel and Kremer (2004) and use variation in a village's exposure to other nearby treated villages after controlling for proximity to all villages.[39] On the consumption side, we find evidence of positive spillovers from nearby terminals in other villages, as previewed above. Yet we find no evidence of cross-village spillovers on retail stores or on the production side. Consistent with the absence of income or price spillovers, we also confirm in microdata from the 2010 census that the fraction of village market access driven by trade with other nearby rural markets is minor (less than 3 percent).[40]

TABLE 5.2. Heterogeneity across Households and Villages

Type of Heterogeneity		Household Has Bought Something through E-Comm Option (Yes = 1)		Monthly Income Per Capita in RMB		Log Local Retail Prices	
		ITT	TOT	ITT	TOT	ITT	TOT
Village Was Previously Connected to Parcel Delivery (Yes = 1)	Treat	0.0578[a]	0.106[a]	−15.00	−27.15	0.0114	0.0215
		(0.0188)	(0.0283)	(77.55)	(140.1)	(0.0144)	(0.0273)
	Treat * Delivery	−0.0606[b]	−0.111[b]	50.17	96.91	0.0417	0.0739
		(0.0253)	(0.0443)	(171.1)	(339.0)	(0.0377)	(0.0572)
	First Stage F	2.682		2.694		17.26	
Village Distance to Township Center	Treat	−0.0144	−0.00652	−23.61	−43.80	−0.0219	−0.0322
		(0.0281)	(0.0411)	(181.7)	(289.1)	(0.0375)	(0.0632)
	Treat * Log Dist Township	0.0384[b]	0.0606[a]	0.422	0.422	0.0216	0.0358
		(0.0161)	(0.0223)	(97.49)	(152.0)	(0.0198)	(0.0336)
	First Stage F	15.55		15.66		16.96	
Primary Earner's Age	Treat	0.141[a]	0.223[a]	−136.5	−238.0		
		(0.0505)	(0.0777)	(172.5)	(286.5)		
	Treat * Age	−0.00172[b]	−0.00251[c]	2.563	4.554		
		(0.000773)	(0.00129)	(2.734)	(4.825)		
	First Stage F	16.04		16.34			
Primary Earner's Education	Treat	0.0408[c]	0.0979[b]	52.81	119.7		
		(0.0206)	(0.0412)	(83.52)	(195.0)		
	Treat * Years of Education	0.00164	−0.000432	−8.672	−17.80		
		(0.00266)	(0.00504)	(12.14)	(24.03)		
	First Stage F	8.456		8.662			

		(1)	(2)	(3)	(4)	(5)	(6)
Household Income Per Capita	Treat	0.00863	0.0220	35.83	59.45		
		(0.0214)	(0.0375)	(96.84)	(165.5)		
	Treat * Log Income	0.00708[b]	0.0120[b]	−9.201	−15.78		
		(0.00327)	(0.00544)	(21.22)	(36.32)		
	First Stage F	22.67	22.57	22.67	22.57		
Household Distance to Planned Terminal	Treat	0.142[b]	0.227[b]	185.8	400.0		
		(0.0600)	(0.110)	(350.6)	(697.5)		
	Treat * Log Dist Terminal	−0.0177[c]	−0.0264	−36.53	−79.65		
		(0.0100)	(0.0196)	(61.53)	(128.5)		
	First Stage F	9.899			9.325		
Combined	Treat	0.153[c]	0.287[b]	174.5	330.1	−0.0398	−0.0435
		(0.0811)	(0.141)	(329.9)	(612.1)	(0.0362)	(0.0531)
	Treat * Delivery	−0.0401	−0.106	102.1	253.3	0.0413	0.0517
		(0.0286)	(0.0690)	(121.1)	(308.1)	(0.0361)	(0.0622)
	Treat * Log Dist Township	0.0457[a]	0.0809[a]	−42.86	−93.17	0.0284	0.0380
		(0.0173)	(0.0296)	(58.39)	(128.5)	(0.0188)	(0.0312)
	Treat * Age	−0.00181[b]	−0.00314[b]	0.587	1.266		
		(0.000775)	(0.00130)	(2.555)	(4.602)		
	Treat * Years of Education	0.000384	−0.00377	−2.230	−1.954		
		(0.00267)	(0.00497)	(10.01)	(21.43)		
	Treat * Log Income	0.00907[a]	0.0162[a]	−8.451	−14.28		
		(0.00339)	(0.00556)	(22.00)	(37.97)		
	Treat * Log Dist Terminal	−0.0248[b]	−0.0411[c]	−16.48	−34.37		
		(0.0109)	(0.0222)	(45.01)	(94.93)		
	First Stage F	0.479	0.479	0.419	0.419		1.579

Notes: Based on the same samples as Table 5.1. Standard errors are clustered at the level of villages: a 1%, b 5%, c 10% significance levels. *Source:* Victor Couture, Benjamin Faber, Yizhen Gu, and Lizhi Liu. 2021. "Connecting the Countryside via E-Commerce: Evidence from China." *American Economic Review: Insights* 3, no. 1: 35–50.

Quantification of Household Welfare

The most robust effect we find is for the substitution of local households' retail expenditures to the new e-commerce shopping option. To quantify the cost of living implications consistent with these estimates, we follow a revealed-preference approach as in recent work by Atkin et al. (2018) and classify household preferences into three tiers: (1) the upper tier is Cobb-Douglas over broad product groups $g \in G$ (durables and nondurables) in total consumption, (2) the middle tier is constant elasticity of substitution (CES) across retailers $s \in S$ selling that product group (e.g., local stores, market stalls, or the e-commerce option), and (3) the final tier is across individual products within groups $b \in B_g$ that can be left unspecified.[41] The direct consumer gains from the arrival of the e-commerce option, measured as a percentage of initial household expenditure, can then be expressed as follows:

$$\frac{Gains_n}{Initial\ Expenditure_h} = \prod_{g \in G} \left(\left(\sum_{s \in S_g^C} \phi_{gsh}^1 \right)^{\frac{1}{\sigma_g - 1}} \right)^{\alpha_{gh}} - 1, \qquad (3)$$

where σ_g is the elasticity of substitution across retail options to source consumption in product group g, a_{gh} is the initial expenditure share of that product group for household group h, and is $\sum_{s \in S_g^C} \phi_{gsh}^1$ the share of retail expenditures that is not spent on the new e-commerce option after the intervention (where $s \in S_g^C$ indexes continuing local retailers and ϕ_{gsh}^1 is the endline expenditure share of retailer s in product group g of household group h).

To estimate this expression, we need information about the program's effect on $\sum_{s \in S_g^C} \phi_{gsh}^1$ and the parameters a_{gh} and σ_g. For the a_{gh}, we use our baseline data on household expenditure shares across product groups. For ex post expenditure shares on the new e-commerce option, we use the treatment effects among the 85 percent of villages without access to parcel deliveries at baseline reported in Table 5.2. These villages experienced the removal of both logistical and transactional barriers to e-commerce. We include mean program usage among control villages in these treatment effects to account for program spillovers, as discussed above.

We perform this welfare computation for two groups of local households: (1) the average sample household, for whom the average effect on the terminal share of total retail consumption is 1.6 percent and (2) households that report ever having used the terminal for consumption, for which this effect is 14 percent. We also estimate price index effects separately for durable and nondurable consumption, and report estimates both with and without reweighting households according to sampling weights. Finally, we calibrate σ_g using estimates from Atkin et al. (2018) for households in Mexico with incomes comparable to those of rural Chinese households in our survey ($\sigma_N = 3.87$ for nondurables and $\sigma_D = 3.85$ for durables).

Table 5.3 reports the estimation results. The average reduction in the retail cost of living among households that experienced the lifting of both logistical and transactional barriers is 0.82 percent. This effect increases to 5.6 percent among the roughly 15 percent of households that ever used the new e-commerce option. These effects are slightly lower at 0.73 percent and 4.7 percent, respectively, when weighting our sample households to represent the average population living in these villages. Underlying these effects are strong consumer gains in durable consumption: 3 percent for the average village household and 16.6 percent among e-commerce users. For reference, retail consumption across all product groups accounts for an average of 55 percent of total household expenditure among the rural households in the sample.[42]

Finally, to investigate the distribution of these gains, we use treatment effects from the joint heterogeneity specification in the bottom panel of Table 5.2. We estimate this specification by defining the household expenditure share spent via the new e-commerce option for either durables or nondurables as the dependent variable. For each sample household in treatment villages without preexisting parcel delivery, we then compute a fitted value of the effect on $\sum_{s \in S_g^C} \phi_{gsh}^{t1}$, based on the primary earner's age, per capita income, residential distance from the planned terminal, and distance from the nearest township center (remoteness), included jointly (see Figure 5.7). Ranking households along each of these dimensions, we find more than a fourfold difference in the price index effect within the sample. For example, the average rural household with a twenty-five-year-old primary earner experiences a reduction in the retail cost of living of about 1.5 percent (without conditioning on uptake), which drops below 1 percent past the age of forty and close to zero past the age of sixty.

Additional Evidence from the Firm's Database

The previous analysis is based on the results of surveys, which could only capture changes over a year due to time and budget constraints. A potential concern is that these findings do not apply to a larger set of villages covered by the program or beyond the experiment period. We therefore use the firm's internal transaction database to supplement the survey findings. In this section, we

TABLE 5.3. Average Effects on Household Welfare

	Unweighted (Effects in Sample)			Weighted (Effects in Village Population)		
	Durables Consumption	Nondurables Consumption	Total Retail Consumption	Durables Consumption	Nondurables Consumption	Total Retail Consumption
Reduction in Retail Cost of Living for All Households	3.379% (0.03)	0.481% (0.003)	0.824% (0.005)	2.962% (0.03)	0.429% (0.003)	0.73% (0.005)
Reduction in Retail Cost of Living among Users	19.884% (0.221)	3.806% (0.028)	5.597% (0.034)	16.637% (0.224)	3.217% (0.025)	4.722% (0.032)

Notes: The table reports average household gains in terms of percentage-point reductions in the retail cost of living for different consumption categories and groups of households. Estimates are based on equation (3) using treatment effects on household substitution into the new e-commerce option. The left panel reports unweighted results, and the right panel adjusts the weight of each household using sampling weights. Standard errors are bootstrapped across 1,000 iterations, considering that the treatment effects are point estimates. *Source:* Victor Couture, Benjamin Faber, Yizhen Gu, and Lizhi Liu. 2021. "Connecting the Countryside via E-Commerce: Evidence from China." *American Economic Review: Insights* 3, no. 1: 35–50.

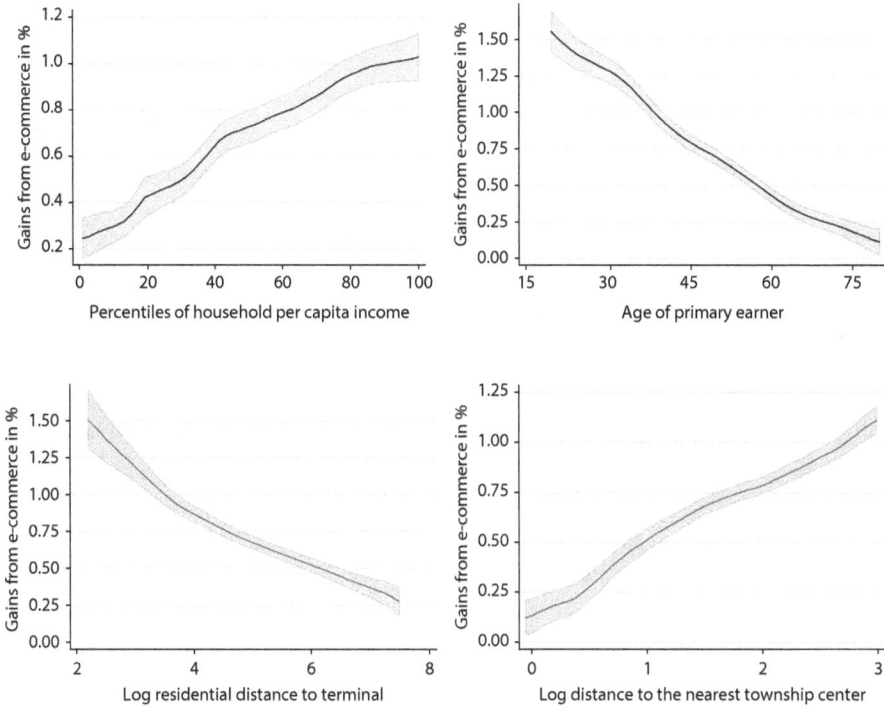

FIGURE 5.7. Heterogeneity of Gains from E-Commerce. *Notes*: The figure shows predicted average gains (users and nonusers) in terms of percentage-point reductions in household retail cost of living as a function of household per capita income (*top left*), age of primary earner (*top right*), residential distance from terminal (*bottom left*), and distance from the nearest township center (*bottom right*). Predictions are based on treatment effects from the bottom panel of Table 5.2. The figure depicts 95 percent confidence intervals that are based on clustering standard errors at the village level. *Source*: Victor Couture, Benjamin Faber, Yizhen Gu, and Lizhi Liu, 2021. "Connecting the Countryside via E-Commerce: Evidence from China," *American Economic Review: Insights* 3, no. 1: 35–50. Copyright American Economic Association; reproduced with permission of the *American Economic Review: Insights*.

focus on two important questions. First, what is the time path of adjustments on the consumption and production sides, and does terminal take-up increase beyond our survey's twelve-month posttreatment time window? Second, is our survey data missing rare but highly successful tail events on the production side that could shift the average effect on local household incomes?

Appendix D reports two additional findings from the firm's database. First, the one hundred RCT villages are broadly representative of all twelve thousand program villages in five provinces, i.e., the three RCT provinces plus Guangxi and Yunnan, where the firm has over 40 percent of all program villages.[43] Second, seasonality of data collection is unlikely to drive our survey findings in the RCT.

What Is the Time Path of Adjustments in Consumption and Production?

A potential concern is that the RCT period may be too short to fully capture the treatment effects. Since the program aimed to continuously roll out e-commerce in the counties where we did the experiment, we could not keep our control group unconnected for more than a year. To what extent did the effects of e-commerce access on consumption and production increase beyond our one-year study period?

To answer this question, we use the universe of transaction records from five provinces and about twelve thousand villages that had been treated by April 2017 to estimate the following event-study specification:

$$y_{vm} = \theta_v + \delta_m + \sum_{j=-3}^{24} \beta_j \text{ Months Since Entry}_{jvm} + \epsilon_{vm}, \tag{4}$$

where v indexes villages, δ_m is a set of month fixed effects between November 2015 and April 2017, and θ_v is a village fixed effect. Each observation in equation (4) is a village v in a given month m. y_{vm} is one of the four village-level monthly outcomes: number of buyers, number of purchase transactions, number of out-shipments, or total weight of out-shipments in kilograms. We created a balanced panel in the sense that each village appears once per month in the panel, for each of the eighteen months for which we have data (sixteen months in the shipment data). This spans terminal observations of up to seventeen months preinstallation for villages connected in April 2017, and up to twenty-eight months postinstallation for the earliest villages connected by the program. A negative index j denotes the number of months prior to program entry. A positive j indexes the number of months since the program began operating, so β_0 is a measure of average outcomes for villages during the month of their installation, β_1 captures averages one month after installation, and so on. We assigned an index of $j = 24$ to all observations at or beyond twenty-four months after program entry, so β_{24} captures average outcomes among villages that have been in operation for more than two years. Each of $\beta_0 - \beta_{24}$ is estimated relative to the omitted category of periods preprogram entry (zeros by construction since the program did not exist).[44]

Figure 5.8 presents the event-study plots for village-level outcomes on the consumption and production sides. On the consumption side, we find little evidence of increased consumption after the endline survey. Program usage increases rapidly for about two to four months after opening and then plateaued at around eighty-five buyers and 280 transactions per month per village.[45] On the production side, we find evidence that the number and total weight of out-shipments increases smoothly over time after program entry and beyond the twelve-month window covered in our survey data. The effect increases by roughly 50 percent when comparing the point estimate on the total weight of out-shipments twelve months post-entry to that of more than two years post-entry. These results suggest that production-side adjustments take longer to fully materialize than our survey's one-year horizon. Despite this positive trend, the average monthly estimated effects at the village level remained small more than two years after implementation, at around ten out-shipments with a combined weight of thirty kilograms.

Are the Survey Data Missing Successful Tail Events on the Production Side?

Our sampling of thirty-eight households per village may be too small to capture rare but highly successful tail events on the production side, leading to biased estimates of average treatment effects on local household incomes. To determine whether this is the case, we examine the universe of e-commerce out-shipments depicted in Figure 5.8.

To obtain an upper-bound estimate for these shipments' potential income creation in the local village economy, we assume that: (1) the entire value of these shipments is local value added and captured by local incomes and (2) the shipments' average value per kilogram is as high as that of Chinese exports to the world (i.e., on average RMB 66.5 per kilogram in 2015 and 2016).[46] Even under these assumptions, we find that e-commerce out-shipments account for on average at most a 0.17 percent increase in local income per capita more than two years after the program's arrival. Therefore, this average longer-term effect—that we can estimate precisely in the firm's administrative data— would still be consistent with the statistical zero result on incomes and the production side that we find using the RCT survey data after one year.

Summary of RCT Findings

The RCT study reveals that access to e-commerce generates significant welfare gains for the rural households that use it. Such access creates welfare gains of roughly 180,000 RMB (approximately $28,000) per village per year, or a total

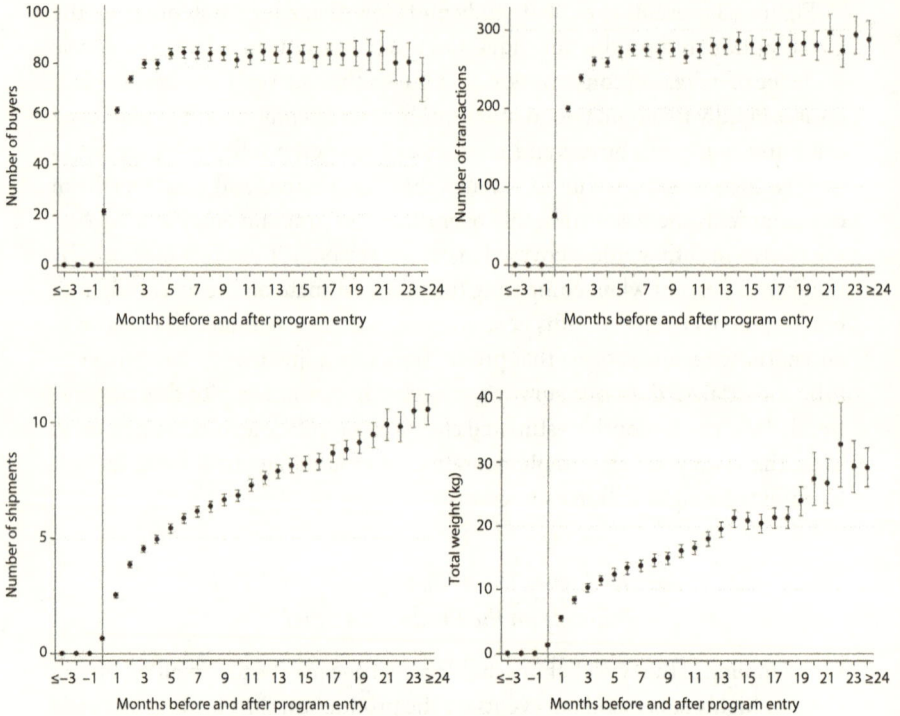

FIGURE 5.8. Timeline of Adjustment: Village E-Commerce Consumption and Out-Shipments. *Notes*: The figure shows point estimates from a regression of depicted outcomes on the number of months since program entry, and village and month fixed effects. The outcomes are the number of buyers (*top left*), number of transactions (*top right*), number of out-shipments (*bottom left*), and the total weight of out-shipments (*bottom right*) for each village. The data are from the e-commerce firm's internal database and contain the universe of village purchase transactions from November 2015 to April 2017 and the universe of sales transactions from January 2016 to April 2017 in the five provinces of Anhui, Guangxi, Guizhou, Henan, and Yunnan (roughly twelve thousand villages in total). The last point estimate of each plot pools months twenty-four to twenty-eight. The figure shows 95 percent confidence intervals based on standard errors clustered at the village level. *Source*: Victor Couture, Benjamin Faber, Yizhen Gu, and Lizhi Liu, 2021. "Connecting the Countryside via E-Commerce: Evidence from China," *American Economic Review: Insights* 3, no. 1: 35–50. Copyright American Economic Association; reproduced with permission of the *American Economic Review: Insights*.

of approximately 5.4 billion RMB ($84 million) each year for the thirty thousand villages participating in the program at the time of writing.

However, not all rural households have embraced the option of e-commerce, leaving ample potential for further expansion. Participating households represent approximately 14 percent of the village population after a year of treatment, which the firm's transaction dataset demonstrates remains constant beyond twelve months. The relatively low adoption rate can be attributed, in part, to the demographic composition of typical Chinese villages. The migration of many young individuals to cities for employment results in a hollowing out of village populations, leaving behind mainly children and elderly family members who are less receptive to e-commerce.

The welfare gains are subject to four types of strong heterogeneity. First, the beneficiaries tend to be younger, wealthier, live closer to the program's terminals, and reside in more remote villages. Second, the welfare gains generated by e-commerce are largely driven by the removal of logistical rather than transactional barriers. For instance, welfare gains are mostly limited to villages that could not previously receive commercial parcel deliveries. Third, the consumption effects are particularly pronounced for durable goods such as electronics and appliances. Last, there is suggestive evidence of knock-on effects on the local retail environment: local storeowners reported slightly higher numbers of new product varieties and a higher likelihood of sourcing their products online in treated villages without prior commercial parcel delivery services. However, we do not find significant procompetitive effects on product prices among local stores.

Importantly, the welfare gains from e-commerce access are mainly driven by the consumption side rather than the production end. E-commerce generates consumption-side welfare by offering cheaper prices, more product variety, better shopping amenities, and reduced travel costs. As a result, e-commerce reduces the cost of living and increases households' purchasing power.

There is little evidence of production-side effects of e-commerce in the RCT area, at least in the short to medium term. No evidence shows that e-commerce access significantly affects entrepreneurship, household production, or online selling activities for average rural areas. It is noteworthy that the null findings on selling activities do not appear to be driven by the effectiveness of program implementation (see Appendix Table A5.16), as the characteristics of terminal managers did not emerge as significant determinants of the program's impact. Rather, it appears to be linked to the general conditions prevalent in rural areas and the specific characteristics of agricultural products. First, many interviews suggest that agricultural products are more difficult to sell online than typical manufactured products such as clothes, as the former are usually not standardized, have special packing requirements, and are difficult to transport and preserve.[47] Selling such products online therefore requires a great deal of effort and expertise, which sets a high bar for entry for the average rural household. Second, rural areas still face many obstacles to online entrepreneurship, including a lack of human capital and complementary resources for selling activities such as education and credits.

The economic effects of e-commerce above have two implications for rural development. First, e-commerce-induced market integration is likely to *concentrate* rather than *decentralize* production. The hope that e-commerce can reverse the fortune of small producers and poor areas by granting cheap market access has been realized to some extent, because e-commerce can bring consumption benefits everywhere and reduce households' costs of living. However, not all areas or producers can exploit this new market opportunity to sell. While the rise of e-commerce villages illustrates that online selling can turn rural locales into highly prosperous production hubs, there are relatively few such villages, and their success is not easy to replicate. Our RCT demonstrates that such transformative production effects are not representative in the short to medium run.

A second, related implication is that the urban-rural economic gap is *not* primarily due to rural areas lacking access to urban markets, but rather the lack of human capital and complementary business resources in rural areas.[48] These factors are difficult to change, even if rural households obtain market access through e-commerce. It seems unlikely that significant production-side effects will emerge organically in average rural areas without complementary interventions such as business training, access to online credit, and targeted online promotions.

E-Commerce's Effects on Urban Areas

To understand the overall effects of e-commerce in China, it is essential to examine urban areas, where the majority of e-commerce activities occur. As previously mentioned, it is impossible to conduct the same RCT in urban areas since e-commerce access was already widespread prior to the research period, leaving little variation to explore.

Although we cannot directly generalize our rural-based RCT results to urban areas, they offer valuable insights. The RCT serves as a "hard test" for the effects of e-commerce. If e-commerce can produce effects even in rural villages where its adoption is less likely, we can reasonably expect stronger effects in urban areas. Therefore, the rural RCT findings can be considered a lower bound estimate of e-commerce's effects in urban areas. By combining our RCT findings with other recent research, I will discuss the differences between rural and urban areas and the inferred effects in urban settings.

Substantial Overall Welfare Generation

The RCT study reveals significant welfare improvements for those who adopt e-commerce. Given the higher adoption rate of e-commerce in urban areas and their more favorable conditions—such as wealth, demographic structure, and logistics infrastructure—urban areas are expected to have significantly larger welfare gains than observed in rural villages.

Only 14 percent of our RCT village population used e-commerce at the end of the one-year study period, compared to 61.4 percent in first- and second-tier cities and approximately 36.8 percent in lower-tier cities in 2018.[49] Urban households also already spent a much higher portion of their disposable income online: 20–30 percent in 2012[50] compared to less than 1 percent found in the RCT study (conducted a few years later).

Distributional Effects across Households and Regions

Although urban areas have more e-commerce activities, I anticipate that the distributional effects will parallel those observed in rural areas. For example, younger, wealthier families spend more on e-commerce, and education does not necessarily significantly affect e-commerce usage.

Consistent with the RCT finding that more remote villages benefit more from e-commerce, there is also evidence that lower-tier cities benefit more from e-commerce, likely because residents of lower-tier cities have fewer offline options. Fan et al. (2016) have shown that the rise of e-commerce has led to a net increase in domestic trade, particularly among cities in the lowest quintile of market potential and population. This suggests that e-commerce can reduce cross-city inequality in terms of living standards, as smaller cities benefit disproportionately from access to a variety of goods.[51]

The Conjunction of Substitution and New Consumption

Some insignificant RCT results may become significant in urban areas due to the high intensity of e-commerce activities. Our RCT findings indicate that the arrival of e-commerce does not significantly change the overall level of retail consumption, which suggests that the new mode of shopping has simply substituted offline retail without generating new consumption.

However, both anecdotal and correlational evidence indicates that e-commerce creates new consumption in urban areas, indicating a degree of osuccess in the government's strategy to boost domestic consumption through e-commerce. Although causality should be approached with caution, a 2011 McKinsey report finds that, at the time, 61 percent of every 1 RMB spent online resulted from the substitution of offline spending, while 39 percent represented new consumption driven by e-commerce.[52] The report also highlights that online shoppers in lower-tier cities spent a higher share of their income online. These findings have been confirmed by a more recent and rigorous empirical study: Fan et al. (2016) have revealed that while e-commerce indeed substitutes for offline trade, the rise of e-commerce has led to a net increase in domestic trade.

Disruptions to Offline Retail

In contrast to the RCT findings, the increase in urban e-commerce has greatly disrupted brick-and-mortar stores. Urban residents have shifted a substantial share of their offline shopping to online stores, leading to a reportedly large wave of store closures and loss of sales. As brick-and-mortar stores cannot compete with e-commerce on price or convenience, there have been efforts to empower offline stores. The concept of "new retail" (新零售) aims to seamlessly merge online and offline shopping experiences. For example, customers can try the products in offline "experience stores" and then order online, so that a small physical store can generate large profits.[53]

Effects Beyond the Scope of the RCT

The RCT analysis focuses on e-commerce's direct effects on household welfare, consumption, production, and entrepreneurship, as these effects are both critical and quantifiable. However, e-commerce also impacts China's technological and logistical capacity, which are often overlooked or difficult to quantify.

The explosive demand generated by e-commerce sales events has forced platforms to build technology capacity, allowing their systems to simultaneously process huge numbers of orders without crashing. For example, on Singles' Day in 2012, Alibaba's system crashed within ten minutes, but in 2019, its cloud and AI technologies successfully handled the first $1 billion in sales within sixty-eight seconds and a peak order rate of 544,000 per second with zero system downtime.[54] The AI algorithms accurately predicted the products and quantities that would be purchased in each area, allowing local warehouses to preload packages before the sales event and deliver them quickly. As a result, many urban residents received products only a few hours after placing orders on Singles' Day in 2020.[55]

E-commerce has also spurred the development of a highly efficient express delivery industry that in 2020 accounted for more than half the global total, at eighty-three billion packages[56]—an average of fifty-nine per person.[57] Express delivery services have penetrated even remote pockets of the country, covering

98 percent of all townships and half of all villages in 2020.[58] By 2018, JD.com could make 90 percent of all deliveries within twenty-four hours, and 57 percent within twelve hours; thirty-minute deliveries are even possible.[59]

While initially designed for the online market, such technological and logistical capacities can create positive externalities for other commercial activities. They can even indirectly strengthen the government's ability to achieve policy goals. For example, the e-commerce and logistics industries contributed substantially to China's coronavirus pandemic control, as they ensured the fast delivery of personal protective equipment, food, and daily products during the lockdown.[60]

Concluding Remarks

This chapter provides the first experimental evidence of the economic effects of e-commerce in China. Its findings have three broad implications.

To begin with, like many other aspects of the digital economy, e-commerce has distributive effects and ramifications for inequality. The study suggests that despite the state's efforts to provide widespread access to digital technologies, inequality persists due to variations in the readiness and willingness of different regions and demographic groups to utilize them. For example, we find that younger, wealthier families are more likely to use e-commerce and reap its benefits. However, the impact of e-commerce on inequality is intricate because it also brings more benefits to remote, economically disadvantaged villages. Similar to global trade, e-commerce as a "digital highway" seems to have a dual effect on inequality: it can alleviate inequality *across* regions by improving conditions in the poorest areas, but it may also widen inequality *within* regions by further empowering already advantaged households.

This finding echoes insights by Paul DiMaggio and Eszter Hargittai (2001): as internet technologies thrive, the source of inequality will move *from a digital divide to digital inequality*. The digital divide concerns "inequality between 'haves' and 'have-nots' differentiated by dichotomous measures of access to or use of the new technologies,"[61] but digital inequality exists within a group of "haves"— those who all have formal access to technologies but do not enjoy the same equipment, skills, social support, and other crucial conditions to exploit them.

Addressing digital inequality is very important because China's rapid digitization has already created a "digital underclass," especially among the elderly. For instance, China's stride toward a cashless society led many businesses, including street vendors, to stop accepting cash. For these businesses, using mobile wallets avoids the hassle of dealing with counterfeit bills and providing change. Yet people who only use cash are essentially deprived of many basic services, such as parking, dining, and even paying health care. In an extreme case that provoked public outrage, the family of a ninety-four-year-old woman had to carry her to a bank branch and prop her up in front of an ATM camera for facial recognition, all to activate her social security account.[62]

Second, while e-commerce has the potential to stimulate rural development, simply introducing e-commerce access is insufficient to transform an ordinary village into an e-commerce hub. To effectively foster online selling, it is crucial to complement online market access with additional interventions, which may encompass providing business training, facilitating access to online credit, implementing targeted online promotions, and creative marketing strategies. For example, China's latest fad, live streaming, has facilitated the sale of agricultural products. Due to the nonstandardized nature of these products and the inherent information asymmetry, customers often exhibit reluctance to purchase agricultural items online. Nevertheless, through live streaming, online streamers can showcase the products' origins and also conduct live tastings. This innovative approach has demonstrated remarkable potential to help villagers sell.

Third, e-commerce—and perhaps other commercial and entertainment facets of internet technologies—appears to actually stabilize the authoritarian regime rather than undermine it. E-commerce is economically stabilizing because it generates significant welfare benefits for its users, comprising over 50 percent of the Chinese population. It increases households' purchasing power by granting citizens access to a wider variety of cheaper products and making shopping more convenient. E-commerce can boost households' real income, even if not their nominal income, which is crucial during China's economic slowdown. Furthermore, e-commerce and related logistics industries have provided flexible employment opportunities and absorbed displaced workers from other sectors, mitigating potential economic hardship and social unrest.

Given the significant employment and welfare impacts carried by e-commerce and other platform-based technologies, China's efforts to regulate tech platforms have become a tricky endeavor, as discussed in the upcoming chapter.

6

Governing the Titans

CHINA'S REGULATORY SHIFTS
TOWARD PLATFORMS

The Regulatory Pendulum

Toward the end of October 2020, global investors were eagerly awaiting what was poised to be the world's largest IPO. Ant Group, China's fintech power-house and an Alibaba affiliate, was set to raise $37 billion on November 5, with an estimated valuation nearing $300 billion. This investment fervor was pro-pelled by the rapid expansion of China's internet industry. In the preceding year, China had already claimed nine of the world's top twenty most valuable internet companies, with the rest all originating in the United States.

However, events took an unexpected turn. Less than two weeks before the planned IPO, Jack Ma, the founder of Alibaba and Ant Group, delivered a bold speech at a summit. Speaking before the country's top financial regulators, he criticized the "pawnshop mentality" of state-owned banks that only lent to borrowers with collateral, suggesting that China's regulatory system was sti-fling innovation. While the outspoken tycoon had made similar points in the past without repercussions, this time, possibly due to the timing and venue, his comments came at a steep cost. A week later, the Chinese government abruptly halted the IPO. Following this, the company underwent a series of tough regulations and restructuring.

To the surprise of many, the suspension of the Ant Group IPO was only the beginning of a 2.5-year government crackdown. This crackdown ex-tended beyond Alibaba to the entire technology sector, particularly target-ing digital platforms. The regulatory blizzard covered a wide range of issues, including antitrust, data security, privacy provisions, content oversight, and algorithmic scrutiny. As a result, the market value of China's internet indus-try plummeted by over $1 trillion from its peak.

In December 2022, the government made another U-turn in its policy. Facing a faltering economy, it reinstated open support for platform companies in an effort to revive economic growth. In the annual Central Economic Work Conference to plan for the next year, the government claimed that it would "support platform firms to play significant roles in spearheading development, creating jobs, and competing globally."[1] In July 2023, China officially ended the crackdown. As a strong signal of support, the newly appointed premier Li Qiang met representatives from major tech companies and stressed the importance of regular communication. This was followed by a series of central and local government policies to bolster the platform economy. As of now, China has indeed relaxed its regulations on platforms, though not to the minimal oversight level seen before 2020.

Preview of the Chapter

What factors contributed to the dramatic shifts in regulatory approaches toward platform companies around 2020? Why did the Chinese government implement such stringent regulations on platforms during the regulatory crackdown, seemingly killing its golden tech goose? Why did China eventually revert its policy? Of relevance to this book, I will also explore: Why did the government opt to crack down on platforms despite outsourcing certain institutional functions to them? Did institutional outsourcing persist during and after the crackdown?

This chapter uses the framework of institutional outsourcing to explain the crackdown and the subsequent policy reversal. As mentioned in chapter 2, ideally, platforms should refrain from arbitrarily exploiting their users, and the state should avoid arbitrarily intervening in the platforms' private governance. This balance produces the best economic outcomes under institutional outsourcing. However, in reality, both sides can overstep their limits. China's turbulent regulatory shifts toward platforms post-2020 can be succinctly described as follows: *the platforms overstep, and the state overreacts.*[2]

As platforms expand and cultivate a loyal user base, they occasionally overstep boundaries and harm consumer interests. Digital platforms can substitute for state institutions due to their scalability and automated digital enforcement capabilities. However, these strengths can also be their drawbacks. For instance, the digital enforcement capacities come from platforms' collection of personal data, leading to privacy concerns and data breach risks. In the absence of proper state regulations, digital governance can also hurt consumer welfare through algorithmic manipulation, monopolistic behavior, and excessive collection of personal information.

The Chinese government, however, overreacted to the challenges posed by platforms. While there is a valid economic rationale to curb platform power, the regulations on Big Tech were enforced with a campaign-style approach, involving a high level of seriousness and intensity, which many referred to as a "regulatory storm." This chapter explores several factors contributing to this overreaction, including communist ideology, the lack of checks and balances in China's political system, as well as the overconfidence displayed by both the government and tech companies in late 2020, when the regulatory crackdown began.

The consequences of this overreaction have been disastrous. The regulatory crackdown severely impacted the market value and profitability of tech firms, abruptly halting their upward trajectory. More importantly, it undermined market confidence by installing policy uncertainty into the whole economy, leading to massive job losses.

As shown by the framework in chapter 2, the state's objective to foster economic growth can serve as a partial check on its arbitrary actions. Indeed, significant economic pressure compelled the government to cease the regulatory storm in 2023. When state regulations become too overbearing, it can undermine the autonomy of platforms and hamper their capacity to innovate and generate job opportunities. Thus, the state had to ease the regulations and reinstate its support for platforms in an effort to bolster the economy.

Finally, this chapter underscores the enduring presence of institutional outsourcing before, during, and after the regulatory crackdown.

The Platforms Overstepped

Prior to 2020, the Chinese government followed a largely hands-off approach toward e-commerce platforms. During this period, platforms benefited from what was referred to as "regulatory dividends" (监管红利), enabling them to capitalize on the lax regulatory environment and expand rapidly.

Nevertheless, this phase of lenient regulation is not without its drawbacks. Unchecked power, whether private or public, tends to corrupt. This tendency becomes particularly noticeable as platforms grow larger and wield greater societal influence. I have previously discussed specific issues related to Taobao's institutions in chapter 3, highlighting design flaws and its failure to address all market concerns. This chapter broadens the scope to explore the overarching problems inherent in digital platforms: excessive data collection and monetization, anticompetitive practices and corruption, challenges in combating fraudulent activities such as brushing and data manipulation, and the implementation of big-data-driven price discrimination.

Overcollection and the Selling of Personal Data

The phrase "If you're not paying for the product, you are the product" reveals a crucial truth about digital products. To access seemingly "free" services, users must agree to give tech companies extensive access to their personal data. These companies then profit by selling advertisements or the data itself. This business model, common in the tech industry, raises global concerns about data privacy.

Cross-national surveys have consistently revealed that Chinese citizens are more willing to trade their personal data for access to digital services than their American and European counterparts.[3] However, in 2018, when tech tycoon Robin Li suggested that Chinese companies could benefit from exploiting this lower concern for privacy, it sparked a notable public outcry.[4] This indicates that privacy awareness has been on the rise in China.

In recent years, the excessive collection and misuse of personal data by tech firms has drawn significant public attention in China. For instance, a user reported that if he kept the JD Financial app running in the background, the app would secretly store all screenshots taken in other apps and photos captured through the camera in the JD app's cache directory.[5] An exhaustive investigation conducted by the Shanghai Consumer Rights Protection Commission revealed that twenty-five of thirty-nine popular apps obtain unnecessarily sensitive information on users' phones, including personal contacts, audio recordings, and messages, even though the apps lack corresponding functions to justify the use of such data.[6]

A more worrisome issue pertains to the unauthorized sale of such data, some of which has even found its way to the black market, with information being sold for as little as 2 yuan (30 cents) per individual. In 2018, the police in Jiangsu Province arrested 288 suspects and confiscated over 468 million pieces of personal information. Before this law enforcement action, the data had changed hands between companies eight times.[7] Given that this type of data is not anonymized and frequently contains sensitive information such as home addresses and phone numbers, it is often exploited for fraudulent activities like scam calls.

Depending solely on the firms' self-regulation cannot adequately address the issue. To begin with, fierce competition among tech firms often motivates them to amass extensive data, even if it is unrelated to their primary business activities. Moreover, businesses can take advantage of the so-called privacy paradox, where users claim to highly value their privacy but continue to use digital services that potentially compromise it. These factors reduce companies' incentives to implement stringent self-regulatory measures to safeguard user data, highlighting the necessity of government regulation.

Anticompetitive Practices and Corruption

Platforms are multisided markets with network effects: as more users join, the platform's value increases, making its services more appealing to even more users. Therefore, big platforms often grow even bigger, which can give rise to anticompetitive practices that unfairly disadvantage their competitors.

One example of their anticompetitive behavior lies in the historical practice of platform companies like Alibaba and Tencent blocking each other's website links and services. For instance, due to their rivalry, users could not open Taobao links on the WeChat app, and Taobao did not support WeChat Pay. It was only after the government's regulatory crackdown in 2021 that these tech giants began to open up their platforms to one another.[8]

Another illustration of anticompetitive behavior is the practice known as "either-or restriction" (二选一). This platform strategy binds sellers to exclusive agreements during major sales events, compelling them to cease operations on competing platforms. In 2017, e-commerce giant JD initiated legal action against Alibaba for implementing such restrictions. Likewise, in 2019, oven manufacturer Galanz sued Alibaba, citing a significant decline in traffic to its Tmall online store and a one-third drop in sales following the launch of its products on Alibaba's competitor platform, Pinduoduo (PDD). In fact, the either-or restriction has a long history and has been used by other major internet platforms as well.[9]

Apart from anticompetitive behavior, corruption poses another significant challenge within platforms, as employees of major platforms may abuse their power for personal gain. Platforms control many resources that are critical to the success of online businesses, including stores' online ratings, penalties, and prime advertisement spots during sales events. Although platform rules are largely executed through algorithms, opportunities for human manipulation remain, which creates room for rent-seeking.

In the 2010s, a bribery scandal emerged within Alibaba: some employees accepted payments to help sellers orchestrate fraudulent sales and delete negative reviews, thus boosting search rankings. The CEO and COO at the time resigned in the wake of the scandal, and the company made a big effort to crack down on employee corruption.[10] It is now common for Chinese internet firms to launch anticorruption investigations against their own employees. In 2020, Meituan, an online food delivery platform, turned in thirty-three individuals suspected of corruption to the police. PDD and Baidu also turned in employees and published anticorruption reports that year.[11]

"Brushing" and Data Manipulation

One of the core institutions on digital platforms is the online rating system and the ratings-based search rankings. Search rank matters substantially for the sales of a product. The first search page of Google captures approximately 70 percent to 90 percent of traffic clicks.[12] Similarly, interviews indicate that the top three search results for a product on Taobao account for 70 percent of sales.[13]

The quest for higher search rankings has led to a pervasive form of fraud in China known as "brushing" (刷单). This involves hiring "brushers" to fabricate sales and reviews—either to inflate the seller's own positive reviews or to post negative reviews on their competitors' products. According to the sellers I interviewed, brushing has become an industry-wide open secret, with sellers frequently factoring its costs into their marketing budgets.[14]

Given brushing's illicit nature, it's interesting that brushing activities frequently face difficulties in contract enforcement. It is not uncommon for "sellers to trick brushers, and brushers to trick sellers," according to my interviews.[15] In some cases, unscrupulous sellers manipulate inexperienced brushers into revealing their bank account information through phishing websites. In another scenario, brushers inadvertently boosted the sales of the hiring seller's competitor. Nevertheless, the seller remained obligated to pay, as brushers threatened to report to the platform and post negative reviews about the seller.

Why can't the platforms eliminate brushing? Partly because it is a game of catch me if you can. Brushers continually enhance their fraudulent techniques as platforms improve their detection capabilities. Some online sellers shared with me how brushers emulate genuine consumers to evade platform detection. For example, authentic buyers typically compare options across various sellers, rarely making an immediate purchase from a single shop. Brushers mimic this behavior by first browsing the stores of the hiring seller's major competitors without making any purchases. Then, they proceed to place orders with the hiring seller. This approach allows brushers to kill two birds with one stone. On certain platforms like Taobao, the click-to-purchase conversion rate—the ratio of purchases to clicks on a product—significantly influences search rankings. By not buying at the competitor's store, brushers reduce the conversion rate and thereby the search rank of competitors. Simultaneously, by buying from the hiring seller's store, they increase their employer's conversion rate and ranking. To make these brushing orders appear genuine, sellers ship empty packages to the brushers. Consequently, these fabricated transactions generate authentic logistics data, making it difficult for the platform to differentiate them from legitimate orders.[16]

Beyond technical hurdles, platforms may face a conflict of interest in combating brushing: the allure of "fake it until you make it." Although platforms have a clear stake in preserving authentic online ratings to uphold consumer trust, the immediate sales surge from brushing can give a misleading impression of market popularity. This could attract more consumers and investors, which may ultimately lead to an actual surge in sales. This aligns with the findings of Wesley Koo (2024), who demonstrates that platforms occasionally allow or even encourage user misconduct if such behavior benefits them.

Especially when specific platform employees are incentivized to meet sales targets, they may turn a blind eye to or even collude with sellers engaged in brushing schemes. During an interview with an online seller, he coincidentally received a call from a platform employee who subtly suggested that the sellers use brushing tactics to help achieve sales targets. According to the seller, noncompliance could lead to exclusion from future sales events. He also mentioned that some employees on another platform would "auction" off advertisement spots during sale events based on sellers' sales projections, which often turned out to be inflated by brushers.[17]

The opportunistic behavior, such as brushing by sellers and even some platform employees, poses a significant challenge to the quality of online institutions. Meanwhile, platforms have limited capacity to effectively regulate such activities. This may be due to conflicts of interest or constraints in their capacity; for instance, while platforms can ban an account, perpetrators may resort to using other accounts to reenter the platform. This underscores the need for public regulation to catch up and elevate the legal costs of such fraudulent activities.

Big Data-Enabled Price Discrimination

In recent years, the issue of "big data-enabled price discrimination against loyal customers" (大数据杀熟) has gained significant attention in China. Numerous news reports unveiled the practice whereby certain digital companies charge long-standing consumers higher prices for the same digital services than new customers. According to a survey in 2021 by Beijing Consumer Association, over 80 percent of respondents reported experiencing such price discrimination, which was most prevalent in online shopping, followed by online travel booking, food delivery, and ride-hailing services.[18]

Other forms of big data-assisted price discrimination have also sparked public outcry. Digital companies appear to segment consumers into subgroups based on factors like the type of device they use, which serves as a proxy for income level. For example, when booking ride-hailing services in China, iPhone users were more frequently matched with premium vehicle options compared to Android users. This often resulted in higher ride fares and diminished discount opportunities, a phenomenon referred to as the "Apple tax" by researchers.[19]

In fact, price discrimination was a common business practice even before the advent of big data. Price discrimination involves charging different prices to different consumers for the same product. Although it may seem unfair, price discrimination is generally lawful and is not necessarily bad for consumers.[20] One common manifestation of price discrimination is group pricing (i.e., third-degree price discrimination): targeting specific subgroups of buyers, such as offering senior or student discounts for park admission. Another prevalent form is quantity discounts (known as second-degree price discrimination); that is, price per unit decreases when purchased in bulk. The most precise form of price discrimination is personalized pricing (or first-degree price discrimination), where prices are determined based on each consumer's willingness to pay. Examples include individually negotiated prices with a vendor. However, this form of price discrimination was deemed impractical before the advent of big data. It is difficult to set individual prices accurately given the seller's lack of complete information about buyer preferences.

While price discrimination has long existed, the rise of big data allows sellers to implement it with unprecedented precision and effectiveness. The wealth of user data unveils consumers' concealed or even subconscious preferences, enabling sellers to better assess an individual's willingness to pay. It allows firms to shift from group pricing, which relies on broad demographic and group-level metrics, to personalized pricing. Consequently, this could lead to unique, dynamically changing prices for each consumer.

This shift to big data-enabled price discrimination has raised significant concerns among Chinese citizens. They worry about the extensive collection of personal data, companies potentially making excessive profits by pricing close to each consumer's maximum willingness to pay, and issues of market fairness and transparency. Many find it unfair that prices vary without the option to opt out, especially when the algorithms behind these variations are opaque.

The State Overreacted

The above issues are not unique to Chinese platforms; they are inherent in the operations of digital platforms globally, providing a compelling economic rationale for government regulations. In fact, the United States and the European Union took steps to address the unchecked influence of platforms concurrently with, or even before, China. Since 2018, the European Union has enacted the General Data Protection Regulation (GDPR), the world's toughest privacy and data security law. Under GDPR, tech companies that fail to comply can face fines of up to 4 percent of their annual global turnover, or 20 million euros, whichever is higher. This resulted in a total of $1.2 billion in fines imposed on prominent tech firms in 2021, including Amazon ($850 million) and Meta ($267 million).[21] While the United States lacks a federal-level privacy law, the state of California adopted the California Consumer Privacy Act of 2018, which resembles GDPR. Later, the US Congress called for antitrust reforms to curtail the influence of Big Tech companies—one of the few areas that has garnered bipartisan support.

Similarly, China's 2020 regulatory tightening on platforms was not purely driven by political reasons. There were valid economic reasons and public backing for regulating platforms. Prior to the crackdown, the problems with unchecked platform power had been widely discussed in public. There was a widespread anticipation that stricter governmental oversight would inevitably be introduced—it was merely a question of when. Thus, while Jack Ma's criticism of regulators before the Ant Group IPO may have accelerated the implementation of regulatory measures, it is not the root cause.

The real question is not whether platforms should be regulated but how. Compared to Western countries, China's regulatory actions stood out for their exceptional speed, intensity, and campaign-like nature. In hindsight, this overzealous response inflicted much greater harm on China's leading platforms than Western regulations did on theirs. This approach seems at odds with China's interests in the global tech race. What motivated China to adopt such a radical approach, even at the risk of jeopardizing its technological prowess?

Triggers of Overreaction

One contributor to the overreaction is the influence of communist ideology, which reinforces the government's resolve to regulate private platforms. The Chinese Communist Party (CCP) has long been wary of powerful private businesses that could potentially capture the state and wield political influence. An important motivation behind China's regulatory crackdown on Big Tech is to "prevent capital from expanding in a disorderly fashion" (防止资本无序扩张).[22] In 2021, following allegations of a manager's sexual assault, a state-media-owned social media account blasted Alibaba for its delayed response and for curbing trending searches on social media. It commented, "Don't fantasize about being too big to fail . . . Also, don't entertain the idea of controlling everything like South Korean business conglomerates; this is China."[23]

Another trigger to China's tendency to overreact lies in its political system, characterized by limited constraints on executive power. Once the leadership decides to regulate digital platforms seriously, it can swiftly and forcefully implement regulations. An example is the antitrust case involving Alibaba on "either-or-restriction." As early as 2015, Alibaba's rivals reported the company's anticompetitive practices to the government, leading to a lawsuit filed by its competitor JD in 2017. The ensuing period saw widespread media coverage and criticism of such anticompetitive behavior. However, it wasn't until December 2020—just a month after the suspension of the Ant IPO and a clear resolution from the leadership to rein in Big Tech—that the regulator initiated an investigation against Alibaba. The investigation was carried out at lightning speed, concluding in only four months—a stark contrast to the average 16.3 months for antitrust cases—and resulting in a record-high fine of 18.2 billion yuan ($2.8 billion).[24] A similar expeditious process occurred for the antitrust case involving another major platform, Meituan. It took only five months in 2021 for the government to conclude the case and impose a fine of 3.4 billion yuan ($527.4 million).

This sharply contrasts with the situation in the United States. Despite facing equally scathing criticisms from the government, US tech companies continue to prosper. This is partly because the US government is constrained by prolonged legal procedures and influenced by business lobbying. For example, the U.S. federal government's antitrust case against Microsoft took over a decade to complete the investigation and legal proceedings. Although the District Court initially ordered Microsoft's breakup, the company successfully appealed, avoiding a split-up and ultimately reaching a settlement with the Department of Justice.

Finally, timing wise, in late 2020, it is likely that overconfidence from both the government and tech companies fueled the regulatory turn and the overreaction.[25] On the government front, it may have been overly confident in its ability to quickly fix problems within the tech sector. By late 2020, China had contained the first wave of COVID-19 through stringent zero-COVID policies. The rapid rebound of the Chinese economy, in contrast to the continued struggles of Western economies, bolstered the government's confidence in its capabilities. It seemed to believe that the same forceful and swift execution of policies that proved successful in handling the health crisis could be applied to a range of other issues. This potentially explains the proliferation of policy objectives in the summer of 2021, wherein the government sought to tackle not only the big-tech challenges but also issues such as inequality, local government debts, housing prices, and many other issues, all at once.[26]

Simultaneously, tech companies overestimated the government's tolerance for criticism and misjudged the industry's resilience. This misunderstanding arises from the government's historically hands-off approach, coupled with the substantial growth of the industry in the preceding two decades. By late 2020, Chinese internet companies were riding a wave of success, further buoyed by the anticipation of Ant Group's potentially record-breaking IPO. This heightened confidence in the tech sector likely prompted figures like Jack Ma to openly criticize regulators without foreseeing the consequences, ultimately precipitating the collision between the tech sector and the government.

Winter Is Coming

China's post-2020 regulatory efforts unfolded with remarkable intensity, characterized by a multitude of measures implemented within a condensed timeframe. Although the crackdown officially lasted for two and a half years, the bulk of government interventions occurred within a single year (November 2020–October 2021), with a notable concentration in the summer of 2021 (see Table 6.1). Illustrating this heightened activity, in early 2021, the government initiated antitrust investigations into nearly all major platforms, resulting in fines imposed on twelve internet giants for various charges, ranging from engagement in anticompetitive practices like the "either-or-restriction" to irregularities related to mergers.

The regulatory crackdown covered all major and highly competitive internet sectors, including e-commerce, fintech, ride hailing, social media, gaming, online food delivery, and online education. Table 6.1 illustrates the extensive array of policy goals and measures implemented. Some are related to the characteristics of digital platforms, such as antitrust measures, data security, privacy protection, and algorithm transparency. Others focus on safeguarding workers and minors using such platforms. For instance, measures have been implemented to ensure minimum wages for platform-based delivery workers. There are also regulations designed to restrict online gameplay hours for minors to prevent addiction, and to restrict online education for the sake of protecting children's sleep.

Many of these regulations were introduced in highly unexpected ways, leading to a widespread sense of policy uncertainty. Beyond the surprise suspension of the Ant Group IPO, the government also intervened in another high-profile IPO. On June 30, 2021, Didi, China's largest ride-hailing platform, went public on the New York Stock Exchange (NYSE) despite receiving mixed signals from different government agencies regarding whether to proceed with the IPO.[27] Just two days after Didi's debut, China's internet watchdog launched a cybersecurity probe into the company. The government also mandated the removal of Didi's main app and its twenty-five affiliated apps from all online platforms, citing "serious" issues related to the collection and use of customer data. A year later, facing pressure from regulators and data security concerns, Didi delisted from the NYSE, experiencing an 87 percent stock price decline

TABLE 6.1 Key Events in China's Big Tech Crackdown (November 2020–July 2023)

Time	Event Description
November 2020	• Ant Group's record-breaking IPO is canceled. • Twenty-seven internet companies are summoned over alleged monopolistic practices. • The State Administration for Market Regulation (SAMR) drafts antitrust guidelines for regulating internet platforms.
December 2020	• Politburo vows to curb Big Tech's influence, marking the first explicit mention of "strengthening antitrust efforts and preventing the disorderly expansion of capital." • The State Administration for Market Regulation fines companies such as Alibaba and Tencent for antitrust violations. • Alibaba faces official antitrust investigation.
February 2021	• SAMR issues new guidelines for antitrust.
April 2021	• Alibaba is fined a record 18.2 billion yuan ($2.8 billion) in antitrust case; thirty-four tech companies are warned to pay full attention to the case. • Meituan is investigated for "either-or restriction," an anticompetitive practice. • Ten companies, including Didi and Tencent, are penalized for failures to disclose mergers; 34 tech companies are ordered to rectify anticompetitive behaviors within the next month. • The Ministry of Education proposes regulations to protect children's sleep, placing limits on online education and gaming services.
June 2021	• The Data Security Law is enacted.
July 2021	• Didi faces unprecedented data and security investigation after going public on the New York Stock Exchange. Didi is ordered to stop new user registration on its app. • Regulator probes Big Tech mergers back to the 2000s; twenty-two fines of 500,000 yuan ($77,000) each—the maximum penalty allowed under China's antimonopoly law—are imposed on companies including Alibaba, Tencent, and Didi. • Reforms are started to ensure minimum wage for delivery workers. • Tencent is ordered to end exclusive agreements with music producers. • A six-month rectification campaign is launched for the internet industry. • Tencent and thirteen other developers are instructed to rectify "intrusive" pop-up windows. • Twenty-five companies are ordered to address data security and consumer rights protection.

TABLE 6.1. (*continued*)

Time	Event Description
August 2021	• State media criticizes gaming as "spiritual opium" and new regulations are introduced to restrict minors' online gaming time on platforms like Tencent. • The Personal Information Protection Law is enacted.
September 2021	• Policy statements on governance rules for algorithms are released.
October 2021	• Meituan is fined 3.4 billion yuan for abusing market dominance by imposing "either-or restriction."
January 2022	• Regulatory guidelines emphasize healthy platform development, with positive tone toward Big Tech's role in the economy.
May 2022	• Government signals support for tech sector development, boosting tech stocks.
July 2022	• Didi is fined 8 billion yuan for data violations, concluding a yearlong investigation.
December 2022	• President Xi Jinping supports internet platforms, highlighting their role in boosting the economy, creating jobs, and helping China in international competition.
January 2023	• Didi resumes new user registrations for its app. • Ant Group and 13 other platforms complete "business rectification."
July 2023	• Ant Group and Tencent's Tenpay are fined 7.1 billion yuan and 3 billion yuan, respectively, for rule violations. • China's tech crackdown officially ends. • Premier Li Qiang issues support to major tech companies.

Notes: The key events are compiled from multiple news sources, including Yahoo News, *South China Morning Post*, and the China Project. Some minor events were omitted.

and a loss of nearly 380 billion RMB ($59 billion). Additionally, Didi incurred a massive fine of 8 billion yuan (about $1.2 billion).

Finally, the regulatory efforts were not confined to ad hoc executive actions but also included an accelerated legislative process, which imposed various compliance costs on businesses within a short timeframe. In 2021 alone, China enacted the Data Security Law to address data security breaches, the Personal Information Protection Law to protect customer privacy, and policy documents such as the "Guiding Opinions on Strengthening the Overall Governance of Internet Information Service Algorithms" to combat issues like price discrimination, algorithmic recommendations, and user addiction.[28]

The Damage and the "Startled Birds"

Although many of the regulations introduced during the crackdown were well-intentioned and arguably long overdue, their implementation was excessively intense, overly broad in scope, and often occurred without warning. This caused significant damage. This regulatory turbulence has made internet firms and investors behave like "birds startled by the mere twang of a bow-string," as a Chinese idiom says. Even when regulatory authorities were only issuing warnings without official intervention, internet companies scaled back their operations, and investors divested. Ironically, it was not foreign competitors but the Chinese government's own regulatory crackdown that halted the rapid rise of China's internet industry.

The 2.5 years of regulatory crackdown wiped out more than $1 trillion in market value from major tech companies—equivalent to the size of the GDP of the Netherlands in 2022.[29] This regulatory intervention has notably disrupted China's progress in catching up with United States in the digital economy and widened the gap between the two countries. In 2018, nine out of the world's top twenty most valuable internet firms hailed from China, leaving the remaining positions to the United States.[30] Fast-forward to mid-2023, after the crackdown, only six Chinese firms remained on the list, while the US contingent has expanded to twelve.[31]

Another compelling benchmark of the damage can be seen through the market value of tech giant Apple, which is the United States' most valuable firm as of 2023. In April 2020, before the crackdown, Apple's market value lagged behind the combined added value of China's top five internet/platform companies—Alibaba, Tencent, Meituan, JD, and Pinduoduo—by $19.2 billion. However, two years later, Apple's market value surpassed the combined value of China's top fifty firms by a staggering $1.26 trillion.[32]

As a result, numerous platform companies reported lackluster profits and resorted to widespread layoffs and salary cuts.[33] In the first quarter of 2022, major Chinese tech giants such as Alibaba, Tencent, and Baidu saw significant year-on-year declines in net profits—53 percent, 23 percent, and 10 percent, respectively.[34] In response, tech companies have prioritized cost reduction and efficiency improvements throughout 2022 and 2023, with employee layoffs being a key strategy. Although specific figures are unavailable, Tencent's Q1 2023 fiscal report hints at a workforce reduction of approximately 10 percent.[35] Notably, reports of layoffs across major tech giants have become increasingly prevalent, marking a contrast to the previous era of workforce expansion in the internet industry. To be sure, other factors have contributed to the layoffs.[36] Nonetheless, regulatory policy certainty emerges as a significant factor influencing the decision to downsize in these companies.

More importantly, the decrease in profits and the escalating regulatory risks have subdued the eagerness of platform companies to pursue innovation. Innovation inherently entails risks and costs, with no immediate returns, and may expose firms to additional regulatory uncertainties. In a strategic and rational response, tech giants have shifted their focus back to their core operations, discontinuing nonessential and risky ventures and cutting back on extensive research initiatives. For example, Tencent significantly scaled back its business operations in 2022, with the founder advocating "cutting off whatever needs to be cut off,"[37] while Alibaba terminated various research projects, including a quantum computing lab.[38] This shift underscores that the tech crackdown has not yielded the intended consequences. Rather than propelling tech giants toward higher-quality innovation and cutting-edge research, it has produced the opposite effect.

The regulatory crackdown has had detrimental effects not only on platform companies but also on other industries. The internet industry serves as a nexus connecting various upstream and downstream service sectors. When it suffers, a ripple effect spreads through interconnected industries, endangering numerous jobs across a broad range of sectors. Additionally, the Chinese government's aggressive targeting of its most competitive industry has caused a chilling effect in other sectors. This, in turn, erodes overall confidence among domestic and international investors, who perceive substantial policy uncertainty in the market.

The Return

From late 2021 onward, China grappled with mounting difficulties in maintaining its zero-COVID policies, facing economic strain due to extended lockdowns and extensive testing. This could explain the reduced frequency of newly introduced regulations post-October 2021, as shown in Table 6.1. Starting January 2022, the government adopted a more accommodating approach toward Big Tech, expressing support for the sector's development and commending the substantial role it played in the economy (Table 6.1).

In 2023, faced with even greater economic pressure and dwindling market confidence, the Chinese government officially concluded the regulatory crackdown. In July 2023, the newly appointed premier, Li Qiang, convened with representatives of major tech firms, sending the "strongest signal" in support of platform firms.[39] Numerous central and local governments then introduced new policies aimed at bolstering the platform economy, with the intention of driving economic growth and job creation.

In spite of the government's shift in stance, the timeline for the recovery of the internet industry remains elusive. The regulatory storm showcased the government's formidable might, leaving a lingering perception of policy uncertainty among entrepreneurs and investors. This has cast a shadow over market confidence, potentially hindering platform innovation and private investments in the long term.

Institutional Outsourcing Persisted

As previously discussed, regulations and outsourcing are not mutually exclusive but rather intricately linked. Under heightened scrutiny from regulatory bodies, private platforms are likely to forge stronger collaborations with the state, aligning themselves even more closely with the state's economic and political objectives. In chapters 3 and 4, I have documented cases of outsourcing both preceding, during, and following the regulatory crackdown, highlighting the enduring nature of this phenomenon. For example, amid the regulatory crackdown, in 2022, the collaboration between the local government's public security agencies and the platform still continued.[40] After the crackdown, in 2023, the Zhejiang provincial government signed a new comprehensive strategic collaboration framework agreements with Alibaba.[41]

A notable change post-crackdown is the uptick in de jure outsourcing, marked by formal contracts outsourcing functions from the state to platforms. This change is a response to heightened policy uncertainty faced by platforms in the aftermath of crackdowns. Platforms proactively seek formal arrangements—such as memoranda of understanding or collaborative contracts—with the government to codify obligations and responsibilities. Additionally, they aim to secure a formal safe harbor, which would exempt them from legal or regulatory liability under specific conditions, as highlighted in Xin Dai's (2023) study.

Importantly, Dai illustrates that during the post-crackdown period, there is an increasing integration of regulatory processes between platforms and the government. Personnel from both sides engage in "routine and close interactions," as exemplified by collaborative efforts in 2023 between regulators and China's food-delivery platforms. The collaboration involves a digital infrastructure enabling two-way data sharing: platforms access government data for vendor license verification and reciprocally provide the government with "data check assistance," offering information on business owners and sales records. Additionally, they jointly manage consumer claims, utilizing the platform's existing framework. The government channels complaints collected from official channels (e.g., 12315) to platforms, which process and report outcomes back to regulators. This indicates the persistence of institutional outsourcing, although it is more likely to transform from de facto to de jure outsourcing.

Conclusion

The late historian Renyu (Ray) Huang asserted that ancient China grappled with a notable weakness: "mathematically unmanageable" (无数目字管理). He argued that the cornerstone of modernization lies in the use of accurate data, statistics, and a robust property rights system for effective governance and resource exchange in society.[42]

In the contemporary era, it may be tempting to conclude that big data provides a convenient path to achieving mathematical management. With platforms amassing vast data and employing analytical tools, one might assume that effective governance would emerge spontaneously.

However, as this chapter underscores, our increasing reliance on digital governance goes hand in hand with the growing issue of digital *mis*governance. Unbridled private powers can result in a decline in the quality of services and institutions they offer. Therefore, appropriate public regulations on platforms are crucial for ensuring the efficacy of institutional outsourcing.

Yet, achieving the ideal level of state regulation poses a challenge. Insufficient government oversight fails to fix the problem presented by platforms, while excessive regulation hampers their ability to innovate and experiment with new institutions. Since the early 2000s, China's regulations on digital platforms have oscillated between extremes of leniency and stringency, often missing the optimal midpoint.

Striking the right balance between public and private regulatory powers is challenging, and the state's learning process is ongoing.

7

Bridging the Past and the Present

UNDERSTANDING THE INTERPLAY OF STATE AND MARKETS

The Contemporary Law Merchant

This book is not merely about a nascent technology, a burgeoning market, or China alone. I endeavor to connect China's technological advancements with several enduring challenges faced by all societies throughout human history: the tricky nexus between institutions and growth, the long and winding road to good governance, and the delicate interplay between public and private regulatory powers.

The Western world encountered similar challenges in an earlier stage of development. After the collapse of the Roman Empire, Europe descended into a long "dark age" characterized by chaos and economic deterioration. It was medieval long-distance trade—encompassing exchanges across jurisdictional boundaries—that generated significant profits and laid the groundwork for the eventual Rise of the West.[1] The expansion of long-distance trade, however, raised questions of trust. At the time, there existed no modern form of state or international laws to govern such transactions. Merchants convening at medieval fairs often hailed from different regions, seldom knew one another, and might never meet again. How did they establish trust and engage in trade with strangers? An influential explanation, posited by Paul Milgrom, Douglass North, and Barry Weingast (1990), focuses on the development of a private code of laws governing transactions, called *lex mercatoria* or the Law Merchant. Private judges at trade fairs enforced this legal code via a reputation mechanism: they kept a public record of every trader's past conduct to incentivize merchants to honor contracts and behave honestly. This private-order institution helped sustain long-distance trade in the absence of strong public enforcement power.[2]

Drawing parallels between medieval Europe and contemporary China helps put China's e-commerce market into perspective.[3] China has strived to sustain its economic development as the old growth engines (e.g., export and investment) sputter. The new sources of growth—domestic consumption and innovation—require expanding domestic trade and encouraging widespread impersonal exchange. E-commerce provides a means to achieve this goal. Much like the bustling trade fairs of medieval Europe, online platforms in China serve as marketplaces where individuals from different regions can connect and engage in trade. However, this long-distance trade faces challenges such as fraud and deception, which were especially pronounced in China during the 2000s when the legal infrastructure was inadequate to address these problems. In the absence of strong public institutions, private platforms such as Taobao had to create their own online versions of the Law Merchant. While the modern iteration of the Law Merchant is significantly more complex and relies on digital enforcement, certain core institutions persist. Online rating systems, reminiscent of the role of private judges in medieval Europe, publicly disclose every trader's rating history, leveraging reputation mechanisms to regulate market transactions.

This institutional perspective of the e-commerce market lays the foundation for institutional outsourcing—a state's strategic decision to leverage private governance by using key private actors as proxies of state power and, importantly, *building state capacity outside the state apparatus*. From this perspective, large digital platforms are not simply private entities; they also perform some public functions. These platforms help the state enforce institutional functions, experiment with various rules, and advance economic reforms.

In this book, I mainly focus on how the Chinese state outsources economic functions to online trading platforms. In the previous chapters, I discussed why it outsources institutional functions (chapter 2), how it does so (chapter 3), the economic and political effects of e-commerce (chapters 4 and 5), and the relationship between outsourcing and state regulation on platforms (chapter 6). It is worth noting that institutional outsourcing occurs beyond the e-commerce market. The Chinese state has also outsourced political and social functions to tech platforms in recent years, for example, in the areas of censorship, surveillance, and pandemic control.

In this concluding chapter, I discuss how the book's findings have broad implications.

Changes Seen from the Vantage Point of E-Commerce

In the preface of *Civilization and Capitalism*, French historian Fernand Braudel wrote that "the economic history of the world is the entire history of the world, but seen from a certain vantage-point—that of the economy."[4] Similarly, I view the e-commerce market as a lens through which I can observe several profound changes in China's economic and political landscape. The findings from this book carry broader implications across four domains:

China's growth trajectory, state-business relations, governance, and the politics of the internet.

The Shifting Growth Model

The book's findings help reflect on China's evolving political foundations of markets and the relationship between institutions and economic development more generally. I juxtapose my findings with existing theories to help identify the continuities and differences in China's growth strategy over time.

Many political economists have provided insights into how China grew despite weak-rule-of-law institutions. Theories such as "market-preserving federalism" by Montinola et al. (1995), "local state corporatism" by Oi (1992), and "the M-form hierarchy" by Qian and Xu (1993) emphasize the role played by local governments in conducting policy experiments and steering economic growth. Zhou and Li (2005) further delve into why local governments are driven to do so, positing that local officials compete for promotion in a "political tournament." Drawing upon prior research, Xu (2011) further argues that China's growth is driven by "regionally decentralized authoritarianism," a combination of economic decentralization and political centralization. Other contributing factors to China's growth include embracing foreign direct investment[5] and selectively providing property rights to private entrepreneurs.[6]

Building on and advancing this line of inquiry, Yuen Yuen Ang's highly acclaimed monograph, *How China Escaped the Poverty Trap*, offers two lessons. First, the state harnessed weak institutions—practices and features that defy standards of good governance—to build markets. Second, the state created the right conditions for institutions and markets to mutually adapt and coevolve. The key, in Ang's terms, is "directed improvisation," in which central reformers set the direction of reform and local authorities tailor the policy details to fit the local conditions.[7]

In line with prior research, I acknowledge that growth can be generated under weak formal institutions through institutional experiments and improvisation. However, there are two differences between institutional outsourcing and other theories. The first is who gets to improvise and implement the reform. Prior research primarily focuses on the role of local officials or other state agents in reforming the Chinese economy. My work, by contrast, examines the state's outsourcing of reform functions to nonstate actors such as digital platforms. The second difference is local versus national solutions to development problems. When considering China's substantial regional variations, Ang and other scholars stress the importance of local solutions to development problems—China's decentralized economic system allows local governments to adapt policies to local conditions. Local solutions remain critical in today's China. However, as the Chinese economy grows and cross-regional trade expands, there is a growing need for national-level solutions to tackle broader development challenges.[8] National platforms, equipped with digital enforcement capabilities and high scalability, provide such means. Outsourcing to these platforms therefore aids in overcoming local protectionism, addressing challenges that transcend the capacity of local governments, and facilitating nationwide coordination of cross-regional trade.

In many respects, my theory of institutional outsourcing complements rather than replaces prior theories about China's growth. Scholars like Ang have explored China's journey from poverty to a middle-income status, while my focus is on the subsequent phase: how China aspires toward even higher income and sustainable growth, striving to avoid the middle-income trap by encouraging domestic trade and consumption. In this process, while the classic model—locally driven development strategies and directed improvisation—remains critical, institutional outsourcing emerges to mitigate some downsides of the previous development model and fuel new sources of growth.

The Blurring State-Business Boundaries

This book enriches our understanding of the political role played by the private sector, in particular Chinese tech firms, which have ignited a great deal of geopolitical controversy. My overarching findings concur with a long-standing consensus among China scholars that the rise of the private sector does not undermine authoritarian rule. Prior research on Chinese politics finds that private entrepreneurs do not seek regime change; they are instead status quo oriented,[9] co-opted by the regime,[10] and benefit from a symbiotic alliance with government officials.[11] My work likewise suggests that the rise of powerful private platforms would not pose political challenges to the authoritarian regime. This observation diverges from a corollary of the modernization theory applicable in many other countries, which posits that the emergence of private entrepreneurs, who control autonomous sources of economic power, will be a key catalyst of democratic transition.[12]

Meanwhile, I show that China's private sector has become much more politically relevant than previously thought.[13] Many prior studies take formal institutions as exogenous and demonstrate how private actors cope with existing institutions created by the authoritarian state. I instead show that key private actors (e.g., digital platforms) proactively develop their own institutions to substitute for formal ones. They serve as sources of institutional development and governance innovation within the authoritarian state.

My emphasis on the private sector's contribution to formal institutional changes parallels Kellee Tsai's insightful theory of "adaptive informal institutions."[14] We both argue that institutions devised by private entrepreneurs can trigger formal institutional development. According to Tsai's theory, private entrepreneurs often develop informal coping strategies to bypass the restrictive formal institutions, which may end up inspiring government officials to change the original formal institutions.

Yet our studies also diverge in at least three ways. First, Tsai's theory focuses on the collaboration between *local* officials and private entrepreneurs to bypass the formal institutional restrictions imposed by the central government. In contrast, my study reveals that both central and local governments outsource certain governance functions to platforms, with central government-platform collaboration being more prominent. A second, and more important, difference is that the informal institutions in Tsai's analysis are based on repeated interactions and personal relationships between entrepreneurs and local officials. By contrast, the institutions created by platforms are largely impersonal and scalable, governing economic agents who are strangers. Third, Tsai's theory applies to a broad range of private actors, whereas in my theory, very few actors are eligible to privately supply market-supporting institutions.

The rising political role played by key private actors such as platforms points to another implication of this book: the blurring of boundaries between state and nonstate sectors.

The conventional wisdom has overwhelmingly relied on firm ownership to predict the Chinese state's reach within the corporate sector. Many analyses portray state-owned enterprises (SOEs) as vehicles of the state that fulfill political goals domestically and exert economic statecraft globally. Private businesses, on the contrary, are found to be less favored by the state than SOEs: they face restricted market access in strategic sectors (e.g., energy, aviation, telecom); discriminatory access to bank loans; and an unfavorable regulatory environment. As the Chinese Communist Party has historically distrusted the private sector, private entrepreneurs are largely excluded from—or only peripherally connected to—the political process.

Nonetheless, my book indicates that the state-business boundaries have become increasingly porous, elusive, and fluid. Unlike traditional private companies that are marginalized in state initiatives, privately held Big Tech firms have performed many strategic roles previously reserved for SOEs. The state collaborates extensively with digital companies on a wide range of issues.

This finding joins a growing number of studies that challenge the notion that the Chinese state only patronizes SOEs. For example, Fuller (2016) argues that state-favored firms also include two tech giants: the privately managed Lenovo and privately controlled Huawei. Rithmire and Chen (2022) show that certain nonstate conglomerates (e.g., the "Tomorrow System" 明天系) were able to manipulate the state through "mafia"-like organizations. At the most fundamental level, even ownership itself is a fuzzy concept. Waves of Chinese corporate reforms have created many mixed-ownership firms (also called hybrid firms), in which the state and private shareholders share ownership and management responsibilities, blurring the line between the state and nonstate sectors.[15]

Together, my research and the above studies suggest that the conventional typology—state versus private firms—no longer adequately describes the variations within the Chinese corporate sector. Hence, there is a necessity for a new typology in future research.

The Collaborative Provision of Governance

This book highlights the importance of online institutions and the collaboration between the state and digital platforms to jointly supply governance. This aligns with an emerging model of governance promoted by the Chinese government known as "collaborative governance" (协同治理): the sharing of power and discretion between public and private sectors in certain areas. While "collaborative" does not imply an equal partnership—the state remains in the driver's seat in this "collaboration" and has increasingly tightened its grip on the private sector—the private sector nonetheless plays an essential role. With the continuous emergence of new technologies and the increasing complexity of the domestic economy, the state faces increasing challenges in addressing all governance issues on its own. Consequently, it turns to the private sector for innovative solutions.

Beyond the e-commerce market, many other areas have engaged in public-private collaborations to provide public services, such as building high-speed rail and managing the healthcare system.[16] Karen Eggleston, Jack Donahue, and Richard Zeckhauser (2021) show that this parallels the United States despite the drastic political differences between the two countries.[17] While prior research has often focused on joint infrastructure projects involving public and private actors, my findings highlight that such collaboration also involves setting and enforcing the rules.

How does this new model advance our understanding of governance in China? My findings regarding the state's tolerance of private governance echo a consensus among China scholars: China is not a monolithic state where the central government dictates governance from the top down. Rather, as best depicted by the theory of fragmented authoritarianism, its governance system is fragmented, disjointed, and involves numerous actors.[18]

My research departs from prior literature in at least two respects. First, many analytical frameworks, including fragmented authoritarianism, have mainly focused on the state as the sole and direct provider of governance. My research highlights the growing regulatory power of private actors, as well as the state's strategic use of such actors to indirectly fill the governance gap. I show that governance is not necessarily provided by the government,[19] and that competition among private providers of governance facilitates institutional innovation.[20]

Second, my research demonstrates that platforms are akin to "semi-governments" in many governance areas, providing institutional substitutes for the state. This new perspective reverses the traditional direction of intellectual inquiry. In the 1980s and 1990s, a prominent strand of the literature treated governments as "industrial firms."[21] For example, some studies modeled the Chinese government as a giant corporation, with each local government operating like a profit-generating unit, where local officials leverage state-owned enterprises and government resources to generate growth. With the rise of the digital economy, an opposite trend has emerged. As private platforms host a great number of citizens and businesses, they gain substantial public influence and are obliged to shoulder certain governance responsibility, albeit sometimes reluctantly. Exploring the institutional parallels between the government and industrial organizations will help enrich our understanding of the nature of governance.

The Dual-Faceted Politics of the Internet

Investigating the e-commerce sector also prompts us to reconsider the political effects of the internet, particularly its implications for authoritarian regimes. Previous political science research has primarily focused on the media and informational aspects of the internet, such as how online news, web campaigns, and social media influence citizens' ideologies and behavior.[22] However, the internet is also a vast marketplace affecting citizens' material interests. My research emphasizes the economic and institutional dimensions of the internet—e-commerce and online institutional development—demonstrating their profound sociopolitical effects.

By incorporating the internet's economic and institutional aspects into political analysis, the book sheds light on the democratic implications of the internet. At the outset of the digital era, many politicians and technophiles believed information technology would expedite the demise of autocracies. For example, this techno-liberal belief led then-US President Bill Clinton, in 2000, to grant China the status of permanent normal trade relations. He claimed:

> In the new century, liberty will spread by cell phone and cable modem [. . .]
> When China joins the WTO [World Trade Organization], by 2005, it will
> eliminate tariffs on information technology products, making the tools of
> communication even cheaper, better, and more widely available. We know

how much the internet has changed America, and we are already an open society. Imagine how much it could change China. Now, there's no question China has been trying to crack down on the internet—good luck. That's sort of like trying to nail Jello to the wall [. . .] In the knowledge economy, economic innovation and political empowerment, whether anyone likes it or not, will inevitably go hand in hand.[23]

In this case, the internet was regarded as a decentralized and people-empowering innovation that would spread democracy. This belief was so entrenched that scholars even call the Arab Spring a "Twitter revolution" to emphasize its digital origins.[24]

A more recent thread of the literature, however, contends that authoritarian regimes can survive in the digital era. Autocracies can defuse collective actions against the ruler through online censorship,[25] use paid online propagandists to manipulate public opinion,[26] and garner information about their citizens via digital surveillance.[27] In extreme cases, authoritarian governments can even shut down or restrict internet services to curb security threats.[28]

In line with the latter group of studies, my findings also show that the internet does not necessarily lead to democratic transitions. I go a step further by suggesting that the internet might have *delayed* democratization in China due to its economic and institution-building functions. As chapters 4 and 5 demonstrate, e-commerce and other commercial apps promote citizens' economic welfare—an important benefit for the CCP, which relies on performance-based legitimacy. Furthermore, institutional outsourcing allows private platforms to provide substitutes for state institutions. This helps authoritarian regimes to partially close the institutional gap vis-à-vis Western democracies and further postpone political reforms on formal institutions. The takeaway here is that technology is inherently neutral; the effects of the internet largely depend on who gets to use it and how.

My work also adds to past studies by providing a more nuanced account of China's internet policy. Unlike prior research that pinpoints the suppressive features of autocracies' internet policies, my work shows that China's stance is *area-dependent*. While notorious for stringent online content censorship, the Chinese state was surprisingly tolerant of e-commerce and other commercial applications of the internet and left considerable regulatory power to private platforms for almost two decades before 2020.

These two faces of China's internet policy—control and commerce—seem contradictory, but they are intricately interwoven. To some extent, online commerce thrived in China *not in spite of* strategic censorship but partially *because of* it. During the 2000s and 2010s, online censorship and other suppressive measures impeded Western firms' access to China, which gave Chinese indigenous firms time to grow and thrive commercially. Censorship also increased the Chinese government's confidence that it could embrace the internet without inciting instability. As a result, the Chinese government's approach to the internet exhibited a clear bifurcation: stringent censorship over social media alongside more autonomy and support for e-commerce and other commercial internet applications. Even after 2020, when the state heightened its overall internet regulations, this duality persists, with the government maintaining stricter controls over social media compared to the economic sphere.

Generalizing beyond China and E-Commerce

Can institutional outsourcing to digital platforms explain cases beyond China and the realm of e-commerce? Applying the concept to different contexts requires caution. Not all countries possess the necessary prerequisites for institutional outsourcing, such as internet access, logistics networks, and adequate road connectivity. Additionally, in many countries, dominant platforms are foreign rather than homegrown, making governments reluctant to entrust them with institutional functions. It is also important to acknowledge that each country is unique and that many of the market dynamics discussed earlier may be specific to China.

Despite above caveats, institutional outsourcing does offer insights into similar dynamics elsewhere. In many developing countries, various obstacles have impeded the development of strong rule of law in markets. With the global rise of online markets and the diffusion of online institutional practices across borders, platforms in various countries may have developed a strong institutional capacity to handle tasks that the state is unable to perform. Once such online institutions emerge, the state can partner with platforms to deliver governance.

For instance, SafeBoda, the "Uber for motorcycles," is the dominant ride-hailing app in Uganda, where accidents are common due to the poor enforcement of traffic regulations. The app, founded in 2015, seeks to address this institutional gap by focusing on building a strong safety record. All SafeBoda drivers must follow a strict code of conduct that includes obeying the traffic rules, providing high-quality helmets to passengers, regularly maintaining their vehicles, and taking safety training classes that SafeBoda provides through a partnership with the Ugandan police.[29]

The state and other public organizations have outsourced institutional functions to SafeBoda's safe delivery network. During the COVID-19 pandemic, HIV tests and reproductive health supplies were in short supply due to lockdowns and supply chain disruptions. In response, international organizations and local health officials partnered with SafeBoda to create an online shop within its app, allowing individuals to order free or government-subsidized health items for home delivery. This outsourcing practice greatly enhanced the delivery efficiency, as well as the population base that the government service could cover.[30]

Similarly, Grab, Southeast Asia's leading platform offering services such as ride-hailing, food delivery, and digital payments, has collaborated with multiple governments to make and enforce rules in ride hailing. For example, Grab has a mission statement featured on a Singaporean government website:

> Grab continues to prioritise community welfare—going beyond drivers and passengers to helping governments and local communities at large. Grab's approach is collaborative: for example, helping governments think about how ride-hailing regulations should come into effect, based on what the local infrastructure needs are. In turn, governments appreciate that we are aligned to their policy agendas and that we work together to provide long-term solutions.[31]

During the COVID-19 pandemic, Grab also partnered with the Indonesian government to set up drive-through vaccination centers and with the Malaysian government to help distribute pandemic relief funds through the app's digital wallets.[32]

In the cases discussed above, as well as the core context of the book—China's e-commerce market—both enabling conditions of institutional outsourcing are met: (1) private regulatory intermediaries (PRIs) such as digital platforms exist, and (2) the state acquiesces to or explicitly endorses them. To assess whether a new case fits the framework of institutional outsourcing, it is essential to revisit the two enabling conditions. Next, I examine three ancillary cases in the context of developed economies: the darknet market (condition 1 is met but not 2); online child pornography in the United States (both conditions are met); and Facebook's "Supreme Court" (condition 1 is met but 2 is unstable). This exercise not only helps determine whether a case qualifies as institutional outsourcing but also indicates the potential usefulness of the framework beyond the developing world.

The Darknet Market

The darknet market is a case of *private institution building without state acquiescence*. It does not fit the theory of institutional outsourcing, but it informs us why both enabling conditions need to be present for institutional outsourcing.

Darknet markets are black markets run on the dark web, a segment of the internet not indexed by conventional search engines. Accessible only through specialized software that anonymizes users' web traffic, the dark web fosters a range of criminal activities. Darknet markets often sell illicit goods such as drugs, weapons, forged currency and documents, and stolen credit card details.

Every market encounters challenges in enforcing contracts, and the darknet market is no exception. Furthermore, what makes the darknet attractive to illicit behaviors—being anonymous and unregulated by the state—also makes it vulnerable to fraud. Even cybercriminals desire to trade with "honest crooks," as illustrated by an anonymous comment:

> I have been scammed more than twice now by assholes who say they're legit when I say I want to purchase stolen credit cards. I want to do tons of business but I DO NOT want to be scammed. I wish there were people who were honest crooks. If anyone could help me out that would be awesome! I just want to buy one at first so I know the seller is legit and honest.[33]

In the absence of law enforcement, these online contraband markets had to develop private institutions to govern their transactions. A prime example is the first modern darknet market, called Silk Road. Launched in 2011, Silk Road was a global platform for trading illegal drugs, using the Tor hidden service for anonymity and Bitcoin as currency. It was founded and operated by "Dread Pirate Roberts," a pseudonym based on a fictional character in the movie *The Princess Bride*.

Silk Road developed various community and hierarchical enforcement mechanisms to facilitate honest transactions of illegal commodities. In an interesting parallel with China's e-commerce market, it also developed an escrow system to mitigate risk and provide trust. Political scientist Henry Farrell described it as follows:

> "People looking to buy commodities via Silk Road would transfer money to Silk Road's escrow account. Silk Road would then communicate the fact that the money had been received to the seller. Once both buyer and seller were happy that the deal had gone through as it should, the money in escrow would be sent, minus commission, to the seller."[34]

According to him, the escrow system proved highly effective:

> A trustworthy escrow mechanism clearly greatly eases problems of trust and trustworthiness between buyers and sellers. So long as both trust the escrow, there is far less incentive to cheat, since the cheated party can either refuse to pay (if she is the buyer and has not gotten the good as promised) or refuse to send the good (if she is the seller and the money

has not been placed in escrow). Feedback on transactions suggests that this mechanism was highly successful . . . 97.8% of feedback on consummated transactions was positive. While this likely exaggerates people's happiness with the service, it suggests that incidents of fraud were relatively rare.[35]

However, without the state's acquiescence or support, such private institutions tend to collapse. In October 2013, the FBI shut down the Silk Road website and arrested Ross Ulbricht, who was charged with being Dread Pirate Roberts. Silk Road 2.0 was created the following month under a new Dread Pirate Roberts, but it was closed a year later by another law enforcement operation.

Even without government intervention, such private institutions tend to collapse due to security issues and "exit scams," in which the market organizers grab the money in escrow and disappear. According to Nick Weaver, a Berkeley researcher who studied Silk Road and other darknet markets:

"[T]he most viable exit strategy . . . is to rip and run."[36] Silk Road 2.0 reported all the bitcoins in its escrow accounts hacked, worth approximately $2.6 million.[37] The descendant of Silk Road, Evolution, also vanished with its users' bitcoins valued at $12 million.[38] Other replacement sites, including Abraxas, Amazon Dark, Blackbank, and Middle Earth, also disappeared, "likely having pulled their own exit scams."[39]

The Silk Road escrow system echoes the observation that private economic institutions emerge in markets where state enforcement is lacking. It also indicates why state acquiescence or endorsement is an important condition for institutional outsourcing. Without the state providing ultimate backup to minimize the risk of malfeasance, private institutions tend to collapse from within and outside.

Section 230, Child Pornography, and US Platforms

Unlike the darknet market, US regulation of online child pornography is an example that exhibits both enabling conditions for institutional outsourcing: private governance and the state's backing in outsourcing.

Child pornography is considered a criminal offense in the United States, at both federal and state levels. However, the rise of the internet made it challenging for the US government to directly pursue individual "publishers" of such illegal content, as these users often remain anonymous. Therefore, rather than targeting individual users, some lawsuits shifted focus to the internet service providers for disseminating such content.[40]

To deal with such issues, in 1996 the US Congress enacted a federal statute, the Communications Decency Act (CDA), to prohibit the provision of indecent or obscene material to minors online. However, the following year, the Supreme Court deemed the act unconstitutional, citing its vagueness and potential to excessively curtail free speech. Internet advocates also expressed apprehension that the CDA could prompt platforms to overly censor content to avoid violating its provisions.

However, some parts of the CDA, including Section 230, survived. It empowers internet platforms (which it calls "interactive computer services") to police content such as child pornography on a voluntary, rather than mandatory, basis. Section 230 has established two pillars of internet governance in the United States. First, the section exempts internet platforms from legal liability for content published by third-party users. For example, Facebook cannot be charged for harmful information posted by its users. Second, it allows internet platforms to remove or moderate content "in good faith."

Essentially, Section 230 outsources the regulation of harmful online content, such as child pornography, to online platforms. Although these platforms are not legally liable for content published by third parties, external factors like public pressure, the protection of corporate image, and ethical considerations compel them to restrict such content. To regulate child pornography, major social media platforms have developed various private institutions that usually combine auto-detection (by machine-learning algorithms) and human moderation. Users can also report content to the platform or appeal a content moderation decision.

In this scenario, platforms establish private governance to regulate child pornography, a federal crime, with platforms' online regulatory authority acknowledged by Section 230. In recent years, there is growing pressure on platforms to strengthen their private regulations. Efforts to narrow the scope of Section 230 are gaining momentum in the US Congress, with the aim of increasing legal accountability for companies that do not adequately address the problem.[41]

Hate Speech Regulation and Facebook's "Supreme Court"

Another case to study is the regulation of hate speech on US social media platforms. Unlike the case of child pornography, the second enabling condition—state acquiescence and/or explicit endorsement—is much weaker and more unstable in the realm of hate speech regulation.

In the United States, while hate speech is offensive, it is generally shielded by the First Amendment. Unlike the European Union, the United States lacks hate speech laws. However, in recent years, social media platforms have faced growing criticism for hosting hate speech and misinformation. Responding to public pressure, and empowered by Section 230, American platforms have started establishing private institutions to regulate and moderate such content. These regulations often spark controversy, leading certain platforms to institutionalize the removal of offensive content.

A notable institutional development in this field is Facebook's Oversight Board, often referred to as its "Supreme Court," which began operations in 2020. The board is an independent, quasi-judicial body responsible for reviewing and potentially overturning Facebook's content moderation decisions. Its twenty members include academics, lawyers, and political leaders. So far, it has reviewed several cases, including Donald Trump's ban from Facebook and Instagram following the January 2021 Capitol Hill riots.

There are parallels between Facebook's Oversight Board and Taobao's jury system. Both platforms struggle with growing complaints from users, whether concerning harmful content or user disputes. Outsourcing justice to a third party allows platforms to shift the responsibility for making unpopular decisions: Facebook relies on a group of external experts to establish content moderation standards, while Taobao randomly selects experienced users to serve as jurors for resolving online disputes. In both scenarios, private institutions emerge when public institutions are absent or incapable of enforcement, which meets the first condition of institutional outsourcing.

However, the second enabling condition (state acquiescence or endorsement) is uncertain in the case of hate speech regulation. On the one hand, Section 230 grants internet platforms the authority to restrict content they deem harmful, regardless of whether such material is constitutionally protected. Platforms thus have discretion to categorize hate speech as harmful content and remove it. On the other hand, the United States has a strong tradition of freedom of speech, which is upheld by the First Amendment. It's important to differentiate between the regulation of hate speech and child pornography. While child pornography is illegal under federal law, hate speech is not, and it is unlikely to be criminalized in the foreseeable future. Without the support of public regulations, platforms' private content regulations remain highly contentious. The tension between their content moderation and the nation's free speech tradition renders outsourcing unstable.

The Uncertain Path Forward

What does the future hold for China's e-commerce industry? For the rapidly evolving technology sector, change is the only constant.

Truly, the history of e-commerce in China is a saga of sweeping transformations and unexpected turns. When I began my research in 2013, the burgeoning e-commerce market in China remained unnoticed by most Westerners.

However, it didn't take long for Alibaba, Jack Ma, and the entire Chinese internet industry to burst onto the global stage, capturing the attention of wary US tech giants. Then, in 2020, a seismic regulatory shift occurred. China's sudden crackdown halted the highly anticipated IPO of Ant Group, triggering a regulatory storm that stalled the meteoric rise of Chinese tech titans. By early 2023, the Chinese government pivoted back to supporting the platform economy. Nevertheless, a sluggish domestic economy has since tempered the once-unstoppable momentum of e-commerce growth in China.

While predicting the precise trajectory of the industry's future is challenging, I can identify two key risk factors that will influence it.

The first risk factor revolves around the robustness of China's overall economy. This will influence the purchasing power of Chinese citizens and, ultimately, their inclination to make online orders. Prior to 2020, despite indications of saturation, China's e-commerce market consistently expanded, owing to rising disposable income, general optimism about future economic prospects, and the younger generation's propensity for more generous spending compared to their frugal parents. However, post-2022, the Chinese economy faced unprecedented challenges due to earlier coronavirus lockdowns and unfavorable global environments. Numerous industries witnessed salary cuts and layoffs, with the youth unemployment rate reaching alarming levels. Consequently, citizens, including young Chinese consumers, curtailed their expenditures and prioritized savings. If China's macroeconomic conditions continue to struggle, consumers are likely to further reduce spending on nonessential items and opt for more affordable products. This trend of "consumption downgrade" has fueled growth for e-commerce platforms that prioritize low prices, like Pinduoduo. It may also prompt other platforms to follow suit, prioritizing price over product quality.

Despite the lackluster performance in domestic sales, there is a silver lining for the industry: cross-border e-commerce has flourished since 2020. Chinese sellers have asserted dominance on third-party marketplaces like Amazon. Traditional e-commerce giants such as Alibaba have also increased their investments in this area, leading to impressive revenue growth in overseas e-commerce sales. Moreover, other China-originated e-commerce platforms like Shein and Temu have swiftly gained popularity in the US market, potentially marking a new chapter in the global e-commerce landscape.

The second risk factor concerns the government's role in the economy, particularly how it treats large platforms. According to Barry Weingast (1995), fostering markets requires a government strong enough to uphold property rights and enforce contracts, yet not too strong that it can arbitrarily revoke these rights. An excessively strong government can hinder market growth by instilling fear of property and rights seizures, thereby discouraging investment and innovation among firms and individuals.

It is difficult to have a government that is *strong enough but not overly strong*. In many countries, markets fail to develop because the government is not strong enough—either lacking the capacity to implement policies or being captured by private interests. China faces the opposite problem: the government tends to be overly powerful and decisive, leaving firms with few means to challenge arbitrary government actions. Therefore, to nurture market growth, it requires the government to exercise self-restraint and resist the temptation of excessive intervention in the economy.

This logic is evident in China's e-commerce market development. As highlighted in the book, the key contributor to the e-commerce boom was the state's deliberate choice to avoid excessive regulation. Before 2020, the government exercised great tolerance toward the institutional innovations of private platforms, even when their operations ventured into legally ambiguous terrain and challenged vested interests. This effectively formed an implicit contract between the platforms and the government, with platforms committed to fostering growth and innovation, while the state refrained from exerting undue control. Such an implicit contract bolstered market confidence, incentivizing private investments, risk-taking, and the overall growth of e-commerce.

Unfortunately, China's regulatory shift in 2020 shattered the implicit contract and indicated the perils of unconstrained governmental powers. While there were legitimate reasons for regulating Big Tech firms, the regulations were executed in a radical and heavy-handed approach, resulting in a significant loss of market value in the internet sector, amounting to trillions of dollars. Although the Chinese government later eased regulations and resumed support for the platform economy, the regulatory storm showcased the government's formidable might, leaving a lingering perception of policy uncertainty. This has greatly undermined market confidence, discouraging platform innovation and private investments.

In contemplating the future, the critical question is how long it will take to restore market confidence and what actions the government can undertake to accomplish this. Despite recent actions by the Chinese government to bolster the private sector, including establishing supportive government bodies[42] and acknowledging private entrepreneurs as integral contributors to the nation,[43] there has been limited success in stimulating the economy. Perhaps the answer lies in the timeless wisdom of the revered Chinese philosopher Mencius: "Doing what should be done while refraining from what should not be done (有所为有所不为)." The industry's future hinges not just on the government's active support but, more significantly, on its judicious practice of "non-doing"—resisting excessive control, exercising restraint when necessary, and granting greater autonomy to the market.

Appendix A

A.1 China Entrepreneurs Survey (CES): Implementation Notes

SURVEY PLATFORM AND SAMPLING FRAME

A premier Chinese survey company, QQSurvey (Quality & Quick), implemented the survey. The firm maintains an online panel of over 2.7 million registered users throughout China who take surveys for cash rewards. QQSurvey charges a high cost per completed survey (three times more than its competitors) due to its rigorous identity verification and quality control procedures.

The survey sampling employed a nonprobabilistic approach because of the difficulties in identifying and reaching the entire online merchant population. Online merchants are often scattered across various digital platforms, operate from mobile workplaces, and lack official registration. Neither QQSurvey nor other online survey companies had access to comprehensive occupational information about their participants, which made it challenging to specifically target the online merchant group.

To tackle this issue, survey invitations were sent to registered users with generic information, intentionally withholding the specific occupation for which the survey was designed. Only those users who self-identified as "online merchant" or "brick-and-mortar storeowner" were allowed to proceed. Additionally, respondents had to pass screening questions to ensure the authenticity of their information, such as providing store details and having a unique IP address. In total, the firm dispatched 27,597 survey solicitation links, resulting in a preliminary sample of 3,801 responses. Subsequently, several postsurvey quality checks were performed to eliminate poor-quality data. The final sample comprised 3,280 business owners, with 1,920 being online merchants and 1,360 being traditional, offline merchants. An oversampling of online merchants was conducted since they received additional questions about their online store operations.

As a probabilistic sample was not feasible, I assessed the representativeness of my online merchant sample by comparing it with a benchmark—the Taobao Online Merchant Survey (TOMS), conducted by Alibaba in 2012 on a nationally representative sample of online merchants on Taobao. I demonstrate later that the two surveys exhibit resemblances along major dimensions. Although the sampling frame had limitations, it was the best possible approach given the constraints I faced during the study.

STRATEGIES TO ENSURE DATA QUALITY

The survey data is of high quality due to a variety of rigorous procedures to screen out respondents who are insincere or inattentive. The survey firm employs a variety of measures to ensure data quality and verify respondent identity. It identifies unique IP addresses to prevent respondents from participating more than once. It also conducts additional checks that are more stringent than industry standards. For example, respondents are asked classification questions (e.g., gender, occupation, income, and other identity information) that they have answered previously to check for consistency. Survey response time, trap questions, and attention filters are also used to ascertain survey quality. If a respondent fails any of the quality checks, no reward is given and the response is dropped. Respondents are also constantly ranked by their history of "integrity" based on the number of times they survive quality checks. Those with high "integrity" scores will be more likely to receive a survey invitation, and those who receive three warnings will be cut from the panel. These measures incentivize respondents to provide high-quality data.

In addition to quality controls imposed by the online panel, I designed additional procedures to preempt two concerns common to all online surveys: survey satisficing and self-selection.

Survey satisficing occurs when respondents do not fully engage with the questions and only choose the answers that require the least cognitive effort.[1] For example, respondents may select a random answer or the first one displayed instead of going through all the alternatives. As such, satisficing activities increase measurement errors and jeopardize data reliability. I use three measures to reduce satisficing and exclude inattentive subjects. First, I drop respondents who spent an extremely short time responding or fail the trap questions. Second, at the beginning of the survey, I use instructional manipulation checks to screen out respondents who do not carefully read the instructions.[2] Lastly, I embed hidden timing tools into the survey to record the amount of time spent on important questions (those to be coded as dependent and independent variables). If these questions are used in the analysis, I include and exclude low-quality responses (measured by time spent on the questions) in regressions to check the robustness of the results. These tools address the possibility that even the most attentive respondents may get fatigued at some point and rush through the rest of the survey.

Another concern is that the respondents can self-select into a survey, hence skewing the sample toward entrepreneurs who have strong opinions about the subject. If this is the case, the sample may not be representative of the general population of interest. I do not find this to be a major problem for the China Entrepreneurs Survey because the survey invitation is purposefully designed to be generic. Respondents are only informed about the survey's subject after accepting the survey invitation, and the dropout rate after seeing the subject is below 5 percent.

A.2 *Additional Analysis*

TABLE A4.1. Descriptive Statistics of the CES Dataset

Var.	N	Mean	Min	Max	SD
Online	3280	0.5854	0	1	0.4927
TimeGovRelations	2941	1.3410	0	13	1.9627
RegulatoryIntensity					
1	3269	0.1778	0	1	0.3823
2	3269	0.2600	0	1	0.4386
3	3269	0.3044	0	1	0.4602
4	3269	0.1340	0	1	0.3407
5	3269	0.0728	0	1	0.2598
6	3269	0.0284	0	1	0.1661
7	3269	0.0092	0	1	0.0955
8	3269	0.0135	0	1	0.1154
NumOfficialInspec					
1	3280	0.2138	0	1	0.4100
2	3280	0.4279	0	1	0.4948
3	3280	0.2796	0	1	0.4488
4	3280	0.0787	0	1	0.2693

Var.	N	Mean	Min	Max	SD
Female	3280	0.4851	0	1	0.4998
Age					
Below 20	3280	0.0345	0	1	0.1825
21–30	3280	0.4290	0	1	0.4949
31–40	3280	0.4030	0	1	0.4905
41–50	3280	0.1098	0	1	0.3126
Above 50	3280	0.0238	0	1	0.1524
Education					
1	3269	0.0012	0	1	0.0346
2	3269	0.1190	0	1	0.3238
3	3269	0.2343	0	1	0.4236
4	3269	0.5980	0	1	0.4903
5	3269	0.0474	0	1	0.2125
CCP	3280	0.2240	0	1	0.4169
PCorPCC	3280	0.0857	0	1	0.2799
Employment (level)					

YearOfBiz	3280	6.8840	1	32	4.2730
ValuePC					
1	3280	0.1936	0	1	0.3951
2	3280	0.4457	0	1	0.4970
3	3280	0.2485	0	1	0.4321
4	3280	0.0893	0	1	0.2852
5	3280	0.0229	0	1	0.1496
Area					
1	3280	0.8341	0	1	0.3720
2	3280	0.1381	0	1	0.3450
3	3280	0.0278	0	1	0.1644

1	3280	0.5683	0	1	0.4953
2	3280	0.3071	0	1	0.4613
3	3280	0.1049	0	1	0.3064
4	3280	0.0211	0	1	0.1438
Sales					
1	3280	0.3238	0	1	0.4679
2	3280	0.2902	0	1	0.4539
3	3280	0.2220	0	1	0.4156
4	3280	0.1236	0	1	0.3291
5	3280	0.0414	0	1	0.1992

Note: Online is a dichotomous variable to indicate whether the vast majority of a merchant's income comes from online or offline (online = 1; offline = 0). TimeGovRelations documents the average time per day invested in maintaining and improving local government relations. Regulatory-Intensity shows the time spent per month dealing with the requirements imposed by government regulations (almost zero time = 1; 1 day = 2; 2–3 days = 3; 4–5 days = 4; 6–8 days = 5; 9–12 days = 6; 13–16 days = 7, more than 17 days = 8). NumOfficialInspec is the frequency of visits or required meetings with local officials (never = 1; seldom = 2; sometimes = 3; often = 4). ValuePC reflects whether the private merchant agrees with the statement "making acquaintance with local officials is helpful for my business" (strongly agree = 1; somewhat agree = 2; neither agree nor disagree = 3; somewhat disagree = 4; strongly disagree = 5). YearOfBiz denotes the number of years as an offline/online entrepreneur. Area indicates the location where the merchant operates business (city = 1; county/township = 2; countryside/suburb = 3). Storesales is a categorical variable showing the annual sales of the business (in RMB) in 2015 (under 100k = 1; 100k–360k = 2; 360k–1 million = 3; 1–5 million = 4; more than 5 million = 5). Age is the merchant's age (below 20 = 1; 21–30 = 2; 31–40 = 3; 41–50 = 4; above 50 = 5). Education shows the highest degree earned by this merchant (primary school education or below = 1; junior high school = 2; senior high school = 3; college = 4; graduate school = 5). CCP indicates whether the merchant is a Communist Party member. PCorCPPCC indicates whether the merchant is a member of the People's Congress of Chinese People's Consultative Conference at any level. Employment is the number of employees of the business at the end of 2015 (1–4 = 1; 5–10 = 2; 11–99 = 3; more than 100 = 4).

TABLE A4.2. Regression Results before and after Controlling for Prior Political Ties

	RegulatoryIntensity		NumOfficialInspec		TimeGovRelations		ValuePC	
	(1)	(2)	(3)	(4)	(5)	(6)	(7)	(8)
Online	-0.346***	-0.317***	-0.219***	-0.198***	-0.610***	-0.607***	0.411***	0.394***
	(0.062)	(0.074)	(0.067)	(0.070)	(0.076)	(0.076)	(0.116)	(0.115)
Prior Political Ties		✓		✓		✓		✓
Individual-level Covariates	✓	✓	✓	✓	✓	✓	✓	✓
Business-level Covariates	✓	✓	✓	✓	✓	✓	✓	✓
Province FE	✓	✓	✓	✓	✓	✓	✓	✓
Model	Ordered Logit	Ordered Logit	Ordered Logit	Ordered Logit	Neg. Binom.	Neg. Binom.	Ordered Logit	Ordered Logit
N	3249	3249	3231	3231	2926	2926	3260	3260
Pseudo R-squared	0.0710	0.0690	0.0780	0.0740	0.0740	0.0740	0.0410	0.0390

Note: * $p < 0.1$; ** $p < 0.05$; *** $p < 0.01$. Standard errors are clustered at the provincial level and reported in the parentheses.

TABLE A4.3. Regression Results before and after Controlling for *Sociability*

	RegulatoryIntensity		NumOfficialInspec		TimeGovRelations		ValuePC	
	(1)	(2)	(3)	(4)	(5)	(6)	(7)	(8)
Online	−0.322***	−0.317***	−0.203***	−0.198***	−0.608***	−0.607***	0.417***	0.394***
	(0.062)	(0.074)	(0.070)	(0.070)	(0.077)	(0.076)	(0.120)	(0.115)
Sociability		✓		✓		✓		✓
Individual-level Covariates	✓	✓	✓	✓	✓	✓	✓	✓
Business-level Covariates	✓	✓	✓	✓	✓	✓	✓	✓
Province FE	✓	✓	✓	✓	✓	✓	✓	✓
Model	Ordered Logit	Ordered Logit	Ordered Logit	Ordered Logit	Neg. Binom.	Neg. Binom.	Ordered Logit	Ordered Logit
N	3249	3249	3231	3231	2926	2926	3260	3260
Pseudo R-squared	0.0690	0.0690	0.0740	0.0740	0.0740	0.0740	0.0440	0.0390

Note: * $p < 0.1$; ** $p < 0.05$; *** $p < 0.01$. Standard errors are clustered at the provincial level and reported in the parentheses.

TABLE A4.4. Regression Results before and after Controlling for *Interest in Politics*

	RegulatoryIntensity		NumOfficialInspec		TimeGovRelations		ValuePC	
	(1)	(2)	(3)	(4)	(5)	(6)	(7)	(8)
Online	−0.365***	−0.317***	−0.249***	−0.198***	−0.627***	−0.607***	0.484***	0.394***
	(0.061)	(0.074)	(0.072)	(0.070)	(0.077)	(0.076)	(0.118)	(0.115)
Interest in Politics		✓		✓		✓		✓
Individual-level Covariates	✓	✓	✓	✓	✓	✓	✓	✓
Business-level Covariates	✓	✓	✓	✓	✓	✓	✓	✓
Province FE	✓	✓	✓	✓	✓	✓	✓	✓
Model	Ordered Logit	Ordered Logit	Ordered Logit	Ordered Logit	Neg. Binom.	Neg. Binom.	Ordered Logit	Ordered Logit
N	3249	3249	3231	3231	2926	2926	3260	3260
Pseudo R-squared	0.0730	0.0690	0.0820	0.0740	0.0770	0.0740	0.0530	0.0390

Note: * $p < 0.1$; ** $p < 0.05$; *** $p < 0.01$. Standard errors are clustered at the provincial level and reported in the parentheses.

TABLE A4.5. Regression Results before and after Controlling for *Anti-authority Attitude* (Part I)

	RegulatoryIntensity			NumOfficialInspec		
	(1)	(2)	(3)	(4)	(5)	(6)
Online	−0.332***	−0.361***	−0.317***	−0.232***	−0.249***	−0.198***
	(0.064)	(0.061)	(0.074)	(0.073)	(0.073)	(0.070)
Anti-authority Attitude_Var1	✓			✓		
Anti-authority Attitude_Var2		✓			✓	
Individual-level Covariates	✓	✓	✓	✓	✓	✓
Business-level Covariates	✓	✓	✓	✓	✓	✓
Province FE	✓	✓	✓	✓	✓	✓
Model	Ordered Logit	Ordered Logit	Ordered Logit	Ordered Logit	Ordered Logit	Ordered Logit
N	3249	3249	3249	3231	3231	3231
Pseudo R-squared	0.0690	0.0760	0.0690	0.0760	0.0870	0.0740

Note: $^*p<0.1$; $^{**}p<0.05$; $^{***}p<0.01$. Standard errors are clustered at the provincial level and reported in the parentheses.

TABLE A4.6. Regression Results before and after Controlling for Anti-authority Attitude (Part II)

	TimeGovRelations			ValuePC		
	(1)	(2)	(3)	(4)	(5)	(6)
Online	−0.630***	−0.657***	−0.607***	−0.451***	−0.497***	−0.394***
	(0.075)	(0.080)	(0.076)	(0.116)	(0.117)	(0.115)
Anti-authority Attitude_ Var1	✓			✓		
Anti-authority Attitude_Var2		✓			✓	
Individual-level Covariates	✓	✓	✓	✓	✓	✓
Business-level Covariates	✓	✓	✓	✓	✓	✓
Province FE	✓	✓	✓	✓	✓	✓
Model	Neg. Binom.	Neg. Binom.	Neg. Binom.	Ordered Logit	Ordered Logit	Ordered Logit
N	2,926	2,926	2,926	3,260	3,260	3,260
Pseudo R-squared	0.0760	0.0860	0.0740	0.0460	0.0650	0.0390

Note: $^*p<0.1$; $^{**}p<0.05$; $^{***}p<0.01$. Standard errors are clustered at the provincial level and reported in the parentheses.

TABLE A4.7. Regression Results before and after Controlling for *Risk Preference*

	RegulatoryIntensity		NumOfficialInspec		TimeGovRelations		ValuePC	
	(1)	(2)	(3)	(4)	(5)	(6)	(7)	(8)
Online	−0.353***	−0.317***	−0.266***	−0.198***	−0.681***	−0.607***	0.484***	0.394***
	(0.062)	(0.074)	(0.068)	(0.070)	(0.074)	(0.076)	(0.118)	(0.115)
Risk Preference		✓		✓		✓		✓
Individual-level Covariates	✓	✓	✓	✓	✓	✓	✓	✓
Business-level Covariates	✓	✓	✓	✓	✓	✓	✓	✓
Province FE	✓	✓	✓	✓	✓	✓	✓	✓
Model	Ordered Logit	Ordered Logit	Ordered Logit	Ordered Logit	Neg. Binom.	Neg. Binom.	Ordered Logit	Ordered Logit
N	3249	3249	3231	3231	2926	2926	3260	3260
Pseudo R-squared	0.0700	0.0690	0.0820	0.0740	0.0840	0.0740	0.0530	0.0390

Note: * $p < 0.1$; ** $p < 0.05$; *** $p < 0.01$. Standard errors are clustered at the provincial level and reported in the parentheses.

TABLE A4.8. Did State-Business Interactions Decline after the Switch from Offline to Online Commerce?

Agree	60.00%	Strongly Agree	190
		Somewhat Agree	316
Neutral	20.9%	Neither Agree Nor Disagree	176
Disagree	19.10%	Somewhat Disagree	137
		Strongly Disagree	24
	100.00%	Total	843

TABLE A4.9. Covariate Balance Table: Coarsened Exact Matching (CEM)

	Pre-matching				Post-matching			
Covariates	L_1	Mean	Min	Max	L_1	Mean	Min	Max
Age	0.10895	0.41532	0	0	1.6e-16	2.2E-15	0	0
Education	0.06154	0.13303	0	0	1.8E-16	1.8E-15	0	0
YearOfBiz	0.18939	−2.10630	−1	−9	0.05569	0.02936	−1	−1
Employment	0.27906	−1.25630	0	0	2.9E-16	4.4E-16	0	0
Gender	0.08167	0.08167	0	0	3.3E-16	−1.1e-16	0	0
CCP	0.02280	0.02280	0	0	2.8E-16	−1.1e-16	0	0
Area	0.08639	−0.09974	0	0	1.5e-16	−6.9E-17	0	0
Sales	0.27654	−1.9872	0	0	1.6e-16	−1.1e-15	0	0
PCorPCC	0.00311	−0.00311	0	0	6.4E-17	−1.7e-17	0	0

Note: L1 is a multivariate imbalance statistic proposed by Iacus, King, and Porro (2011). L1 varies in [0,1] where L1 = 0 indicates perfect global balance, and L1 = 1 means no overlap in the multidimensional histograms.

Appendix B

B.1 Web-Scraped Store Information: Data Notes

GENERAL DESCRIPTION

The raw dataset contains web-scraped, product-level data of 1,761,339 online stores that actively operated in December 2014 on Taobao.com. The raw data was scraped by an anonymous software engineer who made the data public for downloads for a short period of time in 2015. Each data entry is at the product level. For each store, the dataset includes information about store name, store location, product description, unique product id, product category, unique category id, and product price. The dataset has 9,987,432 product-level observations. The data constitutes a nationally representative sample of all active stores on Taobao.com during the same period.

EXAMPLE OF OBSERVATION IN THE DATASET

{"name": "冲冠秒杀草编换鞋凳收纳凳储物箱储物凳收纳箱坐箱颜色可定特价", "nick": "博兴魏位888", "_id": 10138775967, "category": 50023172, "query": "收纳凳", "area": "滨州", "price": 35.0}

VARIABLES

Variable	Description	Variable	Description
name	Product description	nick	Unique store name
_id	Unique id for a product	category	Unique id for a product category
query	Product category name	area	City or prefectural-level city
price	Price of the product (RMB)		

B.2 Constructing Online Store Index at the City/Prefecture Level

As the second step, a prefectural-level dataset on e-commerce selling is constructed based on the raw data. The purpose of the prefectural-level dataset is to uncover the macrolevel features of China's online retailing industry. The goal of the data processing is to aggregate store information to the city/prefecture level. The output reflects the regional distribution of (a) store number, (b) product diversity, which is measured by the number of products/categories of a region, and (c) local specialty products that cover the top twenty product categories sold in an area.

B.3 Summary of the Output Dataset

TABLE B4.1. Number of Stores by Location

Store Location	Number of Stores
Municipalities	291,970
Prefectural-level Divisions	1,441,751
Hong Kong	12,187
Macau	228
Taiwan	658
Other*	732
Overseas	12,223
Missing Location Information	1,590
Total	1,761,339

Notes: *Other locations refer to the county-level administrative units directly governed by provinces.

TABLE B4.2. Distribution of Taobao Stores across Municipalities

English Name	Chinese Name	Type	Number of Stores	Number of Product Categories	Number of Products
Beijing	北京	Municipality	106,052	2,571	716,422
Chongqing	重庆	Municipality	8,099	2,191	48,412
Tianjin	天津	Municipality	12,067	2,274	71,301
Shanghai	上海	Municipality	165,752	2,592	1,272,373

Notes: A municipality, which is directly governed by the central government, enjoys the same political and economic status as a province.

TABLE B4.3. Distribution of Taobao Stores across Prefectural-level Divisions

English Name	Chinese Name	Province/ Autonomous Region	Type	Number of Stores	Number of Product Categories	Number of Products
Anqing	安庆	Anhui	C	1,127	1,054	5,944
Bengbu	蚌埠	Anhui	C	1,052	1,048	6,474
Bozhou	亳州	Anhui	C	650	396	1,514
Chizhou	池州	Anhui	C	209	353	922
Chuzhou	滁州	Anhui	C	792	782	4,360
Fuyang	阜阳	Anhui	C	721	811	2,698
Hefei*	合肥*	Anhui	C	9,922	2,217	52,310
Huaibei	淮北	Anhui	C	256	443	1,298
Huainan	淮南	Anhui	C	341	489	1,746
Huangshan	黄山	Anhui	C	531	572	2,819
Lu'an	六安	Anhui	C	854	709	3,123
Ma'anshan	马鞍山	Anhui	C	418	569	2,484
Suzhou, Anhui	宿州	Anhui	C	515	642	2,468
Tongling	铜陵	Anhui	C	149	358	1,886
Wuhu	芜湖	Anhui	C	1,836	1,417	13,563
Xuancheng	宣城	Anhui	C	1,153	644	11,611
Fuzhou, Fujian*	福州*	Fujian	C	12,594	2,200	67,893
Longyan	龙岩	Fujian	C	954	871	2,989
Nanping	南平	Fujian	C	1,171	885	5,391
Ningde	宁德	Fujian	C	2,155	1,076	7,317
Putian	莆田	Fujian	C	6,456	1,158	22,079
Quanzhou	泉州	Fujian	C	51,892	2,264	214,316
Sanming	三明	Fujian	C	707	673	2,660
Xiamen	厦门	Fujian	C	19,473	2,283	81,531
Zhangzhou	漳州	Fujian	C	2,193	1,329	11,029
Baiyin	白银	Gansu	C	31	37	57
Dingxi	定西	Gansu	C	28	26	38
Gannan	甘南	Gansu	AP	6	9	20
Jiayuguan	嘉峪关	Gansu	C	13	11	23
Jinchang	金昌	Gansu	C	13	23	71
Jiuquan	酒泉	Gansu	C	72	61	174
Lanzhou*	兰州*	Gansu	C	585	588	2,078
Linxia	临夏	Gansu	AP	18	18	49
Longnan	陇南	Gansu	C	142	48	232
Pingliang	平凉	Gansu	C	25	30	38
Qingyang	庆阳	Gansu	C	41	29	81
Tianshui	天水	Gansu	C	73	100	178
Wuwei	武威	Gansu	C	26	30	83
Zhangye	张掖	Gansu	C	21	22	30
Chaozhou	潮州	Guangdong	C	10,695	1,445	60,594
Dongguan	东莞	Guangdong	C	36,419	2,409	172,582
Foshan	佛山	Guangdong	C	38,465	2,311	234,409
Guangzhou*	广州	Guangdong	C	192,869	2,593	1,030,937

English Name	Chinese Name	Province/ Autonomous Region	Type	Number of Stores	Number of Product Categories	Number of Products
Heyuan	河源	Guangdong	C	369	444	1,221
Huizhou	惠州	Guangdong	C	8,794	1,950	37,552
Jiangmen	江门	Guangdong	C	6,523	1,857	41,100
Jieyang	揭阳	Guangdong	C	14,946	1,701	64,473
Maoming	茂名	Guangdong	C	731	732	3,322
Meizhou	梅州	Guangdong	C	844	796	3,333
Qingyuan	清远	Guangdong	C	508	742	2,948
Shantou	汕头	Guangdong	C	18,110	2,013	104,018
Shanwei	汕尾	Guangdong	C	1,479	726	6,796
Shaoguan	韶关	Guangdong	C	499	606	3,543
Shenzhen	深圳	Guangdong	C	113,032	2,530	569,543
Yangjiang	阳江	Guangdong	C	1,816	853	10,581
Yunfu	云浮	Guangdong	C	371	420	1,580
Zhanjiang	湛江	Guangdong	C	1,449	880	6,414
Zhaoqing	肇庆	Guangdong	C	1,180	946	6,424
Zhongshan	中山	Guangdong	C	26,438	2,086	137,990
Zhuhai	珠海	Guangdong	C	3,308	1,720	17,100
Baise	百色	Guangxi	C	111	92	257
Beihai	北海	Guangxi	C	325	286	979
Chongzuo	崇左	Guangxi	C	231	161	956
Fangchenggang	防城港	Guangxi	C	707	257	4,206
Guigang	贵港	Guangxi	C	177	216	673
Guilin	桂林	Guangxi	C	1,844	1,124	9,833
Hechi	河池	Guangxi	C	124	107	313
Hezhou	贺州	Guangxi	C	99	143	312
Laibin	来宾	Guangxi	C	52	62	138
Liuzhou	柳州	Guangxi	C	1,097	953	5,356
Nanning*	南宁*	Guangxi	C	3,826	1,706	16,825
Qinzhou	钦州	Guangxi	C	156	175	431
Wuzhou	梧州	Guangxi	C	247	316	914
Yulin, Guangxi	玉林	Guangxi	C	680	614	2,933
Anshun	安顺	Guizhou	C	69	85	346
Bijie	毕节	Guizhou	C	45	48	162
Guiyang*	贵阳	Guizhou	C	941	845	3,310
Liupanshui	六盘水	Guizhou	C	44	54	178
Qiandongnan	黔东南	Guizhou	AP	133	130	412
Qiannan	黔南	Guizhou	AP	71	71	170
Qianxinan	黔西南	Guizhou	AP	37	45	76
Tongren	铜仁	Guizhou	C	80	64	212
Zunyi	遵义	Guizhou	C	234	167	467
Danzhou	儋州	Hainan	C	16	17	68
Haikou*	海口	Hainan	C	1,065	643	6,474

(*continued*)

English Name	Chinese Name	Province/ Autonomous Region	Type	Number of Stores	Number of Product Categories	Number of Products
Sansha	三沙	Hainan	C	5	5	5
Sanya	三亚	Hainan	C	599	159	2,053
Baoding	保定	Hebei	C	16,244	1,635	60,820
Cangzhou	沧州	Hebei	C	3,046	1,220	13,916
Chengde	承德	Hebei	C	255	309	1,192
Handan	邯郸	Hebei	C	1,410	1,041	5,214
Hengshui	衡水	Hebei	C	5,222	1,167	17,665
Langfang	廊坊	Hebei	C	3,834	1,415	16,264
Qinhuangdao	秦皇岛	Hebei	C	812	836	3,700
Shijiazhuang*	石家庄	Hebei	C	18,480	2,241	96,763
Tangshan	唐山	Hebei	C	1,840	1,326	10,123
Xingtai	邢台	Hebei	C	11,012	1,296	38,815
Zhangjiakou	张家口	Hebei	C	345	428	1,792
Daqing	大庆	Heilongjiang	C	229	267	612
Daxing'anling	大兴安岭	Heilongjiang	P	192	39	1,011
Harbin*	哈尔滨	Heilongjiang	C	3,384	1,717	16,624
Hegang	鹤岗	Heilongjiang	C	48	56	112
Heihe	黑河	Heilongjiang	C	140	116	743
Jiamusi	佳木斯	Heilongjiang	C	114	147	482
Jixi	鸡西	Heilongjiang	C	51	77	144
Mudanjiang	牡丹江	Heilongjiang	C	459	309	3,370
Qiqihar	齐齐哈尔	Heilongjiang	C	177	198	687
Qitaihe	七台河	Heilongjiang	C	33	40	80
Shuangyashan	双鸭山	Heilongjiang	C	25	40	57
Suihua	绥化	Heilongjiang	C	104	141	466
Yichun, Heilongjiang	伊春	Heilongjiang	C	191	92	552
Anyang	安阳	Henan	C	815	659	3,492
Hebi	鹤壁	Henan	C	286	252	765
Jiaozuo	焦作	Henan	C	646	660	3,886
Kaifeng	开封	Henan	C	520	544	2,416
Luohe	漯河	Henan	C	990	607	4,247
Luoyang	洛阳	Henan	C	2,184	1,376	10,605
Nanyang	南阳	Henan	C	2,676	927	15,094
Pingdingshan	平顶山	Henan	C	390	509	2,003
Puyang	濮阳	Henan	C	341	446	1,407
Sanmenxia	三门峡	Henan	C	129	151	350
Shangqiu	商丘	Henan	C	1,046	872	5,753
Xinxiang	新乡	Henan	C	1,122	908	5,104
Xinyang	信阳	Henan	C	459	501	1,745
Xuchang	许昌	Henan	C	831	733	3,285
Zhengzhou*	郑州	Henan	C	19,086	2,347	99,363
Zhoukou	周口	Henan	C	662	535	2,217

English Name	Chinese Name	Province/ Autonomous Region	Type	Number of Stores	Number of Product Categories	Number of Products
Zhumadian	驻马店	Henan	C	400	440	1,421
Enshi	恩施	Hubei	AP	224	228	810
Ezhou	鄂州	Hubei	C	130	179	451
Huanggang	黄冈	Hubei	C	487	523	1,602
Jingmen	荆门	Hubei	C	359	565	1,923
Jingzhou	荆州	Hubei	C	1,053	966	4,936
Shiyan	十堰	Hubei	C	317	403	1,232
Suizhou	随州	Hubei	C	248	334	1,157
Wuhan*	武汉	Hubei	C	21,285	2,377	120,751
Xiangyang	襄樊	Hubei	C	942	865	4,247
Xianning	咸宁	Hubei	C	235	318	834
Xiaogan	孝感	Hubei	C	412	410	1,302
Huangshi	黄石	Hubei	C	288	405	1,037
Yichang	宜昌	Hubei	C	1,045	939	3,860
Changde	常德	Hunan	C	548	638	3,021
Changsha*	长沙	Hunan	C	12,528	2,297	70,730
Chenzhou	郴州	Hunan	C	1,299	554	2,576
Hengyang	衡阳	Hunan	C	732	685	2,614
Huaihua	怀化	Hunan	C	412	401	1,787
Loudi	娄底	Hunan	C	407	435	1,213
Shaoyang	邵阳	Hunan	C	803	589	3,160
Xiangtan	湘潭	Hunan	C	980	790	8,374
Xiangxi	湘西	Hunan	AP	170	134	461
Yiyang	益阳	Hunan	C	1,682	580	6,473
Yongzhou	永州	Hunan	C	307	402	1,151
Yueyang	岳阳	Hunan	C	858	698	3,467
Zhangjiajie	张家界	Hunan	C	193	193	625
Zhuzhou	株洲	Hunan	C	2,426	1,082	10,195
Alxa	阿拉善	Inner Mongolia	L	10	11	27
Baotou	包头	Inner Mongolia	C	262	289	912
Bayannur	巴彦淖尔	Inner Mongolia	C	111	98	556
Bayingolin	巴音郭楞	Inner Mongolia	C	257	54	656
Chifeng	赤峰	Inner Mongolia	L	134	131	389
Hinggan	兴安盟	Inner Mongolia	L	1	1	4
Hohhot*	呼和浩特	Inner Mongolia	C	638	458	2,635
Hulunbuir	呼伦贝尔	Inner Mongolia	C	94	89	393
Ordos	鄂尔多斯	Inner Mongolia	C	259	106	643
Tongliao	通辽	Inner Mongolia	C	72	73	228
Ulanqab	乌兰察布	Inner Mongolia	C	44	56	161
Wuhai	乌海	Inner Mongolia	C	19	23	67
Xilingol	锡林郭勒	Inner Mongolia	L	53	40	573

(*continued*)

English Name	Chinese Name	Province/ Autonomous Region	Type	Number of Stores	Number of Product Categories	Number of Products
Changzhou	常州	Jiangsu	C	11,173	2,173	73,807
Huai'an	淮安	Jiangsu	C	2,385	1,550	13,509
Lianyungang	连云港	Jiangsu	C	7,586	1,790	47,091
Nanjing*	南京	Jiangsu	C	23,097	2,442	161,996
Nantong	南通	Jiangsu	C	27,606	2,048	104,383
Suqian	宿迁	Jiangsu	C	4,819	1,615	21,594
Suzhou, Jiangsu	苏州	Jiangsu	C	46,653	2,928	258,693
Taizhou, Jiangsu	泰州	Jiangsu	C	4,256	1,735	24,665
Wuxi	无锡	Jiangsu	C	12,802	2,384	89,523
Xuzhou	徐州	Jiangsu	C	20,463	2,181	97,062
Yancheng	盐城	Jiangsu	C	4,124	1,814	22,599
Yangzhou	扬州	Jiangsu	C	9,972	1,895	56,151
Zhenjiang	镇江	Jiangsu	C	4,615	1,568	26,015
Fuzhou, Jiangxi	抚州	Jiangxi	C	438	607	2,058
Ganzhou	赣州	Jiangxi	C	2,598	1,150	9,055
Ji'an	吉安	Jiangxi	C	812	449	2,417
Jingdezhen	景德镇	Jiangxi	C	3,589	821	35,401
Jiujiang	九江	Jiangxi	C	1,474	808	4,638
Nanchang*	南昌	Jiangxi	C	4,711	1,944	23,797
Pingxiang	萍乡	Jiangxi	C	302	385	1,222
Shangrao	上饶	Jiangxi	C	940	822	4,130
Xinyu	新余	Jiangxi	C	235	314	819
Yichun, Jiangxi	宜春	Jiangxi	C	660	627	2,498
Yingtan	鹰潭	Jiangxi	C	266	313	1,144
Changchun*	长春	Jilin	C	2,244	1,419	10,142
Jilin	吉林	Jilin	C	456	589	2,037
Liaoyuan	辽源	Jilin	C	80	90	343
Siping	四平	Jilin	C	119	208	679
Songyuan	松原	Jilin	C	85	104	308
Tonghua	通化	Jilin	C	185	163	584
Baicheng	白城	Jilin	C	60	90	204
Baishan	白山	Jilin	C	208	139	566
Yanbian	延边朝鲜族	Jilin	AP	635	457	3,752
Anshan	鞍山	Liaoning	C	2,046	963	7,800
Benxi	本溪	Liaoning	C	204	293	992
Chaoyang	朝阳	Liaoning	C	110	147	532
Dalian	大连	Liaoning	C	4,981	1,898	31,031
Dandong	丹东	Liaoning	C	419	512	2,068
Fushun	抚顺	Liaoning	C	349	575	2,307
Fuxin	阜新	Liaoning	C	112	173	404
Huludao	葫芦岛	Liaoning	C	1,189	444	3,837
Jinzhou	锦州	Liaoning	C	429	571	1,840

English Name	Chinese Name	Province/ Autonomous Region	Type	Number of Stores	Number of Product Categories	Number of Products
Liaoyang	辽阳	Liaoning	C	319	380	1,052
Panjin	盘锦	Liaoning	C	194	241	757
Shenyang*	沈阳	Liaoning	C	8,118	2,185	58,833
Tieling	铁岭	Liaoning	C	184	275	898
Yingkou	营口	Liaoning	C	467	580	1,884
Guyuan	固原	Ningxia	C	12	15	18
Shizuishan	石嘴山	Ningxia	C	31	41	87
Wuzhong	吴忠	Ningxia	C	31	42	71
Yinchuan*	银川	Ningxia	C	410	304	1,187
Zhongwei	中卫	Ningxia	C	64	31	168
Golog	果洛	Qinghai	AP	1	1	1
Haibei	海北	Qinghai	AP	9	14	19
Haidong	海东	Qinghai	C	25	27	42
Hainan	海南藏族	Qinghai	AP	1	5	6
Haixi	海西	Qinghai	AP	18	25	49
Huangnan	黄南	Qinghai	AP	6	7	9
Xining*	西宁	Qinghai	C	227	162	560
Yushu	玉树	Qinghai	AP	5	5	7
Ankang	安康	Shaanxi	C	85	86	234
Baoji	宝鸡	Shaanxi	C	306	307	1,262
Hanzhong	汉中	Shaanxi	C	130	171	340
Shangluo	商洛	Shaanxi	C	42	35	88
Tongchuan	铜川	Shaanxi	C	21	31	49
Weinan	渭南	Shaanxi	C	406	161	1,153
Xi'an*	西安	Shaanxi	C	6,694	2,088	34,790
Xianyang	咸阳	Shaanxi	C	245	227	679
Yan'an	延安	Shaanxi	C	56	43	84
Yulin, Shaanxi	榆林	Shaanxi	C	93	72	329
Binzhou	滨州	Shandong	C	2,498	1,016	12,282
Dezhou	德州	Shandong	C	1,604	1,106	6,521
Dongying	东营	Shandong	C	567	761	2,331
Heze	菏泽	Shandong	C	9,537	1,252	40,340
Jinan*	济南	Shandong	C	13,227	2,325	78,615
Jining	济宁	Shandong	C	2,061	1,374	12,787
Laiwu	莱芜	Shandong	C	204	304	839
Liaocheng	聊城	Shandong	C	2,129	1,264	11,912
Linyi	临沂	Shandong	C	12,069	2,153	75,521
Qingdao	青岛	Shandong	C	14,988	2,285	80,631
Rizhao	日照	Shandong	C	872	925	4,022
Tai'an	泰安	Shandong	C	1,573	1,171	8,569
Weifang	潍坊	Shandong	C	6,521	1,855	34,113

(*continued*)

English Name	Chinese Name	Province/ Autonomous Region	Type	Number of Stores	Number of Product Categories	Number of Products
Weihai	威海	Shandong	C	2,939	1,316	14,988
Yantai	烟台	Shandong	C	3,612	1,721	17,980
Zaozhuang	枣庄	Shandong	C	1,390	1,179	6,327
Zibo	淄博	Shandong	C	3,456	1,566	16,639
Changzhi	长治	Shanxi	C	167	235	542
Datong	大同	Shanxi	C	247	378	1,294
Jincheng	晋城	Shanxi	C	111	151	423
Jinzhong	晋中	Shanxi	C	293	293	1,528
Linfen	临汾	Shanxi	C	274	406	984
Lüliang	吕梁	Shanxi	C	153	181	341
Shuozhou	朔州	Shanxi	C	50	103	175
Taiyuan*	太原	Shanxi	C	2,258	1,498	9,504
Xinzhou	忻州	Shanxi	C	135	205	423
Yangquan	阳泉	Shanxi	C	86	127	289
Yuncheng	运城	Shanxi	C	444	454	1,519
Bazhong	巴中	Sichuan	C	46	51	110
Chengdu*	成都	Sichuan	C	23,510	2,394	129,211
Dazhou	达州	Sichuan	C	136	163	464
Deyang	德阳	Sichuan	C	344	489	1,578
Garzê	甘孜	Sichuan	AP	6	7	7
Guang'an	广安	Sichuan	C	110	169	395
Guangyuan	广元	Sichuan	C	112	127	330
Leshan	乐山	Sichuan	C	547	342	4,811
Liangshan	凉山	Sichuan	AP	118	89	305
Luzhou	泸州	Sichuan	C	234	221	749
Meishan	眉山	Sichuan	C	614	346	3,510
Mianyang	绵阳	Sichuan	C	604	643	2,447
Nanchong	南充	Sichuan	C	246	267	824
Neijiang	内江	Sichuan	C	191	209	623
Ngawa	阿坝	Sichuan	AP	49	22	75
Panzhihua	攀枝花	Sichuan	C	99	59	211
Suining	遂宁	Sichuan	C	119	234	653
Ya'an	雅安	Sichuan	C	100	111	352
Yibin	宜宾	Sichuan	C	244	242	813
Zigong	自贡	Sichuan	C	272	288	1,064
Ziyang	资阳	Sichuan	C	219	228	550
Lhasa*	拉萨	Tibet	C	192	108	707
Lhoka	山南	Tibet	C	1	1	1
Nagqu	那曲	Tibet	C	2	4	191
Nyingchi	林芝	Tibet	C	19	16	32
Qamdo	昌都	Tibet	C	2	2	2
Xigazê	日喀则	Tibet	C	3	6	14
Aksu	阿克苏	Xinjiang	P	252	39	647

English Name	Chinese Name	Province/ Autonomous Region	Type	Number of Stores	Number of Product Categories	Number of Products
Altay	阿勒泰	Xinjiang	P	24	19	60
Bortala	博尔塔拉	Xinjiang	AP	12	11	29
Changji	昌吉	Xinjiang	AP	95	63	360
Hotan	和田	Xinjiang	P	130	23	340
Ili	伊犁	Xinjiang	AP	170	59	468
Karamay	克拉玛依	Xinjiang	C	74	44	176
Kashgar	喀什	Xinjiang	P	109	34	298
Kizilsu	克孜勒苏	Xinjiang	AP	13	8	21
Kumul	哈密	Xinjiang	P	65	22	136
Tarbagatay	塔城	Xinjiang	P	16	12	24
Turpan	吐鲁番	Xinjiang	C	65	39	262
Ürümqi*	乌鲁木齐	Xinjiang	C	2,153	641	10,170
Baoshan	保山	Yunnan	C	141	86	596
Chuxiong	楚雄	Yunnan	AP	88	129	273
Dali	大理	Yunnan	AP	316	206	1,082
Dehong	德宏	Yunnan	AP	310	128	945
Dêqên	迪庆	Yunnan	AP	15	17	37
Honghe	红河	Yunnan	AP	174	147	643
Kunming*	昆明	Yunnan	C	3,681	1,583	18,553
Lijiang	丽江	Yunnan	C	247	181	774
Lincang	临沧	Yunnan	C	38	31	62
Nujiang	怒江	Yunnan	AP	6	4	11
Pu'er	普洱	Yunnan	C	58	70	195
Qujing	曲靖	Yunnan	C	147	121	604
Wenshan	文山	Yunnan	AP	32	30	59
Xishuangbanna	西双版纳	Yunnan	AP	284	168	1,498
Yuxi	玉溪	Yunnan	C	105	131	315
Zhaotong	昭通	Yunnan	C	56	41	122
Hangzhou*	杭州	Zhejiang	C	88,832	2,560	499,415
Huzhou	湖州	Zhejiang	C	8,926	1,754	44,916
Jiaxing	嘉兴	Zhejiang	C	23,001	2,179	93,782
Jinhua	金华	Zhejiang	C	82,417	2,440	726,244
Lishui	丽水	Zhejiang	C	5,846	1,702	32,969
Ningbo	宁波	Zhejiang	C	25,954	2,507	142,743
Quzhou	衢州	Zhejiang	C	2,096	1,462	12,577
Shaoxing	绍兴	Zhejiang	C	10,827	2,062	60,986
Taizhou, Zhejiang	台州	Zhejiang	C	35,201	2,459	221,541
Wenzhou	温州	Zhejiang	C	46,375	2,444	249,150
Zhoushan	舟山	Zhejiang	C	481	658	2,189

Notes: A prefecture-level division marked with a star is the capital city of a province or an autonomous region. There are four types of prefecture-level divisions (C = City, P = Prefecture, AP = Autonomous prefecture, L = League). Since the data is from 2014, it includes Laiwu, which ceased to exist as a prefecture in 2019 and became a district of Jinan.

Appendix C

Alibaba's Five Requirements for County Governments in the Rural Taobao Project[3]

To join the program, a county government needs to satisfy five prerequisites:

Land Requirement: (a) Providing a logistics site as the program's county-level operation center (1,000–1,500 m², free of rent for five years, close to the main street of the county seat, equipped with all the basic infrastructure ready for use, e.g., building, lighting, water, and heating); (b) Providing a store site in each participating village, which will be used to establish the e-commerce terminal (50–100 m², close to the village center).

Organizational Requirement: Establishing a leading small group (LSG) and a program implementation small group (PISG) within the county government to help implement the program. (a) The LSG should include the county governor (or a member of the standing committee of the CCP county committee) to lead the LSG. The rest of the team should include heads of different departments (with a clear action plan and division of responsibilities). (b) Each of the relevant departments (e.g., the Bureau of Commerce, the Communist Youth League, the Government Office, and the township governments) should send one or two officials to work in the PISG full- or part-time. The PISG is responsible for collaborating with Alibaba on follow-up work such as selecting villages for the program, training e-commerce merchants, and operating village terminals.

Advertising and Promotion Requirement: Fully exploiting local channels to promote the program, such as state-run TV stations, government websites, newspapers, outdoor advertising facilities, and radio stations. The government should also promote e-commerce within villages, for example, using wall slogans and posters to advertise e-commerce, with at least two hundred wall advertisements completed.

Operation and Subsidy Requirement: Having a plan for e-commerce-related issues, such as subsidies, operation, and training. For example, the government can provide regular subsidies and bonuses to incentivize the managers running the e-commerce terminals. In some places, the firm would even ask the local governments to prepare special funds for e-commerce-related expenses.

Training Requirement: Having local officials (with ranks above township head) participate in at least one e-commerce training session. It is not a must but a plus if the "first hand" official can go to Hangzhou and participate in the e-commerce training session designed for county governors and offered by Taobao University, Alibaba's training facility.

APPENDIX TO CHAPTER 5

Portions of Appendix Chapter 5 were originally published as Couture, Victor, Benjamin Faber, Yizhen Gu, and Lizhi Liu, 2021, "Connecting the Countryside via E-Commerce: Evidence from China," *American Economic Review: Insights* 3, no. 1: 35–50, and they are reproduced with permission of *American Economic Review: Insights*.

Appendix A

Appendix A presents additional figures and tables. Appendix B describes the construction of the K-L-K outcome indices. Appendix C presents additional analysis on the role of GE spillovers. Appendix D provides additional estimation results using the firm's admin database. Appendix E provides details on the welfare analysis. Appendix F presents details on the program, experimental design, field staff training, quality management, and data.

TABLE A5.1.A. Descriptive Statistics: Individual Level (All Household Members)

		Full Sample at Baseline	Treatment Villages at Baseline	Control Villages at Baseline	P-Value (Treat- Control=0)	Control Villages at Endline
Age	Median	44.000	44.000	43.000		46.000
	Mean	38.950	39.329	38.407	0.208	39.943
	Standard Deviation	23.580	23.658	23.460		23.759
	Number of Obs	8491	5001	3490		4194
Gender	Median	1.000	1.000	1.000		1.000
(Female = 1)	Mean	0.534	0.526	0.546	0.025	0.537
	Standard Deviation	0.499	0.499	0.498		0.499
	Number of Obs	8484	5001	3483		4188

(continued)

217

		Full Sample at Baseline	Treatment Villages at Baseline	Control Villages at Baseline	P-Value (Treat-Control=0)	Control Villages at Endline
Employed	Median	1.000	1.000	1.000		1.000
(for age>15)	Mean	0.767	0.766	0.769	0.882	0.762
(Yes = 1)	Standard Deviation	0.423	0.424	0.422		0.426
	Number of Obs	6070	3590	2480		3015
Farmer (for	Median	1.000	1.000	1.000		1.000
age>15)	Mean	0.527	0.527	0.526	0.971	0.513
(Yes = 1)	Standard Deviation	0.499	0.499	0.499		0.500
	Number of Obs	6369	3760	2609		3144
No Schooling (for	Median	0.000	0.000	0.000		0.000
age>15) (No	Mean	0.270	0.273	0.266	0.745	0.319
School = 1)	Standard Deviation	0.444	0.446	0.442		0.466
	Number of Obs	6368	3758	2610		3132
Completed Junior	Median	0.000	0.000	0.000		0.000
High School	Mean	0.437	0.429	0.449	0.419	0.422
(for age>15)	Standard Deviation	0.496	0.495	0.498		0.494
(Yes = 1)	Number of Obs	6368	3758	2610		3132
Completed Senior	Median	0.000	0.000	0.000		0.000
High School	Mean	0.104	0.104	0.104	0.969	0.097
(for age>18)	Standard Deviation	0.305	0.305	0.305		0.296
(Yes = 1)	Number of Obs	6286	3719	2567		3096

Notes: See Design/Data Section and Appendix F for discussion. *Source*: Victor Couture, Benjamin Faber, Yizhen Gu, and Lizhi Liu, 2021. "Connecting the Countryside via E-Commerce: Evidence from China," *American Economic Review: Insights* 3, no. 1: 35–50. Copyright American Economic Association; reproduced with permission of the *American Economic Review: Insights*.

TABLE A5.1.B. Descriptive Statistics: Individual Level (Survey Respondents Only; Demographics)

		Full Sample at Baseline	Treatment Villages at Baseline	Control Villages at Baseline	P-Value (Treat-Control=0)	Control Villages at Endline
Age	Median	51.000	51.000	50.000	0.138	53.000
	Mean	50.391	50.797	49.779		52.264
	Standard Deviation	13.172	13.094	13.270		12.943
	Number of Obs	2725	1637	1088		1403
Gender (Female = 1)	Median	1.000	1.000	1.000	0.993	1.000
	Mean	0.635	0.635	0.635		0.625
	Standard Deviation	0.482	0.482	0.482		0.484
	Number of Obs	2726	1639	1087		1403
Employed (for age>15) (Yes = 1)	Median	1.000	1.000	1.000	0.587	1.000
	Mean	0.801	0.807	0.793		0.804
	Standard Deviation	0.399	0.395	0.406		0.397
	Number of Obs	2639	1593	1046		1371
Farmer (for age>15) (Yes = 1)	Median	1.000	1.000	1.000	0.760	1.000
	Mean	0.617	0.622	0.609		0.610
	Standard Deviation	0.486	0.485	0.488		0.488
	Number of Obs	2727	1639	1088		1402

(continued)

TABLE A5.1.B. (*continued*)

		Full Sample at Baseline	Treatment Villages at Baseline	Control Villages at Baseline	P-Value (Treat-Control = 0)	Control Villages at Endline
No Schooling (for age>15) (No School = 1)	Median	0.000	0.000	0.000		0.000
	Mean	0.284	0.289	0.277	0.662	0.334
	Standard Deviation	0.451	0.453	0.448		0.472
	Number of Obs	2727	1639	1088		1398
Completed Junior High School (for age>15) (Yes = 1)	Median	0.000	0.000	0.000		0.000
	Mean	0.403	0.394	0.417	0.410	0.381
	Standard Deviation	0.491	0.489	0.493		0.486
	Number of Obs	2727	1639	1088		1398
Completed Senior High School (for age>18) (Yes=1)	Median	0.000	0.000	0.000		0.000
	Mean	0.091	0.090	0.093	0.804	0.086
	Standard Deviation	0.288	0.286	0.291		0.280
	Number of Obs	2722	1638	1084		1398

Notes: See Design/Data Section and Appendix F for discussion. *Source:* Victor Couture, Benjamin Faber, Yizhen Gu, and Lizhi Liu, 2021. "Connecting the Countryside via E-Commerce: Evidence from China," *American Economic Review: Insights* 3, no. 1: 35–50. Copyright American Economic Association; reproduced with permission of the *American Economic Review: Insights.*

TABLE A5.1.C. Descriptive Statistics: Individual Level (Survey Respondents Only; Sociopolitical Beliefs)

		Full Sample at Baseline	Treatment Villages at Baseline	Control Villages at Baseline	P-Value (Treat-Control=0)	Control Villages at Endline
Intention to migrate if a good job presents itself (a definite yes to a definite no, 1 to 4)	Median	4.000	4.000	4.000		4.000
	Mean	3.020	3.023	3.017	0.927	3.159
	Standard Deviation	1.188	1.193	1.181		1.177
	Number of Obs	2686	1619	1067		1402
Life satisfaction (very low to very high, 0 to 10)	Median	7.000	7.000	7.000		7.000
	Mean	6.722	6.704	6.749	0.747	7.061
	Standard Deviation	2.324	2.332	2.313		2.294
	Number of Obs	2632	1581	1051		1362
China's economic prospects in a year (much better to much worse, 1 to 4)	Median	2.000	2.000	2.000		2.000
	Mean	2.294	2.331	2.239	0.204	2.150
	Standard Deviation	0.931	0.943	0.912		0.865
	Number of Obs	2122	1249	873		1238
Economic growth as govt. goal (not important at all to extremely important, 0 to 10)	Median	9.000	9.000	9.000		9.000
	Mean	8.504	8.471	8.552	0.489	8.386
	Standard Deviation	1.789	1.807	1.764		1.797
	Number of Obs	2127	1268	859		1189
Democracy in local policymaking as govt. goal (not important to extremely important, 0 to 10)	Median	9.000	9.000	9.000		8.000
	Mean	8.253	8.195	8.340	0.238	8.041
	Standard Deviation	2.138	2.196	2.047		2.127
	Number of Obs	2091	1249	842		1166

(continued)

TABLE A5.1.C. (*continued*)

		Full Sample at Baseline	Treatment Villages at Baseline	Control Villages at Baseline	P-Value (Treat-Control=0)	Control Villages at Endline
Government priority (economic growth = 1, democracy in local policymaking = 2)	Median	1.000	1.000	1.000		1.000
	Mean	1.428	1.413	1.451	0.210	1.403
	Standard Deviation	0.495	0.493	0.498		0.491
	Number of Obs	1877	1103	774		1125
Perceived conflicts between rich and poor citizens (very high to very low, 1 to 4)	Median	3.000	2.000	3.000		3.000
	Mean	2.520	2.486	2.570	0.193	2.549
	Standard Deviation	1.065	1.064	1.066		1.086
	Number of Obs	2397	1435	962		1305
Perceived conflicts between urban and rural citizens (very high to very low, 1 to 4)	Median	3.000	3.000	3.000		3.000
	Mean	3.061	3.056	3.067	0.843	2.954
	Standard Deviation	0.940	0.935	0.948		0.966
	Number of Obs	2192	1303	889		1274
Political interest (very high to very low, 1 to 4)	Median	4.000	4.000	4.000		4.000
	Mean	3.428	3.426	3.431	0.921	3.245
	Standard Deviation	0.929	0.931	0.926		1.034
	Number of Obs	2494	1497	997		1360
Generalized Trust (very low to very high, 0 to 10)	Median	8.000	8.000	8.000		8.000
	Mean	7.365	7.364	7.366	0.987	7.130
	Standard Deviation	2.439	2.439	2.439		2.345
	Number of Obs	2032	1235	797		1169

Notes: See Design/Data Section and Appendix F for discussion. *Source:* Victor Couture, Benjamin Faber, Yizhen Gu, and Lizhi Liu, 2021. "Connecting the Countryside via E-Commerce: Evidence from China," *American Economic Review: Insights* 3, no. 1: 35–50. Copyright American Economic Association; reproduced with permission of the *American Economic Review: Insights.*

TABLE A5.2. Descriptive Statistics: Household Level

		Full Sample at Baseline	Treatment Villages at Baseline	Control Villages at Baseline	P-Value (Treat-Control = 0)	Control Villages at Endline
Age of Primary Earner	Median	50.000	50.000	50.000		52.000
	Mean	49.824	49.953	49.631	0.634	51.395
	Standard Deviation	12.673	12.710	12.621		13.547
	Number of Obs	2548	1530	1018		1348
Gender of Primary Earner (Female = 1)	Median	0.000	0.000	0.000		0.000
	Mean	0.288	0.295	0.276	0.457	0.295
	Standard Deviation	0.453	0.456	0.447		0.456
	Number of Obs	2547	1530	1017		1348
Primary Earner Went to School (Yes = 1)	Median	1.000	1.000	1.000		1.000
	Mean	0.815	0.814	0.817	0.874	0.750
	Standard Deviation	0.388	0.389	0.386		0.433
	Number of Obs	2550	1531	1019		1342
Primary Earner Is Farmer (Yes = 1)	Median	1.000	1.000	1.000		1.000
	Mean	0.590	0.600	0.577	0.620	0.587
	Standard Deviation	0.492	0.490	0.494		0.493
	Number of Obs	2549	1531	1018		1348
Primary Earner Self-Employed (Yes = 1)	Median	0.000	0.000	0.000		0.000
	Mean	0.073	0.087	0.053	0.036	0.072
	Standard Deviation	0.261	0.282	0.224		0.259
	Number of Obs	2549	1531	1018		1348
Household Size	Median	3.000	3.000	3.000		3.000
	Mean	3.114	3.053	3.205	0.075	2.987
	Standard Deviation	1.422	1.420	1.421		1.397
	Number of Obs	2740	1647	1093		1405

(continued)

TABLE A5.2. (*continued*)

		Full Sample at Baseline	Treatment Villages at Baseline	Control Villages at Baseline	P-Value (Treat-Control=0)	Control Villages at Endline
Household Monthly Income Per Capita in RMB	Median	350.000	339.000	375.000		466.667
	Mean	876.412	841.198	929.473	0.365	1028.960
	Standard Deviation	1717.456	1687.169	1761.560		2005.311
	Number of Obs	2740	1647	1093		1405
Household Monthly Retail Expenditure Per Capita in RMB	Median	381.000	372.833	400.500		364.000
	Mean	732.017	663.034	835.966	0.135	686.616
	Standard Deviation	2304.540	1139.788	3368.220		1512.058
	Number of Obs	2735	1644	1091		1405
Household Monthly Expenditure on Business Inputs Per Capita in RMB	Median	0.000	0.000	0.000		0.000
	Mean	123.417	123.007	124.033	0.981	128.464
	Standard Deviation	1033.757	1076.656	966.070		1069.516
	Number of Obs	2736	1644	1092		1405
Any Member of the Household Has Ever Used the Internet (Yes=1)	Median	0.000	0.000	0.000		0.000
	Mean	0.368	0.354	0.390	0.249	0.427
	Standard Deviation	0.482	0.478	0.488		0.495
	Number of Obs	2739	1646	1093		1402
Household Owns a Smartphone (Yes=1)	Median	1.000	1.000	1.000		1.000
	Mean	0.526	0.509	0.552	0.153	0.551
	Standard Deviation	0.499	0.500	0.498		0.498
	Number of Obs	2731	1642	1089		1400

Notes: See Design/Data Section and Appendix F for discussion. *Source:* Victor Couture, Benjamin Faber, Yizhen Gu, and Lizhi Liu, 2021. "Connecting the Countryside via E-Commerce: Evidence from China," *American Economic Review: Insights* 3, no. 1: 35–50. Copyright American Economic Association; reproduced with permission of the *American Economic Review: Insights*.

TABLE A5.3. Descriptive Statistics: Household Level, Continued

		Full Sample at Baseline	Treatment Villages at Baseline	Control Villages at Baseline	P-Value (Treat-Control=0)	Control Villages at Endline
Share of Household Monthly Expenditure on E-Commerce Deliveries	Median	0.000	0.000	0.000		0.000
	Mean	0.007	0.006	0.007	0.693	0.008
	Standard Deviation	0.050	0.046	0.057		0.049
	Number of Obs	2720	1637	1083		1397
Share of E-Commerce Sales in Household Monthly Income	Median	0.000	0.000	0.000		0.000
	Mean	0.003	0.001	0.006	0.103	0.003
	Standard Deviation	0.052	0.030	0.074		0.051
	Number of Obs	2055	1244	811		1161
Distance in Meters to Planned Terminal Location	Median	231.556	232.891	231.454		203.629
	Mean	290.346	293.364	285.797	0.789	286.631
	Standard Deviation	243.450	247.778	236.820		267.061
	Number of Obs	2740	1647	1093		1405
Share of Retail Expenditure Outside of Village	Median	0.553	0.489	0.623		0.598
	Mean	0.500	0.470	0.545	0.193	0.531
	Standard Deviation	0.395	0.402	0.379		0.385
	Number of Obs	2720	1637	1083		1397
Share of Business Input Expenditure Outside of Village	Median	1.000	1.000	1.000		1.000
	Mean	0.613	0.610	0.618	0.916	0.633
	Standard Deviation	0.465	0.470	0.457		0.463
	Number of Obs	926	558	368		544

(continued)

TABLE A5-3. (*continued*)

		Full Sample at Baseline	Treatment Villages at Baseline	Control Villages at Baseline	P-Value (Treat-Control=0)	Control Villages at Endline
Travel Time One-Way to Main Shopping Destination Outside Village (minutes)	Median	20.000	20.000	20.000		20.000
	Mean	29.892	29.941	29.826	0.962	28.862
	Standard Deviation	27.825	27.380	28.429		26.187
	Number of Obs	2234	1284	950		1188
Travel Cost One-Way to Main Shopping Destination Outside Village (RMB)	Median	2.000	2.000	1.500		1.000
	Mean	3.739	3.847	3.591	0.715	4.236
	Standard Deviation	10.092	11.774	7.196		16.780
	Number of Obs	2216	1278	938		1185
Household Owns a PC or Laptop (Yes=1)	Median	0.000	0.000	0.000		0.000
	Mean	0.283	0.276	0.295	0.631	0.284
	Standard Deviation	0.451	0.447	0.456		0.451
	Number of Obs	2731	1642	1089		1400
Household Owns a Car (Yes=1)	Median	0.000	0.000	0.000		0.000
	Mean	0.108	0.107	0.110	0.851	0.131
	Standard Deviation	0.311	0.309	0.313		0.337
	Number of Obs	2731	1642	1089		1400
Household Owns a Motorcycle (Yes=1)	Median	0.000	0.000	1.000		0.000
	Mean	0.486	0.456	0.532	0.031	0.467
	Standard Deviation	0.500	0.498	0.499		0.499
	Number of Obs	2731	1642	1089		1400
Household Owns a TV (Yes=1)	Median	1.000	1.000	1.000		1.000
	Mean	0.977	0.977	0.977	0.953	0.977
	Standard Deviation	0.149	0.148	0.150		0.150
	Number of Obs	2731	1642	1089		1400

Notes: See Design/Data Section and Appendix F for discussion. *Source:* Victor Couture, Benjamin Faber, Yizhen Gu, and Lizhi Liu, 2021. "Connecting the Countryside via E-Commerce: Evidence from China," *American Economic Review: Insights* 3, no. 1: 35–50. Copyright American Economic Association; reproduced with permission of the *American Economic Review: Insights*.

TABLE A5.4. Descriptive Statistics: Local Retail Prices

		Full Sample at Baseline	Treatment Villages at Baseline	Control Villages at Baseline	P-Value (Treat-Control=0)	Control Villages at Endline
Number of Stores at Village Level	Median	3.00	3.00	2.00		2.00
	Mean	4.15	4.38	3.79	0.33	3.61
	Standard Deviation	2.94	2.91	2.98		2.99
	Number of Obs	99	60	39		38
Establishment Space in Square	Median	50.00	50.00	40.00		50.00
Meters	Mean	99.07	74.42	146.76	0.35	121.33
	Standard Deviation	320.38	89.60	532.73		375.35
	Number of Obs	361	238	123		126
Number of Establishment's New	Median	0.00	0.00	0.00		0.00
Products Added Over Last	Mean	1.43	1.56	1.17	0.57	0.63
Month	Standard Deviation	7.44	8.88	3.42		2.26
	Number of Obs	330	215	115		126
Prices of All Retail Consumption	Median	7.00	7.00	6.00		6.00
(9 Product Groups) in RMB	Mean	71.03	76.74	61.43	0.47	71.23
	Standard Deviation	411.24	433.67	370.33		390.31
	Number of Obs	9382	5884	3498		3259
Price Was Not Displayed on Label	Median	1.00	1.00	1.00		1.00
(Needed to Ask = 1)	Mean	0.67	0.66	0.67	0.97	0.73
	Standard Deviation	0.47	0.47	0.47		0.44
	Number of Obs	8977	5597	3380		3370
Prices of Business or Production	Median	10.00	10.00	8.80		9.00
Input in RMB	Mean	45.63	42.88	49.78	0.76	43.84
	Standard Deviation	195.09	206.23	177.46		97.92
	Number of Obs	444	267	177		111
(1) Prices of Food and Beverages	Median	4.38	4.60	4.00		4.00
in RMB	Mean	11.58	11.81	11.21	0.73	10.05
	Standard Deviation	24.35	23.31	25.99		17.75
	Number of Obs	4853	3021	1832		1834
(2) Prices of Tobacco and Alcohol	Median	12.00	13.00	12.00		13.00
in RMB	Mean	28.81	30.35	26.36	0.46	29.32
	Standard Deviation	53.97	59.45	43.77		55.16
	Number of Obs	1331	818	513		531

(continued)

TABLE A5.4. (continued)

		Full Sample at Baseline	Treatment Villages at Baseline	Control Villages at Baseline	P-Value (Treat-Control=0)	Control Villages at Endline
(3) Prices of Medicine and Health Products in RMB	Median	10.00	10.00	9.98		8.40
	Mean	26.13	24.40	29.31	0.66	18.50
	Standard Deviation	43.35	38.46	51.11		33.77
	Number of Obs	399	258	141		90
(4) Prices of Clothing and Accessories in RMB	Median	15.00	12.00	20.00		22.00
	Mean	46.31	45.69	47.79	0.90	57.00
	Standard Deviation	74.71	71.49	82.13		85.66
	Number of Obs	401	282	119		65
(5) Prices of Other Everyday Products in RMB	Median	10.00	10.00	9.00		9.00
	Mean	14.68	14.53	14.93	0.93	13.10
	Standard Deviation	31.03	32.69	28.06		18.17
	Number of Obs	1462	916	546		626
(6) Prices of Fuel and Gas in RMB	Median	5.00	5.00	5.00		5.83
	Mean	11.65	15.36	8.08	0.26	5.82
	Standard Deviation	21.46	28.88	9.59		0.23
	Number of Obs	53	26	27		4
(7) Prices of Furniture and Appliances in RMB	Median	110.00	85.00	187.00		398.00
	Mean	1009.49	1001.66	1026.34	0.95	1167.30
	Standard Deviation	1504.81	1583.03	1333.52		1350.70
	Number of Obs	183	125	58		43
(8) Prices of Electronics in RMB	Median	449.00	609.50	17.50		1799.00
	Mean	917.05	976.41	782.14	0.59	1782.71
	Standard Deviation	1224.37	1242.82	1184.20		871.58
	Number of Obs	144	100	44		45
(9) Prices of Transport Equipment in RMB	Median	1440.00	1980.00	30.00		2800.00
	Mean	1700.66	1794.74	1534.21	0.71	2578.24
	Standard Deviation	1822.07	1770.33	1922.34		1697.82
	Number of Obs	108	69	39		21

Notes: See Design/Data Section and Appendix F for discussion. *Source:* Victor Couture, Benjamin Faber, Yizhen Gu, and Lizhi Liu, 2021. "Connecting the Countryside via E-Commerce: Evidence from China," *American Economic Review: Insights* 3, no. 1: 35–50. Copyright American Economic Association; reproduced with permission of the *American Economic Review: Insights*.

TABLE A5.5. Descriptive Statistics: Firm's Transaction Data

	Number of Purchase Transactions	Number of Buyers	Number of Out-Shipments	Number of Terminals	Number of Counties	Number of Provinces	Number of Days	Number of Months	Sum of Payments (RMB)	Sum of Out-Shipments (Weight in kg)
Full Sample	27,270,532	3,785,019	500,743	11,941	175	5	547	18	4,480,424,896	1,169,673
3 Provinces	20,647,373	2,832,872	442,319	8,561	116	3	547	18	3,409,227,245	1,019,373
8 Counties	1,835,897	216,529	44,148	706	8	3	503	17	330,930,097	95,908
RCT Villages	130,769	15,099	3,158	40	8	3	482	16	17,618,900	7,817

Notes: The table provides information from the purchase and the sales transaction databases. The purchase database covers all village transactions in five provinces over the period November 2015 until April 2017. The sales transaction database covers all out-shipments from the same locations over the period January 2016 to April 2017. See Design/Data Section for discussion. *Source:* Victor Couture, Benjamin Faber, Yizhen Gu, and Lizhi Liu, 2021. "Connecting the Countryside via E-Commerce: Evidence from China," *American Economic Review: Insights* 3, no. 1: 35–50. Copyright American Economic Association; reproduced with permission of the *American Economic Review: Insights*.

TABLE A5.6: Average Effects: Consumption

Dependent Variables		Intent to Treat	Treatment on Treated	Log Distance (IV using Treat)
Monthly Total Retail Expenditure Per Capita	Treat or Log Dist	-22.09 (31.99)	-41.2 (60.22)	10.79 (15.67)
	R-Squared	0.038		
	First Stage F-Stat		44.01	48.31
	Number of Obs	3,436	3,436	3,436
Household Has Ever Bought Something through E-comm Option (Yes=1)	Treat or Log Dist	0.0484*** (0.0167)	0.0894*** (0.0268)	-0.0234*** (0.00697)
	R-Squared	0.008		
	First Stage F-Stat		45.31	49.83
	Number of Obs	3,518	3,518	3,518
Household Has Bought Something through E-comm Option in Past Month (Yes=1)	Treat or Log Dist	0.0263*** (0.00981)	0.0490*** (0.0171)	-0.0128*** (0.00445)
	R-Squared	0.009		
	First Stage F-Stat		43.93	47.95
	Number of Obs	3,482	3,482	3,482
Share of E-Comm Option in Total Monthly Retail Expenditure	Treat or Log Dist	0.00668*** (0.00239)	0.0124*** (0.00435)	-0.00326*** (0.00114)
	R-Squared	0.006		
	First Stage F-Stat		44.03	47.98
	Number of Obs	3,434	3,434	3,434

Dependent Variables		Intent to Treat	Treatment on Treated	Log Distance (IV using Treat)
Share of E-Comm Option in Monthly Tobacco and Alcohol (2)	Treat or Log Dist	0.000608 (0.000515)	0.00123 (0.00109)	-0.000330 (0.000287)
	R-Squared	0.001		
	First Stage F-Stat		33.02	32.67
	Number of Obs	1,653	1,653	1,653
Share of E-Comm Option in Monthly Medicine and Health Products (3)	Treat or Log Dist	0.000693 (0.000689)	0.00126 (0.00124)	-0.000329 (0.000324)
	R-Squared	0.000		
	First Stage F-Stat		51.06	54.55
	Number of Obs	2,416	2,416	2,416
Share of E-Comm Option in Monthly Clothing and Accessories (4)	Treat or Log Dist	0.0466*** (0.0140)	0.0736*** (0.0217)	-0.0201*** (0.00594)
	R-Squared	0.019		
	First Stage F-Stat		70.53	65.25
	Number of Obs	1,268	1,268	1,268
Share of E-Comm Option in Monthly Other Household Products (5)	Treat or Log Dist	0.00437 (0.00396)	0.00816 (0.00715)	-0.00217 (0.00190)
	R-Squared	0.001		
	First Stage F-Stat		43.87	47.76
	Number of Obs	2,336	2,336	2,336

	(1) ITT	(2) TOT	(3) TOT (Log Dist)
Share of E-Comm Option in Monthly Business Inputs			
Treat or Log Dist	−0.00707 (0.00779)	−0.0155 (0.0195)	0.00403 (0.00507)
R-Squared	0.003		
First Stage F-Stat		15.59	17.85
Number of Obs	1,191	1,191	1,191
Share of E-Comm Option in Monthly Nondurables			
Treat or Log Dist	0.00538*** (0.00196)	0.0100*** (0.00356)	−0.00262*** (0.000933)
R-Squared	0.003		
First Stage F-Stat		44.11	48
Number of Obs	3,433	3,433	3,433
Share of E-Comm Option in Monthly Durables			
Treat or Log Dist	0.0408** (0.0160)	0.0686** (0.0263)	−0.0191** (0.00727)
R-Squared	0.012		
First Stage F-Stat		52.43	44.14
Number of Obs	768	768	768
Share of E-Comm Option in Monthly Food and Beverages (1)			
Treat or Log Dist	0.00121 (0.000823)	0.00223 (0.00152)	−0.000582 (0.000398)
R-Squared	0.001		
First Stage F-Stat		45.63	49.84
Number of Obs	3,359	3,359	3,359
Share of E-Comm Option in Monthly Heating, Fuel, and Gas (6)			
Treat or Log Dist	0 (0)	0 (0)	0 (0)
R-Squared	·		
First Stage F-Stat		·	·
Number of Obs	1,463	1,463	1,463
Share of E-Comm Option in Monthly Furniture and Appliances (7)			
Treat or Log Dist	0.0546** (0.0217)	0.0908** (0.0368)	−0.0253** (0.0101)
R-Squared	0.019		
First Stage F-Stat		47.51	42.04
Number of Obs	380	380	380
Share of E-Comm Option in Monthly Electronics (8)			
Treat or Log Dist	0.0698** (0.0347)	0.111** (0.0527)	−0.0339** (0.0159)
R-Squared	0.023		
First Stage F-Stat		42.35	26.54
Number of Obs	231	231	231
Share of E-Comm Option in Monthly Transport Equipment (9)			
Treat or Log Dist	0.0357* (0.0203)	0.0565* (0.0319)	−0.0152* (0.00878)
R-Squared	0.014		
First Stage F-Stat		41.19	42.37
Number of Obs	139	139	139

Notes: Table reports point estimates from specification (1). The first column reports ITT and the second column TOT. The third column replaces the binary TOT with log residential distances to the nearest e-commerce terminal (using village-level ITT as instrument as for second column). Standard errors are clustered at the level of villages. * 10%, ** 5%, *** 1% significance levels. *Source*: Victor Couture, Benjamin Faber, Yizhen Gu, and Lizhi Liu, 2021. "Connecting the Countryside via E-Commerce: Evidence from China," *American Economic Review: Insights* 3, no. 1: 35–50.

TABLE A5.7. Average Effects: Incomes

Dependent Variables		Intent to Treat	Treatment on Treated	Log Distance (IV using Treat)	Dependent Variables		Intent to Treat	Treatment on Treated	Log Distance (IV using Treat)
Monthly Income Per Capita in RMB	Treat or Log Dist	-7.864 (70.78)	-14.53 (129.9)	3.974 (35.61)	Member of Household Has Ever Sold through E-Commerce (Yes=1)	Treat or Log Dist	-0.00700 (0.00562)	-0.0129 (0.0104)	0.00353 (0.00282)
	R-Squared	0.038				R-Squared	0.347		
	First Stage F-Stat		45.33	42.83		First Stage F-Stat		45.30	42.71
	Number of Obs	3,437	3,437	3,437		Number of Obs	3,504	3,504	3,504
Monthly Income Per Capita Net of Costs in RMB	Treat or Log Dist	-20.09 (70.80)	-37.20 (129.9)	10.19 (35.51)	Member of Household Has Sold through E-Commerce in Past Month (Yes=1)	Treat or Log Dist	-0.00132 (0.00237)	-0.00244 (0.00438)	0.000667 (0.00119)
	R-Squared	0.037				R-Squared	0.038		
	First Stage F-Stat		44.78	42.54		First Stage F-Stat		44.30	42.34
	Number of Obs	3,390	3,390	3,390		Number of Obs	3,498	3,498	3,498
Monthly Income Per Capita Net of Transfers in RMB	Treat or Log Dist	-12.55 (72.18)	-23.21 (132.4)	6.360 (36.25)	E-Commerce Sales in Past Month in RMB	Treat or Log Dist	-10.09 (12.89)	-18.75 (23.94)	5.109 (6.504)
	R-Squared	0.051				R-Squared	0.012		
	First Stage F-Stat		45.16	42.67		First Stage F-Stat		44.26	42.39
	Number of Obs	3,445	3,445	3,445		Number of Obs	3,498	3,498	3,498
Annual Income Per Capita in RMB	Treat or Log Dist	-45.95 (586.9)	-85.08 (1,080)	23.33 (296.3)	Share of E-Commerce Sales in Household Monthly Income	Treat or Log Dist	-0.00120 (0.00176)	-0.00224 (0.00330)	0.000614 (0.000901)
	R-Squared	0.046				R-Squared	0.032		
	First Stage F-Stat		44.77	42.23		First Stage F-Stat		41.62	38.41
	Number of Obs	3,388	3,388	3,388		Number of Obs	2,830	2,830	2,830

		ITT	TOT	TOT (Log Dist)
Monthly Agricultural Income Per Capita	Treat or Log Dist	−70.23 (140.3)	−130.3 (257.7)	35.61 (70.34)
	R-Squared	0.033		
	First Stage F-Stat		44.23	42.33
	Number of Obs	3,448	3,448	3,448
Monthly Nonagricultural Income Per Capita	Treat or Log Dist	−46.65 (137.3)	−86.06 (249.6)	23.55 (68.28)
	R-Squared	0.157		
	First Stage F-Stat		45.74	43.51
	Number of Obs	3,441	3,441	3,441
Weekly Hours Worked by Primary Earner	Treat or Log Dist	1.008 (3.383)	1.879 (6.285)	0.516 (1.723)
	R-Squared	0.000		
	First Stage F-Stat		43.80	41.21
	Number of Obs	3,310	3,310	3,310
Weekly Hours Worked by Secondary Earner	Treat or Log Dist	−0.0606 (3.886)	−0.110 (7.002)	0.0317 (2.020)
	R-Squared	0.000		
	First Stage F-Stat		45.39	40.21
	Number of Obs	1,866	1,866	1,866
Primary Earner Working as Peasant (Yes = 1)	Treat or Log Dist	−0.0229 (0.0319)	−0.0425 (0.0597)	0.0116 (0.0164)
	R-Squared	0.140		
	First Stage F-Stat		44.42	41.58
	Number of Obs	3,327	3,327	3,327
Member of Household Started a Business Over Last 6 Months (Yes = 1)	Treat or Log Dist	−0.00802 (0.00631)	−0.0149 (0.0120)	0.00407 (0.00327)
	R-Squared	0.001		
	First Stage F-Stat		44.37	42.34
	Number of Obs	3,468	3,468	3,468
New Business Selling in Part Online (Yes = 1)	Treat or Log Dist	0.000212 (0.00159)	0.000394 (0.00294)	−0.000108 (0.000803)
	R-Squared	0.000		
	First Stage F-Stat		44.33	42.37
	Number of Obs	3,468	3,468	3,468

Notes: Table reports point estimates from specification (1). The first column reports ITT and the second column TOT. The third column replaces the binary TOT with log residential distances to the nearest e-commerce terminal (using village-level ITT as instrument as for second column). Standard errors are clustered at the level of villages. * 10%, ** 5%, *** 1% significance levels. *Source:* Victor Couture, Benjamin Faber, Yizhen Gu, and Lizhi Liu, 2021. "Connecting the Countryside via E-Commerce: Evidence from China," *American Economic Review: Insights* 3, no. 1: 35–50. Copyright American Economic Association; reproduced with permission of the *American Economic Review: Insights.*

TABLE A5.8. Average Effects: Local Retail Prices

Dependent Variables		Intent to Treat	Treatment on Treated	Dependent Variables		Intent to Treat	Treatment on Treated
Log Prices (All)	Treat	0.0189 (0.0142)	0.0352 (0.0263)	Log Prices of Food and Beverages (1)	Treat	0.0368** (0.0185)	0.0706* (0.0375)
	R-Squared	0.893	0.893		R-Squared	0.870	0.870
	First Stage F-Stat		41.66		First Stage F-Stat		39.37
	Number of Obs	6,877	6,877		Number of Obs	3,686	3,686
Product Replacement Dummy (Not Counting Store Closures) (Yes=1)	Treat	-0.00516 (0.00947)	-0.00983 (0.0181)	Log Prices of Tobacco and Alcohol (2)	Treat	0.0212 (0.0340)	0.0421 (0.0662)
	R-Squared	0.000	-0.002		R-Squared	0.809	0.810
	First Stage F-Stat		39.82		First Stage F-Stat		32.39
	Number of Obs	8,956	8,956		Number of Obs	1,071	1,071
Store Closure (at Product Level) (Yes=1)	Treat	0.00124 (0.0294)	0.00236 (0.0556)	Log Prices of Medicine and Health Products (3)	Treat	-0.0474 (0.0741)	-0.0756 (0.122)
	R-Squared	0.000	0.000		R-Squared	0.794	0.795
	First Stage F-Stat		39.82		First Stage F-Stat		19.18
	Number of Obs	8,956	8,956		Number of Obs	266	266
Number of New Products Per Store	Treat	2.194** (1.073)	4.020* (2.278)	Log Prices of Clothing and Accessories (4)	Treat	0.0809 (0.111)	0.115 (0.158)
	R-Squared	0.277	0.212		R-Squared	0.845	0.842
	First Stage F-Stat		19.69		First Stage F-Stat		42.80
	Number of Obs	312	312		Number of Obs	152	152
Store Owner Sources Products Online (Yes=1)	Treat	-0.00145 (0.0258)	-0.00261 (0.0461)	Log Prices of Other Household Products (5)	Treat	-0.0328 (0.0382)	-0.0619 (0.0744)
	R-Squared	0.000	-0.001		R-Squared	0.756	0.755
	First Stage F-Stat		23.76		First Stage F-Stat		28.85
	Number of Obs	341	341		Number of Obs	1,268	1,268

Log Prices of Business Inputs	ITT	TOT
Treat	0.00229	0.00337
	(0.129)	(0.186)
R-Squared	0.811	0.811
First Stage F-Stat		24.86
Number of Obs	237	237

Log Prices of Nondurables	ITT	TOT
Treat	0.0211	0.0398
	(0.0146)	(0.0276)
R-Squared	0.860	0.860
First Stage F-Stat		40.36
Number of Obs	6,455	6,455

Log Prices of Durables	ITT	TOT
Treat	-0.0320	-0.0522
	(0.0711)	(0.115)
R-Squared	0.951	0.952
First Stage F-Stat		9.753
Number of Obs	185	185

Log Prices of Heating, Fuel, and Gas (6)	ITT	TOT
Treat	-0.0115	-0.0440
	(0.0955)	(0.332)
R-Squared	0.007	-0.095
First Stage F-Stat		0.795
Number of Obs	12	12

Log Prices of Furniture and Appliances (7)	ITT	TOT
Treat	-0.0347	-0.0617
	(0.0881)	(0.156)
R-Squared	0.952	0.953
First Stage F-Stat		6.757
Number of Obs	109	109

Log Prices of Electronics (8)	ITT	TOT
Treat	-0.0892	-0.163
	(0.305)	(0.570)
R-Squared	0.884	0.890
First Stage F-Stat		3.180
Number of Obs	23	23

Log Prices of Transport Equipment (9)	ITT	TOT
Treat	0.0297	0.0398
	(0.0840)	(0.110)
R-Squared	0.946	0.946
First Stage F-Stat		22.67
Number of Obs	53	53

Notes: Table reports point estimates from specification (1). The first column reports ITT and the second column TOT (using village-level ITT as instrument). Standard errors are clustered at the level of villages. * 10%, ** 5%, *** 1% significance levels. *Source:* Victor Couture, Benjamin Faber, Yizhen Gu, and Lizhi Liu, 2021. "Connecting the Countryside via E-Commerce: Evidence from China," *American Economic Review: Insights* 3, no. 1: 35–50. Copyright American Economic Association; reproduced with permission of the *American Economic Review: Insights*.

TABLE A5.9. Role of Logistical and Transactional Barriers

Effects on Consumption

Dept Variables		Intent to Treat	Treatment on the Treated	Log Distance (IV Using Treat)
Monthly Total Retail Expenditure Per Capita	Treat or Log Dist	−26.91	−49.34	13.67
		(36.29)	(68.00)	(18.71)
	Treat or Log Dist * Delivery	31.64	58.94	−15.50
		(69.36)	(140.5)	(30.43)
	First Stage F-Stat		2.388	19.39
	Number of Obs	3,436	3,436	3,436
Household Has Ever Bought Something through E-Comm Option (Yes=1)	Treat or Log Dist	0.0578***	0.106***	−0.0293***
		(0.0188)	(0.0283)	(0.00775)
	Treat or Log Dist * Delivery	−0.0606**	−0.111**	0.0304***
		(0.0253)	(0.0443)	(0.0102)
	First Stage F-Stat		2.682	19.63
	Number of Obs	3,518	3,518	3,518
Household Has Bought Something in Last Month (Yes=1)	Treat or Log Dist	0.0329***	0.0604***	−0.0168***
		(0.0111)	(0.0189)	(0.00522)
	Treat or Log Dist * Delivery	−0.0422***	−0.0790**	0.0204***
		(0.0155)	(0.0329)	(0.00729)
	First Stage F-Stat		2.513	19.10
	Number of Obs	3,482	3,482	3,482
Share of E-Comm Option in Total Monthly Retail Expenditure	Treat or Log Dist	0.00799***	0.0147***	−0.00407***
		(0.00275)	(0.00489)	(0.00136)
	Treat or Log Dist * Delivery	−0.00835***	−0.0154***	0.00422***
		(0.00295)	(0.00543)	(0.00144)
	First Stage F-Stat		2.413	19.25
	Number of Obs	3,434	3,434	3,434

Effects on Incomes

Dept Variables		Intent to Treat	Treatment on the Treated	Log Distance (IV Using Treat)
Monthly Income Per Capita in RMB	Treat or Log Dist	−15.00	−27.15	7.579
		(77.55)	(140.1)	(39.08)
	Treat or Log Dist * Delivery	50.17	96.91	−25.08
		(171.1)	(339.0)	(86.90)
	First Stage F-Stat		2.694	2.737
	Number of Obs	3,437	3,437	3,437
Monthly Income Per Capita Net of Costs in RMB	Treat or Log Dist	−20.24	−37.09	10.33
		(77.47)	(140.5)	(39.07)
	Treat or Log Dist * Delivery	6.011	9.303	−3.362
		(167.6)	(317.4)	(81.28)
	First Stage F-Stat		2.810	2.852
	Number of Obs	3,390	3,390	3,390
Monthly Income Per Capita Net of Transfers in RMB	Treat or Log Dist	−13.87	−25.27	7.041
		(77.86)	(140.7)	(39.18)
	Treat or Log Dist * Delivery	12.70	23.04	−6.473
		(188.3)	(367.2)	(93.22)
	First Stage F-Stat		2.635	2.696
	Number of Obs	3,445	3,445	3,445
Annual Income Per Capita in RMB	Treat or Log Dist	70.33	124.2	−34.68
		(645.0)	(1,168)	(325.6)
	Treat or Log Dist * Delivery	−734.1	−1,462	368.3
		(1,484)	(2,755)	(692.5)
	First Stage F-Stat		2.501	2.603
	Number of Obs	3,388	3,388	3,388

Effects on Retail Prices

Dept Variables		Intent to Treat	Treatment on the Treated
Log Prices (All)	Treat	0.0114	0.0215
		(0.0144)	(0.0273)
	Treat * Delivery	0.0417	0.0739
		(0.0377)	(0.0572)
	First Stage F-Stat		17.26
	Number of Obs	6,877	6,877
Product Replacement Dummy (Not Counting Store Closures) (Yes=1)	Treat	−0.00680	−0.0129
		(0.0108)	(0.0206)
	Treat * Delivery	0.00907	0.0173
		(0.0213)	(0.0415)
	First Stage F-Stat		2.648
	Number of Obs	8,956	8,956
Store Closure (at Product Level) (Yes=1)	Treat	0.00111	0.00209
		(0.0355)	(0.0668)
	Treat * Delivery	0.000779	0.00162
		(0.0423)	(0.0805)
	First Stage F-Stat		2.648
	Number of Obs	8,956	8,956
Number of New Products Per Store	Treat	1.403*	2.352*
		(0.828)	(1.354)
	Treat * Delivery	3.403	7.993
		(3.876)	(12.77)
	First Stage F-Stat		1.247
	Number of Obs	312	312

Left panel (household consumption)

Share of E-Comm Option in Total Monthly Business Inputs	(1)	(2)	(3)
Treat or Log Dist	-0.00830	-0.0190	0.00501
	(0.00827)	(0.0222)	(0.00589)
Treat or Log Dist * Delivery	0.0179	0.0334	-0.00818
	(0.0113)	(0.0250)	(0.00633)
First Stage F-Stat		6.346	7.094
Number of Obs	1,191	1,191	1,191
Share of E-Comm Option in Total Monthly Non-Durables			
Treat or Log Dist	0.00639***	0.0117***	-0.00325***
	(0.00225)	(0.00401)	(0.00112)
Treat or Log Dist * Delivery	-0.00648**	-0.0119***	0.00329***
	(0.00247)	(0.00453)	(0.00119)
First Stage F-Stat		2.413	19.26
Number of Obs	3,433	3,433	3,433
Share of E-Comm Option in Total Monthly Durables			
Treat or Log Dist	0.0497***	0.0825***	-0.0240***
	(0.0177)	(0.0286)	(0.00823)
Treat or Log Dist * Delivery	-0.0705***	-0.120***	0.0322***
	(0.0258)	(0.0443)	(0.0113)
First Stage F-Stat		3.150	18.33
Number of Obs	768	768	768

Middle panel (household incomes)

Member of Household Has Ever Sold through E-Commerce (Yes=1)	(1)	(2)	(3)
Treat or Log Dist	-0.00857	-0.0156	0.00433
	(0.00608)	(0.0111)	(0.00309)
Treat or Log Dist * Delivery	0.0102	0.0188	-0.00513
	(0.0141)	(0.0280)	(0.00715)
First Stage F-Stat		2.561	2.598
Number of Obs	3,504	3,504	3,504
Share of E-Commerce Sales in Household Monthly Income			
Treat or Log Dist	-0.00172	-0.00316	0.000882
	(0.00210)	(0.00387)	(0.00108)
Treat or Log Dist * Delivery	0.00282	0.00540	-0.00145
	(0.00233)	(0.00441)	(0.00121)
First Stage F-Stat		2.402	2.342
Number of Obs	2,830	2,830	2,830
Primary Earner Working as Peasant (Yes=1)			
Treat or Log Dist	-0.0192	-0.0352	0.00979
	(0.0341)	(0.0624)	(0.0174)
Treat or Log Dist * Delivery	-0.0284	-0.0609	0.0143
	(0.0813)	(0.185)	(0.0464)
First Stage F-Stat		2.503	2.533
Number of Obs	3,327	3,327	3,327
Member of Household Has Started a Business Over Last 6 Months (Yes=1)			
Treat or Log Dist	-0.00328	-0.00601	0.00167
	(0.00635)	(0.0116)	(0.00322)
Treat or Log Dist * Delivery	-0.0297	-0.0604	0.0149
	(0.0183)	(0.0536)	(0.0130)
First Stage F-Stat		2.517	2.566
Number of Obs	3,468	3,468	3,468

Right panel (local retail prices)

Store Owner Sources Products Online (Yes=1)	(1)	(2)
Treat	0.0250**	0.0416**
	(0.0122)	(0.0201)
Treat * Delivery	-0.0911	-0.185
	(0.0814)	(0.166)
First Stage F-Stat		1.320
Number of Obs	341	341
Log Price of Business Inputs		
Treat	-0.0858	-0.108
	(0.134)	(0.182)
Treat * Delivery	0.289	0.473
	(0.273)	(0.447)
First Stage F-Stat		1.972
Number of Obs	237	237
Log Price of Nondurables		
Treat	0.0192	0.0366
	(0.0157)	(0.0308)
Treat * Delivery	0.0137	0.0214
	(0.0362)	(0.0585)
First Stage F-Stat		16.09
Number of Obs	6,455	6,455
Log Prices of Durables		
Treat	-0.118	-0.144
	(0.0880)	(0.104)
Treat * Delivery	0.164	0.288
	(0.134)	(0.366)
First Stage F-Stat		0.488
Number of Obs	185	185

Notes: Left panel shows outcomes related to household consumption, middle panel shows outcomes related to household incomes and right panel shows outcomes related to local retail prices. The first column reports ITT and the second column TOT. The third column replaces the binary TOT with log residential distances to the nearest e-commerce terminal (using village-level ITT as instrument as for second column). Standard errors are clustered at the level of villages. * 10%, ** 5%, *** 1% significance levels. *Source:* Victor Couture, Benjamin Faber, Yizhen Gu, and Lizhi Liu, 2021. "Connecting the Countryside via E-Commerce: Evidence from China," *American Economic Review: Insights* 3, no. 1: 35–50. Copyright American Economic Association; reproduced with permission of the *American Economic Review: Insights*.

TABLE A5.10. Role of GE Spillovers

Dependent Variables		Treatment on Treated without Spillovers	ToT with Spillovers: Number of Terminals within 3 km Outside of Village	ToT with Spillovers: Number of Terminals within 10 km Outside of Village
Any Member of Household Has Ever Sold through E-Comm (Yes = 1)	Treat Dummy	−0.0128 (0.0103)	−0.0134 (0.0101)	−0.0147 (0.0101)
	Exposure to Terminals Outside the Village		−0.00131 (0.0101)	−0.00234 (0.00202)
	Exposure to Other Villages		−0.00334*** (0.00102)	−0.000277 (0.000363)
	First Stage F-Stat	45.30	47.63	44.61
	Number of Obs	3,504	3,504	3,504
Household Has Ever Bought Something through E-Comm Option (Yes = 1)	Treat Dummy	0.0894*** (0.0268)	0.0793*** (0.0263)	0.0873*** (0.0264)
	Exposure to Terminals Outside the Village		0.0658** (0.0312)	−0.00606 (0.00567)
	Exposure to Other Villages		−0.00246 (0.00539)	0.00258** (0.00112)
	First Stage F-Stat	45.31	47.83	44.59
	Number of Obs	3,518	3,518	3,518
Share of E-Comm Option in Total Retail Expenditure	Treat Dummy	0.0124*** (0.00435)	0.0101** (0.00399)	0.0119*** (0.00422)
	Exposure to Terminals Outside the Village		0.0159* (0.00833)	−0.00129 (0.000929)
	Exposure to Other Villages		−0.000595 (0.000524)	0.000507** (0.000228)
	First Stage F-Stat	44.03	46.57	43.50
	Number of Obs	3,434	3,434	3,434
Log Local Retail Prices (All Prices)	Treat Dummy	0.0352 (0.0263)	0.0338 (0.0258)	0.0386 (0.0252)
	Exposure to Terminals Outside the Village		0.00353 (0.0314)	0.00382 (0.00562)
	Exposure to Other Villages		−0.00318 (0.00314)	−0.00135 (0.000950)
	First Stage F-Stat	41.66	43.89	43.95
	Number of Obs	6,877	6,877	6,877

Notes: The first column reports the baseline ToT. The second column adds exposure to other intent-to-treat villages within a 3 kilometer radius, controlling for the total number of eligible villages within this radius. The third column adds exposure to other intent-to-treat villages within a 10 kilometer radius, controlling for the total number of eligible villages within this radius. See Appendix C for discussion. Standard errors are clustered at the level of villages. * 10%, ** 5%, *** 1% significance levels. Source: Victor Couture, Benjamin Faber, Yizhen Gu, and Lizhi Liu, 2021. "Connecting the Countryside via E-Commerce: Evidence from China," American Economic Review: Insights 3, no. 1: 35–50. Copyright American Economic Association; reproduced with permission of the American Economic Review: Insights.

TABLE A5.11. Fraction of Market Access to Other Rural Markets in County

Measure of Market Size:	Fraction of Market Access from Rural Markets in Same County						Fraction of Market Access from Participating Rural Markets in Same County					
	Access to Population			Access to GDP			Access to Population			Access to GDP		
	Median	Mean	Std Dev	Median	Mean	Std Dev	Median	Mean	Std Dev	Median	Mean	Std Dev
Panel A: Distance Elasticity of -1												
All Rural Townships in East, Middle, and Southwest China (10,214 Townships)	0.0082	0.011	0.01	0.0031	0.0044	0.005	0.0014	0.0018	0.0017	0.0005	0.0007	0.0008
Rural Townships in 3 RCT Provinces (2,291 Townships)	0.012	0.016	0.014	0.0037	0.0059	0.0062	0.0020	0.0027	0.0023	0.0006	0.0010	0.0010
Rural Townships in 8 RCT Counties (58 Townships)	0.011	0.012	0.006	0.0031	0.0041	0.0029	0.0018	0.0020	0.0010	0.0005	0.0007	0.0005
Panel B: Distance Elasticity of -1.5												
All Rural Townships in East, Middle, and Southwest China (10,214 Townships)	0.027	0.037	0.042	0.01	0.016	0.024	0.0045	0.0062	0.0070	0.0017	0.0027	0.0040
Rural Townships in 3 RCT Provinces (2,291 Townships)	0.036	0.049	0.055	0.012	0.02	0.028	0.0060	0.0082	0.0092	0.0020	0.0033	0.0047
Rural Townships in 8 RCT Counties (58 Townships)	0.034	0.038	0.033	0.011	0.014	0.013	0.0057	0.0063	0.0055	0.0018	0.0023	0.0022

Notes: Table reports the mean, median, and standard deviation of the fraction of trade market access coming from other rural markets in the same county. See Appendix C for discussion. *Source:* Victor Couture, Benjamin Faber, Yizhen Gu, and Lizhi Liu, 2021. "Connecting the Countryside via E-Commerce: Evidence from China," *American Economic Review: Insights* 3, no. 1: 35–50. Copyright American Economic Association; reproduced with permission of the *American Economic Review: Insights*.

TABLE A5.12. Are Sample Villages Representative?

	(1)	(2)	(3)	(4)	(5)	(6)
	Full Sample			3 Provinces		
Dependent Variables:	Number of Users	Number of Transactions	Sales (RMB)	Number of Users	Number of Transactions	Sales (RMB)
Panel A: Purchase Database						
RCT Sample Village Dummy	−4.110	0.0605	−6,034	0.149	12.65	−3,747
	(7.751)	(25.33)	(4,061)	(7.734)	(25.32)	(4,066)
Months Fixed Effects	✓	✓	✓	✓	✓	✓
Control for Months since Program Entry	✓	✓	✓	✓	✓	✓
Observations	125,204	125,204	125,204	100,098	100,098	100,098
R-squared	0.037	0.047	0.029	0.031	0.046	0.03
Number of Village Clusters	11,731	11,731	11,731	8,471	8,471	8,471

	(7)	(8)	(9)	(10)
	Full Sample		3 Provinces	
Dependent Variables:	Number of Transactions	Weight (kg)	Number of Transactions	Weight (kg)
Panel B: Out-Shipment Database				
RCT Sample Village Dummy	1.712**	5.154	1.364*	4.68
	(0.753)	(4.332)	(0.752)	(4.333)
Months Fixed Effects	✓	✓	✓	✓
Control for Months since Program Entry	✓	✓	✓	✓
Observations	120,483	120,483	95,744	95,744
R-squared	0.06	0.023	0.067	0.026
Number of Village Clusters	11,904	11,904	8,591	8,591

Notes: Table reports point estimates from a regression of the reported outcomes on a dummy equal to one if a village is one of our one hundred RCT villages in addition to month fixed effects and the number of months since program entry. Columns 1 to 3 and 7 to 8 report results for all participating villages in the five provinces of Anhui, Guangxi, Guizhou, Henan, and Yunnan over the period November 2015 to April 2017. The sample in columns 4 to 6 and 9 to 10 are all villages in our three survey provinces Anhui, Guizhou, and Henan. The upper panel presents point estimates from regressions based on the purchase transaction database over the period November 2015 to April 2017. The lower panel presents point estimates from regressions based on the sales transaction database over the period January 2016 to April 2017. See Appendix D for discussion. Standard errors are clustered at the level of village terminals. * 10%, ** 5%, *** 1% significance levels. *Source:* Victor Couture, Benjamin Faber, Yizhen Gu, and Lizhi Liu, 2021. "Connecting the Countryside via E-Commerce: Evidence from China," *American Economic Review: Insights* 3, no. 1: 35–50. Copyright American Economic Association; reproduced with permission of the *American Economic Review: Insights.*

TABLE A5.13. Role of Seasonality

	(1)	(2)	(3)	(4)	(5)	(6)
	Full Sample			3 Provinces		
Dependent Variables:	Number of Users	Number of Transactions	Sales (RMB)	Number of Users	Number of Transactions	Sales (RMB)
Panel A: Purchase Database						
RCT Sample Month Dummy	0.893***	−4.671***	−1,565***	0.568**	−5.290***	−585.9
	(0.255)	(0.818)	(451.5)	(0.274)	(0.863)	(458.0)
Village Fixed Effects	✓	✓	✓	✓	✓	✓
Control for Months since Program Entry	✓	✓	✓	✓	✓	✓
Observations	125,204	125,204	125,204	100,098	100,098	100,098
R-squared	0.694	0.68	0.219	0.679	0.667	0.227
Number of Village Clusters	11,731	11,731	11,731	8,471	8,471	8,471

	(7)	(8)	(9)	(10)
	Full Sample		3 Provinces	
Dependent Variables:	Number of Transactions	Weight (kg)	Number of Transactions	Weight (kg)
Panel B: Out-Shipment Database				
RCT Sample Month Dummy	−0.387***	−1.256***	−0.498***	−1.407***
	(0.0225)	(0.125)	(0.0261)	(0.138)
Village Fixed Effects	✓	✓	✓	✓
Control for Months since Program Entry	✓	✓	✓	✓
Observations	120,483	120,483	95,744	95,744
R-squared	0.592	0.432	0.57	0.422
Number of Village Clusters	11,904	11,904	8,591	8,591

Notes: Table reports point estimates from a regression of the reported outcomes on a dummy equal to one if a village is one of our one hundred RCT villages in addition to village fixed effects and the number of months since program entry. Columns 1 to 3 and 7 to 8 report results for all participating villages in the five provinces of Anhui, Guangxi, Guizhou, Henan, and Yunnan over the period November 2015 to April 2017. The sample in columns 4 to 6 and 9 to 10 are all villages in our three survey provinces Anhui, Guizhou, and Henan. The upper panel presents point estimates from regressions based on the purchase transaction database over the period November 2015 to April 2017. The lower panel presents point estimates from regressions based on the sales transaction database over the period January 2016 to April 2017. See Appendix D for discussion. Standard errors are clustered at the level of village terminals. * 10%, ** 5%, *** 1% significance levels. Source: Victor Couture, Benjamin Faber, Yizhen Gu, and Lizhi Liu, 2021. "Connecting the Countryside via E-Commerce: Evidence from China," *American Economic Review: Insights* 3, no. 1: 35–50. Copyright American Economic Association; reproduced with permission of the *American Economic Review: Insights*.

TABLE A5.14. Quantification Using Alternative Demand Parameters

	$\sigma\_D=2.87, \sigma\_N=2.85$			$\sigma\_D=3.87, \sigma\_N=3.85$			$\sigma\_D=4.87, \sigma\_N=4.85$		
	Durables Consumption	Nondurables Consumption	Total Retail Consumption	Durables Consumption	Nondurables Consumption	Total Retail Consumption	Durables Consumption	Nondurables Consumption	Total Retail Consumption
Reduction in Retail Cost of Living for All Households	5.256% (0.048)	0.739% (0.005)	1.27% (0.007)	3.379% (0.03)	0.481% (0.003)	0.824% (0.005)	2.489% (0.022)	0.357% (0.003)	0.61% (0.003)
Reduction in Retail Cost of Living among Users	32.416% (0.378)	5.904% (0.044)	8.735% (0.054)	19.884% (0.221)	3.806% (0.028)	5.597% (0.034)	14.331% (0.155)	2.808% (0.021)	4.117% (0.025)

Notes: Table reports average household gains in terms of percentage point reductions in household retail cost of living across alternative parameterizations of household demand. Estimates are based on equation (3) using treatment effects on household substitution into e-commerce. Standard errors are bootstrapped across 1,000 iterations. *Source:* Victor Couture, Benjamin Faber, Yizhen Gu, and Lizhi Liu, 2021. "Connecting the Countryside via E-Commerce: Evidence from China," *American Economic Review: Insights* 3, no. 1: 35–50. Copyright American Economic Association; reproduced with permission of the *American Economic Review: Insights.*

TABLE A5.15. Test for Effects on Attrition and Migration

Dependent Variables		Intent to Treat	Treatment on Treated	Log Distance (IV using Treat)
Attrition (Yes = 1)	Treat or Log Dist	0.0138 (0.0239)	0.0258 (0.0445)	−0.00740 (0.0127)
	R-Squared	0.000		
	Number of Obs	2,629	2,629	2,629
	First Stage F-Stat		44.24	35.90
Number of Household Members Who Moved Back to the Village	Treat or Log Dist	0.0255 (0.0400)	0.0472 (0.0734)	−0.0129 (0.0199)
	R-Squared	0.001		
	Number of Obs	3,526	3,526	3,526
	First Stage F-Stat		45.27	42.71
Number of Household Members Who Moved Away from the Village	Treat or Log Dist	−0.00345 (0.0184)	−0.00637 (0.0338)	0.00174 (0.00922)
	R-Squared	0.012		
	Number of Obs	3,523	3,523	3,523
	First Stage F-Stat		45.44	43.84
Would You Be Willing to Migrate to a City if a Good Job Opportunity Presented Itself? (Yes = 1)	Treat or Log Dist	−0.0249 (0.0191)	−0.0458 (0.0348)	0.0125 (0.00953)
	R-Squared	0.025		
	Number of Obs	3,527	3,527	3,527
	First Stage F-Stat		45.76	44.15

Notes: Table reports point estimates from specification (1). The first column reports ITT and the second column TOT. The third column replaces the binary TOT with log residential distances to the nearest e-commerce terminal (using village-level ITT as instrument as for second column). See Appendix F for discussion. Standard errors are clustered at the level of villages. * 10%, ** 5%, *** 1% significance levels. *Source*: Victor Couture, Benjamin Faber, Yizhen Gu, and Lizhi Liu, 2021. "Connecting the Countryside via E-Commerce: Evidence from China," *American Economic Review: Insights* 3, no. 1: 35–50. Copyright American Economic Association; reproduced with permission of the *American Economic Review: Insights*.

TABLE A5.16. Role of Program Implementation

Type of Heterogeneity		Intent to Treat	Treatment on the Treated	Log Distance (IV Using Treat)
		Dependent Variable: Household Has Ever Bought Something through E-Commerce Terminal (Yes = 1)		
Average Effects	Treat or Log Dist	0.0480***	0.0886***	−0.0241***
		(0.0169)	(0.0271)	(0.00721)
	R-Squared	0.008		
	First Stage F-Stat		45.56	43.80
	Number of Obs	3,518	3,518	3,518
Terminal Manager Test Score	Treat or Log Dist	0.0594	0.104	−0.0297
		(0.147)	(0.242)	(0.0679)
	Treat or Log Dist * Score	−0.000214	−0.000384	0.000114
		(0.00164)	(0.00270)	(0.000755)
	R-Squared	0.006		
	First Stage F-Stat		8.786	8.133
	Number of Obs	3,042	3,042	3,042
Terminal Manager Test Score above the Median	Treat or Log Dist	0.0314	0.0616	−0.0172
		(0.0295)	(0.0501)	(0.0136)
	Treat or Log Dist * Above Median	0.0191	0.0182	−0.00504
		(0.0347)	(0.0583)	(0.0158)
	R-Squared	0.006		
	First Stage F-Stat		8.654	7.210
	Number of Obs	3,042	3,042	3,042
County Team without Smooth Planning	Treat or Log Dist	0.0392	0.0656*	−0.0180*
		(0.0247)	(0.0357)	(0.00941)
	Treat or Log Dist * Delay Dummy	0.0167	0.0486	−0.0131
		(0.0335)	(0.0554)	(0.0149)
	R-Squared	0.009		
	First Stage F-Stat		10.93	11.46
	Number of Obs	3,518	3,518	3,518

Notes: Table reports point estimates from specification (1). The first column reports ITT and the second column TOT. The third column replaces the binary TOT with log residential distances to the nearest e-commerce terminal (using village-level ITT as instrument as for second column). See Appendix F for discussion. Standard errors are clustered at the level of villages. * 10%, ** 5%, *** 1% significance levels. *Source:* Victor Couture, Benjamin Faber, Yizhen Gu, and Lizhi Liu, 2021. "Connecting the Countryside via E-Commerce: Evidence from China," *American Economic Review: Insights* 3, no. 1: 35–50. Copyright American Economic Association; reproduced with permission of the *American Economic Review: Insights.*

Appendix B: K-L-K Indices

Table 5.2 reports treatment effects after combining several outcomes related to consumption, incomes, and local retail prices into three indices. We follow Kling et al. (2007) ("K-L-K") and construct equally weighted averages of z-scores that we compute by subtracting outcomes by the mean of the variable in the control group and dividing by the standard deviation of the variable in the control group. The z-scores are signed such that effects on all index components point in the same direction (i.e., price index reductions or income growth). If a household (or store) has a valid response to at least one component measure of an index, then any missing values for other component measures are imputed at the random assignment group mean. This results in differences between treatment and control means of an index being the same as the average of treatment and control means of the components of that index, so that the index can be interpreted as the average of results for separate measures scaled to standard deviation units.[1]

The consumption index is based on eleven variables related to household substitution of expenditures into the new e-commerce shopping option, all entering the index positively. Those outcomes are whether a household reports ever having used the new option, reported usage over the past month, and the shares of household total retail expenditure spent on nine consumption categories (food and beverages, tobacco and alcohol, medicine and health, clothing and accessories, other everyday products, fuel and gas, furniture and appliances, electronics, transport equipment). The treatment effects on each of these outcomes are reported as part of appendix Table A5.6.

The income index is based on fourteen variables related to income generation, labor supply, online selling activity, and online sourcing of inputs. Those outcomes are monthly income per capita, annual income per capita, monthly income from agriculture, monthly income from nonagriculture, monthly hours of work by primary earner, monthly hours of work by secondary earner, whether anyone in the household has ever sold online, sold over the last month, revenues from online sales over the past month, share of online revenues in total monthly income, whether primary earner is a farmer (entering negatively), whether any household member has started a new business over the past six months, whether the new business sells in part online, and the share of monthly online purchases in total expenditures on inputs and materials. The treatment effects on each of these outcomes are reported as part of appendix Table A5.7.

The local retail index is based on four store-level measures related to effects on the local retail cost of living. Those outcomes are the average of log price changes of continuing product items within the store (entering negatively), the number of new product additions over the past month (positively), the number of product replacements (measured as the fraction of products reported in the baseline survey that were no longer available at endline) (negatively), and whether or not the store owner reports sourcing products online (positively). The treatment effects on each of these outcomes are reported as part of appendix Table A5.8.

Appendix C: Role of Spillovers

To investigate the role of spillovers, we pursue two different approaches. First, we follow an approach similar to Miguel & Kremer (2004):

$$y_{hv}^{Post} = \alpha + \beta_1 \text{Treat}_v + \beta_2 \text{Exposure}_v^{treat} + \beta_3 \text{Exposure}_v^{all} + \gamma y_{hv}^{Pre} + \epsilon_{hv}, \quad \text{(A.1)}$$

where $\text{Exposure}_v^{treat}$ measures proximity of village v to other program villages, and Exposure_v^{all} measures proximity to all villages on the candidate list from which we randomly selected our control villages. Even though exposure to other program villages is not randomly assigned, our randomization means that conditional on exposure to all candidate villages, exposure to other treatment villages is plausibly exogenous. Using this design, β_2 is an estimate of the strength of cross-village spillovers. We measure exposure as the number of intent-to-treat villages within 3 or 10 kilometers distance bins of a given village. Table A5.10 reports the estimation results. We find some evidence of positive spillover effects of nearby terminals within 3 kilometers of the village. These effects imply a larger total average effect on e-commerce uptake. Consumption uptake increases from 9 percent in Table A5.6 to 14 percent once we consider positive spillovers from nearby villages, which is 13 percent of the village population after adjusting for sampling weights. In contrast, we find no evidence of cross-village spillovers on local retail stores or on the production side of the economy.

Second, to further investigate these channels in the absence of experimental variation in program saturation rates,[2] we also pursue an approach grounded in trade theory. In particular, we can quantify the fraction of a rural location's total trade market access that is due to trading exposure to other rural markets in the same county. This fraction provides additional information on the extent of rural-to-rural spillovers from other sample villages in our setting. If a sizable share of local market access is due to trading relations with other local rural markets, then indirect effects on local product prices and incomes from treatments in other villages could become an important force. If, on the other hand, local product and factor prices are predominantly determined by access to larger urban markets, then rural-to-rural spillovers could have negligible effects on local prices and incomes across our sample villages.

Following Head & Mayer (2014) and others, the market access of location v to all other rural and urban markets $j \neq v$ is

$$MA_v = \sum_{j \neq v} \tau_{jv}^{-\theta} Y_j \qquad (A.2)$$

where τ_{jv} is the bilateral trade cost, θ is the elasticity of trade flows with respect to trade costs, and Y_j is a measure of j's market size.[3] MA_v is thus a weighted sum of economic activity outside of market v, with weights that are inversely related to bilateral trade costs. To compute the fraction of total market access that is due to bilateral linkages with other rural markets in the same county (i.e., MA_v^R / MA_v), we compute (6) both across bilateral connections to all other markets (denominator), and only summing across bilateral connections with other rural markets in the same county (numerator). Alternatively, we restrict the numerator to bilateral connections with respect to the fraction of rural markets in the county that are participating in the program to compute the share of market access due to rural locations with program terminals. That fraction was about one-sixth of all rural markets in participating counties over our sample period.

To compute these measures, we use the township-level data from the Chinese Population Census in 2010 described in Appendix F below. These data provide us with the populations residing in each of roughly 45,000 township-level administrative units. In addition, we use the coordinates of township centroids to construct the full matrix of bilateral distances in kilometers. Following the trade literature, we use these bilateral distances to parameterize $\tau_{jv}^{-\theta}$: using the finding that the elasticity of trade flows with respect to distance is approximately -1,[4] we measure $\tau_{jv}^{-\theta}$ as the inverse bilateral distance in kilometers when summing across the j market sizes. Alternatively, we also use a larger distance elasticity of -1.5 that gives more weight to markets in closer proximity. For market size Y_j, we use either population or population multiplied by the value added per worker for rural and nonrural workers measured at the province level for 2010. The first metric provides an inverse distance-weighted measure of market access to populations outside the township, while the second provides an approximate measure of access to GDP. Finally, we define rural and urban markets following the administrative classification across township-level units we obtain in the census data. For computational feasibility, when constructing the full matrix of bilateral connections, we compute the total market access of rural townships with respect to all other township units (both rural and urban) within each of the three broad administrative regions of China in which our sample counties are located: East China (seven provinces), Middle China (three provinces), and Southwest China (five provinces).[5]

The above provides us with four measures of the ratio of total market access that is due to access to other rural populations or rural GDP within the same county: measured either in terms of access to population or to GDP, and measured either in terms of access to all rural markets in the county or only the fraction of rural markets that on average participate in the e-commerce program. We compute the median, mean, and standard deviations of these four ratios for all rural townships located in the three regions of China, as well as only for townships in our three sample provinces, or only for townships in the eight sample counties. Furthermore, we compute each of these measures both for the baseline distance elasticity of -1, and when using -1.5 instead.

Appendix Table A5.11 presents the estimation results. Overall, we find that other rural markets in the same county account for a tiny fraction of total trade market access for the median or the average rural market place. This result is driven by the fact that nearby rural markets within the same county account for a small fraction of the market size that is concentrated in vastly larger urban centers. This is particularly the case when using economic output as the measure of market size, but it also holds for raw populations. For example, the median fraction of market access from nearby rural markets in terms of GDP is 0.37 percent in our sample provinces, and 1.2 percent in terms of population access. These fractions slightly increase when giving more weight to nearby markets using a higher distance elasticity, but they remain close to zero in both cases when computing rural-to-rural market access only with respect to the average fraction of rural markets that are participating in the program in any given county over our sample period. These findings are in line with the absence of significant GE spillover effects on market prices or nominal incomes shown in our first approach above, and serve to provide some further corroborating evidence in this context.

Appendix D: Additional Results from the Firm's Database

D1. Are the RCT Sample Villages Representative?

One concern is that the eight counties where our RCT takes place may not be representative of program villages more broadly. To test this, we use the five-province transaction database on both purchases and sales transactions to estimate regressions using the following form:

$$y_{vm} = \theta_m + \beta \text{RCTSample}_v + \gamma \text{MonthsSinceEntry}_{vm} + \epsilon_{vm},$$

where v indexes village terminals and θ_m is a set of monthly dummies indexed by m for the eighteen months of operation from November 2015 to January 2017. y_{vm} is one of five terminal level monthly outcomes (number of buyers, number of purchase transactions, total terminal sales, number of out-shipments, and total weight of out-shipments in kilograms), *RCTSample* is a dummy for whether the terminal is in our RCT sample, and *MonthsSinceEntry* controls for the number of months that the program has been in operation in v as of month m. The standard errors ϵ_{vm} are clustered at the village level.[6]

The results in appendix Table A5.12 indicate no systematic differences between our RCT villages and the population of program villages in these five provinces. The same is true if we compare our RCT villages to all villages in our three survey provinces. The RCT sample seems marginally more successful on the out-shipment side, but the magnitudes are tiny. These results provide some reassurance against the potential concern that the e-commerce firm directed our team toward eight counties that systematically differ from the program's general target locations in Chinese countryside.

D2. Did We Collect the Endline Data during Particular Months?

The timeline of pretreatment data collection was determined by the roll-out schedule of the e-commerce firm, and we could not finance more than a single posttreatment round. As a result of these constraints, our survey cannot measure the impact of seasonality on treatment effects. We therefore use the transaction database to study seasonality effects by estimating:

$$y_{vm} = \theta_v + \beta \text{RCTMonth}_m + \gamma \, \text{MonthsSinceEntry}_{vm} + \epsilon_{vm},$$

where RCTMonth is a dummy for our survey months, i.e., a dummy equal to 1 if month m is either December, January, April, or May, which are the four calendar months during which we conducted our survey. We again cluster standard errors ϵ_{vm} at the terminal level. The results are in appendix, Table A5.13. We find slightly higher numbers of terminal buyers during survey months relative to the rest of the year, and slightly lower numbers of purchase transactions and out-shipments. In both cases, the point estimates are very small: about one additional buyer per month, a reduction of between four to five in the number of monthly purchase transactions, and a reduction of less than one out-shipment per month on the selling side. We conclude that seasonality is unlikely to be a significant driver underlying the findings of the RCT.

Appendix E: Welfare Evaluation

Following recent work by Atkin et al. (2018), we propose a three-tier demand system to describe household retail consumption across product groups, retail shopping options, and products. In the upper tier, shown in equation A.3, there are Cobb-Douglas preferences over broad product groups $g \in G$ (durables and nondurables) in total consumption. In the middle tier, shown in equation A.4, there are asymmetric CES preferences over local retailers selling that product group $s \in S$ (e.g., local stores, market stalls, or the e-commerce option). In the final tier, there are preferences over the individual products within the product groups $b \in B_g$ that we can leave unspecified for now.

$$\mathcal{U}_h = \prod_{g \in G} \left[\mathcal{Q}_{gh} \right]^{\alpha_{gh}} \tag{A.3}$$

$$\mathcal{Q}_{gh} = \left(\sum_{s \in S_g} \beta_{gsh} \, q_{gsh}^{\frac{\sigma_g - 1}{\sigma_g}} \right)^{\frac{\sigma_g}{\sigma_g - 1}}, \tag{A.4}$$

where a_{gh} and β_{gsh} are (potentially household group-specific) preference parameters that are fixed across periods. $\mathcal{Q}_{gh}$ and q_{gsh} are product-group and store-product-group consumption aggregates with associated price indices P_{gh} and r_{gsh} respectively, and σ_g is the elasticity of substitution across local retail outlets. For each broad product group, consumers choose how much they are going to spend at different retail outlets based on the store-level price index r_{gsh} (which itself depends on the product mix and product-level prices on offer across outlets).

While the demand system is homothetic, we capture potential heterogeneity across the income distribution by allowing households of different incomes to differ in their expenditure shares across product groups (a_{gh}) and their preferences for consumption bundles at different stores within those product groups (β_{gsh} and the preference parameters that generate q_{gsh}). As shown by Anderson et al. (1992), these preferences can generate the same demands as would be obtained from aggregating many consumers who make discrete choices over which store to shop in. Building on Feenstra (1994), the following expression provides the exact proportional cost of living effect (CLE) under this demand system as a fraction of initial household expenditures:

$$\frac{CLE}{e\left(\mathbf{P}^0, u_h^0\right)} = \prod_{g \in G} \left(\left(\frac{\sum_{s \in S_g^C} \phi_{gsh}^1}{\sum_{s \in S_g^C} \phi_{gsh}^0} \right)^{\frac{1}{\sigma_g - 1}} \prod_{s \in S_g^C} \left(\frac{\gamma_{gsh}^1}{\gamma_{gsh}^0} \right)^{\omega_{gsh}} \right)^{\alpha_{gh}} - 1 \tag{A.5}$$

where S_g^C denotes the set of continuing local retailers within product group g, $\phi_{gsh}^t = \gamma_{gsh}^t q_{gsh}^t / \sum_{s \in S_g} \gamma_{gsh}^t q_{gsh}^t$ is the expenditure share for a particular retailer of product group g, and the ω_{gsh} are ideal log-change weights.[7]

For each product group g, the expression has two components. The $\prod_{s \in S_g^C} (\frac{\gamma_{gsh}^1}{\gamma_{gsh}^0})^{\omega_{gsh}}$ term is Sato-Vartia (i.e., CES) price-index for price changes in continuing local stores that forms the pro-competitive price effect.[8] The price terms γ_{gsh}^t are themselves price indices of product-specific prices P_{gsb}^t within local continuing stores, which, in principle, could also account for new product varieties or exiting product varieties using the same methodology. While we name these price changes pro-competitive, they may derive from either decreases in markups or increases in productivity at local stores (distinctions that do not matter on the cost-of-living side but that would generate different magnitudes of profit and income effects that we capture on the nominal income side).

The $\left(\dfrac{\sum_{s \in S_g^C} \phi_{gsh}^1}{\sum_{s \in S_g^C} \phi_{gsh}^0} \right)^{\frac{1}{\sigma_g - 1}}$ term captures the gains to customers of the e-commerce option in the numerator from both a direct price index effect due to the new shopping option and potential other local store entry induced by this change, and local store exit in the denominator, i.e., the exit effect.

Now consider the case—as in the final section of the paper—where the program's effect on cost of living is driven by the direct price index effect. In that case, the expenditure share spent on continuing local retailers $\left(\sum_{s \in S_g^C} \phi_{gsh}^1 \right)$ is lower than unity only due to substitution into the new e-commerce option. The consumer gains from the program as a proportion of initial household spending are then:

$$\frac{CLE}{e(\mathbf{P}^0, u_h^0)} = \prod_{g \in G} \left(\left(\sum_{s \in S_g^C} \phi_{gsh}^1 \right)^{\frac{1}{\sigma_g - 1}} \right)^{\alpha_{gh}} - 1 \qquad \text{(A.6)}$$

The welfare gain from a new shopping option is a function of the market share of that outlet post-entry and the elasticity of substitution across stores. The revealed preference nature of this approach is clear. If consumers greatly value the arrival of the new option—be it because it offers low prices P_{gsb}^1, more product variety that reduces r_{gsh}^0, or better amenities β_{gsh}—the market share is higher and the welfare gain greater. Hence, these market share changes capture all the potential consumer benefits of shopping through the e-commerce option. The magnitude of the welfare gain depends on the elasticity of substitution. Observed e-commerce market shares will imply smaller welfare changes if consumers substitute between local shopping options very elastically, and larger welfare changes if they are inelastic. A similar logic would apply to effects on the entry of local retailers, or on the exit of local stores (where a large period zero market share means large welfare losses, again tempered by the elasticity of substitution).

Appendix F: Additional Information about the Program and the RCT

F.1 Surveyor Training and Quality Management

PILOTING AND SURVEYOR TRAINING

Our survey supervisors are professionals from the Research Center for Contemporary China (RCCC) at Peking University. All RCCC supervisors have previous experience conducting large-scale surveys in rural China. Before each of the two survey rounds, we traveled to Beijing to lead a one-day training workshop targeted at the supervisors and a group of graduate students from Renmin University and Jinan University, who were working with us as research assistants on this project. This training walked the RCCC supervisors and our graduate students through each step of the survey design, data collection protocols, and quality control protocols that we had shared with them to study carefully in advance. Given budget and time constraints, the survey was paper based. Prior to our baseline survey, RCCC supervisors and our team of graduate students tested our survey design in a pilot survey of forty-five households in two villages located in the rural parts of Hebei Province.

In the field, each supervisor was in charge of a team of six surveyors. In addition to the supervisors, two of our trained graduate students accompanied each team in the field. The role of the graduate students was to both support and monitor the recruitment and training of the local surveyors and the data collection, and to report back to us with detailed daily progress reports. Given differences in local dialects and rural conditions, the RCCC recruited surveyors among local university students from the provinces in which the data collection took place. All surveyors were familiar with the local dialect and customs of the rural areas in their home province. Each surveyor completed at least two full days of training and supervised practice questionnaire interviews before joining our field survey team. As part of the training, we provided surveyors with a number of supporting documents. In particular, they received an example of a completed representative survey questionnaire, detailed instructions on how to assist households in answering the questionnaire, a set of cards containing descriptions and examples of consumption products within categories or income-generating activities within sectors, and a set of solutions and best practices for common survey challenges. As described in Appendix F.4 below, we also trained surveyors to use separate preprepared spreadsheets to list individual household purchase transactions within product categories or income flows by type of activity. These spreadsheets were used for households to list individual transactions over a given period of time and within categories, before aggregating this information to complete the final survey questionnaire cells. As part of their training, surveyors were trained to double-check with respondents any answer to the questionnaire that appeared inconsistent with a previous answer.

DATA QUALITY MANAGEMENT AND CLEANING

Surveyors conducted the household survey in teams of two. During the interview, surveyors completed the questionnaire, along with supporting documents used to help households recall, categorize, and sum up their consumption expenditures or earnings (we further describe data collection and variable construction for expenditure and earning variables below). As part of quality control, supervisors reviewed one randomly chosen completed questionnaire, supporting documents, and interview audio tape from each surveyor at the end of every day.[9] In addition, our graduate students monitored the survey teams by accompanying them for part of their interviews and reported back to the supervisors and our team in case of concerns. During recruiting and surveyor training, the surveyors had been informed that lack of accuracy, diligence, or patience in the interviews would lead to the termination of employment, while a good record guaranteed a letter of recommendation confirming participation in our research project.

We also asked our surveyors to rate each household respondent along a number of dimensions such as cooperativeness, reliability, level of understanding, and level of interest in our survey. Surveyors also recorded the presence of any other household or nonhousehold member whose presence could affect answers to our questionnaire. In our analysis of the data, we paid special attention to the reliability rating: 1. completely reliable, 2. mostly reliable, and 3. sometimes not reliable. Whenever surveyors rated a respondent as "sometimes not reliable," they also wrote down an explanation for this rating. On the basis of these written explanations, we created a clean household survey dataset. This dataset excludes 0.25 percent of unreliable/uncooperative households entirely from the sample. In other cases, surveyors' explanations suggested that only answers to a particular section of our questionnaire were unreliable. Using this information, we set all income variables to missing for 1.06 percent of all household respondents, all consumption variables to missing for 0.4 percent of households, and all income and consumption variables to missing for 1.31 percent of households. The descriptive statistics in Tables A5.1 to A5.4 are based on this cleaned household survey dataset. When using total nominal retail expenditure or incomes in RMB as the dependent variables on the left-hand side of the regressions, we censor these reported values at the one-percent level from the left and right tails within the survey round.[10] The point estimates remain statistical zeros in all cases, as is the case post-censoring, but the standard errors slightly increase. Appendix F.4 below provides additional information about variable construction.

F.2 Experimental Design

SELECTION OF PROVINCES AND COUNTIES

There are two main factors determining our survey location in Anhui, Henan, and Guizhou, and the eight counties within these provinces. First, our survey location depended on the timing of the program's roll-out across different provinces and counties, which had been decided before our collaboration with the firm. Second, we were guided by the internal evaluation of the program's senior managers as to whether the provincial and county managers in question would be willing to cooperate with our research protocol. To ensure that the experiment could proceed without political interference, we omitted a few e-commerce exemplary counties that were designated by higher-level governments and likely to produce distorted results. These counties are: Huoqiu (Anhui), Linying (Henan), Linzhou (Henan), Minquan (Henan), Suixi (Anhui), Tianchang (Anhui), Xifeng (Guizhou), and Zhenning (Guizhou). In Appendix D, we are also able to investigate the representativeness of our sample villages relative to all participating villages using the firm's internal transaction data in five provinces over this period.

SELECTION OF VILLAGES AND RANDOMIZATION

The unit of randomization is the village. For each county, we obtain a list of candidates that had been extended by five promising village candidates that would have not been part of the list in absence of our research. The three main factors determining the village selection within a county from the firm's operational perspective are i) a sufficient level of local population, ii) accessibility by roads, and iii) the presence of a capable e-commerce store applicant (as measured by the applicant's test score). Overall, we are able to implement randomization on a broad pool of villages selected for participation in the program. This pool, however, is not a random sample of China's rural areas; instead, it is likely a group of villages positively selected within each county, with better expected conditions for e-commerce usage on both consumption and production sides.

Upon receipt of this extended list of village candidates for each county, we randomly select five control villages and seven to eight treatment villages. The remaining villages on the extended list receive program terminals as planned. The full sample thus includes forty control villages and sixty treatment villages across the eight counties, which we selected from a total number of candidates of 432 villages that we received in the extended listings from the eight county operations teams (on average fifty-four villages per county). We restrict the list of villages entering the stratification and randomization to villages with at least 2.5-kilometer distance to the nearest village on the county list, where possible.[11] We then stratify treatment and control villages along four dimensions. First, we balance the selection of treatment and control to both have a ratio of 85:15 with respect to preexisting availability of commercial package delivery (85 percent not available, 15 percent available), which is close to the observed ratio among all candidate villages. We obtain information on the availability of commercial package delivery for each village on the candidate list from the program's local county managers (who are not aware what we require that piece of information for). As we discuss below, having villages in our sample with preexisting commercial delivery services allows us to further investigate the effect of the program that is driven by the terminal access point (i.e., the effect of lifting only the transactional barrier), relative to the effect of providing both the terminal access point and the necessary logistics for local e-commerce deliveries and pick-ups (i.e., the effect of lifting both the transactional and logistical barrier to e-commerce). We further stratify the selection of treatment and control villages on the basis of the equally weighted average of the z-scores for three village variables: the local store applicants' test score, the village population, and the ratio of nonagricultural employment over the local population. We obtain the last variable from the establishment-level data of the Chinese Economic Census of 2008, which surveys every nonagricultural establishment in the counties.

SAMPLING OF HOUSEHOLDS,
RESPONSE RATES, AND ATTRITION

Our team was granted a two-week window for data collection after receiving the extended list of candidate villages from the local operation team in each county. Given this tight timeline, we were unable to conduct a village census for sampling purposes. Instead, our survey teams created detailed maps of all residences in the village to implement a random walk procedure.[12]

From each village's map, we defined an "inner zone" of residences within a 300-meter radius of the planned terminal location, and an "outer zone" outside that radius. In the baseline data collection (December 2015 and January 2016 in Anhui and Henan, and April and May 2016 in Guizhou), the objective was to sample fourteen households from the inner zone and fourteen households from the outer zone. To randomly sample households within these zones, we selected twenty-four residences in both inner and outer zones. The household sampling proceeds as follows: we first randomly assign numbers to all residences within the zone on the map from 1 to n, and then define a rounded integer number n / 24. Starting from household number 1, we then collect survey data from every household number in steps of the integer n / 24 until we have completed fourteen surveys within the zone. For the endline data collection (twelve months after baseline in each village), we implement the same procedure for all households that were not part of the baseline survey to select ten additional households within the inner zone.[13] In the few cases in which there were fewer than twenty-four residences within the inner zone, we extended the radius until we obtain at least twenty-four residences on the map. If either the survey respondent or the primary earner of the initially surveyed household no longer resides at the same address, we record this in our data and replace the household with another randomly sampled household within the same sampling zone (inner or outer). In our welfare analysis, we report results both before and after weighting each sampled household in proportion to the share of the village population in its sampling zone.

After introducing our survey to households, our surveyors asked for the household member with the best knowledge of household consumption expenditures and household incomes to respond to the questionnaire. In case nobody answered the door, or in case this most-suited household member was not at home during our surveyors' first visit, the surveyors returned at least twice to complete the interview, often outside of working hours. Surveyors were also instructed to skip households with a most knowledgeable respondent older than seventy-five. Overall, our surveyors found willing and able respondents in two-thirds of visited residences (66.1 percent).[14] In the endline, we sampled ten additional households from the inner zone. We used the same sampling methodology as in the baseline. Given expected sample attrition and the objective of ten randomly selected additional households, the survey teams created a list of twenty-two new residential addresses in the inner zone and six new addresses in the outer zone. In the endline, we replaced a household respondent from the baseline whenever either the household had moved, the primary earner was no longer living there, or the original baseline respondent was unavailable after three interview attempts. Using this rule, 71 percent of baseline respondents completed our questionnaire in the endline. As documented in appendix Table A5.15, this percentage does not differ in treatment and control villages.

F.3 Retail Price Survey

STORE SAMPLING

Prior to the field survey, RCCC supervisors performed a census of all retail stores and market stalls ("stores" for short) located in the village and within a fifteen-minute walking distance of the boundaries of the natural village. Most villages have fewer than five stores, so in most villages we sampled products from all stores and market stalls in the vicinity of the village. If there were more than fifteen stores in a village, we instructed supervisors to collect a representative sample of local retail information, giving more weight (i.e., more price quotes) to more popular establishments within product groups.

PRODUCT SAMPLING AND DATA COLLECTION

The data collection for the local retail price survey was conducted by the trained RCCC supervisors. We aim to collect data on 115 price quotes for each village. One hundred of these prices are from the same nine household consumption categories for retail products as in our household survey (food and beverages, tobacco and alcohol, medicine and health, clothing and accessories, other everyday products, fuel and gas, furniture and appliances, electronics, transport equipment), and fifteen price quotes are for local production and business inputs. Our protocol for the price data collection closely follows the IMF/ILO standards for store price surveys that central banks collect to compute the CPI statistics. The sampling of products across consumption categories is based on budget shares of rural households in Anhui and Henan that we observed in the microdata of the China Family Panel Study (CFPS) for 2012. Reflecting these consumption weights, supervisors in the baseline survey data aim to collect 47/100 price quotes in food and beverages, 15/100 in tobacco and alcohol, 9/100 in medicine and health, 9/100 in clothing and accessories, 4/100 in other everyday products, 4/100 in fuel and gas, 4/100 in furniture and appliances, 4/100 in electronics, and 4/100 in transport equipment. In addition, we collect fifteen price quotes for purchases of inputs to production or businesses.[15]

We provided supervisors with preprepared price surveys reflecting the number of observations to be collected for each product group. As for the collection of data on household expenses that we discuss above and in Appendix F.4 below, the supervisors were provided with detailed product cards that list product groups within each of the ten broad categories above, as well as examples of product types within those subgroups of products. They also received instructions on product sampling, for instance about how to evaluate the popularity of an individual product by measuring shelf space and recurrence across different stores. To ensure that we can match identical products in both survey rounds, supervisors saved a picture of each product and recorded product characteristics at the barcode-equivalent level, including packaging type, size, and a detailed product description (name, brand, flavor, etc.) wherever possible.[16] For 78 percent of products collected in the baseline, we were able to find the exact same product in the same store one year later in the endline. As documented in appendix Table A5.8, this percentage is somewhat smaller in intent to treat villages than in control villages, but this difference is not statistically significant. One challenge of surveying prices in rural China is a frequent lack of price tags displayed in the store. As shown in Table A5.4, about two-thirds of the surveyed products lacked a price tag. In these cases, supervisors asked the store owner for the price that villagers would pay for the product. As part of quality control, we asked supervisors to rate the reliability of store owners' price quotes as good, average, or poor. None of the reported findings change in sign, size, or statistical significance when limiting the sample to price quotes from labeled products only or excluding reportedly unreliable price quotes.

F.4 Variable Construction

To collect data on household consumption expenditures and incomes from different activities, we trained the surveyors in using separate preprepared spreadsheets before filling out the final survey questionnaires. For expenditures, there is one spreadsheet for each of the nine categories that we include in retail consumption, and a separate sheet for business inputs. This allowed households to recall and list all relevant expenses or income flows within a given product group or type of activity over a given period of time. This transaction-level information was then aggregated in the presence of the household to complete the final survey questionnaire sections on expenditures or income flows.

To help respondent recall and categorize their expenditures, surveyors also received cards with examples of products in each category. The product cards break down the retail consumption space into 169 product types within the ten broad categories we list above. After recording each item in a given category, surveyors go through the list of items and ask respondents how much they paid for each listed purchase. In addition to allocating transactions to different consumption product groups, the surveyors also recorded the modality of each listed purchase transaction (e.g., online vs. offline, in the village vs. outside the village). This procedure was implemented covering a two-week time window for nondurable household consumption, and a three-month time window for durable goods categories. To obtain total monthly retail expenditure, we multiply the biweekly expenditure on nondurables by a factor of two and divide durable good expenditure by a factor of three, and sum up across the nine consumption categories. For expenditures on the new e-commerce option, we include both direct use of the terminal interface as well as remote usage by ordering deliveries to the terminal through the firm's app. The majority of terminal usage is done in person at the terminal rather than remotely. In most village cases, deliveries and pickups can be made at the terminal location (90 percent). In about 10 percent of cases, the logistics operators offered delivery to the home address too.

To construct total household income, our surveyors again used a preprepared spreadsheet to assist households in recording each of their individual income sources over the last month. We defined four income categories: farm earnings, nonfarm earnings, remittances (money or in-kind) from family not living in the home, and all other income (e.g., pension, returns from savings, gifts). In addition, we recorded sector of activity and occupation categories for each economically active member of the household. To help household respondents recall and categorize earnings, surveyors used cards with detailed examples of income sources in each category and proceeded to collect each flow on the spreadsheet before filling out the final survey questionnaire in the presence of the household. Our measure of income per capita is the sum of all income sources in these four categories, divided by the number of household members. Our measure of income net of transfers subtracts gifts and remittances from family not living in the home.[17] Our measure of income per capita net of costs subtracts the recorded household expenses used to generate the reported flows of income. The income variables exclude the market value of home production for own consumption.[18] Including this as part of household income has no effect on the statistical zeros that we report in the analysis.

Finally, for households who were either replaced or added as part of our extended sample in the second round (from twenty-eight to thirty-eight households), we define y_{hv}^{Pre} in specification (1) as the mean pre-treatment outcome of households living in the same zone (inner or outer) in the same village. The implicit assumption is that households were not induced to move within or across villages as a result of the program. As reported in appendix Table A5.15, we find no evidence that households in treated villages are more or less likely to reside at the same address at endline. We also find no treatment effect on migration decisions of members within households.

F.5 Township-Level Data on Trade Market Access

As part of our analysis of potential spillover effects on the control group in Appendix C, we estimate the fraction of a rural location's total trade market access that stems from trading relationships with other rural locations in the same county, as opposed to access to larger urban markets within and outside the county. To do this, we use geocoded township-level data from the Chinese Population Census in 2010, which contains information on the recorded population for each of roughly 45,000 township-level administrative units in China,[19] the coordinates of the centroid of each of those units, the type of township-level unit (e.g., urban zones, rural townships), and data on the value added per rural and urban worker at the province level for 2010. See Appendix C for further discussion and details about the estimation.

NOTES

Chapter One: Introduction

1. Fieldwork in Wantou Village in 2014 and 2015.

2. Celia Hatton, "The Families Revealing Everything They've Ever Bought Online," BBC News, April 28, 2015, http://www.bbc.com/news/magazine-32498456.

3. Ministry of Commerce of the People's Republic of China, *E-Commerce in China*, 2022, http://images.mofcom.gov.cn/dzsws/202306/20230609104929992.pdf.

4. Yujie Xue, "Single's Day: Record-breaking Sales Focus New Attention on Packaging Waste as almost 4 Billion Parcels Are Shipped," Yahoo News, November 18, 2020, https://finance.yahoo.com/news/chinas-singles-day-sales-period-014733212.html.

5. The calculation is made on the assumption that the average length of a parcel is 30 centimeters.

6. China's top four e-commerce platforms alone account for 44 percent of global sales. John Koetsier, "44% of Global E-Commerce Is Owned by 4 Chinese Companies," *Forbes*, October, 21, 2020, https://www.forbes.com/sites/johnkoetsier/2020/10/21/44-of-global-ecommerce-is-owned-by-4-chinese-companies/.

7. Dashveenjit Kaur, "China vs. US E-Commerce—How They're Very Different," January 28, 2021, https://techwireasia.com/01/2021/china-vs-us-e-commerce-how-theyre-very-different/.

8. *China Daily*, "Chinese Robbers Are Forced to Find New Jobs, and Here's Why," May 9, 2017, https://www.chinadaily.com.cn/business/tech/2017-05/09/content_29258929.htm.

9. *Bloomberg Newsweek/Chinese Edition*, "电商改变中国/E-Commerce Has Transformed China," 2016, https://cread.jd.com/read/startRead.action?bookId=30338926&readType=1.

10. Dieter and He, 2000.

11. Haley, 2012.

12. An extensive body of literature has discussed this issue. Examples include North, 1990; Persson and Besley, 2009; Acemoglu and Robinson, 2012; Rodrik, Subramanian, and Trebbi, 2004; and Weingast, 1995.

13. Barnett, Feng, and Luo, 2010.

14. For the distinction between "marketplace" and "independent merchants," see McKinsey Global Institute, "China's E-tail Revolution: Online Shopping as a Catalyst for Growth," March 2013, https://www.mckinsey.com/~/media/McKinsey/Featured%20Insights/Asia%20Pacific/China%20e%20tailing/MGI_China_e%20tailing_Executive_summary_March_2013.pdf.

15. The major exception is JD.com, which follows the Amazon model. JD is a large online retailer, but it also hosts a marketplace for third-party sellers.

16. In the early days, Chinese online shoppers mostly looked for generic products with the lowest prices, paying little attention to brands. Even after the e-commerce market became consolidated in 2014, top brands on Alibaba's platforms still held less than 30 percent of the market share (Alibaba's platforms then accounted for 80 percent of China's e-commerce sales). The majority of sales came from nonbranded products (around 40 percent), lesser-known brands (around 10 percent), and regional and pure online brands (around 20 percent). See Bain & Company, *China's E-Commerce: The New Branding Game*, 2015, https://media.bain.com/Images/BAIN_REPORT_China_ecommerce_The_new_branding_game.pdf.

17. Boston Consulting Group, "What China Reveals about the Future of Shopping," May 4, 2017, https://www.bcg.com/publications/2017/retail-globalization-china-reveals-future shopping.aspx.

18. The Chinese figure is from http://images.mofcom.gov.cn/wzs2/202007/20200703162 035768.pdf. The US figure is from Daniel Keyes, "E-Commerce Sales Surpassed 10% of Total Retail Sales in 2019 for the First Time," *Business Insider*, February 24, 2020, https://www.business insider.com/ecommerce-topped-10-percent-of-us-retail-in-2019-2020-2.

19. The study is based on a nationally representative sample of adults online in each country in 2016. *Interactive Advertising Bureau*, "Understanding Digital Commerce in the US & China," November 2016, https://www.iab.com/wp-content/uploads/2016/11/IAB-US-China-Digital -Commerce-Study_FINAL.pdf.

20. *The Economist*, "A Giant Cage," April 6, 2013, https://www.economist.com/special-report /2013/04/06/a-giant-cage.

21. For example, censorship mainly focuses on the media aspects of the internet; the commercial side is rarely affected. See *Financial Times*, "Chinese Internet: Commerce and Control," March 13, 2015, https://www.ft.com/content/2622e476-c89e-11e4-b43b-00144feab7de.

22. Previous research on e-commerce has focused more on its economic and commercial dimensions. Henry Farrell is one of the pioneers in political science to examine the implications of e-commerce for international relations (Farrell, 2003, 2006, 2012). In recent years, there is a small yet growing strand of literature that delves into the political dynamics of platforms, primarily within Western contexts. This includes works by Culpepper and Thelen (2020), Atal (2021), Lehdonvirta (2022), and Mazur and Serafin (2023).

23. Other scholars had previously used this term in different contexts, including China's integration into the global economic system (Steinfeld, 2010); the study of comparative capitalism (Allen, 2013); and elite-mass relations in Russia (Polishchuk, 2013). I use the term in a distinctly different way from these prior studies. The idea of outsourcing by the Chinese government—China's importing of foreign institutions during the globalization process—is also discussed by Fuller, 2005, 2016; Steinfeld, 2010; and Wilson, 2009.

24. This point echoes Henry Farrell's (2006) argument that private actors in e-commerce are "points of control."

25. North, 1990, 34.

26. Greif, 2006.

27. North, 1990, 34–35.

28. North, 1990, 35.

29. North, 1991; Dixit, 2004.

30. North, 1990, 35.

31. Greif, 2006; North, 1990.

32. Michael Forsythe, "China's Chief Justice Rejects an Independent Judiciary, and Reformers Wince," *New York Times*, January 18, 2017, https://www.nytimes.com/2017/01/18/world/asia/china-chief-justice-courts-zhou-qiang.html.

33. Xin and Pearce, 1996.

34. Haveman et al., 2017.

35. For example, Xu (2011) calls this combination a "regionally decentralized authoritarian system." Landry's (2008) theory of decentralized authoritarianism also describes how the Chinese Communist Party politically controls local officials in a decentralized economic system.

36. For example, Oi, 1992, 1999; Montinola, Qian, and Weingast, 1995; and Weingast, 1995.

37. For example, Li and Zhou, 2005; Zhou, 2007.

38. Ang, 2016.

39. Aziz, 2006.

40. A conservative estimate shows that around twenty million migrant workers returned home jobless in 2009 following the global crisis. See Tania Branigan, "Downturn in China Leaves 26 Million Out of Work," *The Guardian*, February 2, 2009, https://www.theguardian.com/business/2009/feb/02/china-unemployment-unrest.

41. Structural reforms have proven challenging, and while there were some signs of economic rebalancing by the mid-2010s, adverse internal and external factors such as the US-China trade war and the COVID-19 pandemic compelled China to adhere to traditional economic stimulus measures like state-led investments.

42. Poncet, 2003, 2005; Barwick et al., 2021.

43. In chapter 2, I delve further into why digital platforms are well suited for state outsourcing. While various private actors can establish private institutions, digital platforms fall into a distinct category of private entities that I term private regulatory intermediaries (PRIs). PRIs possess the ability to (1) provide private governance and (2) simultaneously meet three criteria: encompassing, impersonal, and capable yet limited. These characteristics make them capable of providing good substitutes or complements for state institutions.

44. *Sohu*, "淘宝售假被芝麻信用加入黑名单. 信用惩戒效用明显 [Taobao sellers of counterfeit goods have been blacklisted by Sesame Credit. The punitive effect of credit discipline is evident]," March 23, 2017, http://www.sohu.com/a/129962460_115443.

45. Interview with a Taobao employee, Tonglu County of Zhejiang Province, July 7, 2015.

46. Phone interview with a former Taobao employee on the rulemaking team, December 7, 2023.

47. Reuters, "China Allows Internet Access in Xinjiang 10 Months after Riots," May 14, 2010, https://www.reuters.com/article/us-china-xinjiang-internet/china-allows-internet-access-in-xinjiang-10-months-after-riots-idUSTRE64D0MB20100514.

48. Reuters, "China Gives P2P Lenders Two Years to Exit Industry," November 28, 2019, https://www.reuters.com/article/us-china-p2p/china-gives-p2p-lenders-two-years-to-exit-industry-document-idUSKBN1Y2039.

49. Policy Research Office of the Ministry of Commerce, "关于我国电子商务快速发展原因的分析 [Analyzing the Factors Behind the Rapid Growth of E-Commerce in Our Country]," May 10, 2016, http://zys.mofcom.gov.cn/article/d/201605/20160501315068.shtml.

50. Chinese central government's official web portal, "税务总局: 年内不得组织针对某新业态的税务检查 [State Administration of Taxation: No tax inspections targeting a specific new business model shall be organized within the year]," May 6, 2015, https://www.gov.cn/xinwen/2015-05/06/content_2857698.htm.

51. *Beijing News*, "工商总局: 个人网店不强制工商登记 应向平台登记[State Administration for Industry and Commerce: Individual online stores are not required to undergo compulsory business registration; instead, they should register with the platform]," Feburary 23, 2016, https://www.chinanews.com.cn/cj/2016/02-23/7768200.shtml.

52. Lecture by a government official, Hangzhou City, July 2, 2016.

53. Dai, 2023.

54. Interview with a China-based legal expert in Germany, July 2023.

55. This is inspired by Susan Shirk's book *Overreach* (2022).

56. For interview effects, see Mensch and Kandel, 1988, and Catania et al., 1996. Biernacki and Waldorf (1981) and Johnson (2005) have discussed snowball sample biases.

57. Yang, 2003; Han, 2015.

Chapter Two: Institutional Outsourcing: A Public-Private Collaboration on Institutional Building

1. NASA, "Korean Peninsula Seen from Space Station," February 24, 2014, https://www.nasa.gov/content/korean-peninsula-seen-from-space-station.

2. Acemoglu, Johnson, and Robinson, 2005.

3. The special case of two Koreas proves that institutions precede growth. Yet more generally there is a scholarly debate on whether good institutions precede or follow growth. While some establish that good institutions cause growth (e.g., Acemoglu et al., 2005, and North and Weingast, 1989), other scholars find institutions to be an outcome of growth (e.g., Glaeser et al. 2004). A more likely scenario is that institutions and growth are endogenous to each other (a chicken and egg situation), and they mutually evolve (Ang, 2016).

4. Weingast, 2008.

5. Weingast, 2008.

6. In the late stage of this project, I discovered that other scholars had used this term in different contexts, including China's integration into the global economic system and the outsourcing of power to foreign entities (Steinfeld, 2010); the study of comparative capitalism (Allen, 2013); and elite-mass relations in Russia (Polishchuk, 2013). I conceptualize the term in a different way from the prior literature. The idea of outsourcing by the Chinese government—China's importing of foreign institutions during the globalization process—is also discussed by Fuller (2005, 2016) and Wilson (2009).

7. North, 1990, 3.

8. Arrow, 1969.

9. Milgrom, North, and Weingast, 1990; Greif, 2000.

10. Greif, Milgrom, and Weingast, 1994; Weingast, 1995.

11. North and Weingast, 1989; Weingast, 1995; Acemoglu, Johnson, and Robinson, 2005.

12. Ang, 2016.

13. Evans, 2004.

14. International Monetary Fund, 1997; Santiso et al., 2001; Graham, Amos, and Plumptre, 2003.

15. Pritchett and Woolcock, 2004; Shirley, 2008; Rodrik, 2006.

16. Rodrik, 2006.

17. North, Wallis, and Weingast, 2009; Weingast, 2008.

18. Hellman, 1998.

19. Ang, 2016.

20. This viewpoint conforms to China's general reform strategy that many people view as undertaking comprehensive economic reforms without major political reforms (Shirk, 1993; He, 2000).

21. For example, China has established a rule-by-law system (Hurst, 2018), or as Whiting (2017) calls it, authoritarian rule of law. In the post-Mao era, China has launched legal reforms that establish various aspects of a formal legal infrastructure, including promulgating numerous laws, training legal professionals, and expanding the court system (Peerenboom, 2002; Stern, 2014), which serves the state's goals of enhancing regime legitimacy and spurring economic growth (Stockmann and Gallagher, 2011; Liebman, 2014; Wang, 2015). Gallagher (2017) finds that China's "half-hearted construction of rule of law" undermines the stability of authoritarian rule in the area of labor rights.

22. Liu and Weingast, 2021.

23. Montinola et al., 1995.

24. Shen, Jin, and Zou, 2012.

25. Ang, 2016; Heilmann, 2008.

26. Oi, 1992, 1999.

27. W. Wang, 2017.

28. Whiting, 2017; Blanchard and Shleifer, 2000; Li and Zhou, 2005; Zhou, 2007.

29. For more discussion on local protectionism, see Rodden and Rose-Ackerman, 1997, and Xu, 2011.

30. Montinola, Qian, and Weingast, 1995.

31. Poncet, 2003, 2005.

32. Xin and Pearce, 1996; Wank, 1996.

33. Kang, 2002, 442.

34. Haber, 2002, xiv, xv.

35. Haber, 2002, xvi.

36. Braudel, 1982, 20.

37. Stringham, 2015, 4.

38. Bernstein, 1992, 2001, respectively.

39. Ellickson, 1991.

40. Leeson, 2009.

41. Ely, 2002; Chandler, 1977.

42. Stringham, 2015, chapters 4–6.

43. Sherman and Phillips, 2020.

44. Sherman and Phillips, 2020, 1.

45. In November 2019, the Chinese government gave peer-to-peer lending platforms two years to exit the industry. Reuters, "China Gives P2P Lenders Two Years to Exit Industry,"

November 28, 2019, https://www.reuters.com/article/us-china-p2p/china-gives-p2p-lenders
-two-years-to-exit-industry-document-idUSKBN1Y2039.

46. Holland, 2017.

47. Acemoglu and Johnson, 2005.

48. I define these categories as discrete for analytical purposes. In practice, an institution
can govern more than one issue area.

49. Different countries and elites may assign different weights to these goals.

50. Gallagher and Miller, 2021.

51. I draw the concepts of encompassing and narrow interests from Olson (1993).

52. Wallis, 2010, 1.

53. Greif, 1993.

54. Parker, Van Alstyne, and Choudary, 2016.

55. Evans, 2003.

56. He Wei, "Vendors Rebel against Taobao Mall Changes," *China Daily*, October 13, 2011,
http://www.chinadaily.com.cn/bizchina/2011-10/13/content_13881570.htm; https://xueqiu
.com/3993902801/126468371.

57. Oi, 1992; Montinola, Qian, and Weingast, 1995.

58. Heilmann, 2008.

59. Li, 2004.

60. For the importance of data and digital trade, see Liu, 2021, and Weymouth, 2022.

61. Liu and Weingast, 2018.

62. Liu and Weingast, 2018.

63. Following the past literature, I mainly use the dichotomy of "private firms versus SOEs"
to describe their differences in connection to the state. While some firms are jointly owned and
managed by state and private shareholders (Milhaupt and Zheng, 2014), this is not the case for
large digital platforms. While many of them have received investments from government-
backed funds, the majority of shares and management responsibilities still lie in the hands of
private actors. I therefore treat them as private firms.

64. Mattli and Büthe, 2005.

65. See Fuller, 2016, chapter 7; Brandt and Thun, 2016.

66. Kornai, 1979; Kornai, Maskin, and Roland, 2003.

67. *China Business Network*, "邓亚萍的互联网教训：'国字头'是把双刃剑 [Deng Yaping's Internet Lesson: 'Being State-Owned' Is a Double-Edged Sword]," December 10, 2014, http://
finance.sina.com.cn/money/cfgs/20141203/142120986480.shtml.

68. Steven Millward, "China Has a New State-run Search Engine that Nobody Will Ever
Use," *Tech in Asia*, March 3, 2014, https://www.techinasia.com/china-new-state-run-search
-engine-chinaso-launches.

69. Interview with an e-commerce expert in Shandong Province, August 21, 2014.

70. Yanjing Zhao, "平台经济的制度演进——一个平台经济的分析框架[Institutional Evolution of Platform Economy—An Analytical Framework for Platform Economy], Guancha,
April 14, 2021, https://www.guancha.cn/zhaoyanjing/2021_04_14_587338_2.shtml.

71. Mark Sweney, "China to Take 'Golden Shares' in Tech firms Alibaba and Tencent,"
Guardian, January 13, 2013, https://www.theguardian.com/world/2023/jan/13/china-to-take
-golden-shares-in-tech-firms-alibaba-and-tencent.

72. Interview with an Alibaba employee in Hangzhou City, December 18, 2013.

73. Phone interview with a platform employee, May 30, 2016.

74. Interview with an online merchant in Boxing County, Shandong Province, August 21, 2014.

75. Jillian D'Onfro, "Google's Chairman Says Amazon—Not Bing—Is Its Biggest Search Competitor," *Business Insider*, October 13, 2014, https://www.businessinsider.com/eric-schmidt -says-amazon-is-googles-biggest-search-competitor-2014-10.

76. Clause 58 of the Cybersecurity Law.

77. Reuters, "China Allows Internet Access in Xinjiang 10 Months after Riots," May 14, 2010, https://www.reuters.com/article/us-china-xinjiang-internet/china-allows-internet-access-in -xinjiang-10-months-after-riots-idUSTRE64D0MB20100514.

78. For antitrust regulations in China, see Zhang, 2021.

79. Jill Disis, "China Fines Alibaba, Tencent and Baidu for More Antitrust Violations," *CNN*, November 22, 2021, https://www.cnn.com/2021/11/22/tech/alibaba-tencent-fines-intl-hnk /index.html.

80. Alan Wong, "China Puts a Stop to Plans for Virtual Credit Cards," *New York Times*, March 14, 2014, https://www.nytimes.com/2014/03/15/business/international/china-virtual -credit-cards.html.

81. Li Guan, "人民网一评《王者荣耀》: 是娱乐大众还是'陷害'人生 [The People's Daily Online Commentary on 'Honor of Kings': Entertainment for the Masses or Life Trap]," *People's Daily Online*, July, 3, 2017, http://opinion.people.com.cn/n1/2017/0703/c1003-29379751.html.

82. Liberthal and Oksenberg, 1988; Mertha, 2009.

83. *Financial Times*, "China Tech Groups Hire Ex-Regulators to Fend Off Beijing's Crack-down," https://www.ft.com/content/71daa106-259e-4dc2-b267-b0289177de1f.

84. Interview with a tech firm employee in Zhejiang Province, July 7, 2015.

85. Reuters, "Beijing Moves to Mollify Tech Bosses as COVID Threatens Economy," April 29, 2022, https://www.reuters.com/technology/china-end-regulatory-storm-over-big -tech-scmp-2022-04-29/; Tracy Qu and Zhou Xin, "China to End Regulatory Storm over Big Tech and Give Sector Bigger Role in Boosting Slowing Economy, Sources Say," *South China Morning Post*, April 29, 2022, https://www.scmp.com/tech/big-tech/article/3175971/china-end -regulatory-storm-over-big-tech-and-give-sector-bigger-role.

86. Note that P2P platforms do not fit here. P2P platforms were shut down because their user bases were small and many of their activities were considered illegal under Chinese law.

87. Pollman and Barry, 2017.

88. *Financial Times*, "Alibaba's Growth Brings Millions of Jobs," https://www.ft.com/content /722e6f0c-bac7-11e2-b289-00144feab7de.

89. Michael Forsythe, "Alibaba's I.P.O. Could Be a Bonanza for the Scions of Chinese Lead-ers," *New York Times*, July 20, 2014, https://dealbook.nytimes.com/2014/07/20/alibabas-i-p-o -could-be-a-bonanza-for-the-scions-of-chinese-leaders/.

90. Ibid.

91. Steven Millward, "Alibaba Confirms Government Investment for its Alipay and Online Banking Business," *Tech in Asia*, June 18, 2015, https://www.techinasia.com/alibaba-confirms -investment-alipay-and-online-banking-business.

92. See *The Paper*, "京东数科股权大起底: 刘强东仍为实际控制人, 国资股东云集 [Deep Dive into JD Digits' Equity: Liu Qiangdong Remains the Ultimate Controller, State-Owned

Shareholders Gather]," December 19, 2018, https://m.thepaper.cn/kuaibao_detail.jsp?contid
=2751324&from=kuaibao.

93. Interview with a China-based legal expert in Germany, July 2023.

94. Yan Yue, "马云: 未来 30 年 计划经济会越来越大 [Jack Ma: Planned Economy Will
Become Increasingly Prominent in the Next 30 Years]," China Business Network, November 20,
2016, https://www.yicai.com/news/5162510.html.

95. *Jiemian News*, "阿里问: 假货这么多, 为何不能像治酒驾一样严刑峻法? [Alibaba Asks:
With So Many Counterfeit Goods, Why Can't We Impose Strict Laws and Punishments
Like Those for Drunk Driving?]," February 27, 2017, https://m.jiemian.com/article/1138879
.html.

96. Rodrick, 2008.

97. It is important to note that China's development strategies at various stages have taken
this "second-best" form. Two examples include developing Township and Village Enterprises
(Oi, 1999) and the strategy of "grasping the large and letting go of the small" in China's SOE
reforms (Cao, Qian, and Weingast, 1999).

Chapter Three: Making Institutions Work:
The Political Foundations of China's E-Commerce Market

1. Jillian D'Onfro, "The Remarkable Story of How Alibaba Defeated eBay in China," *Business
Insider*, April 14, 2014, https://www.businessinsider.com/how-alibaba-defeated-ebay-in-china
-2014-4.

2. Helen H. Wang, "Alibaba Saga II: Meg Whitman Unexpectedly Met Her Match," *Forbes*,
July 2, 2014, https://www.forbes.com/sites/helenwang/2014/07/02/alibaba-saga-ii-whitman
-met-her-match/?sh=4708042e76c6.

3. Chris Nuttall, "eBay To Shut Down its China Site," *Financial Times*, December 19, 2006,
https://www.ft.com/content/cf6b07a4-8ef8-11db-a7b2-0000779e2340

4. Ryan Mac, "The Crocodile and the Shark: Could Alibaba Swallow eBay?" *Forbes*, September 30, 2014, https://www.forbes.com/sites/ryanmac/2014/09/30/the-crocodile-and-the
-shark-could-alibaba-swallow-ebay/.

5. Barnett et al., 2010.

6. Bing Han, "谁创造了蚂蚁金服? [Who Created Ant Financial?]," *PingWest*, December 18,
2018, https://www.pingwest.com/a/181371.

7. Barnett et al., 2010.

8. *36Kr*, "蚂蚁金服 CSO 陈龙: 没有支付宝, 就没有阿里巴巴的今天 [Ant Financial's CSO,
Chen Long: 'Without Alipay, there would be no Alibaba today']," June 3, 2017, https://36kr.com
/newsflashes/3277798899713.

9. If the buyer does not express satisfaction on time, the payment will be sent directly to the
seller after a certain period, e.g., fifteen days.

10. Global Netpreneur, "支付宝历史上的第一笔交易, 居然是跨境支付 [The first transaction
in the history of Alipay was actually a cross-border payment]," *Sina*, April 7, 2017, https://tech
.sina.cn/2017-04-07/detail-ifyecfnu7592017.d.html.

11. Other alternatives include cash upon delivery, online banking, and wire transfer.

12. So and Westland, 2009, 103.

13. The original words by Jack Ma are: "要是我贸然上线一个支付系统, 那是违法的, 因为没有许可......如果有什么麻烦, 如果政府不同意, 如果必须有个人去坐牢的话, 我去坐嘛." See *Sohu*, "马云为什么冒着坐牢的风险也要做支付宝? [Why did Jack Ma risk going to jail to create Alipay?]," June 3, 2017, https://www.sohu.com/a/145798447_631742. Also see Chorzempa, 2022.

14. *Sina*, "马云谈支付宝往事: 当年做好了坐牢准备 [Jack Ma talks about the past of Alipay: At that time, he was prepared to go to jail]," August 9, 2018, https://finance.sina.cn/2018-08-09/detail-ihhnunsp7966247.d.html?from=wap.

15. David Cohen and Jia Minhui, "Online Finance: China's Reform Battleground," *Nikkei Asia*, March 19, 2014, https://asia.nikkei.com/Economy/The-emerging-field-of-Chinese-reform.

16. Hangzhou Xiacheng People's Court, "杭州法院全力配合 北京法院查支付宝账户仅40分钟 [Hangzhou Court Fully Cooperates; Beijing Court Checks Alipay Account in Just Forty Minutes]," *Sina*, July 14, 2018, https://tech.sina.com.cn/roll/2018-07-14/doc-ihfhfwmv2642396.shtml.

17. Chaoyang District Government, "全国首例朝阳警方通过 支付宝APP进行精准反诈预警 [The first case in the country: Chaoyang police use Alipay app for precise antifraud early warning]," March 2, 2022, http://www.chaoyang.gov.cn/html/CYSZF/202203/0164618839859471.html.

18. It's noteworthy that the share of platform-based e-commerce transactions in the United States has increased in recent years, yet the market remains less platform-based than it is in China.

19. In 2008, Taobao introduced the spin-off site Taobao Mall, which became independent in 2010 as Tmall.com. Taobao.com is a customer-to-customer (C2C) site, welcoming both individual vendors and businesses with minimal entry barriers to set up shop. Tmall.com, on the other hand, is the business-to-consumer (B2C) version of Taobao.com. Tmall.com hosts brands and registered businesses, featuring fewer but larger sellers, with significantly higher entry thresholds compared to Taobao. I discuss the two sites together because they are closely intertwined and share a similar institutional design. In fiscal year 2016, Taobao's GMV was $320 billion, and Tmall's was $227 billion.

20. Alibaba Group, "March Quarter 2020 and Full Fiscal Year 2020 Results," May 20, 2020, https://www.alibabagroup.com/cn/ir/presentations/pre200522.pdf.

21. See the auction page on Taobao here: "一拍 (破) 中科建工集团有限公司名下 43笔坏账 [Auction (Bankruptcy): China Construction Science & Industry Corporation Limited Has 43 Bad Debts]," accessed March 14, 2024, https://susong-item.taobao.com/auction/710499595381.htm?spm=a219w.12963282.paiList.5.78823e3cuwkzov.

22. See Dominque Rowe, "The 10 Strangest Things on Taobao, China's Biggest Online Trading Platform," *Time*, September 22, 2016, https://time.com/4502415/taobao-china-ebay-weirdest-strangest-items/.

23. See BBC, "Chinese Skyscraper to Be Auctioned Online," December 27, 2017, https://www.bbc.com/news/world-asia-china-42490297.

24. Bing Sun, "谁打造了 "万能的淘宝" ? [Who Created the 'Omnipotent Taobao'?]," *China Economic Weekly*, December 12, 2019, https://finance.sina.cn/2019-12-12/detail-iihnzhfz5445595.d.html?cre=wappage&mod=r&loc=3&r=9&rfunc=54&tj=none.

25. The analysis explores Taobao's institutional features as of 2020, the period when the research was concluded. While minor institutional adjustments may occur later, the core features are shown to be enduring over time.

26. Sellers and buyers can evaluate each other by giving a positive (+1 point), neutral (+0 point), or negative rating (-1 point) within fifteen days of the conclusion of a transaction. The total credit score is the sum of these user reviews from each transaction, and this score can be translated into four grades ranging from lowest to highest: heart, diamond, crown, and golden crown. Each grade is further disaggregated into five levels. Upgrading to higher levels becomes increasingly difficult.

27. The seller is evaluated for each aspect using a scale ranging from 1 (very unsatisfied) to 5 (very satisfied). The overall store rating is the average of all evaluations from each transaction that occurred in the past six months.

28. Chen et al., 2015.

29. For a detailed analysis of Taobao's counterfeit problem, see Yue Wang and Paul Armstrong, "Is Alibaba Doing Enough to Fight Fakes?" *Forbes*, March 17, 2017, https://www.forbes.com/sites/ywang/2017/03/10/is-alibaba-doing-enough-to-fight-fakes/#4540cdbf5587.

30. Interview with a Taobao employee on the train from Shanghai to Hangzhou, December 18, 2014.

31. Phone interview with a former Taobao employee on the rulemaking team, December 7, 2023.

32. In 2016, the total number of jurors on a panel was reduced from thirty-one (sixteen votes to win) to thirteen (seven votes to win).

33. *Alizila*, "How Taobao Is Crowdsourcing Justice in Online Shopping Disputes," July 17, 2014, https://www.alizila.com/how-taobao-is-crowdsourcing-justice-in-online-shopping-disputes/#:~:text=If%20the%20merchant%20disputes%20the,photos%20of%20the%20product%20purchased.

34. This number is according to real-time statistics at pan.taobao.com.

35. *Alizila*, "How Taobao Is Crowdsourcing Justice."

36. *China Daily*, "Betta 和Doctor Betta 傻傻分不清楚？阿里大众评审：Betta 涉嫌山寨，摘牌 [Confused between Betta and Doctor Betta? Alibaba's Public Jury: Betta Suspected of Counterfeiting, Delisting]," June 14, 2017, https://caijing.chinadaily.com.cn/2017-07/14/content_30117860.htm.

37. Ibid.

38. Nicole Kobie, "The Complicated Truth about China's Social Credit System," *Wired*, July 6, 2019, https://www.wired.co.uk/article/china-social-credit-system-explained.

39. *Sohu*, "支付宝芝麻信用分 900 都能干什么？[What can you do with a Sesame Credit Score of 900 on Alipay?]," July 7, 2017, https://www.sohu.com/a/325258070_613239.

40. Interview with a Taobao employee in Hangzhou City, Zhejiang Province, June 13, 2018.

41. Baidu Baike, "规则众议院(House of Representatives for Taobao Rules)," https://baike.baidu.com/pic/%E6%B7%98%E5%AE%9D%E8%A7%84%E5%88%99%E4%BC%97%E8%AE%AE%E9%99%A2/17872253/1/6a63f6246b600c33696cb827124c510fd8f9a1cc?fr=lemma&fromModule=lemma_content-image#aid=1&pic=6a63f6246b600c33696cb827124c510fd8f9a1cc.

42. The latest voting on rule changes can be found on the website of the House of Representatives for Taobao Rules at https://rule.taobao.com/rulecycle.htm.

43. The voting page explained the reasons for this rule change: improving customer satisfaction and regulating sellers' shipping behavior. The page outlined the key points of the rule change: raising the compensation from one to five for all products except a list of special product categories

(e.g., service, education, restaurant coupon). The end of the webpage asked what the user thought about this rule change and whether he or she would vote that (A) the rule change was appropriate or (B) it should be reconsidered. See Taobao, "关于《淘宝规则》违背承诺（三）未按约定时间发货规则调整公开征求意见 (Regarding the violation of commitments in 'Taobao Rule' (Part 3): Public solicitation of opinions on the adjustment of rules for failure to ship according to the agreed-upon time"), September 9, 2015, https://rulechannel.taobao.com/?taskId=122#/ruleHOR /detail.

44. Taobao, "关于《淘宝规则》违背承诺（三）未按约定时间发货规则调整公开征求意见结果反馈 [Regarding the violation of commitments in "Taobao Rules" (Part 3): Results feedback on the public solicitation of opinions regarding the adjustment of rules for failure to ship according to the agreed-upon time]," October 28, 2015, https://rulechannel.taobao.com/?type =detail&ruleId=3335&cId=161&spm=a2177.7231205.0.0.285917eaOujZ43#/rule/detail ?ruleId=3335&cId=161&spm=a2177.7231205.0.0.285917eaOujZ4.

45. Since many buyers failed to confirm the receipt of the product, Taobao implemented a rule to automatically release the money to the seller after fifteen days if no issues were reported by the buyer.

46. Interview with an Taobao employee in Hangzhou, December 18, 2013.

47. Interviews with online merchants and industry experts in Yangchenghu Township, Suzhou City, August 2014.

48. Interview with a Chinese platform employee in San Francisco, June 1, 2017.

49. Ibid.

50. Ibid.

51. Interview with an e-commerce seller, Lishui City (a prefecture-level city), Zhejiang Province, December 26, 2013.

52. Knowledge @ Wharton, "eBay's Deal with Tom Online Offers Some Timely Lessons for Managers of Global Online Companies," February 14, 2007. http://knowledge.wharton.upenn .edu/article/ebays-deal-with-tom-online-offers-some-timely-lessons-for-managers-of-global -online-companies/.

53. Ibid.

54. Taobao.com remains free to use until today. But it later adopted a monetization model by selling advertisement spots and data services. It also created a separate site called Taobao Mall (Tmall.com), which hosts large online businesses and charges an entry fee and a commission fee.

55. Barnett et al., 2010.

56. Ruo Huang, "淘宝和 eBay 中国：关于那场战争 [Taobao and eBay China: About That War]," Snowball News, May 28, 2019, https://xueqiu.com/3993902801/127383597.

57. This is quoted from the then-premier Wen Jiabao's speech in 2007. See Martin Wolf, "The Chinese Economy Is Rebalancing, At Last," Financial Times, April 3, 2018, https://www.ft.com /content/b54cda40-3659-11e8-8b98-2f31af407cc8.

58. Roula Khalaf, "Downturn Causes 20m Job Losses in China, Financial Times, https://www .ft.com/content/19c25aea-f0f5-11dd-8790-0000779fd2ac.

59. Aziz, 2006.

60. Wolf, "The Chinese Economy Is Rebalancing."

61. Naughton, 2010.

62. Naughton, 2010.

63. Policy Research Office of the Ministry of Commerce, "关于我国电子商务快速发展原因的分析 [Analyzing the Factors behind the Rapid Growth of E-Commerce in Our Country]," May 10, 2016, http://zys.mofcom.gov.cn/article/d/201605/20160501315068.shtml.

64. Interview with an online merchant in Baigou Township, Hebei Province, January 26, 2015.

65. Policy Research Office of the Ministry of Commerce, "关于我国电子商务快速发展原因的分析 [Analyzing the Factors behind the Rapid Growth of E-Commerce in Our Country]."

66. Jiabao Wen, "政府工作报告——2011 年 3 月 5 日在第十一届全国人民代表大会第四次会议上 [Government Work Report—Delivered on March 5, 2011, at the Fourth Session of the Eleventh National People's Congress]," *Xinhua News*, March 15, 2011, https://www.gov.cn/2011lh/content_1825233.htm.

67. Chinese central government's official web portal, "李克强出席中国大数据产业峰会暨中国电子商务创新发展峰会并致辞 [Li Keqiang attended and delivered a speech at the China Big Data Industry Summit and the China E-Commerce Innovation and Development Summit]," May 25, 2016, http://www.gov.cn/guowuyuan/2016-05/25/content_5076764.htm.

68. The original words in Chinese by Premier Li are: "去年在经济增速放缓的情况下，就业不减反增⋯⋯电子商务起到了极大的推动作用." See the Chinese central government's official web portal, "李克强为何一个月内两次为电商'站台' [Why did Li Keqiang endorse e-commerce twice within one month?]," April 2, 2015, http://www.gov.cn/zhengce/2015-04/02/content_2841635.htm.

69. Ibrahim Chowdhury, Ekaterine T. Vashakmadze, and Li Yusha, World Bank Blog, January 12, 2022, https://www.worldbank.org/en/news/opinion/2022/01/12/rebalancing-act-china-s-2022-outlook#:~:text=Instead%2C%20to%20achieve%20sustained%20growth,a%20greater%20role%20for%20markets.

70. Ding, 2018.

71. Ibid.

72. For the full text of the law, see *Xinhua News*, "中华人民共和国电子商务法 [E-Commerce Law of the People's Republic of China]."

73. Ibid.

74. For the full text of the memorandum, see the Supreme People's Procuratorate of the People's Republic of China. "检察机关联合非公企业共建廉洁诚信的市场环境: 最高检反贪总局三局与阿里巴巴、蚂蚁金服签署行贿犯罪档案查询协作备忘录 [The Procuratorate and non-public enterprises jointly establish a market environment of integrity and honesty: The Third Bureau of Anti-Corruption and Bribery Bureau affiliated with the Supreme People's Procuratorate's signed a memorandum of cooperation with Alibaba and Ant Group on file inquiries of bribery crime]," May 9, 2017, http://www.spp.gov.cn/xwfbh/wsfbt/201705/t20170509_190120.shtml.

75. *Sohu*, "淘宝售假被芝麻信用加入黑名单. 信用惩戒效用明显 [Taobao sellers of counterfeit goods have been blacklisted by Sesame Credit. The punitive effect of credit discipline is evident]," March 23, 2017, http://www.sohu.com/a/129962460_115443.

76. Chinalawinfo Database, "Administrative Measures for Online Trading," issued on January 26, 2014, http://lawinfochina.com/display.aspx?id=16309&lib=law.

77. "线下无理由退货'是有益的消费尝试 [The offline 'no-questions-asked return policy' is a beneficial consumer experiment]," *Workers' Daily*, May 21, 2020, http://xiaofei.people.com.cn/n1/2020/0521/c425315-31717686.html.

78. *Sohu*, "电商法要来了，你想知道的都在这里[The E-Commerce Law is coming, and every-thing you want to know is here]," November 24, 2016, http://www.mofcom.gov.cn/article/shangwubangzhu/201603/20160301274283.shtml.

79. Phone interview with a former Taobao employee on the rulemaking team, December 7, 2023.

80. Ibid.

81. *Sohu*, "解决 1500 万起纠纷，腾讯滴滴都学习，阿里首创这项机制成行业共识 [Alibaba's pioneering initiative has successfully resolved 15 million disputes, setting an industry consensus that Tencent and DiDi have since adopted and learned from]," January 7, 2019, https://www.sohu.com/a/287174120_258371.

82. Ibid.

83. Zeyi Yang, "Users are doling out justice on a Chinese food delivery app," *MIT Technology Review*, December 4, 2023, https://www.technologyreview.com/2023/12/04/1084288/food-delivery-user-jury-meituan/.

84. Ibid.

85. Miller and Gallagher, 2021.

86. Shangkun Zhou, "民政部呼吁腾讯阿里开发社区工作软件，比捐十个亿还有用[The Ministry of Civil Affairs calls on Tencent and Alibaba to develop community work software, which is more useful than donating ten billion yuan]," *Jiemian Vnews*, February 10, 2020, https://m.jiemian.com/video/AGQCOAhmB2QBMVVm.html.

Chapter Four: The Invisible State? How E-Commerce Transforms State-Business Relations

1. Interviews in Dongfeng Village, Suining County of Jiangsu Province, August 25, 2014, and March 27, 2015.

2. For a systemic analysis on the relationship between return migration and online entrepreneurship, see Koo and Eesley, 2022.

3. Jealousy and peer pressure appear to have played a significant role in motivating other villagers to adopt e-commerce practices, a phenomenon observed in many Taobao villages. A rural merchant even joked: "To expedite the diffusion of rural e-commerce, the most effective strategy is to encourage the pioneer merchant to show off her wealth, perhaps by buying a car, the more expensive the better, the sooner the better." Interview in Baigou Township, Hebei Province, January 23, 2015.

4. Interviews in Dongfeng Village, Suining County of Jiangsu Province, August 25, 2014.

5. Ibid.

6. Ibid.

7. Ibid.

8. The grabbing hand literature includes Frye and Shleifer (1997), and Shleifer and Vishny (1998). The helping hand literature includes Fisman (2001), Faccio (2006), and Jayachandran (2006).

9. Oi, 1992, 1994; McKinnon, 1992; Montinola et al., 1995; Qian and Weingast, 1996, 1997; Jin et al., 1999.

10. Chen, Hillman, and Gu, 2002.

11. Interviews with two online merchants, Shandong Province, February 11, 2015.

12. Interview with online merchant, Dongfeng Village, Suining County of Jiangsu Province, August 25, 2014.

13. Interview with local official, Suining County of Jiangsu Province, August 25, 2014.

14. Interview with an e-commerce industry expert, Beijing, March 12, 2015.

15. Interviews with two experts who are involved in e-commerce industrial associations, Suzhou City of Jiangsu Province, August 26, 2014.

16. Another factor adding to the challenge is the high threshold required to qualify for the subsidy, or the lack of clear guidelines to allocate the fund. Interviews with two experts who are involved in e-commerce industrial associations, Suzhou City of Jiangsu Province, August 26, 2014.

17. Interview with an e-commerce platform employee, Suzhou City of Jiangsu Province, August 26, 2014.

18. We do not examine merchant vs. central government relations due to China's decentralized economic system, where local governments act as proxies for central governments in regulating local businesses.

19. Culpepper and Thelen, 2020.

20. Maxfield and Schneider, 1997; Dickson, 2003; Evans, 2012.

21. Bai, Hsieh, and Song, 2014; Chen and Dickson, 2010.

22. Landry, 2008; Montinola, Qian, and Weingast, 1995; Xu, 2011.

23. Oi, 1992, 1999; Bai, Hsieh, and Song, 2014.

24. Bai, Hsieh, and Song, 2014; Jiang and Nie, 2014.

25. Fisman, 2001; Dickson, 2003; Kang, 2003; Tsai, 2007; Haber, 2013.

26. Haveman et al., 2017.

27. The exceptions are cities such as Shenzhen, where residential addresses can also be registered as business addresses.

28. *Sohu*, "市场监管总局: 个体户可用网店地址办理工商登记, 无需提供实体经营地址 [State Administration for Market Regulation: Individual Vendors Can Officially Register Using Online Store Addresses without the Need to Provide Physical Business Addresses]," December 8, 2018, https://www.sohu.com/a/280435369_100239955.

29. I also visited a company for smart inventory management in Jieyang, Guangdong Province, July 28, 2014.

30. Interview with an online merchant in a northern city, January 25, 2015.

31. Interview with two merchants, Zhejiang Province, December 27, 2013.

32. For example, Alipay (an app similar to PayPal) ensures that online entrepreneurs are paid within fifteen days.

33. Interview with two online merchants, Shandong Province, February 11, 2015.

34. The online entrepreneur has a Tmall (Taobao Mall) store with annual sales of 10 million RMB in 2014.

35. See World Bank, "Doing Business 2017: China," 2017, https://openknowledge.worldbank .org/bitstream/handle/10986/25444/109799-WP-DB17-PUBLIC-China.pdf?sequence =1&isAllowed=y. Although China's ranking in the 2019 and 2020 Doing Business Reports improved significantly due to domestic reforms, e-commerce had already flourished by this time.

36. Whether all individual sellers should be mandated to undergo official registration sparked heated debates during the preparation phase of China's E-Commerce Law. Some ar-

gued that equal treatment should be applied to online and offline sellers, advocating for registration requirements for both. However, others highlighted the flexible nature of e-commerce and its potential for job creation, contending that mandatory registration would stifle market vitality.

37. For the full text of the E-Commerce Law, see *Xinhua News*, "中华人民共和国电子商务法 [E-Commerce Law of the People's Republic of China]," August 31, 2018, https://www.gov.cn /xinwen/2018-08/31/content_5318220.htm.

38. Article 11 of the E-Commerce Law: "According to the E-Commerce Law of 2018, e-commerce operators shall fulfill their tax obligations in accordance with the law and enjoy preferential tax treatment according to the law."

39. Interviews with two online merchants, Hebei Province, January 25, 2015.

40. Interviews with two online merchants, Shandong Province, February 11, 2015.

41. Eastday, "天猫网店遭遇'查税风暴' [Tmall online stores face a 'tax inspection storm']," May 5, 2015, http://www.xinhuanet.com/politics/2015-05/05/c_127766563.htm.

42. Jin Tian, "电商新法实施前夜：慌乱的代购们 [The Eve of the Implementation of New E-Commerce Law: Panic among Personal Shoppers]," *Economic Observer*, September 22, 2018, http://m.eeo.com.cn/2018/0922/337661.shtml.

43. Online ethnography in a WeChat group with members, including local government officials, e-commerce researchers, and leading online sellers. September 25, 2018.

44. Ibid.

45. Online merchants vary widely. Some sellers are producers selling their own products, with or without physical stores. Others source products from producers or wholesalers. Among these, some use dropshipping and keep no inventory, while others maintain warehouses.

46. The questionnaire design was greatly informed by semi-structured field interviews and prior surveys of private businesses. To make the findings comparable to past studies on private businesses, I incorporated questions from the World Bank Enterprise Survey, the Chinese General Social Survey, and two surveys on Chinese private entrepreneurs designed by Bruce Dickson (2003, 2008). I am grateful to Bruce Dickson for sharing his survey questionnaires.

47. Those who earned equal amounts from online and offline sources were excluded from the sample.

48. Merchants who generate roughly equal income from online and offline sales were dropped from the dataset. Thus, only a small fraction of merchants in the sample run online and offline businesses simultaneously, and their major income comes from one or the other.

49. Some prior face-to-face attempts made by other survey institutes failed as a result, according to three different interviews with an online merchant in Boxing County of Shandong, February 11, 2015, and two Taobao employees in Suzhou City of Jiangsu, August 26, 2014, and in Tonglu County of Zhejiang, July 7, 2015, respectively.

50. The TOMS survey is jointly conducted by Alibaba Research Institute and Peking University. See Qiu and Qiao, 2019.

51. Taobao.com accounted for 95.43 percent of the market share of the C2C e-commerce market in 2016. The data source is iResearch, according to news from Technode. Retrieved from http://technode.com/2012/12/04/china-tech-roundup-taobao-turnover-hit-rmb-1000b -momoclaims-20m-users/. Accessed February 1, 2016.

52. TOMS primarily serves Taobao's need to understand its online seller population. Taobao was therefore very involved in the process of sampling and survey implementation.

53. Daniel Halim, "Women Entrepreneurs Needed—Stat!" World Bank Blog, March 5, 2020, https://blogs.worldbank.org/opendata/women-entrepreneurs-needed-stat.

54. China Business Network, "别以为她只会网购, 淘宝店铺一半都是女老板 [Don't think she only knows how to shop online. Half of the Taobao stores are run by female bosses]," May 21, 2015, https://www.yicai.com/news/4620782.html.

55. Interview with a partner of Alibaba, in Hangzhou City, June 12, 2018.

56. Sara Yin, "Women Entrepreneurs We Love—Founder Stories," Shopify Blog, https://www.shopify.com/blog/women-owned-businesses.

57. Guoliang Zhang, "《女性创业者报告》发布 互联网时代女性创业占半边天 [The 'Female Entrepreneurs Report' Is Released: Women's Entrepreneurship Dominates Half of the Sky in the Internet Era]," China National Radio Web Portal, May 21, 2015, http://politics.people.com.cn/n/2015/0521/c70731-27036470.html.

58. Phone interviews with two online merchants based in Hebei Province, October 11, 2016.

59. The original dataset was scraped by an anonymous software engineer who made it public for downloads for a short period of time in 2015. It took several days and great computational power to aggregate the large amount of raw product-level information to the regional level, thanks to the stellar research assistance of Haotian Xu. See Appendix B after the chapter for more notes on the dataset.

60. Metrodata, "10 张图告诉你, 淘宝跟城市有哪些关系 [The relationship between Taobao and cities: 10 charts tell you]," China Securities Journal, November 12, 2015, https://www.cnstock.com/v_news/sns_rdsm/201511/3621671.htm.

61. Interview with an online merchant in Boxing County, Shandong Province, August 21, 2014; interview with an online merchant in Suzhou City, Jiangsu Province, August 26, 2014.

62. The question asks: "In a typical month over the last year, what percentage of your time was spent on dealing with requirements imposed by government regulations? Some examples of government regulations are taxes, customs, labor regulations, licensing and registration, including dealings with officials and completing forms." The choices are: (1) None or almost zero; (2) 1 day; (3) 2–3 days; (4) 4–5 days; (5) 6–8 days; (6) 9–12 days; (7) 13–16 days; (8) more than 17 days.

63. The question states: "Over the last year (2015), how frequent was your business either inspected by local government officials or required to meet with them?" The choices are: (1) never; (2) seldom; (3) sometimes; (4) often.

64. *ValuePC* is coded on a five-level ordinal scale that reflects whether the respondent tends to (1) strongly agree, (2) somewhat agree, (3) neither agree nor disagree, (4) somewhat disagree, or (5) strongly disagree with the statement "making acquaintance with local officials is helpful for my business."

65. For both the deviance goodness-of-fit test and Pearson goodness-of-fit test for Poisson regression, the null hypothesis is rejected at the 1 percent level of significance.

66. Using robust standard errors instead does not affect the direction or significance of the results. The change in point estimate is remarkably small for all models.

67. Past studies show that newness and smallness constitute liabilities to business survival. Therefore, smaller and newer businesses are more likely than larger ones to seek informal ties,

including political ties, to counteract these organizational disadvantages (Xin and Pearce, 1996; Haveman et al., 2017).

68. I take King and Nielson's (2019) suggestion to use CEM and MDM instead of Propensity Score Matching, which they argue seeks to approximate complete randomization but often increases imbalance, inefficiency, and bias. They recommend CEM and MDM, which attempt to approximate a more efficient fully blocked randomized experiment.

69. The only exception is the treatment effect on *NumOfficialInspec*, which is almost significant after 1-to-1 MDM (p-value = 0.109).

70. Holmes, 1974; Friedman and Amoo, 1999.

71. Interview with a city official in Guangdong Province, July 28, 2014.

72. Interviews with a city cadre, Guangdong Province, July 28, 2014, and with a village cadre in Jiangsu Province, March 27, 2015, and with a village cadre in Shandong Province, August 22, 2014.

73. Interview with a village cadre, Jiangsu Province, March 27, 2015.

74. Interview with a village cadre, Shandong Province, August 22, 2014.

75. For instance, the enterprise income tax (EIT) is calculated based on income attributable to a firm's institutions (机构) or establishments (场所). See Azam, 2013.

76. Phone interview with an e-commerce company employee, May 20, 2015.

77. See Article 24 of the Civil Procedure Law at the *National People's Congress*, "Civil Procedure Law of the People's Republic of China," December 12, 2007, http://www.npc.gov.cn/zgrdw /englishnpc/Law/2007-12/12/content_1383880.htm.

78. Jian Lv, "网购纠纷应如何确定管辖法院[How to determine the jurisdictional court for online shopping disputes]," *People's Court Announcement*, March 28, 2018, https://www .chinacourt.org/article/detail/2018/03/id/3250571.shtml.

79. Ibid.

80. Shunzhong Hou, "网络购物服务协议中对管辖权的约定该如何认定 [How should the jurisdictional clauses in online shopping service agreements be treated?]" People's Court Announcement, March 29, 2017, https://www.chinacourt.org/article/detail/2017/03/id/2647364 .shtml.

81. Jian Lv, "网购纠纷应如何确定管辖法院 [How to determine the jurisdictional court for online shopping disputes]."

82. Ibid.

83. Interview with a Taobao employee on the train from Shanghai to Hangzhou, December 18, 2014.

84. Interview with an e-commerce seller in Hebei Province, January 23, 2015.

85. Ting Zhen, "双 11 购物狂欢节即将打响 马云/刘强东/黄峥被祭拜 [Singles' Day Shopping Carnival is about to kick off, Jack Ma/Liu Qiangdong/Huang Zheng being worshipped]," *Kuai-Keji*, November 10, 2018, https://news.mydrivers.com/1/602/602580.htm.

86. Wang, 2015.

87. Chen Yuxi, "诉腾讯不正当竞争案最新进展：抖音申请撤诉，获福州中院准许[The latest development in the case of Tencent's unfair competition lawsuit: Douyin has applied for withdrawal of the lawsuit and has been granted permission by the Fuzhou Intermediate Court.]," *The Paper*, March 29, 2021, https://www.thepaper.cn/newsDetail_forward _11940729.

88. The Smart City initiative aims to use information technologies to improve the operational efficiency, information transparency, and government services of a city.

89. Przeworski and Wallerstein, 1988.

90. Although central government agencies have much greater bargaining power than local governments over data held by big tech firms, platforms sometimes refuse to comply with data requests. Alibaba and Tencent reportedly once refused to submit their customer loan data to Baihang, a credit-scoring business launched by the Chinese central bank. See *Financial Times*, "Alibaba and Tencent Refuse to Hand Loans Data to Beijing," September 18, 2019, https://www .ft.com/content/93451b98-da12-11e9-8f9b-77216ebe1f17.

91. Interview with a county-level local official of Sichuan Province, July 2, 2016, Hangzhou City.

92. Interview with a platform employee, July 2, 2016, Hangzhou City.

93. A small group is a supra-ministerial coordinating body formed to build consensus and implement policy on issues that cut across the party and different government units when the existing bureaucratic structure fails to do so.

94. Alibaba's major competitor JD also has a similar program, called the "JD county governor program" (京东县长班).

95. Author's calculation based on aggregated statistics of participants of Taobao University's special training program for county governors.

96. Lecture by a government official, Hangzhou City, July 2, 2016.

97. Author's translation from the original sentence from the slides of a class taught in July 2016 by a provincial-level official.

98. Author's translation from the original sentence from the slides of a class taught in July 2016 by a program instructor, who is an e-commerce industry expert.

99. ChinaCourt.Org, "互联网神州租车受阻 老赖主动还款 [Due to the Denial of Services by Internet-based Shenzhou Car Rental, Defaulters Proactively Take Steps to Repay]," July 13, 2016, https://www.chinacourt.org/article/detail/2016/07/id/2020846.shtml.

100. Reuters, "国家统计局与企业展开大数据合作 [The National Bureau of Statistics Collaborates with Enterprises on Big Data]," November 20, 2013, https://www.reuters.com/article /cn-statistic-bureau-baidu-data-share-idCNCNE9AK01I20131121.

101. Interview with a platform employee, Hangzhou City, December 15, 2014.

102. *Financial Times*, "China Tech Groups Hire Ex-regulators to Fend Off Beijing's Crackdown," April 20, 2021, https://www.ft.com/content/71daa106-259e-4dc2-b267-b0289177de1f.

103. Culpepper and Thelen, 2020.

104. Xinjie Yang, "马云刘强东税务总局座谈 [Jack Ma and Richard Liu held discussions with the Taxation Bureau]," *The Paper*, March 31, 2017, https://www.thepaper.cn/newsDetail _forward_1652707.

105. Liu and Weingast, 2018.

Chapter Five: Digital Path to Prosperity or Road to Nowhere? The Economic and Political Effects of E-Commerce Access

1. Sergei Klebnikov, "Alibaba's 11/11 Singles' Day By the Numbers: A Record $38 Billion Haul," *Forbes*, November 11, 2019, https://www.forbes.com/sites/sergeiklebnikov/2019/11/11 /alibabas-1111-singles-day-by-the-numbers-a-record-38-billion-haul/?sh=49a1fad72772.

2. Kate Gibson, "Singles Day 2019's Record Sales Make Black Friday Look Like a Church Bazaar," CBS News, November 11, 2019, https://www.cbsnews.com/news/singles-day-2019 -alibaba-sales-break-records-on-24-hour-shopping-holiday/.

3. *The Economist*, "The Next Big Thing in Retail Comes with Chinese Characteristics," January 2, 2021, https://www.economist.com/business/2021/01/02/the-next-big-thing-in-retail -comes-with-chinese-characteristics.

4. Dobbs et al., 2013.

5. Parts of this chapter are drawn from my paper, coauthored with Victor Couture, Benjamin Faber, and Yizhen Gu (Couture, Faber, Gu, and Liu, 2021, "Connecting the Countryside via E-Commerce: Evidence from China," *American Economic Review: Insights* 3, no. 1: 35–50). Copyright American Economic Association; reproduced with permission of the American Economic Review: Insights. This research was approved by the UC Berkeley Office for the Protection of Human Subjects under IRB Protocol No. 2015-09-7944, and the research design was preregistered under RCT ID AEARCTR-0001582. Stanford University issued a Notice of Determination of Human Subject Research to confirm that the project is subject to review by UC Berkeley and that the Stanford researcher is not engaged in human subject research (the Stanford researcher will not intervene or interact with study participants, i.e., survey subjects), and the researcher's role will be limited to participating in questionnaire/study design and data analysis of coded data with no access to the identifiable information of the subjects.)

6. See, e.g., World Bank publications by Luo and Niu (2019) and Luo et al. (2019). E-commerce villages have also received widespread media attention (e.g., "China's Number One E-Commerce Village" BBC Global Business, May 1, 2013, https://www.bbc.co.uk/programmes /p039q07m; "Inside China's Tech Villages," *The Telegraph*, November 5, 2016, https://www .telegraph.co.uk/news/2016/11/05/inside-chinas-tech-villages-where-farmers-have-replaced -communis/; "Taobao Villages Are Turning Poor Communities into Huge Online Retail Hubs," *Business Insider*, February 27, 2017, https://www.businessinsider.in/chinese-taobao-villages-are -turning-poor-communities-into-huge-online-retail-hubs/articleshow/57382255.cms).

7. This policy statement released annually by the Central Committee of the Communist Party of China and the State Council announces the most important policy theme for the year. It has been devoted to rural areas and agriculture for more than a decade.

8. E.g., Egypt's "National E-Commerce Strategy," https://unctad.org/system/files/official -document/dtlstict2017d3_en.pdf; "Digital India," https://www.digitalindia.gov.in/; "Vietnam's "E-Commerce Development Masterplan," Vietnam's Office of the Prime Minister, 2016; and UNCTAD's technical assistance platform "eTrade For All: Unlocking the Potential of E-Commerce in Developing Countries," https://unctad.org/topic/ecommerce-and-digital -economy/etrade-for-all.

9. OECD, 2009.

10. The villages that were included in the logistics networks were either located in economically developed regions or in close proximity to townships and county centers already covered by the logistics networks.

11. In the logistics industry, there are two primary types of domestic players: state-owned giants such as the China Post and its subsidiary EMS, and private commercial logistics companies. By 2015, the state-owned mail service was able to reach approximately 90 percent of villages to deliver letters on a monthly or bimonthly basis, but package delivery was not included.

Although the postal service received government subsidies, the delivery process was slow, as evident in instances like "ten days to send a package from Shanghai to Chuxiong County in Yunnan Province" mentioned during an in-person interview with a senior expert on China's logistics and distribution industries in Hangzhou City, August 11, 2015. Another interviewee estimated the coverage provided by large private logistics companies such as Sitong Yida and Shunfeng. According to their assessment, "These companies could deliver packages to only 60 percent of the townships, and the large majority of the townships with preexisting commercial logistics network are located in costal and developed provinces. In contrast, the coverage rate in western and other inland provinces was approximately 30 percent. It should be noted that the 60 percent coverage rate includes indirect shipping of packages through secondhand channels. This means that the largest logistics companies would deliver packages to the county level, and then small local firms or individuals would take over the delivery, enabling packages to reach townships. If we consider only the direct delivery by private logistics companies, less than 50 percent of China's townships were able to receive packages," as mentioned during a phone interview with a senior expert on China's logistics and distribution industries based in Hangzhou, September 23, 2016.

12. The Rural Taobao Program was designed by Alibaba and implemented through formal collaboration with various levels of the Chinese government.

13. Following 2020, the program fell short of its original target and underwent downsizing. This decision was influenced by Alibaba's business adjustments and the program's lackluster performance. To some degree, this outcome was anticipated based on our research. Our findings indicate that, regardless of the program's implementation quality, the unfavorable preexisting conditions in rural areas make it challenging to achieve substantial results within a short period of time.

14. Neither the warehouses nor the last-mile subsidy can be used for shipments outside the firm's e-commerce platform.

15. Before deciding on terminal installations, the firm solicits applications from potential local store operators and schedules an exam for the applicants. The score of this exam is one of the criteria the firm uses to determine whether a village is a candidate.

16. Interview with a peasant in Wantou Village, Shandong Province, February 12, 2015.

17. Interview with a platform manager in Tonglu County, Zhejiang Province, July 8, 2015.

18. Rural Taobao experimented with various operational models (see Khanna et al., 2019) but was eventually scaled back in 2019–2020 due to the high costs of logistics subsidies and the limited selling activities triggered by this program—findings corroborated by our study. Similar rural e-commerce programs by other firms also failed to achieve significant impact due to poor conditions in rural areas, which make fostering e-commerce much more difficult than in cities.

19. Interview with the Rural Taobao storeowner in Wantou Village, Shandong Province, February 12, 2015.

20. The funding institutes include the Bill and Melinda Gates Foundation, Weiss Family Program Fund Awards, UC-Berkeley Clausen Center, Hass Dean's Office, and CEGA Grant.

21. These counties are: Huoqiu (Anhui), Linying (Henan), Linzhou (Henan), Minquan (Henan), Suixi (Anhui), Tianchang (Anhui), Xifeng (Guizhou), and Zhenning (Guizhou).

22. Incomplete acceptance rates are standard in this setting and are unrelated to the experiment since applicants were unaware of it.

23. Two missing villages are treatment villages and the other two are controls. This suspension was unrelated to our survey operations, as we followed the same research protocol everywhere, including in this county, and the survey timing within the county was random.

24. The fast pace of the program's expansion places bounds on the timing of the endline. Our control villages were at the top of the list when the firm decided to roll out additional waves of program expansion shortly after the endline.

25. This extended sample was possible due to a small balance in the project account that we decided to invest in enlarging the survey sample. In the endline data collection, one township government blocked our survey activities in four of the twelve villages in that county. Two missing villages were treatment villages and the other two were controls. This suspension was unrelated to our survey operations, as we followed the same research protocol everywhere, including in this county, and the survey timing within the county was random. As a result, we were able to obtain data from ninety-six of the one hundred villages in the endline survey.

26. If this individual was not at home during the first visit, the surveyor would schedule a follow-up visit. If two survey visits failed, the surveyor would replace the household with another randomly sampled household in the same sampling zone ("inner zone" or "outer zone"). As compensation for participating in the survey, the respondent received a gift package of products (e.g., paper towels, soaps, sweets) with a total value of 30 RMB ($4.50).

27. This covers a two-week window for nondurable household consumption, and a three-month window for durable goods categories.

28. The nine product categories include food and beverages, tobacco and alcohol, medicine and health, clothing and accessories, other everyday products, fuel and gas, furniture and appliances, electronics, and transport equipment.

29. In villages with a small number of stores, we sampled all of them.

30. Using these budget shares as consumption weights across categories, we were guided to collect 47/100 price quotes in food and beverages, 15/100 in tobacco and alcohol, 9/100 in medicine and health, 9/100 in clothing and accessories, 4/100 in other everyday products, 4/100 in fuel and gas, 4/100 in furniture and appliances, 4/100 in electronics, and 4/100 in transport equipment.

31. If it was not possible to find the identical product, we replaced it with a new product from the same product category.

32. The five provinces at the time accounted for 40 percent of all participating villages in China.

33. For each e-commerce purchase recorded in our household survey, we asked the respondent whether the product was available in the village and at the most common shopping destination outside the village. If the good was available, we asked how much it would have cost in the offline market.

34. While improving precision, none of the significant findings below rely on the inclusion of baseline outcomes y_{hv}^{Pre}.

35. For households that had purchased durables over the past three months, the treatment effect on uptake is 15.3 percent instead of 9 percent. This yields an effect on the average durable consumption share among uptakers of $0.069 / 0.153 = 45$ percent.

36. See Appendix B for details on the K-L-K indices in Table 5.2.

37. The transport subsidy does not affect villages previously serviced by parcel delivery, as logistics operators offered services in a few rural locations at the same rate as elsewhere in the county prior to program entry.

38. China Internet Network Information Center 2015a, b.

39. See Appendix C for details.

40. Given how small villages are compared to cities, and that only a small fraction of all villages participates in the program, general equilibrium effects on urban centers are unlikely in our setting.

41. See Appendix E for more details.

42. We also evaluate robustness to alternative σ_g Assuming $\sigma_N = 2.87$ and $\sigma_D = 2.85$ yields larger gains (a 1.27 percent reduction in the retail cost of living on average and 8.74 percent among users). Assuming $\sigma_N = 4.87$ and $\sigma_D = 4.85$ yields slightly smaller effects (0.61 and 4.12 percent, respectively).

43. Gaining access to the entire proprietary dataset is beyond our reach. Nevertheless, the five provinces present the most comparable dataset to our experiment villages. This is because all five provinces share key characteristics: a large rural population and a similar level of economic development.

44. In terms of identification, we no longer have experimental variation and a clear counterfactual control group when using the firm's internal database, as we did in the RCT. Instead, we assume that online purchases and out-shipments would be a hard zero in these villages if the program had not arrived in month $j = 0$. This assumption is reasonable given that online purchases and sales remain close to zero at endline in the control villages (Appendix Table A5.4). Reassuringly, we also found that the magnitudes of the program's effect after twelve months were closely aligned with the findings based on the RCT survey data. However, if for some reason we believe this assumption does not hold in the broader set of villages that we are able to observe in the transaction data, then the estimates of the findings of the event study we discuss below can be interpreted as upper-bound estimates of the program's effect (assuming a hard zero for the counterfactual).

45. At the same time, total terminal sales in RMB appear to slightly decline over time, after peaking at about three months after program entry, suggesting that villagers make higher-value purchases first and then switch to buying lesser-value products through e-commerce.

46. From the World Bank's World Integrated Trade Solution (WITS) database, which provides the total value and weight of Chinese exports. For details, see https://wits.worldbank.org.

47. For example, an interview with an Alibaba manager in charge of the rural e-commerce program, Hangzhou City, August 11, 2015.

48. Moreover, compared with urban sellers, rural sellers are particularly poor at adjusting to platforms' rule changes due to the lack of local access to rich information (Koo and Eesley, 2021).

49. *Leading Industrial Research*, "低线城市人口基数庞大，网购人群渗透率不足 40%，未来仍有很大增长空间 [In lower-tier cities, with a large population base, the penetration rate of online shopping is less than 40%, indicating significant growth potential in the future]," December 13, 2019, http://www.leadingir.com/hotspot/view/2163.html.

50. Dobbs et al., 2013.

51. Ibid.

52. Ibid.

53. For more information on New Retail, see Jason Ding, Bruno Lannes, Larry Zhu, Hongbing Gao, Liqi Peng, Fei Song and Zhengwei Jiang, "Embracing China's New Retail," *Bain*, March 13, 2018, https://www.bain.com/insights/embracing-chinas-new-retail/.

54. Yash Wate, "Alibaba Singles' Day 2019 Had a Record Peak Order Rate of 544,000 per Second," *TechPP*, November 19, 2019, https://techpp.com/2019/11/19/alibaba-singles-day-2019-record/.

55. Jian Hong, "送货超快的"双十一", 与阿里、京东、拼多多间的物流暗战 [The lightning-fast deliveries of 'Double Eleven' and the logistics showdown among Alibaba, JD.com, and Pinduoduo]," *Deep Echo*, November 13, 2019, https://mp.weixin.qq.com/s/raaiK0RW17W4FtB4_Xhb5g.

56. Xinping Li, "China's Courier Industry Ships 83 Billion Packages in 2020," *People's Daily*, January 15, 2021, http://en.people.cn/n3/2021/0115/c90000-9809843.html.

57. Author's calculation.

58. Chinese central government's official web portal, "主要快递品牌网点在全国 98% 的乡镇已经实现覆盖 [The main courier service companies have achieved coverage in 98% of towns nationwide]," July 27, 2021, http://www.gov.cn/xinwen/2021-07/26/content_5627438.htm.

59. Steve LeVine, "The Chinese Want Their Packages—Now," *Axios*, June 17, 2018, https://www.axios.com/china-jd-com-package-delivery-logistics-amazon-ups-fedex-d48830af-6a3c-4873-91a1-688a08a784ca.html.

60. Chengyi Lin, "In the Face of Lockdown, China's E-Commerce Giants Deliver," *Harvard Business Review*, April 1, 2020, https://hbr.org/2020/04/in-the-face-of-lockdown-chinas-e-commerce-giants-deliver.

61. DiMaggio and Hargittai, 2001, 1.

62. *The Paper*, "94 岁老人被抱起做人脸识别, 银行道歉 [A 94-year-old was lifted for facial recognition, bank apologizes]," November 23, 2020, https://www.thepaper.cn/newsDetail_forward_10100998.

Chapter Six: Governing the Titans: China's Regulatory Shifts toward Platforms

1. Dai, 2023.

2. This is inspired by Susan Shirk's book *Overreach* (Shirk, 2022).

3. Mary Meaker, "Internet Trends 2018," May 30, 2018, https://cdn.sanity.io/files/ti7si9cx/production/469a9985ce800234dd01dd9ddc8a944856f199e2.pdf?dl.

4. Yiting Sun, "China's Citizens Do Care about Their Data Privacy, Actually," March 28, 2018, MIT Technology Review, https://www.technologyreview.com/2018/03/28/67113/chinas-citizens-do-care-about-their-data-privacy-actually/#:~:text=Baidu%E2%80%99s%20CEO%2C%20Robin%20Li%2C%20is,not%20that%20sensitive%20about%20privacy.

5. Jingli Song, "JD Finance Comes under Fire for Privacy Violations," KrASIA, February 18, 2019, https://kr-asia.com/jd-finance-comes-under-fire-for-privacy-violations.

6. *The Paper*, "上海消保委告诉你, 你手机上的这些 APP 正在'偷看' [The Shanghai Consumer Protection Commission tells you that these apps on your phone are 'snooping']," March 28, 2019, https://www.thepaper.cn/newsDetail_forward_3216470.

7. CCTV, "可怕！这7家科技公司盗取身份证信息，4.68亿个人信息泄露 [Terrifying! These 7 tech companies stole identity card information, resulting in the leakage of 4.68 billion personal records]," November 19, 2019, https://v.cctv.com/2019/11/19/VIDEvR0fpanP7vHEEeTE l0nM191119.shtml.

8. Reuters, "China Tells Alibaba, Tencent to Open Platforms Up to Each Other—Media," September 11, 2021, https://www.reuters.com/technology/china-tells-alibaba-tencent-open -platforms-up-each-other-media-2021-09-11/.

9. Yuxiang Lin, "电商'二选一'简史 [The Brief History of E-commerce 'Either-Or-Restriction']," 36kr, October 16, 2019, https://36kr.com/p/1724518842369.

10. Kelvin Soh, "Alibaba.com CEO Resigns after Jump in Fraudulent Sales," Reuters, February 21, 2011, https://www.reuters.com/article/us-alibaba/alibaba-com-ceo-resigns-after-jump -in-fraudulent-sales-idUSTRE71K1QA20110221.

11. Xiaoning Ren, "100余人因违反腾讯高压线被辞退，这些年互联网反腐已成寻常 [Over 100 people have been dismissed for violating Tencent's strict rules, making anticorruption measures in the internet sector increasingly routine in recent years]," Economic Observer, February 2, 2021, http://m.eeo.com.cn/2021/0202/464394.shtml.

12. Kelly Shelton, "The Value Of Search Results Rankings," Forbes, October 30, 2017, https:// www.forbes.com/sites/forbesagencycouncil/2017/10/30/the-value-of-search-results-rankings /?sh=448d9bc344d3.

13. Interview with a Taobao employee on the train from Shanghai to Hangzhou, December 18, 2014.

14. Interviews of three online merchants in Hebei Province, January 2015, during multiple interviews.

15. Ibid.

16. Ibid.

17. Interviews of three online merchants in Hebei Province, January 2015, during multiple interviews.

18. The Paper, "调查称超八成受访者被大数据"杀熟"，网购问题最多 [The survey indicates that over 80% of respondents have experienced big-data-enabled price discrimination, with e-commerce being the most affected area," March 1, 2022, https://m.thepaper.cn/newsDetail _forward_16902607.

19. Sohu, "网约车大数据杀熟收'苹果税'？复旦副教授花5万多元打车给答案 [Are ride-hailing apps imposing an 'Apple tax' through big-data-enabled price discrimination? A Fudan University associate professor spent over 50,000 yuan on rides to uncover the answer]," March 5, 2021, https://www.sohu.com/a/454306106_802438.

20. See the White House Report, "Big Data and Differential Pricing," February 2015, https:// obamawhitehouse.archives.gov/sites/default/files/whitehouse_files/docs/Big_Data_Report _Nonembargo_v2.pdf.

21. Ryan Browne, "Fines for Breaches of EU Privacy Law Spike Sevenfold to $1.2 Billion, as Big Tech Bears the Brunt," CNBC, January 17, 2022, https://www.cnbc.com/2022/01/18/fines -for-breaches-of-eu-gdpr-privacy-law-spike-sevenfold.html#:~:text=EU%20data%20protec-tion%20authorities%20have,more%20control%20over%20their%20information.

22. Economic Daily, "解读中央经济工作会议精神：防止资本无序扩张 [Interpreting the Spirit of the Central Economic Work Conference: Preventing Unbridled Expansion of Capital]", December 27, 2020, https://www.gov.cn/xinwen/2020-12/27/content_5573663.htm.

23. Yuan Xiang, "人民日报旗下《踏浪青年》：锐评阿里王成文性侵事件 [People's Daily's 'Youth Wading Through Waves': A Sharp Commentary on Alibaba's Wang Chengwen Sexual Assault Incident]," August 8, 2021, https://finance.sina.cn/chanjing/gsxw/2021-08-09/detail -ikqciyzm0393065.d.html.

24. Shan Jiao and Ying Qin, "互联网平台首例反垄断处罚：简析阿里案 [The First Anti-Trust Penalty on Internet Platforms: A Brief Analysis of the Alibaba Case]," Lifang & Partners, April 12, 2021, http://www.lifanglaw.com/plus/view.php?aid=2149.

25. Interview with a China-based legal scholar in Germany, July 2023. Also see Oi et al., 2023.

26. Barry Naughton, "The Summer of 2021: Consolidation of the New Chinese Economic Model with Professor Barry Naughton," online talk on October 5, 2021 at Stanford Center on China's Economy and Institutions, https://sccei.fsi.stanford.edu/news/summer-2021 -consolidation-new-chinese-economic-model.

27. According to an interview by the *Wall Street Journal*, "There were clearly some mixed signals, but we've been told from people who were involved in this process was that some Chinese regulators were broadly supportive of the IPO and were more or less waving it through but others were not. And so DiDi was sort of trapped in this tricky position where they had some regulatory support in China. And they certainly had investors and bankers telling them to speed up and get this thing done and it's great and let's do it. But then they also had at least one Chinese regulator telling them we really think you need to slow this down or there's going to be some issues." See Patrick Barta's interview with Ryan Knutson on the *Wall Street Journal* podcast, "The Journal," July 13, 2021, https://www.wsj.com/podcasts/the-journal/didi-ipo-gets -caught-in-chinas-tech-crackdown/2b8db00f-1178-4d33-abde-a1d9ebbf13cc.

28. See the English translation of the regulation here: China Law Translate, "Guiding Opinions on Strengthening the Overall Governance of Internet Information Service Algorithms," September 29, 2021, https://www.chinalawtranslate.com/en/algorithm-plan/.

29. Donny Kwok and Scott Murdoch, "Beijing's Regulatory Crackdown Wipes $1.1 Trillion off Chinese Big Tech," Reuters, July 12, 2023, https://www.reuters.com/technology/beijings -regulatory-crackdown-wipes-11-trln-off-chinese-big-tech-2023-07-12/#:~:text =HONG%20KONG%2C%20July%2012%20(Reuters,ago%2C%20according%20to%20Re- finitiv%20data.

30. Meaker, "Internet Trends 2018."

31. Companies Market Cap, "Largest Internet Companies by Market Cap," https:// companiesmarketcap.com/internet/largest-internet-companies-by-market-cap/.

32. *China Daily*, "50 家国内企业市值不敌一个苹果？中国科技企业如何过招？[50 domestic companies' combined market value in China falls short of that of a single Apple. How do Chinese technology companies compete?]," April 28, 2022, https://tech.chinadaily.com.cn/a /202204/28/WS626a50efa3101c3ee7ad2fbd.html.

33. Yoko Kubota, "China's Big Tech Firms Are Axing Thousands of Workers," *Wall Street Journal*, March 21, 2022, https://www.wsj.com/articles/chinas-big-tech-firms-are-axing -thousands-of-workers-11647867255.

34. Zijin Caijing, "大厂财报分析报告：财务降本，战略增效，大厂们如何穿越低谷？[The analysis report of major corporations' financial statements: Reducing costs and enhancing efficiency strategically, how are major corporations navigating through the downturn?]," *OFweek*, June 5, 2023, https://tele.ofweek.com/2023-06/ART-8320505-8420-30598829.html.

35. *Sohu*, "为什么互联网大厂大规模裁员，来得如此汹涌？[Why are internet giants laying off employees on such a large scale, coming in such a surging manner?]," June 18, 2023, https://www.sohu.com/a/686915645_121171705.

36. The combined impact of the pandemic, lockdowns, and adverse economic conditions has cast negative effects on the foundational aspects of the Chinese economy.

37. *International Financial News*, "小米关停非主营业务，马化腾"狠话"出圈，互联网行业'冬至'？[Xiaomi shuts down noncore businesses, Ma Huateng's 'tough words' go viral, Internet industry's 'winter is coming'?]," December 22, 2022, https://finance.sina.cn/hkstock/gsxw/2022-12-23/detail-imxxript4100832.d.html?from=wap.

38. Casey Hall, "Alibaba's Research Arm Shuts Quantum Computing Lab amid Restructuring," Reuters, November 27, 2023, https://www.reuters.com/technology/alibabas-research-arm-shuts-quantum-computing-lab-amid-restructuring-2023-11-27/.

39. Iris Deng, "China's internet firms create at least 200 million jobs amid unemployment crisis, report finds," *South China Morning Post*, July 18, 2023, https://www.scmp.com/tech/big-tech/article/3228105/chinas-internet-firms-create-least-200-million-jobs-amid-unemployment-report-finds.

40. In 2022, the Public Security Bureau of Chaoyang District in Beijing also collaborated with Alipay to jointly develop an Anti-Fraud Early Warning System, targeting scammers. See Chaoyang District Government, "全国首例 [The first case in the country]."

41. Xiaoping Li, "浙江省与阿里巴巴签署全面战略合作框架协议 [Zhejiang Province Signs Comprehensive Strategic Cooperation Framework Agreement with Alibaba]," July 5, 2023, *Securities Times*, https://www.stcn.com/article/detail/911347.html.

42. Huang, 1989.

Chapter Seven: Bridging the Past and the Present: Understanding the Interplay of State and Markets

1. Nathan and Trefler, 2014.

2. There are also disagreements with the law merchant thesis. See, for example, Kadens, 2012.

3. I was inspired by Qiang Zhou's working paper (2015) that points out the parallel between the Law Merchant and Taobao. I thank him for sharing this paper with me.

4. Braudel, 1992 [1967], 19.

5. Pearson, 1991; Huang, 2003.

6. Hou, 2019.

7. Ang, 2016.

8. This necessity is emphasized by a 2022 State Council document advocating the creation of a national common market governed by a unified set of rules. The document's central theme is to "accelerate the construction of a national unified market." To this end, China aims to "break down local protectionism and market segmentation, eliminate key barriers constraining economic circulation, and promote the smooth flow of factors of production on a wider scale." See *Xinhua News*, "中共中央 国务院关于加快建设全国统一大市场的意见 [The Opinions of the Central Committee of the Communist Party of China and the State Council on Accelerating the Construction of a Unified National Market]," April 10, 2022, https://www.gov.cn/zhengce/2022-04/10/content_5684385.htm.

9. Pearson, 1997; Dickson, 2003, 2008.

10. Dickson, 2003, 2008.

11. Wank, 1996. For a discussion of the collusion between nonstate firms and the state, also see Chen and Rithmire, 2021.

12. Huntington, 1968; Moore, 1966.

13. Prior research finds that Chinese private businesses do not press for regime change (Pearson, 2000; Dickson, 2003) or major reforms. Instead, private entrepreneurs often create informal coping strategies to bypass the restrictive formal institutions (Tsai, 2006, 2007). Even when they hold legislative seats, they pursue mainly business benefits rather than political goals (Truex, 2014; Hou, 2019).

14. Tsai, 2006, 2007.

15. For instance, the telecommunications giant ZTE is state-owned (51 percent of the shares) but managed by private shareholders (see Milhaupt and Zheng 2015).

16. Leng (2018) finds that, since the late 1980s, China has opened some of its public services to private firms, such as wastewater treatment and environmental improvement projects.

17. See Eggleston, Donahue, and Zeckhauser, 2021.

18. Lieberthal, 1992; Mertha, 2009.

19. Also in Dixit, 2004.

20. Also in Stringham, 2015.

21. Weingast and Marshall, 1988; Oi, 1992, 1999; Walder, 1995.

22. For a review on the past research, see Farrell, 2012.

23. Tech Law Journal, "Clinton Says Trade Deal and Internet Will Reform China," March 9, 2000, http://www.techlawjournal.com/trade/20000309.htm.

24. Mungiu-Pippidi and Munteanu, 2009.

25. King, Pan, and Roberts, 2013.

26. Han, 2015.

27. Xu, 2020.

28. Howard, Agarwal, and Hussain, 2011; Milner, 2006.

29. See Bagire and Silverman (2024) and Jonathan W. Rosen, "Uganda's 'Uber for Motorcycles' Focuses on Safety," *MIT Technology Review*, April 3, 2017, https://www.technologyreview.com/2017/04/03/152808/ugandas-uber-for-motorcycles-focuses-on-safety/.

30. Martha Songa, Cedric Muhebwa, and Rakiya Abby-Farrah, "Ride-hailing App Delivers Contraceptives to Users' Doorsteps," July 17, 2020, https://www.unfpa.org/news/ride-hailing-app-delivers-contraceptives-users-doorsteps.

31. Zafrul Hashim, "Public Value through Private Partnerships: The Grab Story," *Civil Service College Singapore*, January 30, 2018, https://knowledge.csc.gov.sg/ethos-issue-18/public-value-through-private-partnerships-the-grab-story/.

32. Meena Thiruvengadam, "Where Cash Is Still King, Governments Are Partnering with Superapp Grab to Bring People into the Formal Economy," *Fortune*, December 1, 2021, https://fortune.com/2021/12/01/grab-president-ming-maa-super-app-ecommerce-financial-inclusion-ipo-spac-nasdaq/.

33. Farrell 2015, 2017.

34. Farrell 2017.

35. Farrell 2017.

36. Andy Greenberg, "The Silk Road's Dark-Web Dream Is Dead," *Wired*, January 14, 2016, https://www.wired.com/2016/01/the-silk-roads-dark-web-dream-is-dead/.

37. Andy Greenberg, "Silk Road 2.0 Hacked Using Bitcoin Bug All its Funds Stolen," *Forbes*, February 13, 2014, https://www.forbes.com/sites/andygreenberg/2014/02/13/silk-road-2-0-hacked-using-bitcoin-bug-all-its-funds-stolen/?sh=f0257ea20257.

38. Greenberg, "The Silk Road's Dark-Web Dream Is Dead."

39. Greenberg, "The Silk Road's Dark-Web Dream Is Dead."

40. See Gillespie, 2017, for more discussion.

41. Brian Fung, "A Controversial Bill to Protect Kids Online Just Advanced in the Senate. Here's What You Should Know," CNN, February 11, 2022, https://www.cnn.com/2022/02/11/tech/earn-it-act-senate/index.html.

42. Raffaele Huang, "China Creates Government Body to Support Private Sector," *Wall Street Journal*, September 4, 2023, https://www.wsj.com/world/china/china-creates-government-body-to-support-private-sector-cb21a548.

43. *Xinhua News*, "Xi Focus: Xi Stresses Healthy, High-quality Development of Private Sector," March 6, 2023, https://english.news.cn/20230306/486008d94aa1493fa2c1849c0ec1514d/c.html.

Appendix to Chapter 4

1. Krosnick, Narayan, and Smith, 1996.

2. Oppenheimer, Meyvis, and Davidenko, 2009; Huang, 2015.

3. Sources: Alibaba's program introductory slides presented to local governments obtained through fieldwork and an interview conducted in Hangzhou City, July 2, 2016, with a county-level local official of Sichuan Province.

Appendix to Chapter 5

1. For two outcomes of the consumption index discussed below, the control mean and standard deviation were zero. In those cases, we use the standard deviation of the variable observed in the full sample, instead.

2. As part of our negotiations and collaboration with the firm's local implementation teams, it was not feasible to also attempt a two-stage cluster randomization design that would have allowed us to randomly vary saturation rates.

3. To be consistent with structural gravity in trade models, the measure Y_j of j's market size should include a multilateral resistance term capturing j's own degree of access to all other markets (see, e.g., Head & Mayer, 2014).

In the equation, we abstract from this and compute a first-order approximation of the structural gravity expression for MA_v. In practice, both measures have been found to yield very similar results in recent empirical work, as they are highly correlated (e.g., Donaldson & Hornbeck, 2016).

4. See, e.g., Disdier & Head (2008) for a meta-analysis of this point estimate.

5. The eight counties of our RCT fall into one these three zones. Omitting regions outside each zone is somewhat conservative, as their inclusion would increase the denominator of the rural-to-total market access ratios.

6. With very rare exceptions, there is only one terminal per village.

7. In particular, $\omega_{gsh} = \left(\dfrac{\phi_{gsh}^{-1} - \phi_{gsh}^{-0}}{\ln \phi_{gsh}^{-1} - \ln \phi_{gsh}^{-0}} \right) / \sum_{s \in S_g^C} \left(\dfrac{\phi_{gsh}^{-1} - \phi_{gsh}^{-0}}{\ln \phi_{gsh}^{-1} - \ln \phi_{gsh}^{-0}} \right)$, which in turn contain

expenditure shares of different retailers within product groups, where the shares consider only expenditure at continuing retailers $\tilde{\phi}_{gsh}^t = \gamma_{gsh}^t \cdot q_{gsh}^t / \sum_{s \in S_g^C} \gamma_{gsh}^t q_{gsh}^t$.

8. Notice that the assumption of CES preferences does not imply the absence of procompetitive effects as we do not impose additional assumptions about market structure (e.g. monopolistic competition).

9. Some households opted out of audio-recording.

10. Given that more than 1 percent of observations report zero incomes, nominal incomes are only censored at the 1-percent level from the right tail.

11. In counties with relatively short candidate lists, we had to marginally extend this threshold, leading to a small number of villages with distances of less than 2.5 kilometers to the nearest other villages on the candidate list. The mean and median distances for villages without terminals to the nearest terminal location were 10.6 and 9.1 kilometers, respectively. Also see related spillover analysis in Appendix C.

12. We use the boundary of the "natural village" as opposed to the "administrative village." Both of these are known delineations in China. The natural village captures a geographically contiguous rural population. Administrative villages are units with a village committee. In some cases, the administrative village includes more than one natural village.

13. This extended sample was possible due to a small remaining positive balance on the project account that we decided to invest in expanding the household survey sample.

14. Of the one-third of addresses at which our surveyors did not encounter willing and able respondents, 56.6 percent had nobody at home during any of our three visits, 30.5 percent refused to participate in the survey, 7.5 percent had no qualified respondent (due to old age), and 5.4 percent had no one living there.

15. Supervisors sometimes failed to find enough products in a given category within the village. This was often the case for the durable goods categories. In such cases, supervisors replaced products in these missing categories with additional price quotes for products in "other everyday products."

16. Some store owners refused to let supervisors take pictures. In such cases, we identify identical products in the endline data based on the same store and the detailed recorded product description.

17. Remittances represent on average 13 percent of total household income in our sample.

18. The market value of all food and beverages that the household produces for its own consumption amounts to on average less than 10 percent of household incomes.

19. This includes both the registered and nonregistered population currently residing in the unit at the time of the census. Townships are the most disaggregated unit of observation that we can obtain the full census database for. In China's administrative hierarchy, townships are one layer above villages. In the countryside, townships include on average about fourteen villages. In urban regions, township-level units are one level below urban districts.

BIBLIOGRAPHY

Acemoglu, Daron, and Simon Johnson. 2005. "Unbundling Institutions." *Journal of Political Economy* 113, no. 5: 949–95.

Acemoglu, Daron, Simon Johnson, and James A. Robinson. 2005. "Institutions as a Fundamental Cause of Long-run Growth." In *Handbook of Economic Growth*, vol. 1, 385–472.

Acemoglu, Daron, James A. Robinson, and David Woren. 2012. *Why Nations Fail: The Origins of Power, Prosperity and Poverty*, vol. 4. New York: Crown Publishers.

Allen, Matthew MC. 2013. "Comparative Capitalisms and the Institutional Embeddedness of Innovative Capabilities." *Socio-Economic Review* 11, no. 4: 771–94.

Anderson, Simon P., Andre De Palma, and Jacques-Francois Thisse. 1992. *Discrete Choice Theory of Product Differentiation*. MIT Press.

Ang, Yuen Yuen. 2016. *How China Escaped the Poverty Trap*. Ithaca, NY: Cornell University Press.

Arrow, Kenneth J. The Organization of Economic Activity: Issues. *The Analysis and Evaluation of Public Expenditures: the PPB System: pt. 1. The Appropriate Functions of Government in an Enterprise System. pt. 2. Institutional Factors Affecting Efficient Public Expenditure Policy. pt. 3. Some Problems of Analysis in Evaluating Public Expenditure Alternatives*, vol. 1, 47.

Atal, Maha Rafi. 2020. "The Janus Faces of Silicon Valley." *Review of International Political Economy* 28, no. 2: 336–50.

Atkin, David, Benjamin Faber, and Marco Gonzalez-Navarro. 2018. "Retail Globalization and Household Welfare: Evidence from Mexico." *Journal of Political Economy* 126, no. 1: 1–73.

Azam, Rifat. 2013. "E-Commerce Taxation in China." *Journal of Chinese Tax and Policy* 3, no. 1: 66–76.

Aziz, Jahangir. 2006. "Rebalancing China's Economy: What Does Growth Theory Tell Us?" (working paper).

Bagire, Vincent, and Brian Silverman. 2024. "Using Platform Governance to Address Social Problems: Safeboda's Impact on Traffic Safety in Kampala, Uganda." *Working paper*.

Bai, Chong-En, Chang-Tai Hsieh, and Zheng Michael Song. 2014. "Crony Capitalism with Chinese Characteristics" (working paper, University of Chicago 39–58).

Barnett, William, Xue Luo, and Miaomiao Feng. 2010. "Taobao VS. eBAY China" (unpublished, Graduate School of Business, Stanford University).

Barwick, Panle Jia, Shengmao Cao, and Shanjun Li. 2021. "Local Protectionism, Market Structure, and Social Welfare: China's Automobile Market." *American Economic Journal: Economic Policy* 13, no. 4: 112–51.

Bernstein, Lisa. 1992. "Opting Out of the Legal System: Extralegal Contractual Relations in the Diamond Industry." *Journal of Legal Studies* 21, no. 1: 115–57.

————. 2001. "Private Commercial Law in the Cotton Industry: Creating Cooperation through Rules, Norms, and Institutions." *Michigan Law Review* 99, no. 7: 1724–90.

Besley, Timothy, and Torsten Persson. 2009. "The Origins of State Capacity: Property Rights, Taxation, and Politics." *American Economic Review* 99, no. 4: 1218–44.

Biernacki, Patrick, and Dan Waldorf. 1981. "Snowball Sampling: Problems and Techniques of Chain Referral Sampling." *Sociological Methods & Research* 10, no. 2: 141–63.

Blanchard, Olivier, and Andrei Shleifer. 2001. "Federalism with and without Political Centralization: China versus Russia." *IMF Staff Papers* 48, no. 1: 171–79.

Braudel, Fernand. 1982. *Civilization and Capitalism, 15th–18th Century*, vols. 2, 3. Oakland: University of California Press.

Buchak, Greg, Jian Hu, and Shang-Jin Wei. 2021. *FinTech as a Financial Liberator* (No. w29448). National Bureau of Economic Research.

Catania, Joseph A., Dennis Binson, Jorge Canchola, L. M. Pollack, William Hauck, and Thomas J. Coates. 1996. "Effects of Interviewer Gender, Interviewer Choice, and Item Wording on Responses to Questions concerning Sexual Behavior." *Public Opinion Quarterly* 60, no. 3: 345–75.

Cao, Yuanzheng, Yingyi Qian, and Barry R. Weingast. "From Federalism, Chinese Style to Privatization, Chinese Style." *Economics of Transition* 7, no. 1: 103–31.

Chandler Jr, Alfred D. 1977. *The Visible Hand*. Cambridge, MA: Harvard University Press.

Chang, Linchiat, and Jon A. Krosnick. 2009. "National Surveys via RDD Telephone Interviewing versus the Internet: Comparing Sample Representativeness and Response Quality." *Public Opinion Quarterly* 73, no. 4: 641–78.

Chen, Jie, and Bruce J. Dickson. 2010. *Allies of the State: China's Private Entrepreneurs and Democratic Change*. Cambridge, MA: Harvard University Press.

Chen, Jidong, Ye Tao, Haoran Wang, and Tao Chen. 2015. "Big Data Based Fraud Risk Management at Alibaba." *Journal of Finance and Data Science* 1, no. 1: 1–10.

China Internet Network Information Center. 2015a. *Research Report on China's Online Shopping Market in 2014*. Beijing: China Internet Network Information Center.

China Internet Network Information Center. 2015b. *The 36th Statistical Report on Internet Development in China*. Beijing: China Internet Network Information Center.

Chorzempa, Martin. 2022. *The Cashless Revolution: China's Reinvention of Money and the End of America's Domination of Finance and Technology*. Hachette UK.

Cohen, Lizabeth. 1990. *Making a New Deal: Industrial Workers in Chicago, 1919–1939*. UK: Cambridge University Press.

Couper, Mick P. 2000. "Web Surveys: A Review of Issues and Approaches." *Public Opinion Quarterly* 64, no. 4: 464–94.

Couture, Victor, Benjamin Faber, Yizhen Gu, and Lizhi Liu. 2021. "Connecting the Countryside via E-Commerce: Evidence from China." *American Economic Review: Insights* 3, no. 1: 35–50.

Culpepper, Pepper D., and Thelen, Kathleen. 2020. "Are We All Amazon Primed? Consumers and the Politics of Platform Power." *Comparative Political Studies* 53, no. 2: 288–318.

Dai, Xin. 2023. "Towards a Regulatory New Deal for Digital Platforms" (working paper, Peking University).

Dickson, Bruce. 2003. *Red Capitalists in China: The Party, Private Entrepreneurs, and Prospects for Political Change*. UK: Cambridge University Press.

———. 2016. *The Dictator's Dilemma: The Chinese Communist Party's Strategy for Survival*. UK: Oxford University Press.

DiMaggio, Paul, and Eszter Hargittai. 2001. "From the 'Digital Divide' to 'Digital Inequality': Studying Internet Use as Penetration Increases." *Princeton: Center for Arts and Cultural Policy Studies, Woodrow Wilson School, Princeton University* 4, no. 1.

Dimitrov, Martin. 2009. *Piracy and the State: The Politics of Intellectual Property Rights in China*. Cambridge University Press.

Ding, Daoqin. 2018.《电子商务法》平台责任"管道化"问题及其反思 [Problem of "Pipelineization" of Platform Responsibility in E-Commerce Law and Its Reflection]. *Journal of Beijing University of Aeronautics and Astronautics: Social Sciences Edition* 31, no. 6: 1–6.

Disdier, Anne-Célia, and Keith Head. 2008. "The Puzzling Persistence of the Distance Effect on Bilateral Trade." *The Review of Economics and Statistics* 90, no. 1: 37–48.

Dixit, Avinash K.. 2004, 2011. *Lawlessness and Economics*. Princeton, NJ: Princeton University Press.

Dobbs, Richard, Yougan Chen, Gordon Orr, James Manyika, and Elisie Chang. 2013. *China's E-tail Revolution: Online Shopping as a Catalyst for Growth*. McKinsey Global Institute.

Donaldson, Dave, and Richard Hornbeck. 2016. "Railroads and American Economic Growth: A "Market Access" Approach." *The Quarterly Journal of Economics* 131, no. 2: 799–858.

Eggleston, Karen, John D. Donahue, and Richard J. Zeckhauser. 2021. *The Dragon and the Eagle*. UK: Cambridge University Press.

Eisenmann, Thomas, Geoffrey Parker, and Marshall W. Van Alstyne. 2006. "Strategies for Two-Sided Markets." *Harvard Business Review* 84, no. 10: 92.

Ellickson, Robert. 2021. *Order without Law*. Cambridge, MA: Harvard University Press

Ely Jr, James W. 2002. *Railroads and American Law*. Lawrence: University Press of Kansas.

Ernst, Dieter, and Jiacheng He. 2000. "The Future of E-Commerce in China." *Report from the East-West Center*. https://scholarspace.manoa.hawaii.edu/server/api/core/bitstreams /14a2457c-9028-4cc1-bc24-45f91dd53843/content.

Evans, David S. 2003. "The Antitrust Economics of Multi-sided Platform Markets." *Yale Journal on Regulation* 20: 325.

Evans, Peter B. 2012. *Embedded Autonomy*. Princeton, NJ: Princeton University Press.

Fan, Jingting, Lixin Tang, Weiming Zhu, and Ben Zou. 2018. "The Alibaba Effect: Spatial Consumption Inequality and the Welfare Gains from E-Commerce." *Journal of International Economics* 114: 203–20.

Farrell, Henry. 2003. "Constructing the International Foundations of E-Commerce—The EU-US Safe Harbor Arrangement." *International Organization* 57, no. 2: 277–306.

———. 2006a. "The Political Economy of the Internet and E-Commerce." In *Political Economy and the Changing Global Order*, edited by Richard Stubbs and Geoffrey R. D. Underhill, 211–22. UK: Oxford University Press.

———. 2006b. "Regulating Information Flows: States, Private Actors, and E-Commerce." *Annual Review of Political Science* 9: 353–74.

———. 2012. "The Consequences of the Internet for Politics." *Annual Review of Political Science* 15: 35–52.

———. 2015. "Dark Leviathan." *Aeon Essays*. https://aeon.co/essays/why-the-hidden-internet -can-t-be-a-libertarian-paradise.

———. 2017. "A State of Trust without the State: The Political Economy of Pseudonymity and Cybercrime" (unpublished paper).

Feenstra, Robert C. 1994. "New Product Varieties and the Measurement of International Prices." *American Economic Review* 84, no. 1: 157–77.

Fisman, Raymond. 2001. "Estimating the Value of Political Connections." *American Economic Review* 91, no. 4: 1095–1102.

Friedman, Hershey H., and Taiwo Amoo. 1999. "Rating the Rating Scales." *Journal of Marketing Management* (Winter): 114–23.

Fuller, Douglas Brian. 2005. "Creating Ladders Out of Chains: China's Technological Development in a World of Global Production." PhD diss., Massachusetts Institute of Technology.

———. 2016. *Paper Tigers, Hidden Dragons: Firms and the Political Economy of China's Technological Development.* UK: Oxford University Press.

Gallagher, Mary E. 2017. *Authoritarian Legality in China: Law, Workers, and the State.* UK: Cambridge University Press.

Gallagher, Mary, and Blake Miller. 2021. "Who Not What: The Logic of China's Information Control Strategy." *China Quarterly* 248, no. 1: 1011–36.

Gerth, Karl. 2013. "Compromising with Consumerism in Socialist China: Transnational Flows and Internal Tensions in 'Socialist Advertising.'" *Past & Present* 218, supplement 8: 203–32.

Glaeser, Edward L., Rafael La Porta, Florencio Lopez-de-Silanes, and Andrei Shleifer. 2004. "Do Institutions Cause Growth?" *Journal of Economic Growth* 9, no. 3: 271–303.

Gillespie, Tarleton. 2017. "Governance of and by Platforms." In *SAGE Handbook of Social Media*, edited by Jean Burgess, Alice Marwick, and Thomas Poell, 254–78. Thousand Oaks, CA: SAGE.

Glickman, Lawrence B. 2012. "Consumer Activism, Consumer Regimes, and the Consumer Movement: Rethinking the History of Consumer Politics in the United States." In *The Oxford Handbook of the History of Consumption,* edited by Frank Trentmann. UK: Oxford Press.

Graham, John, Timothy Wynne Plumptre, and Bruce Amos. 2003. *Principles for Good Governance in the 21st Century.* Ottawa, Canada: Institute on Governance.

Greif, Avner. 1989. "Reputation and Coalitions in Medieval Trade: Evidence on the Maghribi Traders." *Journal of Economic History* 49, no. 4: 857–82.

———. 1993. "Contract Enforceability and Economic Institutions in Early Trade: The Maghribi Traders' Coalition." *American Economic Review* 83, no. 3: 525–48.

———. 2000. "The Fundamental Problem of Exchange: A Research Agenda in Historical Institutional Analysis." *European Review of Economic History* 4, no. 3: 251–84.

———. 2006. "History Lessons: The Birth of Impersonal Exchange: The Community Responsibility System and Impartial Justice." *Journal of Economic Perspectives* 20, no. 2: 221–36.

Greif, Avner, Paul Milgrom, and Barry R. Weingast. 1994. "Coordination, Commitment, and Enforcement: The Case of the Merchant Guild." *Journal of Political Economy* 102, no. 4: 745–76.

Haber, Stephen. 2002. *Crony Capitalism and Economic Growth in Latin America: Theory and Evidence.* Stanford, CA: Hoover Institution Press.

Haley, George T. 2002. "E-cCmmerce in China: Changing Business as We Know It." *Industrial Marketing Management* 31, no. 2: 119–24.

Han, Rongbin. "Defending the Authoritarian Regime Online: China's 'Voluntary Fifty-Cent Army.'" *China Quarterly* 224: 1006–25.

Haveman, Heather A., Nan Jia, Jing Shi, and Yongxiang Wang. 2017. "The Dynamics of Political Embeddedness in China." *Administrative Science Quarterly* 62, no. 1: 67–104.

Hayek, Friedrich A. 1939. "The Economic Conditions of Interstate Federalism." *New Commonwealth Quarterly* 5, no. 2: 131–49.

———. 1960. *Constitution of Liberty*. Chicago, IL: University of Chicago Press.

He, Zengke. 2000. "Corruption and Anti-corruption in Reform China." *Communist and Post-Communist Studies* 33, no. 2: 243–70.

Head, Keith, and Thierry Mayer. 2014. "Gravity Equations: Workhorse, Toolkit, and Cookbook." In *Handbook of International Economics*, vol. 4, 131–95. Elsevier.

Hellman, Joel S. 1998. "Winners Take All: The Politics of Partial Reform in Postcommunist Transitions." *World politics* 50, no. 2: 203–34.

Holland, Alinsha C. 2017. *Forbearance as Redistribution: The Politics of Informal Welfare in Latin America*. UK: Cambridge University Press.

Holmes, Cliff. 1974. "A Statistical Evaluation of Rating Scales." *Journal of the Market Research Society* 16, no. 2: 87–107.

Hou, Yue. 2019. *The Private Sector in Public Office: Selective Property Rights in China*. UK: Cambridge University Press.

Howard, Philip N., Sheetal D. Agarwal, and Muzammil M. Hussain. 2011. "When Do States Disconnect Their Digital Networks? Regime Responses to the Political Uses of Social Media." *Communication Review* 14, no. 3: 216–32.

Huang, Haifeng. 2015. "International Knowledge and Domestic Evaluations in a Changing Society: The Case of China." *American Political Science Review* 109, no. 3: 613–34.

Huang, Ray. 1989. *China, a Macro History*. Armonk: ME Sharpe.

Huang, Yasheng. 2003. *Selling China: Foreign Direct Investment during the Reform Era*. UK: Cambridge University Press.

Huang, Jingyang, and Kellee S. Tsai. 2022. "Securing Authoritarian Capitalism in the Digital Age: The Political Economy of Surveillance in China." *China Journal* 88, no. 1.

Huntington, Samuel P. 1968. *Political Order in Changing Societies*. New Haven, CT: Yale University Press.

Hurst, William. 2018. *Ruling before the Law: The Politics of Legal Regimes in China and Indonesia*. UK: Cambridge University Press.

Iansiti, Marco, and Roy Levien. 2004. *The Keystone Advantage: What the New Dynamics of Business Ecosystems Mean for Strategy, Innovation, and Sustainability*. Cambridge, MA: Harvard Business Press.

International Monetary Fund. 1997. *Good Governance: The IMF's Role*. Washington.

Jiang, Ting, and Huihua Nie. 2014. "The Stained China Miracle: Corruption, Regulation, and Firm Performance." *Economics Letters* 123, no. 3: 366–69.

Johnson, Timothy P. 2014. *Snowball Sampling: Introduction*. Wiley StatsRef: Statistics Reference Online.

Kadens, Emily. 2011. "Myth of the Customary Law Merchant." *Texas Law Review* 90: 1153.

Kang, David C. 2002. "Transaction Costs and Crony Capitalism in East Asia." *Comparative Politics*, 439–458.

Kling, Jeffrey R., Jeffrey B. Liebman, and Lawrence F. Katz. 2007. "Experimental Analysis of Neighborhood Effects." *Econometrica* 75, no. 1: 83–119.

Khanna, Tarun, and Krishna Palepu. 1997. "Why Focused Strategies." *Harvard Business Review* 75, no. 4: 41–51.

Khanna, T., R. Allen, A. Frost, and W. Koo. 2019. "Rural Taobao: Alibaba's expansion into rural e-commerce." *Harvard Business School Case*, 719–433.

King, Gary, and Richard Nielsen. 2019. "Why Propensity Scores Should Not Be Used for Matching." *Political Analysis* 27, no. 4: 435–54.

King, Gary, Jennifer Pan, and Margaret E. Roberts. 2013. "How Censorship in China Allows Government Criticism but Silences Collective Expression." *American Political Science Review* 107, no. 2: 326–43.

Koo, Wesley W. 2024. "Hybrid Governance of Platform Entrepreneurs." *Research Policy* 53, no. 2: 104916.

Koo, Wesley W., and Charles E. Eesley. 2021. "Platform Governance and the Rural-Urban Divide: Sellers' Responses to Design Change." *Strategic Management Journal* 42, no. 5: 941–67.

———. Forthcoming. "Take Me Home, Country Roads: Return Migration and Platform-Enabled Entrepreneurship." *Organization Science*.

Kornai, Janos. 1979. "Resource-Constrained versus Demand-Constrained Systems." *Econometrica: Journal of the Econometric Society* 47, no. 4: 801–19.

Kornai, Janos, Eric Maskin, and Gerald Roland. 2003. "Understanding the Soft Budget Constraint." *Journal of Economic Literature* 41, no. 4: 1095–1136.

Krosnick, Jon A., Sowmya Narayan, and Wendy R. Smith. 1996. "Satisficing in Surveys: Initial Evidence." *New Directions for Evaluation* 70: 29–44.

Landry, Pierre F. 2008. *Decentralized Authoritarianism in China: The Communist Party's Control of Local Elites in the Post-Mao Era*, vol. 1. New York: Cambridge University Press.

Lardy, Nicholas R. 2016. "China: Toward a Consumption-Driven Growth Path." In *Seeking Changes: The Economic Development in Contemporary China*, edited by Yanhui Zhou, 85–111.

Leeson, P. T. 2009. *The Invisible Hook*. Princeton, NJ: Princeton University Press.

Lehdonvirta, Vili. 2022. *Cloud Empires: How Digital Platforms Are Overtaking the State and How We Can Regain Control*. MIT Press.

Leng, Ning. 2018. "Visible Development First: The Political Economy of Restructuring China's Public Service Sectors." PhD diss., University of Wisconsin-Madison.

Lei, Zhenhuan, and Lizhi Liu. 2023. "Turning the Blade Inward: Demystifying China's Deregulation Program" (working paper).

Li, Hongbin, and Zhou, Li-An. 2005. "Political Turnover and Economic Performance: The Incentive Role of Personnel Control in China." *Journal of Public Economics* 89, no. 9–10: 1743–62.

Li, Lianjiang. 2004. "Political Trust in Rural China." *Modern China* 30, no. 2: 228–58.

Lieberthal, Kenneth G. 1992. "Introduction: The Fragmented Authoritarianism Model and Its Limitations." In *Bureaucracy, Politics and Decision Making in Post-Mao China*, edited by Kenneth G. Lieberthal and David Lampton, 1–32. Berkeley: University of California Press.

Lieberthal, Kenneth, and Michel Oksenberg. 1988. *Policy Making in China*. Princeton, NJ: Princeton University Press.

Liebman, Benjamin L. 2014. "Legal Reform: China's Law-Stability Paradox." *Daedalus* 143, no. 2: 96–109.

Lindtner, Silvia M. 2020. *Prototype Nation*. Princeton, NJ: Princeton University Press.

Liu, Lizhi. 2021. "The Rise of Data Politics: Digital China and the World." *Studies in Comparative International Development* 56, no. 1: 45–67.

Liu, Lizhi, and Jian Xu. 2022. "Playing Catch-up: How Authoritarian Courts Handle Transnational IP Litigations" (working paper).

Liu, Lizhi, and Barry R. Weingast. 2018. "Taobao, Federalism, and the Emergence of Law, Chinese Style." *Minnesota Law Review* 102: 1563.

———. 2021. "Law, Chinese Style: Solving the Authoritarian's Legal Dilemma through the Private Provision of Law" (working paper).

Luo, Xubei, and Chiyu Niu. 2019. "E-Commerce Participation and Household Income Growth in Taobao Villages" (*World Bank Policy Research* working paper 8811).

Luo, Xubei, Yue Wang, and Xiaobo Zhang. "E-Commerce Development and Household Consumption Growth in China" (*World Bank Policy Research* working paper 8810).

Malesky, Edmund, and Jonathan London. 2014. "The Political Economy of Development in China and Vietnam." *Annual Review of Political Science* 17: 395–419.

Manion, Melanie. 2015. *Information for Autocrats: Representation in Chinese Local Congresses*. UK: Cambridge University Press.

Mattli, Walter, and Tim Büthe. 2005. "Global Private Governance: Lessons from a National Model of Setting Standards in Accounting." *Law and Contemporary Problems* 68, no. 3–4: 225–62.

Maxfield, Sylvia, and Ben Ross Schneider, eds. 1997. *Business and the State in Developing Countries*. Ithaca, NY: Cornell University Press.

Mazur, Joanna, and Marcin Serafin. 2023. "Stalling the State: How Digital Platforms Contribute to and Profit from Delays in the Enforcement and Adoption of Regulations." *Comparative Political Studies* 56, no. 1: 101–30.

Meng, Tianguang, and Jing Ning. 2018. 互联网"去政治化"的政治后果 [The Political Consequences of Internet "Depoliticization"]. 探索 [Probe] 3, no. 201: 63–76.

Mensch, Barbara S., and Denise B. Kandel. 1988. "Underreporting of Substance Use in a National Longitudinal Youth Cohort: Individual and Interviewer Effects." *Public Opinion Quarterly* 52, no. 1: 100–24.

Mertha, Andrew. "'Fragmented Authoritarianism 2.0': Political Pluralization in the Chinese Policy Process." *China Quarterly* 200: 995–1012.

Mertha, Andrew C. *The Politics of Piracy: Intellectual Property in Contemporary China*. Ithaca, NY: Cornell University Press.

Micheletti, Michele, and Dietlind Stolle. 2007. "Mobilizing Consumers to Take Responsibility for Global Social Justice." *Annals of the American Academy of Political and Social Science* 611, no. 1: 157–75.

Miguel, Edward, and Michael Kremer. 2004. "Worms: Identifying Impacts on Education and Health in the Presence of Treatment Externalities." *Econometrica* 72, no. 1: 159–217.

Milgrom, Paul R., Douglass C. North, and Barry R. Weingast. 1990. "The Role of Institutions in the Revival of Trade: The Law Merchant, Private Judges, and the Champagne Fairs." *Economics & Politics* 2, no. 1: 1–23.

Milhaupt, Curtis J., and Wentong Zheng. 2014. "Beyond Ownership: State Capitalism and the Chinese Firm." *Georgetown Law Journal* 103: 665.

Milner, Helen V. 2006. "The Digital Divide: The Role of Political Institutions in Technology Diffusion." *Comparative Political Studies* 39, no. 2: 176–99.

Montinola, Gabriella, Yingyi Qian, and Barry R. Weingast. 1995. "Federalism, Chinese Style: The Political Basis for Economic Success in China." *World Politics* 48, no. 1: 50–81.

Moore, Barrington. 1966. *Social Origins of Dictatorship and Democracy: Lord and Peasant in the Making of the Modern World*. Boston, MA: Beacon.

Mungiu-Pippidi, Alina, and Igor Munteanu. 2009. "Moldova's 'Twitter Revolution.'" *Journal of Democracy* 20, no. 3: 136–42.

Naughton, Barry. 2010. "Reading the NPC: Post-crisis Economic Dilemmas of the Chinese Leadership." *China Leadership Monitor* 32: 1–10.

North, Douglass C. 1990. *Institutions, Institutional Change and Economic Performance*. UK: Cambridge University Press.

———. 1991. "Institutions." *Journal of Economic Perspectives* 5, no. 1: 97–112.

North, Douglass Cecil, John Joseph Wallis, and Barry R. Weingast. 2009. *Violence and Social Orders: A Conceptual Framework for Interpreting Recorded Human History*. UK: Cambridge University Press.

Oi, Jean C. 1985. "Communism and Clientelism: Rural Politics in China." *World Politics* 37, no. 2: 238–66.

———. 1992. "Fiscal Reform and the Economic Foundations of Local State Corporatism in China." *World Politics* 45, no. 1: 99–126.

———. 1999. *Rural China Takes Off: Institutional Foundations of Economic Reform*. Oakland: University of California Press.

Oi, Jean C, Jason Luo, and Xu Yunxiao. 2023, November 21–22. "A Perfect Storm: COVID, Collapse of the Property Sector, and Local Government Debt in China." Paper prepared for the China Journal Workshop: How COVID Changed China, at the Australian National University, Canberra, Australia.

Olson, Mancur. 1993. "Dictatorship, Democracy, and Development." *American Political Science Review* 87, no. 3: 567–76.

Oppenheimer, Daniel M., Tom Meyvis, and Nicolas Davidenko. 2009. "Instructional Manipulation Checks: Detecting Satisficing to Increase Statistical Power." *Journal of Experimental Social Psychology* 45, no. 4: 867–72.

Parker, Geoffrey G., Marshall W. Van Alstyne, and Sangeet Paul Choudary. 2016. *Platform Revolution: How Networked Markets Are Transforming the Economy and How to Make Them Work for You*. New York: W. W. Norton & Company.

Pearson, Margaret M. 1997. *China's New Business Elite*. Oakland: University of California Press.

Peerenboom, Randall. 2002. *China's Long March toward Rule of Law*. UK: Cambridge University Press.

Peng, Mike W., and Yadong Luo. 2000. "Managerial Ties and Firm Performance in a Transition Economy: The Nature of a Micro-Macro Link." *Academy of Management Journal* 43, no. 3: 486–501.

Polishchuk, Leonid. 2013. "Institutional Outsourcing." *Voprosy Economiki* 9.

Pollman, Elizbeth, and Jordan M. Barry. 2016. "Regulatory entrepreneurship." *Southern California Law Review* 90: 383.

Poncet, Sandra. 2003. "Measuring Chinese Domestic and International Integration." *China Economic Review* 1, no. 14: 1–21.

———. 2005. "A Fragmented China: Measure and Determinants of Chinese Domestic Market Disintegration." *Review of International Economics* 13, no. 3: 409–30.

Pritchett, Lant, and Michael Woolcock. 2004. "Solutions When the Solution Is the Problem: Arraying the Disarray in Development." *World Development* 32, no. 2: 191–212.

Przeworski, Adam, and Michael Wallerstein. 1988. "Structural Dependence of the State on Capital." *American Political Science Review* 82, no. 1: 11–29.

Putnam, Robert D. 2000. *Bowling Alone: The Collapse and Revival of American Community*. New York: Simon and Schuster.

Qian, Yingyi, and Chenggang Xu. 1993. "The M-form Hierarchy and China's Economic Reform." *European Economic Review* 37, no. 2–3: 541–48.

Qiu, Zeqi, and Tianyu Qiao. 2021. 组织退出: 生命周期还是企业家自主选择? [Organization Quit: Enterprise Life Cycle or Entrepreneur's Choice? A Study on Small Enterprises Based on the Taobao Platform]. 社会学评论 [Sociological Review of China] 9, no. 5: 42–64.

Rithmire, Meg, and Hao Chen, H. 2021. "The Emergence of Mafia-like Business Systems in China." *China Quarterly* 248, no. 1: 1–22.

Rochet, Jean-Charles, and Jean Tirole. 2003. "Platform Competition in Two-sided Markets." *Journal of the European Economic Association* 1, no. 4: 990–1029.

Rodden, Jonathan, and Susan Rose-Ackerman. 1997. "Does Federalism Preserve Markets?" *Virginia Law Review* 83, no. 7: 1521–72.

Rodrik, Dani. 2006. "Goodbye Washington Consensus, Hello Washington Confusion? A Review of the World Bank's Economic Growth in the 1990s: Learning from a Decade of Reform." *Journal of Economic Literature* 44, no. 4: 973–87.

Rodrik, Dani, Arvind Subramanian, and Francesco Trebbi. 2004. "Institutions Rule: The Primacy of Institutions over Geography and Integration in Economic Development." *Journal of Economic Growth* 9, no. 2: 131–65.

Santiso, Carlos. 2001. "Good Governance and Aid Effectiveness: The World Bank and Conditionality." *Georgetown Public Policy Review* 7, no. 1: 1–22.

Shah, Dhavan V., Douglas M. McLeod, Eunkyung Kim, Sun Young Lee, Melissa R. Gotlieb, Shirley S. Ho, and Hilde Breivik. 2007. "Political Consumerism: How Communication and Consumption Orientations Drive 'Lifestyle Politics.'" *Annals of the American Academy of Political and Social Science* 61, no. 1: 217–35.

Sharman, Jason Campbell, and Andrew Phillips. 2020. *Outsourcing Empire: How Company-States Made the Mmodern World*. Princeton, NJ: Princeton University Press.

Shen, Chunli, Jing Jin, and Heng-fu Zou. 2012. "Fiscal Decentralization in China: History, Impact, Challenges and Next Steps." *Annals of Economics & Finance* 13, no. 1.

Shirk, Susan L. 1993. *The Political Logic of Economic Reform in China*, vol. 24. Oakland: University of California Press.

———. 2023. *Overreach: How China Derailed Its Peaceful Rise*. UK: Oxford University Press.

Shirley, Mary M. 2005. "Institutions and Development." In *Handbook of New Institutional Economics*, edited by Claude Menard and Mary M. Shirley, 611–38. Boston, MA: Springer.

Shleifer, Andrei, and Robert W. Vishny. 1993. "Corruption." *Quarterly Journal of Economics* 108, no. 3: 599–617.

Smith, Adam. 2010. *The Wealth of Nations: An Inquiry into the Nature and Causes of the Wealth of Nations*. 1776. UK: Harriman House Limited.

So, Suet Ying, and Westland, J. Christopher. 2009. *Red Wired: China's Internet Revolution*. Singapore: Marshall Cavendish International Asia Pte Ltd.

Steinfeld, Edward S. 2010. *Playing Our Game: Why China's Rise Doesn't Threaten the West*. UK: Oxford University Press.

Stern, Rachel E. 2014. The Political Logic of China's New Environmental Courts. *China Journal* 72: 53–74.

Stockmann, Daniela, and Mary E. Gallagher. 2011. "Remote Control: How the Media Sustain Authoritarian Rule in China." *Comparative Political Studies* 44, no. 4: 436–67.

Stockmann, Daniela, and Ting Luo. Forthcoming. *Governing Digital China*. Cambridge University Press.

Stringham, Edward. 2015. *Private Governance: Creating Order in Economic and Social Life*. New York: Oxford University Press, USA.

Sun, Yu. "China Tech Groups Hire Ex-regulators to Fend Off Beijing's Crackdown." *Financial Times*, April 20, 2021. https://www.ft.com/content/71daa106-259e-4dc2-b267-b0289177de1f.

Thompson, Craig J. 2011. "Understanding Consumption as Political and Moral Practice." *Journal of Consumer Culture* 11, no. 2: 139–44.

Tiebout, Charles M. 1956. "A Pure Theory of Local Expenditures." *Journal of Political Economy* 64, no. 5: 416–24.

Truex, Rory. 2014. "The Returns to Office in a 'Rubber Stamp' Parliament." *American Political Science Review* 108, no. 2: 235–51.

———. 2016. *Making Autocracy Work: Representation and Responsiveness in Modern China*. UK: Cambridge University Press.

Tsai, Kellee S. 2006. "Adaptive Informal Institutions and Endogenous Institutional Change in China." *World Politics* 59, no. 1: 116–41.

———. 2007. *Capitalism without Democracy: The Private Sector in Contemporary China*. Ithaca, NY: Cornell University Press.

Walder, Andrew G. 1995. "Local Governments as Industrial Firms: An Organizational Analysis of China's Transitional Economy." *American Journal of Sociology* 101, no. 2: 263–301.

Wallis, John Joseph. 2011. "Institutions, Organizations, Impersonality, and Interests: The Dynamics of Institutions." *Journal of Economic Behavior & Organization* 79, no. 1–2: 48–64.

Wang, Jingdi. 2017. "诞生、前进与发展——探析淘宝退货运费险 [Emergence, Progression, and Evolution—Analyzing Taobao's Return Shipping Insurance]." 法律与新金融 [*Law and New Finance*] 18, no. 2. https://www.finlaw.pku.edu.cn/flyxjr/gk_hljryfl_20181025180041616718/2017_jrfy_20181029112500112638/zdsbq3y/239868.htm.

Wang, Wen. 2017. "The Effects of Political and Fiscal Incentives on Local Government Behavior: An Analysis of Fiscal Slack in China." *International Public Management Journal* 20, no. 2: 294–315.

Wang, Yuhua. 2015. *Tying the Autocrat's Hands*. UK: Cambridge University Press.

Wank, David L. 1996. "The Institutional Process of Market Clientelism: Guanxi and Private Business in a South China City." *China Quarterly* 147: 820–38.

Weingast, Barry R. 1995. "The Economic Role of Political Institutions: Market-Preserving Federalism and Economic Development." *Journal of Law, Economics & Organization*, 11, no. 1.

———. 2013. "Why Developing Countries Prove So Resistant to the Rule-of-Law." In *Global Perspectives on the Rule of Law*, edited by James Heckman, Robert Nelson, and Lee Cabatingan, 44–68. UK: Routledge-Cavendish.

Weingast, Barry R., and William J. Marshall. 1988. "The Industrial Organization of Congress; Or, Why Legislatures, Like Firms, Are Not Organized as Markets." *Journal of Political Economy* 96, no. 1: 132–63.

Weymouth, Stephen. 2022. *Digital Globalization*. UK: Cambridge University Press.

Whiting, Susan H. 2017. "Authoritarian 'Rule of Law' and Regime Legitimacy." *Comparative Political Studies* 50, no. 14: 1907–40.

———. 2017. "The Cadre Evaluation System at the Grass Roots: The Paradox of Party Rule." In *Critical Readings on the Communist Party of China*, 4 vols., edited by Kjeld Erik Brodsgaard, 461–78. Leiden, The Netherlands: Brill.

Wiesen, S. Jonathan. 2012. "National Socialism and Consumption." In *The Oxford Handbook of the History of Consumption*, edited by Frank Trentmann.

Wilson, Steven H. 2009. *Remade in China: Foreign Investors and Institutional Change in China*. UK: Oxford University Press.

Xin, Katherine K., and Jone L. Pearce. 1996. "Guanxi: Connections as Substitutes for Formal Institutional Support." *Academy of Management Journal* 39, no. 6: 1641–58.

Xu, Chenggang. 2011. "The Fundamental Institutions of China's Reforms and Development." *Journal of Economic Literature* 49, no. 4: 1076–1151.

Xu, Xu. 2021. "To Repress or to Co-opt? Authoritarian Control in the Age of Digital Surveillance. *American Journal of Political Science* 65, no. 2: 309–25.

Yang, Fan. 2015. *Faked in China: Nation Branding, Counterfeit Culture, and Globalization*. Bloomington: Indiana University Press.

Yang, Guobin. 2003. "The Internet and the Rise of a Transnational Chinese Cultural Sphere." *Media, Culture & Society* 25, no. 4: 469–90.

Yang, Mayfair Mei-hui. 1994. *Gifts, Favors, and Banquets: The Art of Social Relationships in China*. Ithaca, NY: Cornell University Press.

Zhang, Lin. 2023. *Labor of Reinvention: Entrepreneurship in the New Chinese Digital Economy*. New York: Columbia University Press.

Zhou, Li-an. 2007. "Governing China's Local Officials: An Analysis of Promotion Tournament Model." *Economic Research Journal* 7: 36–50.

Zhou, Qiang. 2015. 信任与互联网商务的秘密-以对于淘宝的分析为例 [Trust and Secrets of Internet Commerce—Examples from Analyzing Taobao] (working paper).

A NOTE ON THE TYPE

This book has been composed in Arno, an Old-style serif typeface in the classic Venetian tradition, designed by Robert Slimbach at Adobe.

GPSR Authorized Representative: Easy Access System Europe - Mustamäe tee 50, 10621 Tallinn, Estonia, gpsr.requests@easproject.com